Medieval Costume,
Armour and
Weapons

university for the **creative arts**

Medieval Costume, Armour and Weapons

Selected and Illustrated by
Eduard Wagner

Text by
Zoroslava Drobná
&
Jan Durdík

With a New Introduction by
Vladimír Dolínek, Ph.D.
Vojenské Museum, Prague

DOVER PUBLICATIONS, INC.
Mineola, New York

Bibliographical Note

This Dover edition, first published in 2000, is an unabridged republication of the work translated by Jean Layton, originally published in 1958 by Andrew Dakers, London. The only alteration consists in printing the color plates from the original edition in black and white, several of which are repeated in color on the front and back covers, inside and out. A new Introduction has been specially prepared for this edition.

Library of Congress Cataloging-in-Publication Data

Wagner, Eduard, major.
    [Kroje, zbroj a zbrane doby predhusitské a husitské. English]
    Medieval costume, armour, and weapons / selected and illustrated by Eduard Wagner ; text by Zoroslava Drobná & Jan Durdík ; with a new introduction by Vladimír Dolínek.
        p. cm.
    Originally published: Medieval costume, armour, and weapons (1350–1450). London : Andrew Dakers, 1958.
    Includes bibliographical references.
    ISBN-13: 978-0-486-41240-5
    ISBN-10: 0-486-41240-7
    1. Costume–History–Medieval, 500–1500. 2. Arms and armor. 3. Harness. I. Drobná, Zoroslava. II. Durdík, Jan. III. Title.

GT575 .W29313 2000
399–dc21

                                        00-038419

Manufactured in the United States by Courier Corporation
41240703
www.doverpublications.com

INTRODUCTION TO THE DOVER EDITION

Almost half a century has elapsed since this book, *Medieval Costume, Armour and Weapons*, came into existence. The first edition–in the Czech language–was published in 1956; the English and German translations appeared two years later, and subsequent editions in these languages followed thereafter. Three authors participated: two wrote the text and one did the illustrations.

The portion of the text that covers clothing worn in the period 1350–1450 is provided by Zoroslava Drobná (1907–1988), who studied art history at the university in Brno and finished her studies in 1933–1934 at the university in Florence, Italy. Upon graduation, Drobná worked at the municipal museum in Brno. Following the occupation of Czech regions by Nazi Germany and after the outbreak of World War II, she was imprisoned for a time. In 1940, she was employed by the National Museum in Prague. Drobná's primary focus was medieval art (she published the paper "Gothic drawing" in 1956, among others) and medieval handicrafts, particularly textile and ceramics.

The author of the text concerning arms and armor is Jan Durdík (born 1923). He studied history at Charles University in Prague and then–until his retirement in 1985–worked in the military museum in Prague. His specialty was medieval warfare, and in the 1950s his book on Hussite warfare was published in several editions: in Czech, German, and Polish. Durdík then devoted himself to the history of edged weapons and firearms, and published several scientific papers and books. He also co-authored the book *Firearms*, first issued in 1981, and later published in French and German editions. I remember that at the beginning of my preoccupation with ancient arms, I learned a great deal from Durdík's work which, in turn, had considerable influence on the book we co-authored, *The Encyclopaedia of European Historical Weapons*, published in 1993, and translated in the same year into a French edition, and later into a German one.

The lion's share of the credit for the success of this book in achieving an accurate representation of medieval clothing and arms must be ascribed to the illustrator–Eduard Wagner–despite the fact that he was not a professional historian, making his approach to the subject quite different from that of his co-authors. Eduard Wagner (1905–1984) lost his father at the age of fourteen. After leaving elementary school, young Eduard opted for a military career, following the example of his elder brother, Otto Wagner (1902–1974), who was expatriated after the Nazi occupation of Bohemia and later achieved officer's rank in the French foreign legion. Eduard attended the military academy in 1923–1925, and became an officer in various combatant branches. He began his military career in the mountain infantry, then served as a military horse-trainer, and after that in the air force. In 1929, he survived a plane crash, with the consequences of his injury resulting in a slight speech impairment. Nevertheless, he continued in his military service, first with the army engineers unit, and later, for many years, in his beloved cavalry. After World War II–in October of 1945–he was assigned at his own request to the military museum in Prague. Both in painting–which had been his hobby since boyhood–and in military history, Eduard Wagner is an exemplar of the self-taught man. He possessed an outstanding ability to match theoretical knowledge with the practical experience of a professional soldier, expert horseman and swordsman.

While Eduard Wagner's expertise in the current book is shown mainly in the illustrations, in subsequent books his contribution fully entailed both text and drawings. The most interesting of his books are *Cut and Thrust Weapons*, issued in many languages (the first English edition was in 1967), and *European Weapons and Warfare, 1618–1648* (the English and

German editions appeared in 1979, the French in 1981). Wagner's illustrations also accompany the text of many other authors in numerous publications on the subject of military history. Worth mentioning too is the fact that he was the founder of the group "Musketeers and Bandits," who have been staging fencing events since 1960 in Prague and abroad. In fact, it was the first group of its kind to organize around the popularity of historic fencing, and continues to flourish in the Czech republic to the present day.

Medieval Costume, Armour and Weapons thus combines the knowledge of renowned historians with the experience of the practitioner well acquainted with matters equestrian and the art of fencing. The authors have drawn from many written and pictorial resources, illuminated manuscripts and period art works, and artifacts from collections in museums and castles. The era from 1350 to 1450 was a crucial one in the development of arms and armor. During this time, firearms became established in European warfare, ending the dominance of armored cavalry and contributing to its replacement by mercenary infantrymen. This was a long and gradual process, and the earliest defeats of armored cavalry can only be inferred by the inception of firearms. However, political and social changes in medieval society are not the preferred topics of the authors, who instead concentrate on the material aspects of warfare and the clothing of the period. Their complex scrutiny is unrivalled in the contemporaneous literature. The book encompasses not only all items of medieval clothing and armor, and all types of arms, but also the technical fittings usually omitted by many authors, as well as various work tools and utensils. It contains not only the appearance of the arms, but also indicates how they had been handled, carried, prepared and used in combat. In its range and complexity of viewpoint lies the prime worth of this publication. And Eduard Wagner had a unique ability to depict the function of the weapon mechanism even to the layperson.

Originally, this volume was intended primarily for artists, costume and stage designers, and filmmakers, to help them attain the authentic representation of reality within the described era. Subsequently, however, this book was seized upon by historians, archivists, collectors and students of medieval history. Naturally, many new and important studies have appeared in recent decades which cover the same topics, but their existence in no way diminishes the value of *Medieval Costume, Armour and Weapons*. For its complexity and versatility, this book remains unsurpassed up to the present time; and its reissue in this Dover edition will undoubtedly find readers among a whole new generation of researchers, and all those concerned with medieval history.

Vladimír Dolínek, Ph.D.
Vojenské Museum, Prague
November, 1999

CONTENTS

Chapter I was written by Zoroslava Drobná, Chapter VIII by Eduard Wagner and Jan Durdík, the remainder by Jan Durdík.

INTRODUCTION

The main core of the work which we hereby offer to the public lies in the illustrations. Our aim in gathering together and working this material has been, above all, to provide as faithful an illustration as possible of that period of Czech national history which culminated in the great Hussite revolutionary movement. The Hussite movement was not the work of a moment, but was in process of preparation within Czech society over a long period of time. This crisis in feudal society in Bohemia was also reflected in the costumes and weapons of the time, on the one hand by a demand for luxury almost amounting to eccentricity and on the other by a worsening of the position of the poorer sections of the population. Hence we have chosen the middle of the 14th century as our point of departure. But not merely for this reason. Particularly in the development of armour and weapons, this milestone in the century forms a distinct break with the past. It is very shortly after this that we first come across firearms, there were basic changes in battle armour, and a number of other phenomena all point to these changes. We have set the limit at the other end of our work to a hundred years later, the chief reason being the fact that works of art and other sources often register changes in dress, arms and armour up to a somewhat later date than they are in use, frequently using older patterns which to-day are no longer known to us. And last but not least we have also considered it necessary to indicate the direction which further development would take.

For the preparation of the illustrations it was necessary to turn to a number of manuscripts which have been preserved in Czech libraries and which are illustrated with outstanding examples of the Czech art of illumination from the 14th and 15th centuries; likewise to panel paintings which have been reproduced or are preserved in the Prague National Gallery. Naturally we could not be satisfied merely with that. Important material was provided by the photographic archives of the State Documentary Centre, above all in connection with the reproduction of the miniatures of the Vienna King Wenceslas Bible. In addition, a number of literary works, with pictorial reproductions, were made use of, also many expert treatises. The drawings of the figures in this work preserve, in colour and form, the precise outlines of costume and armour as they are to be found in the original sources. But in the majority of cases, for the sake of clarity, the posture of the individual figures in the originals has purposely not been adhered to.

It was also necessary to turn to literature and pictorial material from other countries. This was not merely because the type of civilian clothes and military armour in use in other parts of Europe corresponds at least in general outline to Czech types, but also because in this way it was possible to indicate types and details of armour and weapons which Czech sources do not mention. And finally also, so that we could determine the differences and peculiar characteristics of Czech development in the various types.

We are aware of important shortcomings in this work, which in no way tries to pretend that it has dealt exhaustively with all problems connected with the theme. From every point of view we look upon it as being merely a starting point for further expert work on the problems presented here. Such work would necessarily entail further analysis of archive material and, above all, the assembly and evaluation of actual preserved source material, which is at present still scattered and of which there is as yet no catalogued evidence.

EDUARD WAGNER
ZOROSLAVA DROBNÁ
JAN DURDÍK

THE BOHEMIAN COSTUME
FROM 1350 TO 1450

It is possible to learn from several direct sources what the costumes were like which were worn by the various classes of feudal society in Bohemia during the hundred years dating from 1350 to 1450. Mostly these consist of actual remains of costumes that have been preserved, or individual parts of such costumes. Such material is of course very precious, because there is so little of it and what little there is comes almost exclusively from the highest classes of society of those times. For instance, in the royal tombs in St. Vitus's Cathedral in Prague remains have been found, dating from the 14th and 15th centuries, of the cloaks and costumes in which the Bohemian rulers and their wives were buried. In certain exceptional cases fairly large pieces of the material have been preserved, and they enable us to know what the clothes of the two wives of the Emperor Charles IV, who died in the 2nd half of the 14th century, looked like. This is almost a unique case however, not only in Bohemia but in the whole of Europe.[1] There is only one other case anywhere else where, by even greater chance, a complete woman's costume has been preserved from about the year 1400. It is the dress that Margaret, Queen of the united Scandinavian lands, presented from her own wardrobe to the cathedral in Roskilde, and which was probably to have been converted into an ecclesiastical robe of some kind. This robe, which is of purple velvet with a cross-woven gold pattern, is to-day preserved in Upsala Cathedral. As it was not re-worked, it provides us with a rare example of the costume of those times.[2]

Liturgical robes, chasubles and altar frontals have been preserved in much greater quantities. It is true that these are not civilian clothes but we learn something of the materials used, brocades and velvets, and the way in which they were adorned; for instance the embroidery, which was similar to that used in secular clothes. We have quite a large number of examples of leather goods, such as high boots and shoes dating from the 14th and 15th centuries, remains of men's leather jerkins, studded with ornamentations, and dress accessories, such as a plaited leather belt of the 14th century, which was found buried in a tomb in the Emmaus Cloister in Prague. From the graves of noblemen and burghers there are clasps, brooches and circlets of silver wire, rings and jewelry, which were not actually part of the apparel but which were an important accessory to it.[3] At the same time it shows the method by which these very old relics can be found; in so far as they are not articles that have been kept in good condition in church inventories, the majority of them are the result of archaeological research.

Another source, more important than the rest in helping us to learn something of the costumes of the 14th and 15th centuries, is the evidence of contemporary works of art of those times, such as the sculptures, pictures and miniatures. In the period which we have

1] Jitka Gollerová-Plachá, *Látky z pražské královské hrobky*, Prague, 1937. Milada Lejsková, *Dvojí šat královen z hrobky českých králů v chrámu sv. Víta v Praze*, P A XXXVII, 1931 skup. hist., p. 5 ff. Fragments of these materials are preserved in the St. Vitus's Cathedral treasures, in the Prague National Museum and in the Prague Town Museum. From the individual pieces, exact reproductions of the materials were made in 1929, which are now in the collections of the National Museum and the Industrial Art Museum in Prague.

2] Hans Mützel, *Kostümkunde für Sammler*, Berlin, 1919, p. 18. According to the author's description, it is an example of a fashionable gown in one piece, consisting of a close-fitting bodice and a full skirt.

3] Whole shoes or parts of them (usually the uppers), pieces of leather, and the belt from the Emmaus Cloister are to be found in the collections belonging to the archaeological section of the Prague National Museum. The shoes and high boots from the filled-in well beneath the Vladislav Hall in Prague Castle are now preserved in the collection at Prague Castle. The Prague City Museum possesses parts of shoes which were found in the Old Town Square. The prehistoric section of the Prague City Museum has a pair of shoes found in the Ungelt House in Prague. Jewels, rings and diadems of woven silver wire are to be found in greater numbers in various museums such as the Prague National Museum, the collection at Prague Castle, and so on.

under consideration, we hardly ever come across a secular subject; the artists of the Middle Ages restricted themselves to religious scenes. Secular themes only make their appearance round the border of the main subject, and are only slipped in as a small genre picture. The sculptor, painter or illuminator of the Middle Ages worked in such a way that inevitably even in his religious scenes he would portray people from his own surroundings, in the sort of clothes that he was accustomed to see. For the artist of the Middle Ages was not recording history; that was not in keeping with the character of his time, but was a much later phenomenon, which in its clearly-defined form really only dates from the time of the European romanticism of the 19th century. Hence it did not even occur to the sculptor and painter of the 14th and 15th centuries to invent some vague, fantastic clothes for the figures in their biblical or religious scenes. In the simplicity of his heart and artistic attitude the painter depicted his heroes in the kind of clothes he wore himself and in those which he saw worn by the people around him. Hence he is reliable and we can trust him when he depicts people of various classes, from the king and his nobles and the rich man to the poor woman who serves at the bedside of the Virgin Mary and her newborn child, or the ragged-clothed shepherds in the pictures of the Birth of Christ. At most we can perhaps blame him for contenting himself with a few basic, simple types of clothes – the tunic and the cloak – and of avoiding the eccentric changes in fashion. Certainly this is the case if we take Bohemian panel painting between the years 1350 and 1450, for here we do not get a picture of the full development of the costume of that period in all its richness. The illuminator, on the other hand, who was not bound by the idea of monumentalising – and it is obvious that this was one of the driving impulses of Bohemian painters of large pictures – offers us a much richer insight into the costumes of the period. We are also able to verify the testimony of the artistic works of those times, and every examination has only gone to prove the reliability of this medieval artistic material.

Such research is also supported by another substantial source, namely written accounts. These are extremely plentiful and varied. In chronicles and songs, in contemporary satires, in the sermons of the moralists. in actual documentary sources, such as legacies, town records and guild regulations, we find rich and detailed evidence of the costumes and clothes of the time. We can also learn much from the regulations and prohibitions issued by the secular and religious authorities, who were interested in preventing too great an exuberance of fashion extravagances, for which conditions at that time, not only in Bohemia but also throughout European society, were for many reasons extremely favourable.[1] No sooner was there an interval between the wars, famines, epidemics and plagues, which harassed the people of Europe throughout the Middle Ages, than there immediately arose, among all classes of society, an irrepressible desire to live, to enjoy life and, as far as the means permitted, to dress as grandly as possible. There were no bounds to the inventiveness and richness of ideas and these were also applied in the case of clothing. Naturally these eccentricities and the general available luxury spread beyond what had formerly been the sharply outlined bounds between the various classes of feudal society and this was not exactly to the liking of the higher ruling classes. They therefore tried, by means of regulations and prohibitions, to prevent the fashions of the privileged classes of society being used by the lower classes, to prevent the fashions of the rulers, nobles and the higher church hierarchy even being used by the nouveau riche townsmen and the rich peasants. These attempts, needless to say, proved more or less useless and in vain, but they

1] We find numerous examples of this and quotations from all the old literature and editions in Čeněk Zíbrt and Zikmund Winter, *Dějiny kroje v zemích českých (The History of Costume in the Czech Lands)*, I–II, Prague, 1892–3. The authors tell us something of conditions in other countries by providing certain foreign costume studies; see bibliography.

prove very clearly, nevertheless, the desire that prompted them: that the differentiations of feudal society should be clearly visible at a glance, that the poorer and non-aristocratic classes of feudal society, however wealthy they might have become, should be clearly distinguishable, at a glance, from the privileged, rich upper classes. When we look at this phenomena today from the point of view of historical development, we see very clearly what a brake the feudal upper classes were on the general trend of development which slowly, though inevitably, was leading towards an ever greater levelling out of class differences in clothing, towards the slow creation of what was in essence a common uniform fashion and a uniform costume for the entire entity of national society. It was a development which was only solved in principle and with ultimate effect by the French Revolution in 1789.

In the middle of the 14th century, however, we find ourselves still firmly bound by the ties of feudal society. The various classes were differentiated by their clothing, above all by the richness and costliness of the work and material – even though the lower classes, the burghers and peasants, tried hard to imitate the conspicuous and gaudy splendour of the rich ruling classes. When we look at this period more closely and try to analyse the fashions and clothes of the time in greater detail, we come up against an unequal balance between the rather meagre amount of actual material that has been preserved – such as the costumes and their parts – and the numerous written documents. It is often difficult to determine and describe exactly the individual parts of the dress which we come across so many times in literary relics and dictionaries of the time, as probably in many cases it is a question of one and the same costume, which only varies in length, belting, cut of the sleeves, adornments and so on.[1] In those cases where the preserved costumes and relics to be found in Czechoslovakia do not suffice, we have had to turn to the art treasures of both the neighbouring and more distant lands of Europe, to the art of France, Burgundy, the Netherlands and Germany. For in those days, fashion and costume was more or less a common affair for the whole of western and central Europe.

To begin with, in those days, it originated in France, but later in the 15th century it was from Burgundy; these were the countries which created luxurious fashions in their rich ruling court circles and thus set the tone for the entire elegantly dressed world of the time. But in addition, of course, each land had its own individual note, which varied at different times. Take, for instance, Germany at the end of the 15th and the beginning of the 16th century, or say Italy, which had its own particular style of dress and merely shared certain elements of the basic European costume of the time.

At that time Bohemia was by no means separated from this general European stream. We know that good relations between Bohemia and its neighbours and the exchange of goods and cultural commodities stem from old tradition. From time immemorial foreign goods and foreign materials came to Bohemia, which also probably caused the introduction of new modes in fashions and later entailed the arrival of foreign craftsmen – tailors from Germany, Italy and elsewhere.[2] At any rate it is clear that the development of the native costume is directly connected with local production and the import of foreign materials. The oldest textiles produced in Bohemia included linen and cloth, both of which provided the basic elements of Bohemian costume. Then there came furs, which were generally to be found amongst the aristocracy and gradually also among the burghers, and

---

1] Compare Václav Flajšhans, *Klaret a jeho družina*, I–II, Prague, 1926–8. In order to list them in precise relation to the various known whole pieces and parts of the costume, it would be necessary to make an exhaustive study analysing all the details of the costume and all the known names of the different parts. In this case it is not necessary as I do not use the types and names of the various parts to be found in old dictionaries. I have consciously limited myself to the simplest basic types, namely the dress, the tunic (over and undertunic), coat and cloak.

2] See Zíbrt and Winter, *op. cit., passim*, and W. W. Tomek, *Dějepis města Prahy (History of the City of Prague)*, Prague, 1892, etc.

less elaborately worked and of poorer quality even in general use among the common folk. With the increase and extension of foreign trade, the home market began to be enriched with rare foreign materials. In the earlier Middle Ages it had been silks from the East and rich brocades from Byzantium; during the 13th and 14th centuries there were still the rich Byzantine brocades, but there were also, more frequently, Italian brocades from Lucca and Venice, and even Chinese silk brocades, which probably came via the trade routes through the Mediterranean and found their way to Bohemia. They were magnificent, costly and at that time in Bohemia very rare materials. Hence it is not surprising that they were kept almost exclusively for the clothing of the ruling monarchs and the rich secular and ecclesiastical aristocracy. During the 14th and 15th centuries the Bohemian kings were buried in the royal tombs in Prague Cathedral, dressed in their costly robes and mantles of velvet and silk brocade, as we can see from the relics and remains of materials that have been found there.[1] In the second half of the 14th century the silk brocades gave place more and more and were finally almost ousted by new materials, such as lengths of Italian and Spanish velvets. They became the great fashion and we come across them not only in robes for the clergy and in other ecclesiastical garments, which have been preserved in many cases in good condition to this day, but also as clothes for the secular and ecclesiastical nobility and in the dress of the wealthy burgher class, which grew rich with the rise of the towns and crafts and tried to imitate the external display of magnificence of the nobles. At the same time we should remember that the upper and lower ecclesiastics of those times lived like the secular nobility and the monarchs, that they usually dressed in the same manner as the most luxurious feudal lords, and that as a result the disciplinary pastoral letters and interdicts of the archbishops and Synods were often also directed against them.

In addition to the red and green velvets which, during the course of the 15th century, were more and more frequently ornamented with motifs based on the fruit and flowers of the pomegranate, on palm leaves, lotus flowers and other rich plant designs, replacing the older animal motifs, the wonder birds, which had originated in the art of the Orient, we find more and more examples of Flemish, Italian and Rhineland cloth and fine Bavarian linen making their way into Bohemia.

The richly-coloured brocades and the velvets with their decorative ornamental designs were of course not the only ornate material used for the clothes and costly dresses of the feudal overlords and the well-to-do burghers. Under the skilled hands of the embroideress even simple common linen was turned into a valuable robe. Apart from the nuns in the convents this work had been done from oldest times by serf women, later the craft embroideresses, organised in craft guilds. To be able to embroider beautifully was considered part of the good education of the wives and daughters of the ruling and noble families. The chronicler Petr Žitavský tells – in so far as it was not just a polite form of compliment in admiration of the lady – of the admiration aroused by the young Eliška of the House of Přemyslid. For she wore a wedding dress that she had embroidered herself when she married the fourteen-year-old John of Luxembourg.[2] The art of embroidery flourished in Bohemia throughout the whole 14th century, even longer, and it is to our great regret that no example of clothes of that time thus ornamented have survived to this day. But here again the only place from which we can learn something of the art of embroidery, its technical perfection, its beauty and purity of style, so closely connected with the art of monumental painting, is the remains of ecclesiastical robes that have been preserved in part.

1] J. Gollerová-Plachá, *op. cit., passim.* Z. Drobná, *Les trésors de la broderie religieuse en Tchécoslovaquie*, Prague, 1950, *passim.*

2] *Fontes rerum Bohemicarum* IV, p. 130. *Kronika zbraslavská*, Prague, 1952, p. 305.

Between the years 1348 and 1419, a period of rich economic and cultural life accompanied by the dark shadows of conflicts that were sharpening and growing more acute, and already heading for the outburst of the Hussite revolutionary movement, that is during the reigns of Charles IV and Wenceslas, Prague was a city of about 30,000 inhabitants and was at that time larger than either Paris or London.[1] One may be sure that those who could afford it were provided with all that they needed in the way of fine clothes. Among the inhabitants there was quite a considerable number of craftsmen occupied in the various trades directly or indirectly connected with clothes and the making of the various accessories. However, the numbers are not known exactly, as the various lists and registers are incomplete, usually only containing the names of master craftsmen, owners of houses in Prague, and omitting those who in many crafts constituted the majority of the workers in that craft, but in most cases did not own a house. But even if we make allowances for the incompleteness of these reports, they are nevertheless of interest to us, for they at least enable us to get a better picture of what it was like in Prague at that time, and consequently also, in other places. There were altogether 22 different trades and crafts concerned with clothing and dressing the inhabitants of Prague and also to a certain extent with the export of such goods to other places.[2]

At the same time we see to what an extent the clothing industry, like other crafts, was already subject to specialization. Apart from the tailors, who made new clothes for both men and women, there were second-hand dealers, who altered, mended and improved old clothes, coat-makers who concentrated only on coats, hosiers who dealt in stockings, and smockers who made rough smocks. Some furriers made up new furs, while others only repaired old ones. A special group was known as the black furriers.

Even the shoemakers were divided into several groups. The actual shoemakers sewed new boots and shoes, the cobblers mended and soled old footwear; the wooden pattens or clogs so often worn with the soled hose, which were shoe and stocking in one, were again made by special craftsmen. It was the same with the hatters. The hatters worked in felt or fur (beaver), the cap-makers made caps, the beret-makers berets, the men and women veil-makers made head-scarves, wimples, hoods and veils for women, and the wreath-makers made wreaths, circlets and other hair ornaments. In this field there were also many women workers. The silk embroiderers embroidered silk with silk thread, and gold and precious stones. There were also the glovers, belt-makers, bag- and purse-makers, who were likewise an essential element of the fashionable clothing trade.

Let us now take a look at the kind of clothes worn during the second half of the 14th century and the first half of the 15th, and also note what kind of materials were used. We have already mentioned the most precious materials, such as velvet and brocade. In the clothes' chests of the rich and of the more modest burghers, of whose wardrobes we have comparatively the greatest quantity of written evidence, there were numerous different kinds of imported and homemade materials.[3] The native material most frequently mentioned is Tábor cloth; of those imported there is often mention of Flemish cloth, from Brussels, Ghent, Ypres and Louvain, which the Czech merchants themselves went and bought in the Netherlands. From the Walloons they used to bring back fine linen, known as *kment*. Another fine linen was that already mentioned from Bavaria, *tela Bavaricalis*, or *bayerische Leinwand*. Of the Rhineland cloths mention is often made of Aachen and Frankfurt cloth. Furs were imported into Bohemia from Poland.

1] Fr. Graus, *Chudina městská v době předhusitské (The Town Poor in the Pre-Hussite Era)*, Prague, 1949, pp. 116–17.
2] According to W. W. Tomek, *op. cit.*, II, p. 528, VIII, p. 494; and Zíbrt and Winter, *op. cit., passim*.
3]See Zíbrt and Winter, *op. cit.* Fr. Graus, *Český obchod se suknem ve 14. a počátkem 15. století*, Prague, 1950.

As clothes were very expensive in those days, they were usually expressly mentioned in legacies in fairly great detail. Elderly people left their coats and cloaks to their children and grandchildren, on condition that they wore them as they found them, or that they preserved them until they grew into them, only sometimes allowing them to be adapted. The following facts are also quite remarkable and at the same time indicate the comparative costliness of the clothes and the care with which they were treated; even in those days clothes were repaired, altered, adapted and turned, indeed even sometimes dyed. Last wills and testaments from the second half of the 14th century and the first half of the 15th century give us a very clear, interesting picture of the medieval costumes of the nobility and the merchant class of Bohemia. The most important items were the tunics and the cloaks, which were nearly always mentioned; in addition there were furs and skins and more rarely pelissons. The cloaks, like the winter tunics, were lined with fur.

In addition to the heavy furs and skins, in winter light soft furs and fur jackets were worn. They were made of fox (the back and the belly are those parts mentioned), lambskins, marten fur, goatskins, sables and skunk. Once there is mention of a fur of fox-back skin with narrow sleeves, an azure blue skin of marten fur and a long skin, also of marten. Craftsmen working out-of-doors in winter used to wear short furs.

In addition to the long circular pelts or fur cloaks, one also comes across the short cape.

As for other types of clothing, we shall be speaking of them later, when we come to analyse the development of Czech costume.

There is always the question of what parts of ancient Slavonic costume were preserved in the Bohemian costume of the 14th and 15th centuries. It will be necessary to make a much more detailed study and careful comparison and research, and above all more finds, both in the field of Slavonic archaeology and that of historical archaeology, before we shall be in a position to throw real light on this problem on the basis of fresh knowledge. For the time being, therefore, we cannot say whether anything of the old costume was preserved in the national costume of the 14th and 15th century. In any case, it could only be a question of some basic section of the costume, a name or a specifically preserved form. In fact, if we compare the costume of the poorer common folk of Bohemia with that of their neighbours, we do not find any fundamental differences. And as in the works of the poets, satirists and moral preachers, likewise in various regulations and prohibitions, we continually come across the fact that the peasant farmers liked to adopt the costume of the master and thus imitate him, and we are forced to the conclusion that during the period that we are dealing with there were no very great fundamental differences in the cut and various parts of the costumes of the individual classes of society; the differences lay rather in the splendour and cost of the clothes, in the materials and furs of which they were made, in their number, the expensive ornaments, in the linings, gilding and other accessories. Basically, therefore, it seems that the costume of the various classes of society in Bohemia did not differ either in style or fashion, neither was there a fundamental difference between the costume of Bohemia and that of the other countries of western and central Europe. Here, as there, the rich wore three or four parts to the dress, the poor only one.

During the 14th century Bohemian costume was closely linked with that of France. In the above-mentioned description by the chronicler Petr Žitavský of Eliška Přemyslid's marriage to John of Luxembourg, he speaks of the long, French-styled, bridal dress.[1] Under the Luxembourgs this contact with France was of course strengthened and extended. The first wife of the Emperor Charles IV, the French princess Blanche of Valois, came to Bohemia with her husband in 1334 and according to the writer of the Zbraslav Chronicle introduced

1] *FRB* IV, p. 150. *Kronika zbraslavská*, p. 346.

the costume worn by the women of her home country.[1] If we consider the present-day speed with which fashions, cut and ornamentation change, then in comparison the costume of those days lasted for a very long time without significant change, or at least its basic elements remained unchanged. This is most marked if we take the costume as worn during the first half of the 14th century.

The costume of this period had at most four main elements, which were almost identical in both the male and the female costume. The main item was the shirt, a name known already from far older times, but of whose shape and material, as used at that time, we have no exact knowledge. If, in contemporary miniatures of that time, we find a sleeper in bed, in most cases he lies naked, without a shirt. Over the shirt he wore what was known as a tunic, which was not a tunic in the present sense of the word. It was a long dress with long sleeves, which was put on over the head. Wherever in connection with the Middle Ages, we come across the term *sukně*, skirt or tunic, it is this long kind of garment, cut and sewn in one piece, which is meant. Sometimes it also had a small slit at the neck, which was fastened by a clasp or a few buttons; later, as the general line changed, it was a longer row of buttons or even a laced fastening, but it always remained a long dress, cut from one piece, which was put on over the head. Over this undertunic both men and women used to wear an overtunic, though by this time it was often discarded as part of the regular dress, and it was worn in various forms and variations, with corresponding different names. Basically, however, it was always an overtunic. A circular cloak was needed to complete the costume, and this was worn lightly thrown over the shoulders, from which it hung down over the back. Until the end of the 13th century and even till the middle of the 14th century it was fastened with a cord or a neckband that lay across the breast. The ends of the cords were fastened to the cloak with richly ornamented clasps. This, in fact, was what the costume of both men and women of aristocratic society looked like during the first third of the 14th century. There was no difference in the costumes of the two sexes; on the contrary the men tried to imitate the women with their various kinds of accessories, such as the way the hair was arranged, circlets in the hair, and so on.

We can see the costume of the first third of the 14th century, as we have described it, in the drawings of the manuscript of the Abbess Kunhuta's Passional, dating from about the year 1420.[2] There is a picture in this of a young aristocratic couple. The man is wearing a long undertunic, over which he wears an overtunic as an outer garment; it is broader and voluminous in cut, and has a slit from the waist down to the ground over the right hip. This opens as he walks and shows the material of the undertunic. The overtunic, as it is called, has broad sleeves from the shoulder to the elbow, which then narrow down to the wrist. In other cases this overtunic has broad half sleeves, under which we see the long sleeves of the undertunic. The overtunic is girded by a smooth, narrow belt. The neck opening is small, slightly heart-shaped, and from the shoulder down the back there hangs a broad circular cape which is fixed by a cord or string strung across the breast from shoulder to shoulder. The cloak reaches to just below the ankles so that it trails slightly on the ground, and the neck is lined with fur. The woman, who stands to the right and is taking the ring from the knight, is dressed in a fairly narrowly cut overtunic which is gathered into a band fastened with a belt that we cannot see. The tunic has narrow sleeves right to the wrist. As in the case of the man, over her shoulders she wears a cape, which is fastened

1] *FRB* IV, p. 320: "*habitum muliebrem secundum suae gentis consuetudinem secum attulit...*" *Kronika zbraslavská*, p. 703.
2] The Abbess Kunhuta's Passional is to be found in the Prague University Library under the index mark

XIV. A–17. See A. Matějček, *Pasionál abatyše Kunhuty*, Prague, 1922. The drawing reproduced is on fol. 3b. It is also reproduced by Zíbrt and Winter, *op. cit.*, I, p. 267, plate 153.

at the shoulders and hangs down her back. Both the young people have wreaths in their loosely flowing hair. We may take these clothes as examples of the simplest, most typical form of dress and as characteristic examples of the costume as worn before the basic changes in fashion which took place about the middle of the 14th century.

What is for us, perhaps, the most interesting type of costume of this kind is the style in which the overtunic is sleeveless and has only small armholes for the undersleeves. This tunic or smock-frock, which is worn over an undertunic with sleeves, is known by the name *sukně*, both in French and in German, using the Czech word, with the necessary orthographical changes: German *Sukeny*, *Sukkenie*, French *Souquenille*.[1]

As this name obviously has the sound of the Czech word *sukně* and as it is most probable that this word, as used in the German and French fashion vocabulary, derived from the Czech, and from no other Slavonic language, we are perhaps justified in assuming that the sleeveless Bohemian overtunic, together with its original name, was generally adopted as a European form of dress in the 13th century.

What was the great change that took place in European costume about the middle of the 14th century and what are its most important features? Above all, there now appears a permanent separation of the male and female costumes. From now on the individual parts of the male and female costumes begin to develop independently along their own lines, even though, of course, still in the same style groupings. They consist of a narrow, close-fitting bodice that reaches below the hips and the waist, from which there flows a long full skirt, falling in folds right down to the ground. In order to make the bodice close-fitting, it had to be cut down the front and fastened together again with buttons or heavy lacing. This tunic, or should we say dress, was still however cut in one piece and put on over the head. But by now we have come to an important change in costume: the wearing of two tunics of the older fashion begins to disappear, the undertunic becoming a dress in the modern sense of the word, even though the overgarment still undergoes a short further stage of development with very pronounced change in shape, as we shall see later.

This modified undergarment, adapted in the way we have described, has a broad oval neckline cut from shoulder to shoulder. This was another novelty of the new fashion. And since there was now no second tunic, and it was no longer possible to combine the narrow sleeves of the undergarment with the armholes of the overtunic, there also appeared a further novelty, namely the changeable sleeves, which could be fixed into the dress and varied as desired. They tended to be made of colours and materials that contrasted with those of the dress. Such would be the case, for instance, if the tunic, or rather dress, had half-length sleeves with dags at the elbow, which gradually developed into the long, narrow hanging tippets of flowing material which reached to the ground from the elbow. These tippets sometimes even hung right from the shoulder, from the broad border of the oval neckline or from the cuff of the tunic's short sleeves, from just above the elbow, or straight from a short sleeve if they were of the same material as the dress. In very costly dresses these tippets were usually made of ermine. Sometimes pieces of the material also flowed down back over the shoulders, and were known as wings. We only come across them, however, in the sharply defined form of the costume of the second half of the 14th century, as it has been reconstructed according to the remains of the costumes of two Czech queens, found in a tomb in St. Vitus's Cathedral in Prague. The wings, in this case, were fixed

1] Frequently used in foreign literature, often with a note that the word is taken from the Slavonic word *sukno* (woollen cloth). There is no mention in such sources of the possibility that this old Czech name was taken over complete with this style of clothing. See Hans Mützel, *Vom Lederschurz zur Modetracht*, Berlin, 1925, pp. 103, 172; Rosanne Leclère, *Histoire du costume*, Lausanne, 1949, plate IV; H. Skarbina, *Kostüm und Mode*, Leipzig, 1938, p. 14.

to the shoulders of the bodice and flowed down behind. Both the dresses were of silk brocade, lined with silk taffeta. Probably the sleeves were independent parts and were only hooked in, and they may even have been made of other material.[1]

So much for feminine costume. In the case of male costume there was also a similar change in the shape of the overtunic, first into a short tunic, then into an even shorter, close-fitting jacket, which at first reached to the hips, and later to very little below the waist. Here we also see a basic change taking place in the line of fashion: the doublet is close-fitting, and in the front it is cut open down its whole length and made to fasten with buttons or hooks. Such a jacket obviously also needed hose, which were another novelty and one that became a permanent element in male costume. To complete it, the costume also required a cloak, as in the woman's costume. But even the cloak, though it kept more or less to its original circular form, gradually underwent change in the course of the years.

The chroniclers of the time paid considerable attention to these great changes in costume. For instance, the scribe of the Great French Chronicle commented on them, when he was lamenting the defeat of France at the Battle of Crécy, which he considered to be a punishment for excessive human foolishness.[2] The Limburg chronicler mentioned them from a different point of view in the year 1350: "... the great deaths and catastrophes had come to an end, the world was growing green again, flourishing and enjoying itself... and the people made new clothes for themselves."[3]

In that precious old Bohemian manuscript, the Velislav Bible, which dates from about the year 1340 and which contains so many drawings, this change can be seen very well.[4] Here we find women in costumes that show without doubt that this basic change of line had already taken place before the middle of the century. For instance, if we take a look at the woman in the long undertunic, which widens from below the hips and falls to the ground in folds on all sides, we find that it completely covers the wearer's shoes. The tunic has a low-cut oval neckline from the shoulders. The upper part of the tunic, even though hidden beneath another dress, is obviously close-fitting, without a girdle. It is not possible to say how the sleeves of this undergarment are fitted in, because the woman also wears a close-fitting jacket of another contrasting material, with long, narrow sleeves, an oval neckline cut low to the shoulders, with scallops on the neckline and down round the waist. The jacket does not meet at the front and is not fastened anywhere else either. At the edge it is usually bordered with either a broad or narrow band of material that contrasts with that of the jacket. This jacket reminds one most of that part of the costume that developed in France out of the overtunic, but which has no sleeves and was known as the surcoat. Sometimes we come across it as a short bodice with deep-cut armholes, but more often by now as a small cloak. In this case this article was used as a small jacket with sleeves.

Judith is dressed in the same way in the second scene with Holofernes; however she wears a jacket that is even more closely related to the genuine French surcoat.

In another part of the Velislav Bible we come across a picture of a lady of fashion, dating from about the middle of the 14th century, who is again dressed in an over-and undergarment; of the undergarment we only see the close-fitting sleeves, which end in

1] See M. Lejsková, *Dvojí šat královen* etc. (see note p. 1). The same source shows a drawing of the reconstructed dress.
2] Paul Lecroix, *Moeurs, usages et costumes au moyen âge et à l'époque de la Renaissance*, Paris, 1871, p. 574.
3] Herman Weiss, *Kostümkunde*, 3/1, Stuttgart, 1872, p. 201.

4] Velislav Bible in the National and University Library, Prague, No. XXIII C 124. Ant. Matějček, *Velislavova bible a její místo ve vývoji knižní ilustrace gotické*, Prague, 1926. The first drawing for comparison is reproduced by Zíbrt and Winter, *op. cit.*, I, p. 260, plate 147. For Judith and Holofernes on fol. 126, see reproduction in Matějček, *op. cit.*, p. 1 ff.

a sharp point on the back of the hand (unless this is already a case of freely interchangeable sleeves, which could be buttoned in underneath or fixed to the overtunic in some other way). Apart from this undergarment, which otherwise is not visible anywhere and which is possibly not even present, the woman wears an overgarment, a tunic or dress, which in cut is already strikingly different from the former overtunic, as in the case we just mentioned in the Abbess Kunhuta's Passional. The long dress, which is close-fitting down to below the waist, constituting a longish, narrow ungirdled bodice, widens below the hips and falls to the ground in rich folds. The neckline, which is moderate, though substantially lower in comparison to former times, is cut as a broad oval round the shoulders. The sleeves are narrow half-sleeves, which reach exactly to the elbow and from there hang long narrow tippets, which reach to below the knees of the upright figure.[1] These long pointed tippets remained in fashion for a long time, till as late as the second half of the 14th century, where we still come across them in extravagant costumes, as they were the height of fashion. Consequently they were also incorporated in the town burgher's costume and provided the moralists and preachers with much cause for derision and reproof. Already as early as 1330 the chronicler Petr Žitavský, in his Zbraslav Chronicle, complains that the majority of people wear short, tight-fitting clothes, with some sort of tippets, which hang from the elbow down over the tunic and wave about like donkey's ears.[2]

At about the same time, in 1339, the chronicler František Pražský likewise complains about the tippets at the elbows of the male costume, about the tight male tunics, in which the master can scarcely be attired even with the patient help of two servants. Apparently, many people also wore loose capes with hoods, which had a tippet reaching to the ground at the back and which was often trimmed with a fringe.[3]

What František Pražský has to say about the feminine costume almost exactly corresponds with what we have just seen in the Velislav Bible: apparently the tunics had a tight close-fitting bodice top, and were full at the bottom. The cloaks and tunics had broad borders, and shoes were tight and narrow.

In the Velislav Bible we also find beautiful examples of women's hair styles with decorative spiral wimples, of which some, on the one hand, still show signs of the earlier fashion, which was beginning to disappear, and others have little veils and coils which were developing and remained in fashion for a long time. The earlier style, which at that time was really already beginning to disappear, consisted of a head-dress in the form of a garland (known as a chaplet), often very richly decorated with fresh flowers and hung with precious silver ornaments and gold rings and the like. Another very becoming combination was a broad chaplet and a linen band that went right round the head and chin, and was often indented like a crown round the upper edge. There were, however, other styles which remained in vogue much longer, such as the veil with several decoratively indented edges, which enveloped the neck and fell in cascades down the side of the face; then there was also the loose veil, thrown lightly over the head, which left the neck free and surrounded the face with charming little scallops or dags. The Velislav Bible itself also already provides some examples of fashion eccentricities: for instance, the veil was arranged in several flounces around the head and apparently rested at the back of the head on a rectangular wire frame. It had the effect of surrounding the face with a halo. These veils or nebula head-dresses were usually made of fine linen or silk, but sometimes they were even of ordinary linen that had been starched. This is confirmed by Tkadleček, when he speaks

---

1] Velislav Bible, fol. 13. Reproduced by Zíbrt and Winter, *op. cit.*, p. 266, plate 151.
2] *FRB* IV, p. 301: *De novitatibus morum.* Kronika

zbraslavská, p. 660.
3] *FRB* IV, p. 404: *De novitatibus morum, quae temporibus regis Johannis ortum habuerunt.*

of the townswoman, "with her starched veil."[1] It seems probable that it was this form of head-dress that was taken over from Bohemia by the neighbouring state of Germany, where it was mentioned in the Limburg Chronicle in the year 1389. The writer complained that women now wear *böhmische Kogeln* (Bohemian hoods), which are fixed up around the head so that from the front they look like halos.[2]

It seems that during the last quarter of the 14th century the fashions of Bohemia, though closely linked with those of the rest of Europe, seemed to foreigners to have their own particular aroma and a special flavour that was highly valued and much sought after. It is said that the French King Charles VI was particularly intrigued by them and by the fashions of Germany, because at that time they were the most bizarre of all Europe.[3]

Unfortunately we have no direct written evidence to show that it was Bohemian fashions that so intrigued foreigners. It can surely only have been the fashions of the reign of King Wenceslas IV, of which we have evidence in the numerous splendid manuscripts that have been preserved, and which were completed for King Wenceslas around the end of the 14th century; it was a fashion that certainly had a slightly bizarre, exaggerated, elegant and courtly tone.

Although it is not the first time that we come across the influence of Bohemian costume abroad, and its reflection in the clothes of other lands, yet nevertheless we are frequently told by the Czech chroniclers and writers of the time that the Czechs imitated foreign fashions and light-heartedly gave up their own good costumes, morals and habits.

Although in Bohemian chronicles we often come across these complaints about the splendour and luxury indulged in in clothes, and the readiness to imitate foreigners, it is not purely a Czech indulgence, as might seem to be the case, to judge by the severe condemnation and descriptions of the chroniclers. In France and Germany the writers of chronicles and similar works also complained against the luxury and extravagant splendour of the clothes of the time, likewise the light-hearted way in which the native costume was abandoned and foreign fashions were imitated and became the vogue. These lamentations were obviously an indicative feature of serious-minded criticism of the evils of the time; sometimes, however, they refer so far back into the past that we are perhaps justified in asking when it was that this golden age of native simplicity and originality in fact really existed? With the best of intentions we are not able to determine it and we suspect that the chroniclers themselves were inclined to fall for the desire to imitate in another sense, and that they sometimes simply repeated old complaints and slanders as a form of literary polish to their writings.

Once we have clarified for ourselves the principles on which the new fashions of about the year 1350 were based, it is quite easy to find our way through the maze of medieval male and female tunics, jackets, coats and cloaks. It opens our eyes to the way in which costume developed and helps to explain the manner in which new variations arose. It enables us to find our way through the wider field of European costume, especially that of France and Germany, and to see the connections between the foreign fashions and those of Bohemia. Until the victory of the Burgundian fashion, the costume of Bohemia corresponded to the general lines of the new fashion which came into being about the year 1350. This Burgundian fashion, however, did not really affect Bohemia, as the country was too busy trying to solve its own burning problems with weapons in its hands.

Direct sources of pictorial material are our best guide in this instance. If we search among them for evidence and examples of the female costume of the common people,

1] Tkadleček, *Hádka milence s Neštěstím, které ho připravilo o jeho milenku*, ed. Frant. Šimek, Prague, 1940.

2] See Zíbrt and Winter, *op. cit.*, I, pp. 213, 262.
3] See Zíbrt and Winter, *op. cit.*, I, p. 282.

we find a picture by the Master of Vyšší Brod, dating from about the year 1350, which depicts the Birth of Christ, and in which there is a woman preparing a bath on the ground for the child. She wears a costume in two parts, which consists of a skirt, as we know it, with a shortish sleeved blouse partly rolled up and tucked into it. The blouse has a fastening, hidden by the braid, from the waist upwards to the neck. In the miniatures of the *Liber Viaticus* manuscript, dating from the year 1364, there are pictures of a family on a journey, the members of which are well-dressed burghers, though without any extravagance. The woman wears a long tunic gathered in at the waist by a narrow belt, and it spreads out in folds from the waist downwards. Over this she wears a full cloak, fastened at the front over the breast. A veil or wimple is wound round her head and neck. The child is wearing a little tucked-up tunic that reaches to the calf of the leg and has long, narrow sleeves. The tunic and cloak of the man are about the same length and the cloak fastens over the breast with a row of buttons. The man is also wearing a straw hat with a wide brim. In the Wenceslas manuscripts and later we often come across an apron tucked up into the belt.

The illuminator of the Tomáš of Štítný manuscript, dating from about the third quarter of the 14th century, gives us a very true picture of the clothing of his time, by introducing us to the social life of the nobility and the landowners. Here we come across girls in long beltless dresses with close-fitting bodices and narrow sleeves; the skirt (in the modern sense of the word), falls in broad folds right to the ground.

In this manuscript we also come across the circular cape fastened with a clasp at the front in the centre. Other women are dressed in more magnificent dresses, sewn together in one piece, but obviously cut out of two. The bodice, which is close-fitting, has a broad oval open neckline, which comes right down over the shoulders. The sleeves are narrow, but broaden out somewhat over the wrist and end in a point over the back of the hand. There is an ornamental belt placed low over the hips, and below it the skirt falls in broad folds to the ground. At the lower hem there is a broad border of ermine and from the neckline over the shoulders there hang long, thin strips of ermine, which the moralist preachers used to ridicule with such names as noses, points or beaks.

We should also note the hair-styles. The women have long flowing curls down their backs and on their heads they wear ornamental garlands or wreaths.

The fashions of about the year 1400 are depicted very well in the miniatures of the Wenceslas manuscripts.[1] The costume of the well-to-do women remained almost the same as we found it in the Štítný manuscript, dating from about 1376: the tunic is in one piece, with a close-fitting longish bodice and a skirt flaring out to the ground; it is so long that it completely hides the feet. The sleeves are narrow, though broadening out bell-shaped over the wrist and gradually reaching as far as the middle of the hand. The neck is cut as a broad oval shape leaving the shoulders bare. Above the elbows there is a broad ermine cuff from which there hangs a long ermine tippet right down to the ground. In another place a woman wears over this tunic a circular mantle of rich brocade embroidered with an impressive plant design. This mantle is bordered all round with ermine. Sometimes the broad oval neckline of the tunic (the dress) is bordered with a narrow fur collar.

At the beginning of the 15th century new variations began to appear. In addition to the time-honoured tunic with the longish close-fitting bodice that broadens out at the bottom and which is often fastened with buttons, occasionally also with a row of little buttons on the narrow sleeves, we now find tunics with lacing which was obviously often used for

1] Photo-copies of the manuscripts, which are preserved in the National Library in Vienna, are to be found in the Documentation Institute (formerly the Photometric Institute) of the State Relics and Treasures Service in Prague. See also Julius v. Schlosser, "Die Bilderhandschriften Königs Wenzel I", *Jhb. d. Ksthist. Smlgen d. AK*, Vienna, 1893, p. 214.

drawing in the upper half of the costume tight to the body. The lacing runs down the middle of the front of the skirt to below the waist, making in fact a long fastening. Another novelty was the new shape of the sleeves. In addition to the narrow sleeves, which we have seen so far, we now sometimes come across half-sleeves, which broaden out at the ends into a long hanging tippet, often ornamented with fur. Such a sleeve required an under-sleeve and here we must quite definitely assume that it was a question of buttoned-in sleeves which could be changed at will, and that the undergarment, which we know to be an essential part of the costume at the beginning of the 14th century, had now entirely disappeared. The shape of these undersleeves also varied. There was often still the narrow sleeve with the trumpet-shaped cuff broadening down to the hand; later, however, this alternated with a broader sleeve, even a very broad one which was gathered together into a narrow band. Another extravagance of fashion was the sleeve with bag-shaped closed lappets hanging to the ground from the elbow, where there was a hole for the hand. In this way there developed a half-length sleeve which required a second undersleeve. The example which we give for this fashion is the new one in which the undersleeve is broad and gathered together at the wrist. The undersleeves could be fastened in and changed at will and were made of different material from the dress and of a contrasting colour. It should be pointed out that throughout the whole hundred years with which we are dealing, there was a noticeable use of contrasting colours and colourful accessories. The tunic was usually lined with a material in contrasting colour and the undersleeves and linings of the broad oversleeves were often emphasized in the same manner. In men's costume a determining influence on the overall effect was the colour of the stockings and so on.

Another and quite different manner in which the oversleeve was used for decorative effect is shown us by a painting of a queen dating from the year 1405. It is a costume which might almost seem to us improbably fantastic, and yet it is precisely in conformity with the times and has all the elements that are characteristic of the beginning of the 15th century, most of which we know already. It is actually the same type of tunic, or rather dress, as we have previously described in detail. The dress is cut from two pieces but nevertheless forms a single whole: a close-fitting bodice fastened from the top to below the waist with lacing, and below this a skirt flaring out to the ground, often trimmed at the lower edge with a broad hem of ermine. The large oval-shaped neckline, leaving the shoulders bare, is also trimmed with a scallop-shaped border of ermine. The sleeves are only closed as far as the elbow and from there they are cut so as to form a long flowing tippet broadening towards its end, which can either be thrown over the arm or left to hang down to the ground. They are also lined with ermine. Beneath these, the queen wears the narrow sleeves of the earlier style. The ornamentation of the broad, costly belt might also seem somewhat eccentric to us – little bells hanging from a metal chain! They were popular at this time, especially in Germany, where we often come across them, above all in the male costume.[1] The hair style is also already familiar to us. At that time there were only two styles. The young unmarried ladies went bare headed, with their hair falling in loose curls down their backs, and decorated with silver or even more precious garlands. The married women wore a veil which was wound round the head in various ways, from the simple method of throwing it lightly over the head or of covering

1] The drawing comes from the Kyeser Bellifortis MS, dating from the year 1405, of which we shall hear more in the following chapters. Concerning the Czech origin of the manuscript, see Heinrich Jerchel, "Das Hasenburgische Missale von 1409, die Wenzelwerk-statt... und die Mettener Malereien von 1414", *Zeitschrift des deutsch. Verein für Kunstwissenschaft*, Prague (?), IV, *193*, p. 218, and Jan Durdík, *Historie a vojenství*, No. 3, Prague, 1953.

the neck, to the complete thorough binding of the head, neck and chin known as the wimple. The lappets that hung from the veil often gave the effect of forming a little hood. These styles, with minor alterations, were worn all the time. The married women, however, were not content to be restricted to the use of these severe veils and did not accept the idea that only unmarried women should be allowed to wear their hair loose and have their heads uncovered. The representatives of the richer classes used to wear their hair loose and adorned with garlands even after they were married. For instance, the wives of the Emperor Charles IV are depicted in this manner in the well-known stone busts in the triforium of the St. Vitus's Cathedral in Prague.

There is another type of costume of which we have knowledge not only from a unique written source but also from the paintings of the Wenceslas manuscripts: it is the costume of the woman bath attendant, who worked in the medieval public baths. It is an extremely simple costume consisting of a thin, long white shirt, which hangs from just above the breasts on two thin shoulder straps and is drawn in at the waist with a belt. Apparently this costume did not undergo any change throughout the century, for at the beginning of the 16th century it was depicted in exactly the same manner by the illuminator of the Jena Codex, when illustrating for us the frivolous lives of the monks.

In order to complete the picture of Bohemian fashions so far assembled, we must consider at least a few of the most characteristic examples of the feminine costume of other parts of Europe. This glance at foreign costumes will, at the same time, confirm what we have already said, namely that Czech costume also belongs to that complex which in essence constituted the unified medieval costume of Europe and that it always remained closely allied to it.

A French lady of the 14th century wore tunics of the same cut as those of the Bohemian lady, with the broad oval neckline, the ermine hems and ermine tippets. But only occasionally in Czech costume do we come across anything similar to the typical French surcoat of the 14th and first half of the 15th centuries. This was really a developmental form of the overtunic. The long surcoat with the typical deep-cut armholes and the charmingly decorative use of fur trimmings, which we find in the foreign example, is only rarely to be found in Bohemia in the Wenceslas manuscripts. In the fashions of the west it was popular until the middle of the 15th century, even though it naturally underwent various changes. In Burgundian costume we meet with it in the form of a short sleeveless bodice, but this is really only the upper half of the long surcoat, such as we have before us.

The openings in the tunics for the hands, as seen in the French and German costume, are still to be seen in the Bohemian male costume of the end of the 14th century. At the beginning of the 15th century the rich German woman wore a tunic with exaggeratedly wide sleeves ending in pointed tippets that was similar to that worn by the rich Bohemian woman. In other respects, however, German costume had its own peculiarities – too much decoration, perhaps, for our taste and too many lobe-shaped cut-outs, especially in male costume.[1]

At the time when the Táborite women of Bohemia were dispensing with and severely condemning every kind of frivolity and luxury in dress and when, with weapons in their hands, they themselves were taking part in the fight against the old order, there was developing, at the other end of Europe, a courtly splendour of unprecedented proportions and of a character that was strictly bound by court regulations. The Burgundian fashion, originating among the rich ruling nobility, took over the lead from the French and in

1] The art of richly ornamenting the costume and the lappets, etc., by cutting out lobe-shaped patches, which were often similar in form to an oak leaf, was very common in the French-Burgundian fashions, and also well-known in the Rhineland.

a short while the lower classes of society, notably the rich burghers, found ways and means of adapting it to their purposes. For the first time since the middle of the 14th century this fashion introduced a basic alteration in line and cut in female costume; it introduced the train, which from that time on became an essential ceremonial form in all European courts; it tended to have a low neckline and a high waistline and the dress was divided into two clearly discernible parts by an artificial seam forming the bodice and skirt (in our sense of the word); it excelled itself in luxuriousness and richness of ideas in regard to the covering of the female head, such as the high coils, steeple head-dresses and cones known as "hennins" from which flowed whole cascades of fine veiling. Another variant was the so-called "horned head-dress", in which complicated double-horned flexible shapes were artificially bound up in scarves and veils. Something still remains of these head-dresses to this day in the caps and hoods worn by nuns. We have mentioned this fashion chiefly for its significance in regard to the further development of European fashions, for in Bohemia itself it was little known – we only come across it once in the Wenceslas manuscripts – and it is only later, in its more modest, bourgeois form, that it was more common. In essence it is in this fashion that the many sinful women are depicted in the Hussite Jena Codex, dating from the end of the 15th and the beginning of the 16th century.[1]

When we examine the development of the Czech male costume of this time, we find that the miniatures offer us quite a rich variety of types of people. There are shepherds, peasants, gardeners, carpenters, blacksmiths, fishermen and even vintners and barmen, and finally we come across an example of the miner in his ceremonial white overall. In these miniatures we even find the hangman and his accomplice. The foundation garment of countryfolk and handicraftsmen, such as smiths and men of similar professions, is the short tunic reaching to the knees; in the case of peasants it is sometimes just a roughly-woven linen smock, but the craftsman usually has a somewhat better, more expensive garment, such as a cloth tunic in various colours. This form of dress scarcely underwent any change throughout the period with which we are dealing, so that we can take the short loose tunic, cut and sewn from one piece and drawn in at the waist, with its long narrow sleeves or sometimes slightly looser open ones, to be the typical, usual costume of the working people of Bohemia during the 14th century and the beginning of the 15th. Even the poorest clothes sometimes had a hood attached to the shoulders, or there would be a cap with a curved brim, a hood or a straw hat with a broad brim. We also come across rough peasant furs. The smith wore a leather apron when working, many a craftsman, woodcutter or shepherd wore a useful sort of hood and cape right down over his shoulders, and these would sometimes have a dagged edge. The poorest landworkers and the fishermen, however, worked in a rough, sleeveless linen shirt, with a coarse linen undershirt, or a worn, threadbare smock; the very poor wore merely a torn tunic with shoulder cape and hood. But even in these instances it is possible to note the influence of the fashionable costume – by 1405 the countryfolk were already coming under its influence – for in one case a peasant wears quite a short little jacket, the pleated tail of which scarcely covers his buttocks, and another has a jacket or doublet, fringed at the ends and gathered into a belt at the waist, with broad, pointed sleeves, cut in lobes at the edges.

The tunic worn by the burgher was similar to that which we have seen in the case of

1] The richly illustrated Hussite Jena Codex, dating from the beginning of the 16th century, was presented to Czechoslovakia. It was handed over to the National Museum in Prague, where it is deposited under the reference number IV A 24. See Z. Drobná, "Český život 15. století v zrcadle Jenského kodexu", *Český lid* 39, 1955, p. 5.; Z. Drobná, "Janíček Zmílelý z Písku a Jenský kodex", *Umění* III, Prague, 1955, p. 191.

certain craftsmen. It is a tunic of many colours, reaching to the knees, gathered into a belt at the waist, or later, i. e. after 1370, close-fitting with a girdle round the hips. In fact, during the second half of the 14th century, we still come across both the short, wide tunic of the older type, and the narrower, close-fitting tunic which was already assuming the new line of the fashionable doublet. This developed out of the overtunic, that had become so slim that it had to be cut down the middle, so as to enable the fashionable fop to put it on – and then it was fastened tight by a long row of buttons or hooks. He would also sometimes wear an ornamental girdle low down over his hips, from which hung either his purse or a short weapon. The narrow sleeves were often sewn up to the elbow with a close row of buttons, sometimes even as far as the shoulder. In fact buttons were altogether very popular at that time.[1] This jacket was often scalloped at the lower edge. At the beginning of the 15th century the doublet, as far as this was still possible, became even narrower until it completely fitted the shape of the body; it was very close-fitting, very short, reached only a short way below the waist and beneath it was the girdle that rested on the hips.

From the year 1376 we also come across the typical little cape of the dandy. It is short and full, and fastened with buttons in the front. The Wenceslas Bible, dating from the end of the 14th century, also provides us with examples of the long cloak which fastened in the front at the neck, of various forms of hoods or capuche, often scalloped around the head, with a long or short tippet, and finally of the kind of cloak that was slit from the elbow to the ground on the left side and otherwise covered the whole figure.

Here we also come across the short riding cloak, again fastened at the neck, but with only one button.

In the year 1432, that is already during the Hussite period, the squires, and possibly also the higher nobility in Bohemia, used to wear a rather long, severe tunic or jacket (reaching below the knee), that was fuller at the bottom but close-fitting around the upper part of the body and had a girdle resting low over the hips. The jacket sometimes had short sleeves that only reached to the elbow, and so had to be completed by an undersleeve, usually of contrasting material, or alternatively it had a short sleeve to the elbow from which hung long tippets, which of course also enabled one to see the undersleeve.

These basic styles are equally valid as a description of the dress of the nobility, with the difference, however, that the latter were not restricted in any way in satisfying their desire for luxury and eccentricity. Hence the costume is more extravagant, more elegant and, of course, more expensive. The most typical examples of this style have been preserved from the time of King Wenceslas IV at the end of the 14th and the beginning of the 15th centuries, since from all accounts it seems that King Wenceslas was himself an elegant young dandy – at least that is how he was often represented in the famous manuscripts that were specially painted for him – and that he himself encouraged these eccentricities.

As in the case of female costume, here also there was a certain development in the shape of the sleeve. The fashionable dandy of 1405 wore a close-fitting jacket which was pleated at the bottom and finished off round the edge with a decorative belt. The sleeves were, however, noticeable in that they grew wider right from the shoulder and formed long, wide sacklike tippets below the elbow. These were closed, for the sleeve continued further and ended tightly at the wrist. Another style from the beginning of the 15th century was the jacket with sleeves that were slit the whole length of the sleeve from the shoulder

---

1] The Industrial Art Museum in Prague, or rather its branch, the Museum of Fashions and Social Culture in the state castle at Jemniště near Benešov, has a fine collection of buttons, including examples of buttons from the Middle Ages (from the former Waldes Factory Museum). The plans to extend the amenities of the museum include the installation of a display of reconstructed medieval costumes.

and hung down to the lower edge of the jacket. The edge of the sleeves in this case was also dagged from the bottom. From this period we also get the wide, sacklike sleeves, with two openings for the hands, one just below the shoulder and the other somewhat lower. There appeared to be either a short sleeve with a long sacklike tippet (the arm itself was covered by the buttoned-in undersleeve) or else a long wide, balloon-shaped one, according to which opening was used by the hand. Another variation was a similar sack-like sleeve, but with only one opening. Apart from these sacklike sleeves, there were also the long open sleeves which broadened out into a pointed lappet, under which the man of fashion also wore a full undersleeve that was gathered in at the wrist, as we see it in the costume dating from the year 1405. And to judge by the decorative elements this was influenced by the German fashions of the time.

We know from literary sources, and also from a closer examination of the shapes, that the fashionable tight-fitting doublets were fairly firmly padded. And to complete the true picture we should here point out that it was often the fashion to wear tight-fitting parti-coloured hose, the one half contrasting with the other.

What we have already said regarding the relationship between the type of costume. worn by the nobility and that of the burghers applies also to that worn by the monarch. Apart from the question of the ceremonial robe, prescribed by coronation procedure, the king wore the same clothes as the richer nobility – sometimes they were more modest, if he was a sober, straightforward person like the Emperor Charles IV; on the other hand they were sometimes more eccentric, as in the case of King Wenceslas IV. Hence there were no new types of costume, and we shall only cast a swift glance over the royal wardrobe, in order to complete the picture.

In the votive picture of Jan Očko of Vlašim (circa 1370), the young prince Wenceslas is dressed in red hose and a close-fitting red, gold-woven brocade surcoat, from the shoulders of which long ermine strips hang right down to the ground. The belt is worn round the hips. The royal cloak, fastened at the front, is also similar in type to that of the normal medieval costume; it is only the richness of the materials that make it more distinguished. The ermine collar covering the shoulders is apparently just a survival of the former cape. We come across King Wenceslas IV in the illuminations to his Bible as a young, extravagantly-dressed dandy; he usually wears parti-coloured hose (mi-parti), and a short close-fitting jacket, obviously heavily padded over the breast, which either has full sleeves that narrow at the wrist and on which one often finds symbolic love knots,[1] or else club-shaped sleeves that widen out from the shoulder and are cut and dagged in scallops round the edge.

The king's costume which dates from 1405 is an example which shows us how foreign elements immediately seem out of place in a Bohemian context. Here he wears parti-col-oured hose, and a doublet with a stiff, upstanding collar and broad sleeves, narrowing at the wrist. The doublet is covered by a cloak thrown over the shoulders; the latter is deeply laciniated and dagged at the bottom. We have already come across this style of full slit-up sleeve for the jacket as worn by the king.

We should get too far away from our subject if we tried to deal in detail with the vestments of the clergy, the habits of the monks, and so on. I have therefore purposely limited myself to secular costumes. But I hope nevertheless that in the few examples shown

1] See J. v. Schlosser, op. cit., p. 276, for the signifi-cance of this symbol, which was a favourite one in the manuscripts and other works completed for King Wenceslas IV, and where it appears in the form of a garlanded wreath, often with a kingfisher in the middle. Since it appears so often in connection with Wenceslas IV, many present-day authors of specialist works on the subject often speak of it as Wenceslas's personal symbol.

here of clerical and monastic vestments the reader will himself observe elements of the secular costume of the time and that in many cases he will get a clear idea of the origin of certain elements in these clothes which have remained unchanged right to our time. Examples have been taken from the Jena Codex and here we must bear in mind the fact that this codex belongs to the beginning of the 16th century. One of the miniatures depicts Žižka on horseback at the head of the Hussite army. In front of him marches a priest with a monstrance, wearing a blue tunic and a white surplice. This is a Hussite priest as depicted by an illuminator at the beginning of the 16th century.[1]

Considering what we already know of Bohemian fashions and their relationship to other European fashions of the time, we should not be surprised when we find, on examining the male costume of France, Germany and elsewhere, that we repeatedly come across the same or similar basic parts to the costumes and their accessories. The more remote the costumes are, such as those we have mentioned from Italy and England, the more they have their own characteristics, not to speak of those from Hungary and further still, from Kuman, and so on. I think, however, that even these were all in some way subject to the overall basic characteristic style of the time and to the most expressive fundamental trends of that style. Even though we come across local variants, we can always trace them back to a type which we know, to some European form or other. What we have come across least of all so far in our fashion styles is the costume made on the lines of the Burgundian pattern, and so here we must still mention the typical short coat or jerkin of this style from the end of the 14th century, with outer and under sleeves and with thick padding on the shoulders (mahôitres).

In order to characterize Bohemian costume of the first half, and especially the first third, of the 15th century, we should mention that it consciously broke away from contact with the rest of the world and continued to follow the lines inherited from the previous century. It is not necessary to go into detail over the reasons that led to this – they are quite obvious. During this period of great conflict and endeavour, a period in which Hussitism was dominant, every form of luxury, both secular and ecclesiastical, was inevi ably condemned and by none more severely than the strictest and most consistent adherents of Hussitism, the Táborites. In fact, we know that it was the Táborite women, who were strictest in this respect.[2] Of course there were also moderate and more conciliatory elements, and there is no doubt that they were also more compromising in the field of clothing, and that they did not altogether give up or put aside their secular magnificence for very long. It is quite true that during the Hussite period the dominant colour in clothes seems to have been somewhat gloomy or black, but nevertheless the wives of the burghers seem to have preserved and continued to wear expensive ornaments on their heads and their veils. It is also interesting that the wife of King George of Poděbrady loved beautiful dresses and that by the end of the 15th century the nobles and burghers once more displayed a rich luxuriousness in their dress which led to the adoption of the new Renaissance style. What was inherited from the costume of the 14th century, what ascetic Táborite elements influenced the further evolution of dress in the following years, how and when Bohemian costume came once more into close contact with the fashions of the rest of Europe, are all questions which lead beyond the bounds of the first half of the 15th century, the boundary in time to which this short essay is limited.

1] Jena Codex, fol. 76a.
2] Anna Císařová-Kolářová, Žena v hnutí husitském

(Woman in the Hussite Movement), Prague, 1915, p. 179.
Zíbrt and Winter, op. cit., II, p. 50.

BATTLE EQUIPMENT
1. ARMOUR

In the days when the decisive, in fact the only, method of warfare consisted of the head-on clash of armies, of hand-to-hand combat between warrior and warrior, and when engagements fought at greater distances by means of cannon fire were treated as a subordinate part of the battle, in those days it was quite natural that the individual warriors tried to protect their bodies as much as possible by the use of various kinds of personal armour. This was very much the case in the period covered by this book. Firearms were at that time in their infancy and cannonfire, though used more and more as time went on, did not as yet have such devastating effect as in later centuries.

Just as with all other forms of clothing in the Middle Ages, military dress clearly reflected the social and class divisions of society. Only rich people could afford to wear the full suit of armour; even the lesser gentry, though members of the ruling class, had to be content with only partial protection. The same was true in the towns; and the common soldier possessed very few of the individual parts of the suit worn by the knights-at-arms.

During the comparatively long period of which we shall be speaking – in fact a period of more than one hundred years – armour naturally underwent a certain evolution. In Czech sources up to the end of the first half of the 14th century, we still continue to meet with a preponderance of chain armour, made of small iron or steel rings linked together either by rivets or welded so that it formed a closely-knit network of chain mail that provided quite good protection against cut and thrust. In the Velislav Bible[1] of the first half of the 14th century and in other outstanding Czech drawings of that time, also in the *Liber Depictus* MSS, dating from about 1350,[2] the majority of warriors are still dressed in chain armour.

The body is covered by a mail shirt or long, below knee-length, tunic known as a coat of mail or hauberk with sleeves, which fitted right into the armoured gloves, or gauntlets. The warrior wore mail stockings of one piece which covered the whole leg. From the helmet there also hung a piece of mail covering the nape of the neck, the neck itself and the chin of the warrior, known as the aventail. Only a few of the warriors as yet had plate poleyns and shins protected by plate. Over the coat-of-mail all warriors wore a cloth tunic or jupon, which was sleeveless and slit open down both sides from below the waist.

It would seem that by the middle of the 14th century plate armour was still at a very early stage of development and that mail still predominated. However it is also quite clear that the draughtsmen of both of these remarkable manuscripts of Czech origin kept to the older tradition in depicting armour, whereas the evolution of armour itself had progressed considerably.

Already in the Zbraslav Chronicle by Petr Žitavský, dating from the first quarter of the 14th century, we come across the term "thorax" as well as mail. In the Old Town statutes of 1335 we find either coats of mail or plate armour mentioned as part of the equipment for battle. By the first half of the 14th century the battle dress consisted of a combination of mail and plate armour. Throughout the 14th century plate armour more and more took pride of place and during the last quarter and in certain cases at the very beginning of the following century the complete suit of plate armour was evolved, in which the armed knight was literally welded in iron. But even so chain armour does not completely disappear.

1] Manuscript in the Prague University Library.   2] MSS in the Vienna State Library.

Let us just compare how two master painters – the Master of Vyšší Brod, from about the middle of the century, and the Master of Třeboň, about thirty years later – depicted soldiers in their paintings of the same scene, namely the Resurrection. Among the soldiers in the picture by the Master of Vyšší Brod there is a man in chain armour, in which the sleeves and gauntlets are in one piece; he has mail stockings or chausses with plate poleyns and leg coverings or greaves, probably made of leather. Over his chain armour he wears a sleeveless tunic reaching to his knees; his neck is protected by a mail gorget, or collar (II., Pl. 1).

In his picture of the same theme, the Master of the Třeboň altar-piece, dating from about 1380, depicted a richly-dressed soldier in a fundamentally different manner. The best dressed of the guards here wears a helmet with a lattice-shaped visor and mail aventail, or neck protection. The coat of mail with sleeves is only visible on the under part of the upper arm and elbow and beneath the edge of the tunic; otherwise both arms and legs are completely covered by the plate-metal parts of the suit. Over his elbows he has golden couters, the lower part of them being protected on both sides by vambrace. The upper part of the arm and most of the body is covered by a tunic, which is slit open down the sides from the waist and has a dagged border all round the lower edge and round the edges of the short, open sleeves. The soldier's legs are completely covered in mail. Over the mail stockings he has metal plates or cuisses covering the upper part of his legs; his knees are protected by gilt poleyns of oblong shape, which form a point when the knee is bent, the calves of the legs are also completely covered by metal plate to which are attached iron sabbatons with fairly short points. A fine dagger hangs from the narrow belt at the right thigh. The armour is supplemented with a round shield which runs out into a long spike in the centre. The gilt edge to the helmet, the gilt poleyns and the couters point to the luxuriousness of the armour, such as would be worn by the rich nobility when going into battle (II., Pl. 3).

The great differences between the armour of this soldier and that of the warrior depicted by the Vyšší Brod Master are an indication of the changes which had been taking place during this period in the evolution of armour. We notice the marked increase in plate sections and we can assume the existence of a breastplate, which is probably covered by the tunic. Further stages in these evolutionary changes are to be seen in a number of pictures of knights on horseback to be found in the illuminations to that great work of the Bohemian school of painting, dating from the turn of the 14th and 15th centuries, known as the King Wenceslas (Václav) Bible.[1] In one of the miniatures there is a mounted soldier in armour, which includes a helmet with aventail and coat of mail with sleeves. But the armour already described above is further supplemented with other pieces (II., Pl. 8). The shoulders are protected by circular besagues or shoulder pieces, the upper part of the arm by rerebrace, oblong plates bent to the shape of the arm which are fastened round the underarm by a special band. On his elbows he has couters, covering the lower arm are the vambrace and he wears metal gauntlets. Over the coat of mail the soldier wears an overtunic, in chequered pattern, and over this is a breastplate. Again his legs are completely covered in plate armour.

Both the last two armours described above completely disprove Winter's claims that overall protection for the arms and legs by the use of welded plates was not known till the 15th century. Possibly the soldier in the Vyšší Brod Master's Cycle has a leather covering for his legs. The painting by the Master of Třeboň, however, speaks quite clearly for metal. And it would be completely unthinkable that during the 14th century the main parts of

1] The original is in Vienna; a photo-copy is in the State Documentary Centre in Prague.

the armour were made of leather and only a century later of metal, when we know that even before the middle of the 14th century welders constituted one of the most numerous groups of craftsmen employed in the making of armour in Czech towns – especially in the larger towns of Prague and Brno. It would be quite incomprehensible, since they would have had no work to do. The further development of the knight's armour only goes to confirm this opinion.

In the miniatures of the King Wenceslas Bible we can find plenty of material helpful to our researches. A number of pictures of knights-at-arms give us the complete development of plate armour for the arms and legs (II., Plate 12). We can trace a number of different styles for the various parts of the armour. For instance the shoulder piece of the first warrior (II., Pl. 11, No. 1) has an egg-shaped pointed form, with the point turned down towards the elbow; in the case of the soldier with the open helmet (II., Pl. 12, No. 3) it is a raised plate with the edge sloping slightly downwards like a roof; another (II., Pl. 12, No. 4) has a plate lined with what is probably a five-leaved rosette, and yet another (II., Pl. 12, No. 5) has quite a unique shape that runs out from the curved piece protecting the shoulder down over the arm in an oblong shape bent to fit the arm and joining the plate covering for the upper arm.

The same is true of the knee pieces or poleyn. The figure in the jupon decorated with Gothic ornamentation (II., Pl. 12, No. 5), has knee pieces that are really independent of the rest of the covering for the leg, and they are in the form of an oblong bulging in the middle which extends into two split points on the outer side of the leg. In all other cases it is incorporated as part of the armour protecting the leg and its flexibility is achieved by the use of riveted straps at the top and the bottom (II., Pl. 12, Nos. 2—4, 6). The various types and the development of plate coverings for the leg are shown in II., Pl. 78—81.

Armour of this period is, of course, by no means unified, either as regards form or type. It is not so even in the case of the individual sections. We still come across, and as we shall see much later, shall continue to come across, the coat of chain mail or tunic with sleeves but without any plate protection. And as for the cloth tunics, known as soldiers' surcoats, here there was marked diversity of cut and design. Most of them were sleeveless; some with elbow-length sleeves or even longer were turned up above the elbow.

The armour itself, however, showed even more variations. The soldier with the mace (II., Pl. 16, No. 1), who has complete plate armour covering his arms and legs, wears mail reaching to half way down his thighs over which there is a front plate reaching to his waist. The second soldier (*ibid.*, No. 2) is dressed similarly, but in addition to the front plate he has one covering his back and in the third case the plate covering of the upper part of the body for the first time includes a form of skirt, for the time being fairly short and covering only the thighs but running out into a tongue in the centre front.

All these fighters still wore a great many mail parts to their armour. The figure of Goliath in the Krumlov manuscript of the Mirror of Redemption,[1] dating from the beginning of the 15th century, differs considerably from all these. It is the first picture of a soldier completely clothed in plate armour. Apart from the collar, which is apparently of mail, we cannot find the slightest trace of mail on this type of knight. The full suit of plate covering the body is supplemented by a skirt, made of four rows of plates, joined by rivets. The arms and legs are completely covered by sections of plate mail (II., Pl. 17).

It does not mean, of course, that the older types of armour disappeared altogether. On the contrary, in the same manuscript we come across a fighter clothed entirely in the traditional coat of mail with long sleeves fitting into mail gauntlets (II., Pl. 20). In contrast

1] Prague National Museum Library; ref. no. III B. 10. f. 31.

to the warriors of old, however, his legs are completely covered by plate mail. This combination of chain and plate mail, similar to that which we noted already in the Wenceslas Bible, appears in a number of cases here (e. g. II., Pl. 27).

The old type of armour still persisted, one could almost say predominated, if it were not for the fact that one must allow for the conservative concept that persisted in the minds of the individual illuminators concerning armoured figures. Right at the beginning of the 15th century we come across the complete suit of plate armour, for the time being only as an exception, but nevertheless indicating the direction of development. Before we follow this development any further, however, we must still deal with various types of mixed armours.

The most common knight's armour at the beginning of the 15th century was still the combination of chain and plate together with a tunic of cloth or surcoat. We see this very closely in a number of figures taken from the Krumlov manuscript (II., Pl. 21, Nos. 1 and 4; Pl. 22, and Pl. 23).

Another example, however, of the complete suit of plate armour as worn by the feudal lords, is to be found in a drawing in the Kyeser Bellifortis manuscript, showing two knights in combat. Both are wearing full battle dress including the helmet with visor, the breast and back-plates, the metal skirt, the pauldrons, besaques and other pieces and coverings for the arms, and finally also the legs are completely covered in plate armour (II., Pl. 32). The date of the manuscript is indisputable and thus, apart from the figure of Goliath in the Krumlov manuscript, we here have further proof that full plate armour was already in use in Bohemia right at the beginning of the 15th century.

Dating from about the same time we also have the manuscript *Libri XX de anatomia*, belonging to the Prague Chapter Library.[1] In this we again find the complete suit of metal armour, but it is once more a combination of mail and plate armour. The camail, the coat of mail, reaching halfway down the thighs, and the stockings are of chain mail. But with the exception of the camail and the lower edge of the coat of chain mail, taking the place of the skirt (it is not necessarily a mail skirt) the rest is all hidden under plate armour (II., Pl. 34). The figure of the king, with a golden crown on the top of his helmet, is dressed in similar armour (II., Pl. 35), but in his case the armour of the body is covered by a tunic with short sleeves, slit up at the lower edge in the centre so that one can see the weave of the mail skirt. Perpendicular from a gold-embossed belt on the right hand side hangs a dagger with a plate-shaped cross-guard and a bone hilt.

A fairly unique figure is that of the soldier in the picture by the Master of the Rajhrad altar-piece, dating from the period before 1420 (II., Pl. 36).[2] The gilt elbow and knee couter and the fine, embossed belt indicate a wealthy member of the ruling class, but he only has armour on his arms and legs. The body is not protected at all. He is dressed in a tunic with rolled-up sleeves and beneath the open neckline one can see his blue undertunic. He wears a simple iron hat or chapel de fer, but this, however, is an exception. Perhaps he is meant to be a mercenary, and the painter was trying to indicate his leading function by giving him ornamental elbow and knee pieces.

The nearer we come to the end of the Hussite wars the more the amount of plate increases in the individual suit of armour, the more often we come across it, and the more perfectly it serves its purpose. The knight from the Prague University Library manuscript XVII A 34, dressed in full armour and dating from about the year 1430 (II., Pl. 39, No. 1), has his neck protected by a mail camail, the breastplate is ornamented with six narrow, curved bands, which are most probably done in relief, and their purpose is possibly not

1] Prague Cathedral Chapter Library, ref. no. 111.   2] Matějček, *Gothic Painting in Bohemia*, Pl. 184.

only to ornament but also to strengthen the fore-plate against blows. Attached to this the soldier has a skirt made up of flexible metal splints or individual tasse, beneath which one can see the lower edge of the coat of mail, finished off in triangular points. The pauldrons are also made in three parts, allowing greater mobility of movement to the arms and fitting exactly over the rerebrace. The elbow pieces have heart-shaped side-wings. The legs are also protected by metal plates. From the embossed belt, which he wears very low – almost at the bottom edge of the tasses – there hangs a straight sword in a simple scabbard.

How the ornamentation of plate armour was developed even further can well be seen from the figure of Jindřich of Stráž on a tomb dating from 1466 (II., Pl. 39, No. 2). Here there are no new parts to the armour, it is only a question of the development of their forms. The oblong knee pieces have curved protrusions at the sides and a knob-like disc; similarly the shoulder pieces are also more ornamental: the round palette is not fixed straight on to the surrounding plates, but is set in a four-leaved plate that is linked to the rerebrace by a further metal plate which is indented at the edge. The breastplate, which is ornamented with narrow bands cut vertically in relief, bends fairly sharply in at the waist. This curve may be of older origin however. We come across it in Flanders and in Switzerland as early as the thirties of the 15th century. Below the elbow one no longer sees the sleeves of the coat of mail. The arm is covered by a broader band of the elbow piece, which is supplemented with further plates.

As early as the first half of the 14th century the knights on horseback already wore cloaks over their battle clothes, a type of surcoat which was usually lined with fur and known as a *kuršít*. It was a piece of clothing that was certainly very expensive and therefore very precious. A fine example of a fighter in one of these cloaks is the figure of St. Wenceslas in the Mulhouse altar-piece, dating from the year 1385 (II., Pl. 4). He still wears the traditional, but at that time already old-fashioned, coat of mail, which only has ornamental elbow and knee pieces made of plate, similarly to the warrior in the picture of the Crucifixion from Skalice, dating from about 1430 (II., Pl. 37). The latter is dressed in a red tunic with a fine embossed belt, he wears a breastplate and complete plate armour for his arms and legs (no gauntlets); over his shoulders he has a long red cloak, lined with ermine and with a wide ermine collar.[1]

We have now covered a hundred years of development of the knight's armour. From armour made almost entirely of mail, consisting of metal rings welded together, sometimes even of gold or silver, it progressed to the full suit of plate armour. From the beginning of the second half of the 14th century the number of plate sections or parts increased and the armour became a combination of mail and plate. At the turn of the 14th and 15th centuries we come across the first examples of the complete suit of plate armour and these examples gradually increase during the course of the first half of the 15th century. Naturally one continues to find the combination of chain and plate, but gradually mail gives place to the plate sections, which increase in size and number.

All this, of course, only applies to the armour of the heavy cavalry, which was provided by the knights. And even though, throughout this period up to the Hussite wars – and of course on the part of the enemy even during these wars – this cavalry was the main and decisive section of the army, nevertheless the feudal armies, in addition to these knights, also had light cavalry, shield-bearers and archers, and, of course, foot soldiers. The light cavalry usually only differed from the "iron-clads" in that they merely wore certain parts of the armour, of which we have already spoken. An example of one of these types is the

1] Matějček, *op. cit.* Pl. 239.

rider in a picture in the Krumlov manuscript, who, apart from a helmet and aventail, does not have any armour (II., Pl. 24).

A type of horseman who would probably have been common amongst the Hussite riders is the rider depicted in a miniature in the so-called Padeřov Bible, dating from between 1433—1435. He also wears a basinet helmet and aventail and only his legs are protected by plate armour. Apart from this he simply wears a cloth tunic with long sleeves (II., Pl. 43). The majority of Hussite mounted warriors, excluding the small number of landed gentry, and in the case of the Prague army, the rich burghers and the feudal lords who fought with them, clearly only wore incomplete suits of armour, usually just a helmet and aventail or an iron hat or casque with mail hood, a coat of mail and perhaps occasionally certain plate armour sections for the upper part of the body. But even amongst the Hussite cavalry one sometimes comes across fighters in more complete suits of plates which they had won as booty from enemy cavalry riders. Such cases, however, were certainly only exceptions, and full suits of armour were rare among the Hussites.

By the 14th century foot soldiers were far from all being those feudal lieges, assembled together from among the feudal serfs and bondsmen and miserably armed, of whom Frederick Engels rightly wrote that they were of no use for anything. The Old Czech poem, *Alexandreis*, supposed to date from the beginning of the 14th century, no doubt depicts what the author saw around him, even though it is concerned with the almost legendary king of ancient Greece.

According to these verses one can assume that the foot soldier of the first half of the 14th century wore a breastplate or a coat of mail and an iron hat. In fact, basically it was only the upper part of the body that was protected. And this style can be said to have predominated, as far as the infantry were concerned, for the whole period with which we are dealing.

As elsewhere, it was in the expanding towns of Bohemia that a new, more capable, type of foot soldier began to appear. The towns of Bohemia had to be ready to defend themselves during the ever-recurrent smaller wars and against the attacks of the feudal lords; in the Bohemian towns, as elsewhere, the development came about through the establishment of a local militia. According to a Prague Old Town Statute of 1371, the inhabitants, if need arose, had to be ready to go out and fight personally, at their own expense and according to the quarter in which they lived; the quarters took it in turns, two taking part in the expedition and two always remaining at home.[1]

At a very early stage, however, the burghers tried to exempt themselves from this personal obligation, most frequently by the hiring of mercenaries, whom they paid and also often armed. For this purpose the Czech and Moravian towns often had armouries well stocked with arms and armour. In 1362 the towns of Vysoké Mýto and Hradec Králové received a certain quantity of suits of armour from the king, which they then supplemented at their own expense, so that in all, Vysoké Mýto had a total of 300 pieces of armour and Hradec Králové 400. The arms thus acquired consisted of the following pieces: breastplates, helmets (basinets) with aventails, pauldrons and gorgets, rerebrace, vambrace and gauntlets.[2] A year later Plzeň was also equipped with 400 similar pieces.

The supplies of armour in the town armouries were primarily intended for the hired mercenaries and poorer citizens, who could not afford to equip themselves with the necessary armour. Sometimes perhaps individual pieces were also lent out to the burghers to supplement their own suits of armour. That plenty of such pieces were used by the burghers and that the tenant town craftsmen also had them on loan can be seen clearly

1] Tomek, *Dějepis Prahy*, II, p. 369.   2] Jireček, *Cod. Jur. Boh.*, II/3, pp. 103–4.

from the securities for the debts that were forfeited and registered in the towns' books. Sometimes they are only single pieces, most frequently a coat of mail or iron hat or other kind of helmet, sword or cross-bow, but at other times it would be several pieces, from which it would be possible to make up a complete suit of armour.

There were, however, some burghers who were so rich that their armoury inventories could often compare well with those of the landed gentry, in fact sometimes surpassed those of quite a number of them. Documents show that the town militia and mercenaries, the one section of the infantry that was at least comparatively battle-ready in the pre-Hussite period, were equipped with armour that usually only protected the upper part of the body.[1] That this was the case even before the middle of the 14th century can easily be seen from the works of the Bohemian Gothic painters.

As proof let us once more turn to the work of the Master of Vyšší Brod (II., Pl. 1.). In his picture of the Resurrection he painted not only the knight, whom we have already mentioned previously, but also the less well-equipped foot soldiers. One of them, without a helmet and with just a cap, wears a coat of mail and a mail hood. Otherwise he only wears a sleeveless knee-length tunic and cloth hose. From the centre front of his ornamental belt hangs a dagger. The other mercenary in the same picture, holding a halbard, wears a helmet with aventail and a coat of mail with sleeves. Over the coat of mail he wears a cloth tunic girded by a belt with a dagger, cloth stockings and shoes that are fastened with a strap tied above the ankle.

The King Wenceslas Bible, a source which we have already drawn on previously, also provides us with several figures dressed in a similar manner. A bowman with a crossbow and an archer (II., Pl. 6) only have protection for their heads, necks and shoulders. The archer wears a basinet helmet with a scale cape attached; the bowman is wearing an iron hat with a mail hood. The rest of their clothing is no different from that of the ordinary civilian. In both cases they are wearing a simple short jacket with sleeves and hose. The halbardier in II., Plate 15, is dressed in the same way as the archer. The mercenary from II., Plate 7, No. 1 also has just an iron casque, but instead of the hood he wears a mail collar, whereas the soldier with the basinet (II., Pl. 7, No. 2) has a mail camail covering the shoulders of his short tunic which has very wide sleeves.

Figures equipped with similar armour are to be found in other pictorial sources, for instance in the Krumlov manuscript, dating from the beginning of the 15th century, and so on.

Other mercenary soldiers from the King Wenceslas Bible differ from the figures so far mentioned chiefly in the fact that instead of chain or plate armour they wear a gambeson or padded coat to take the place of the tunic or jacket. But at the time of the creation of the Bible this was again nothing new. In the Old Czech *Alexandreis*, created not long after the so-called Dalimil Chronicle, dating from the beginning of the 14th century, the stiff coat or "coats of plates" are considered alternatives for the foot soldiers.[2] Various types of gambeson can be seen in II., Pl. 10. These stiff coats were quilted either horizontally or vertically, both in the body of the garment and in the sleeves. In a number of cases the direction of the sewing varies for the individual parts. Other parts of armour were then added to the gambeson. Thus one of the mercenaries has an iron hat with a mail hood, another, with a sword and lance, has a basinet with aventail, the halbardier has a gambeson without sleeves, but on his shoulders he has metal shoulder-pieces lined with cloth or perhaps leather.

It would be a mistake, however, to consider the gambeson as a subordinate part of the

---

1] Strnad, *Listář města Plzně*, I, p. 91 (1363). 2] *Alexandreis*, Prague, 1947, p. 38.

armour. In a number of the miniatures of the King Wenceslas Bible we come across warriors dressed in such gambesons, but in addition they are equipped with other parts of the suit. For instance there is a lancer with an iron hat and mail hood, metal gauntlets and complete plate protection for the legs (II., Pl. 15, No. 3).

The gambeson was undoubtedly also part of the battle dress of the Hussite soldiers. It probably often made up for the lack of plate armour and at the same time had the advantage of giving the wearer greater power of movement and, of course, of giving him less to carry.

The intermediary type of coat between the gambeson and the full metal covering was the brigandine, a garment lined with small plates of iron or steel overlapping upwards. This type of clothing, strengthened in addition by chains hung across the breast to ward off the blows of the enemy's swords, is worn by at least two of the soldiers depicted in the miniatures of the Wenceslas Bible (II., Pl. 14, Nos. 2 and 3).

The armour of the foot soldiers was, of course, not merely limited to those parts already described above. A great number of examples from pictorial sources indicate that more complicated arrangements of the armour were fairly frequent. A lancer from the Wenceslas Bible (II., Pl. 14, No. 1), apart from his iron hat and chain-mail hood, also wears plate metal gauntlets and plate metal couters on his otherwise unprotected legs. In the Krumlov manuscript (II., Pl. 27, No. 1.) there is a very similarly dressed fighter, though in this case he does not wear metal vambrace, and he holds a sword. From the same source we have illustrations of two warriors wearing helmets with aventail and scale skirts (II., Pl. 19, Nos. 2 and 3). One of them, a lancer, also has a shield. The rest of their clothing is made of cloth.

Sometimes one comes across a coat of mail which is supplemented with a breastplate, as we find in several of the drawings in the Kyeser Bellifortis manuscript (II., Pl. 29, No. 2; Pl. 30, No. 5). Elsewhere the plate armour of the upper part of the body is riveted straight on the cloth tunic (II., Pl. 27, No. 3). We even come across examples of plate protection for the arms as in the case of the warrior dating from about 1430 (Pl. 42), who is equipped with an iron hat, a mail hood, shoulder pieces, greaves, poleyns and vambrace.

An interesting style of dress, and for us a particularly interesting one because it is a question of a type from the period of the Hussite wars, is the figure of an armed cross-bowman in a manuscript in Prague University Library (II., Pl. 41, No. 1).[1] He has an iron casque, beneath which he wears a cloth hood, a short tunic with sleeves and with the exception of iron foot defences his legs are completely protected by metal plate. He is armed with a sword, hanging from a simple girdle, an arbalest and a buckler. Judging by the time when the manuscript was written (circa 1430), one is justified in assuming that the majority of Hussite crossbowmen, especially during the later years of the wars, were probably equipped in a similar manner, although their clothing was certainly colourful and by no means uniform.

When speaking of a greater or lesser number of parts to the armour one is, of course, primarily speaking of the warriors from the towns and of those who had won individual parts of suits of armour as booty. The mass of Hussite foot soldiers, the majority of whom were the common people from the countryside and the town poor, were obviously very poorly equipped, in fact they really had no arms at all.

The miniatures and panel paintings by Bohemian Gothic masters enable us to get an idea of what these "unarmed" warriors looked like. For many of them their only piece of armour was probably the iron casque. The Master of the Rajhrad altar-piece has

1] Ref. no. XVII-a-34.

depicted just such a warrior for us. And there are other cases where they do not even have any protection for the head.

Like the armour of the heavy cavalry of the knights-at-arms, during the period of over a hundred years with which we are dealing, the armour of the infantry underwent considerable development. A common feature was the growth of the use of tin-plate parts as part of the armour. The best equipped of the foot soldiers, namely the burghers and the well-armed mercenary soldiers, for the most part only had armour for the upper part of the body and the arms. Protection for the legs was, in the best of cases, only partial, as full plate armour on the legs made walking difficult and was not suitable for infantry. The great majority of the foot soldiers, especially of the Hussite field armies, scarcely had any armour at all, at most a helmet or iron casque with hood or camail, possible also a gambeson and a weapon. Many of them, however, obviously had no armour at all and fought just as they came into the army, in simple civilian clothes.

If we take a look at similar pictorial material sources from other countries of central and western Europe of that time, we find that a similar development to that which we have followed in Bohemia took place there too. The combination of chain and plate armour persisted for a very long time. Dating from the first third of the 15th century we find a German warrior wearing a conical helmet with aventail, also a long cloth tunic reaching to his knees with wide sleeves laciniated at the edges. The arms, from the elbow downwards, and the legs are completely protected by plate armour and on the body, plate is worn over the tunic (II., Pl. 54, No. 4). In other cases a complete coat of mail is visible (II., Pl. 50, No. 2). There is not even any difference in Italy, as can be seen from the figure of the knight on the tomb of Giovanni de Lalata (died 1421; II., Pl. 52, No. 4), or in France (II., Pl. 50, No. 2).

As in Bohemia, in all these lands the amount of plate armour sections used gradually increased, until by the beginning of the 15th century we find examples of full suits of plate armour. Sometimes we can assume that there was more plate at an earlier stage than is indicated by works of art of the time, for it is clear that a cloth tunic was often worn over what was already the complete suit of armour, so that often the breastplate and even the back-plate would have been covered by it. This is shown very clearly by the figure of a fighter from the second half of the 14th century, who is dressed in a fine tunic ornamented with circles inscribed with a cross; from this tunic, however, there projects the collapsible hook, designed to support the lance when levelled for attack (II., Pl. 49). Very often, however, we come across a combination of the brigandine and chain and plate armour (II., Pl. 54, No. 3).

There is also an interesting figure of a French knight, dating from the end of the 14th century, who wears a type of basinet or "dog's head" helmet, a mail hood and cape and a tunic with sleeves which, in contrast to the others, is not drawn in at the waist, but falls freely and has a jagged edge (II., Pl. 53, No. 1). In Germany, in the second half of the 14th century, particularly in the western parts, we often come across the so-called Westphalian gambeson, such as is worn by the figure on a tomb dating from after 1376 (II., pl. 48). During the same period in Germany and elsewhere we come across the sword or dagger – often both together – secured, in addition to the normal fastening at the waist, by means of a special chain hanging either from a rosette on the right-hand side above the breast, in this case obviously part of the breast-plate hidden beneath the tunic – (II., Pl. 47, No. 1), or each hanging separately from the two rosettes on either side of the breast (II., Pl. 52, No. 1).

The chains were probably designed to prevent the weapon from getting lost if knocked out of the hand during battle. A similar fastening for cut and thrust weapons is to be seen in a Gothic relief in the Týn Church in Prague, dating from the end of the 14th century.

In order to be recognized, a knight, encased almost entirely in metal armour, would wear his coat-of-arms not only on his shield, but also on various forms on his armour. He would often wear small escutcheons on the right- and left-hand sides of his chain aventail, which would rest on the front parts of the fighter's shoulders (II., Pl. 54, No. 4); in other cases a single escutcheon would be fixed to the centre lower edge of the aventail (II., Pl. 46, No. 2). The most frequent manner, however, was to divide the tunic in tinctures, according to the tinctures of the coat-of-arms (II., Pl. 50, No. 2), or even to place the armorial bearings in the corresponding coloured fields (II., Pl. 51, No.1); in other cases the actual armorial bearings would be indicated on the tunic itself (see three escutcheons in II., Pl. 46; also the cross of an Order dividing the tunic, II., Pl. 52, No 1). The escutcheon on the cloth or padded hood of the warrior, dating from the end of the 14th century, is there for the same purpose (II., Pl. 54, No. 2).

At the beginning of the 15th century a further stage in the development of plate armour, apart from metal tasses, is provided by the emergence of armour for the upper part of the body made up of small oblong plate splints (the French knight – II., Pl. 55, No. 1). Often a double protection for the lower part of the body was provided by the fact that beneath the plate tasses, there would also be the "loripedium" or "fauld" – a mail skirt or the lower part of the coat of mail, as we see in Jan van Eyck's painting of a warrior, dating from between 1415—1417 (II., Pl. 58, No. 1) or the knight, dating from 1443 (II., Pl. 70, No. 4); in this case it is interesting to note the long mail sleeves, only protected at the elbows by elbow pieces. A soldier from about the year 1430 (II., Pl. 70, No. 3) wears a particular combination of chain and plate armour. In addition to a helmet with visor and circular cheek protectors, fitted with a plate bevor, or under-chin piece and firmly fixed to the plate collar, he also wears a tunic over his coat of mail, to which is attached a breastplate; in place of the tasses he merely has a mail apron, protecting the front part of his body. Likewise he has small pauldrons and narrow plate rerebrace, which are riveted to the chain-mail sleeves and just protect the outer part of the upper arm.

A peculiar feature of the German, Flemish and Swiss battle armour of the thirties of the 15th century are the long, tippet-sleeved tunics flowing from beneath plate pauldrons (II., Pl. 61, Nos. 2 and 3; Pl. 62). The warrior from the Basle altar-piece, dating from about this time, is interesting because his tasses, made of metal plates, reach almost down to his knees, thus giving the appearance of a kind of plate tunic (II., Pl. 61, No. 3). Almost contemporary with this is the figure of the knight, in a picture by Konrad Witz, who is wearing a full suit of plate armour, but instead of the usual tunic he has a long cloak over his shoulders which is put over his head rather in the manner of a priest's chasuble. On top of the cloak he then wears his helmet with plate gorget, bevor and cheek protectors (II., Pl. 59., No. 5). It is also during the thirties that we come across the profiling of the breastplate in bands done in relief (II., Pl. 58, No. 2; Pl. 61, No. 1) and the use of hinged plates over the thighs, known as tuilles (II., Pl. 58, No. 2; Pl. 61, No. 1; Pl. 64, No. 3). There are only individual instances of a warrior in full plate armour, wearing an iron casque and chain-mail hood instead of the usual helmet (II., Pl. 63).

The picture by the Italian painter, Andrea del Castagno, dating from about 1430, is interesting because it depicts the Italian warrior Pippo Spano de Ozora; he was one of those in the service of that cruel enemy of the Hussite revolutionary movement, Sigismund of Luxembourg, who led a number of expeditions of reactionary European feudal lords into Bohemia and who, in spite of his wealth of experience, was soundly beaten by the peasant Hussite armies. The figure of Pippo Spano presents us with a type of Italian armour dating from the first third of the 15th century. Over his short-sleeved coat of mail with breastplate and lance rest, he wears a short cloak, girded at the front but falling freely at the back; it is richly ornamented with jagged patterns. He wears pauldrons over the cloak. The left-hand-side one, which is made of four splints and supplemented by a club-shaped besaque, protects not only the shoulder, but also a considerable part of the left side of the breast; the right-hand-side one is smaller and the besaque is missing, as it would be a hindrance when using the lance. His elbows are protected by mighty two-winged cowters, composed of three layers of plate; the two-winged projections on the outer sides of the poleyns are made similarly. In addition to cowters he also has vambrace and his legs are protected by complete plate greaves (II., Pl. 57, No. 2).

It is a type of armour found in Italy as early as the beginning of the 15th century. As for the uneven size of the shoulder-pieces, we find them also in England during the first quarter of the same century (II., Pl. 57, No. 1). This type of Italian plate armour from about the middle of the 15th century represents the kind of armour that came from the hand of the famous armourer Tomaso da Missaglia (II., Pl. 65, No. 2).

As far as foot soldiers are concerned, those from foreign countries were not dressed very differently from those we have come across in Bohemia (II., Pl. 67, 68, 72). The iron casque or chapel de fer with mail or cloth hood and cape, sometimes a coat of mail, some of the various parts of the plate armour used for protecting the arms and legs, the breast-plate, sometimes even a gambeson or brigandine – these constituted the parts of armour most frequently in use. And, as in Bohemia, this, of course, applied chiefly to the better-off sections of the infantry, such as the strong-bowmen and those with primitive guns. The great majority of foot soldiers, apart from the iron casque, which was also often missing, clearly had no other kind of armour at all.

2. HELMETS

One of the most important parts of the armour was the helmet protecting the head. Throughout the period with which we are dealing, that is even during the 15th century, we keep coming across the small conical-shaped helmet, which left the nape of the neck and the sides of the head uncovered and originated from a type of helmet known in Bohemia right at the beginning of the Middle Ages. Even in the Emmaus Monastery panel painting, dating from about the year 1375, the helmet still fundamentally preserves a shape already known in the 11th and 12th centuries. It is conical in shape and its lower edge and keel, a ridge running from the centre forehead over to the nape of the neck, are ornamented with a flat band, bordered on each side with a row of rivets (III., Pl. 1, No. 2). This type is also to be found in the Krumlov manuscript of the Mirror of Redemption (II., Pl. 21, No. 2; Pl. 27, No. 1). In the first case the lower edge is bordered with a narrow band of gold, in the second case the helmet has no ornamentation. In nearly all cases this helmet is supplemented with a mail aventail, protecting the nape of the neck, the sides of the head and the throat. The figure in the Krumlov manuscript is an exception to this, as the soldier has a chain-mail collar instead of aventail, so that the whole of his throat and the nape of his neck is uncovered (II., Pl. 27, No. 2).

In Bohemian pictorial sources the most usual type was the conical-shaped helmet, with peak rather towards the back of the head, so that it covered the nape of the neck and the sides of the head; it had an oblong opening for the face that was usually curved off at the corners. We find it already in the first half of the 14th century in the *Liber Depictus* manuscript; it appears again in the works of the Master of Vyšší Brod and in all Czech illuminated manuscripts through the century and in the first half of the 15th century. In most cases they are simple helmets without any ornamentation (II., Pl. 6, Nos. 1,2; Pl. 7, No. 2 and others), but a number of them have an ornamented lower edge and border to the opening for the face. In some cases it is only a narrow gold band (II., Pl. 18, No. 5), elsewhere a double band, as in the case of the warrior in the miniature from the Krumlov manuscript (II., Pl. 20). In the Kyeser Bellifortis manuscript, dating from the years 1402—1405, the ornamentation is often a band scalloped on one side (II., Pl. 29, Pl. 30). Sometimes these are extended in the shape of a Gothic trefoil, so that finally the ornamentation creates a sort of crown over the head, as in the picture from the Master of Třeboň's school of painting, dating from about 1380 (III., Pl. 1, No. 3). The figure of King Saul, from the Prague Chapter Bible, wears a crown over his helmet and the border of the face opening and the lower edge are lined with a red, probably leather, band, held in place by square gold rivets (II., Pl. 35).[1] We very often come across this kind of ornamentation in Germany and elsewhere. Occasionally we find cases where the front of the helmet over the forehead is strengthened in such a way that the piece of plate otherwise cut out for the face opening is bent upwards in a curve, thus giving extra protection. A helmet of this kind is worn by a soldier in the picture of the Resurrection by the Master of Vyšší Brod, dating from about 1350 (III., Pl. 1, No. 1).

An interesting conical-shaped helmet is one depicted in a picture by the Master of the Rajhrad altar-piece, dating from before 1420, which also has a plate bevor or chin piece (III., Pl. 1, No. 7). This type of helmet was also known in Germany, about the year 1420 ("The Carrying of the Cross", in Lorch am Rhein; III., Pl. 10), but in this case there was also a movable visor. In Italy the opening for the face was usually narrowed to form

---

1] Library of Prague Cathedral Chapter; ref. no. A10, fol. 104.

a small vertical opening, which was sometimes combined with a slanting rounded - off slit for the eyes (II., Pl. 14, Nos. 4, 8, 10).

The conical helmet with protection fot the nape of the neck and the sides of the head, sometimes known in Latin sources as a *cassis*, constituted the basis for the further evolution of battle headgear. In his picture of the Resurrection, dating from about 1380, the Master of Třeboň depicted the figure of a warrior with a helmet of this type, which has a gilt ornamental border or orle and also a grating or lattice visor (III., Pl. 1, No. 6). The visor, fixed to a pivot above the forehead, consists of a vertical bar, bent to the curve of the profile, which is interlaced with five curved transverse bars. By lowering this visor the soldier could protect his face well without inconveniencing his sight or breathing.

This was, however, only the first stage in the development of the helmet and visor, which gradually came to enclose the whole head and face of the fighter, only leaving slits for the eyes. These helmets came into use in Bohemia in the third quarter of the 14th century, as they did in Germany and elsewhere in western Europe. The oldest known depiction of such a helmet in Bohemia comes from the works of the Master of Třeboň. We also fairly frequently come across helmets with visors in the miniatures of the King Wenceslas Bible. They are really the cassis or basinet type with the peak placed well to the back, so that the back part of the helmet falls almost perpendicular to the neck. The plate visor had oblong slits running to the front, a sharp projection for the nose with breathing holes for letting in air and a slit where the mouth comes. The visor turned on two pivots fixed on either side of the helmet (III., Pl. 1, No. 4; II., Pl. 12, No. 4). In some cases these visors turned on a single pivot placed over the forehead, as mentioned in the case of the picture by the Master of Třeboň (III., Pl. 1, No. 6).

The older helmet of this type was supplemented by an aventail or neckguard (III., Pl. 4, No. 1), but it was not long before a plate collar was fixed direct to the helmet, thus protecting the neck and throat and reaching often as low as the breast (III., Pl. 7). The original shape of the visor also soon underwent change. At the beginning of the 15th century, apart from the visor with the sharp nose projection, one begins to come across basinets with similar oblong slits for the eyes but otherwise more curved and only having small holes for breathing. This type is worn by two soldiers in the Kyeser Bellifortis drawing (II., Pl. 32). These basinets were also to be met with during this same period both in France and Germany; once again one can see that at that time Bohemia was in no way behindhand in comparison to the rest of western Europe, on the contrary she was as advanced as the most progressive countries of the western world. This type of protective battle headgear finally evolved into the armet – a helmet that was nicely turned to fit the shape of the face and head and which remained for a long time as part of the complete suit of armour and was particularly common during the 16th century.

The most common type of helmet used by the lightly-armed cavalry, and even more by foot soldiers, was the iron casque, iron hat or chapel de fer. This iron casque had been in use as a piece of armour from long before the middle of the 14th century and with the emergence of the importance of light cavalry, and, even more so, of the burgher and mercenary foot soldiers, its popularity increased tremendously. The extensive and frequent use of this type of helmet accounts for the great variety of its forms which we meet with in the various medieval sources.

One type of casque had a curved or conical keel ridge set on a vertical band. This is the kind of helmet depicted by the Master of the Rajhrad altar-piece prior to 1420 (III., Pl. 2, No. 2), likewise the foreign casque from the beginning of the 15th century (III., Pl. 9, No. 4), the Swiss one from the 15th century (III., Pl. 9, No. 1 and III., Pl. 8, No. 4).

Fairly frequently we find that in helmets of Bohemian origin the brim over the forehead forms a small triangular nosepiece, as, for instance, in the picture of the Crucifixion in the Emmaus Monastery, dating from about 1375, and the St. Jacob altar-piece, dating from the years 1430—1440 (III., Pl. 2, No. 6); also in the King Wenceslas Bible from the turn of the 14th and 15th centuries (II., Pl. 14, No. 1) and that of the Skalice Crucifixion, which dates from about 1430 (III., Pl. 2, No. 6).

An interesting shape is that of a German casque dating from between 1440—1480. Over a fairly gently dipping brim there is a band which broadens upwards slightly into a narrow semi-cylindrical rim and it is only from here that there is a rather flat crown which runs out, however, into a high oblong keel ridge (III., Pl. 9, No. 2). Similar casques had been known much earlier in Bohemia, for prior to 1420, in the picture by the Master of the Rajhrad altar-piece, we find just such a helmet, only differing in the fact that it has less exaggerated openings for the eyes and a very small indication of the nosepiece; there is also a helmet of exactly that shape, including the semi-cylindrical rim above the vertical band, in a manuscript in Prague University Library, dating from 1432 (II., Pl. 42, No. 1).

In the King Wenceslas Bible we come across still another type of helmet of this kind. It is a conical casque with the peak set markedly towards the back; in the front the crown gradually merges with the brim, but at the back the join is clearly visible (II., Pl. 7, No. 1). The casque worn by the bowman with a crossbow, from the same source, is a very similar shape, only here the join is at the front and the peak is blunt (II., Pl. 6, No. 3); a similar type was depicted by the illuminator of the Krumlov manuscript, the Mirror of Redemption, when to the casque he added a mail hood and plate bevor, so that the whole thing looks like a precursor of the salett (II., Pl. 17). Even more like the salett is the helmet worn by the man in the brigandine in the King Wenceslas Bible, which has a very wide, slightly curved brim, and which almost entirely covers the nape of the neck and the forehead down to the eyes (II., Pl. 14, No. 2). And it is not a unique case. Between the years 1430—1440 the Master of the St. Jacob altar-piece depicted a similar helmet, but it is wound round with some kind of veiling (III., Pl. 2, No. 7).

On examining the various documentary sources one comes across a whole variety of other shapes and forms. For instance there is the helmet, from the period prior to 1420, depicted by the Master of the Rajhrad altar-piece, which has a rhomboid crest on a vertical band and a brim which is drawn out at the front and the back but rounded off at the sides and bordered with an ornamental band or orle (III., Pl. 2, No. 5). A very peculiar type is represented by the helmet now in the Kutná Hora Museum, found near Miskovice, which with its high crest resembles the casque in the work by the Master of Třeboň (III., Pl. 2, No. 10). It has, however, a very sharply falling brim which is so bent as to form small projections on either side of the head and one over the middle of the forehead. The peak of the crown is set markedly to the back, so that the brim covers the nape of the neck (III., Pl. 8, No. 1). To ascertain its date we should refer both to the above-mentioned iron casque depicted in the Czech panel painting and also to a helmet of German origin from the turn of the 14th and 15th centuries (III., Pl. 8, No. 2), of which the crown is regular in shape and the projections not so marked.

In general one can say that from the third quarter of the 14th century this vital part of the armour of the foot soldier increased in variety and richness of form. There was obviously a trend towards the broadening of the brim and attempts by other means to achieve the best possible protection for the head and neck. The documentary material so far discovered does not as yet permit us to categorize the changes of form in any kind of systematic or chronological order.

As a result of the above-mentioned tendency to acquire more protection, the iron casque gradually developed into the new type of helmet, known as the salett. The changes at first were not very great. Chief among them was the shape of the brim, which from being sharply bent was widened into a broad band not only covering most of the face but also the greater part of the nape of the neck. At first, openings were simply cut in the front for the eyes (III., Pl. 3, Nos 3, 5), later the under part of the brim at the front was somewhat arched, so that the lower edge of the eye holes formed a projection (III., Pl. 3, Nos. 6—8).

The oldest type of salett is usually considered to date from the beginning of the 15th century in France and Germany.[1] In Bohemia we do not find any written documentary evidence of it until the year 1441. That does not, of course, mean that helmets of this kind were not in use in Bohemia at an earlier date, especially as the report speaks of a "silver salade", in fact an ornamented, luxurious example of such a helmet, which inevitably presupposes the previous existence of simpler examples of the same kind.

The development of the salett did not, of course, stop at these older types. About the middle of the 15th century the front part of the helmet was transformed into a movable visor, which could be raised by means of pivots placed on each side of the crown. The join between the crown and the brim was displaced by a nicely turned metal plate and at the back the helmet ran out into a sharp point, reaching almost right over the back and completely protecting the nape of the neck (III., Pl. 11, No. 3). The final improvement was the transformation of the formerly stiff covering for the neck into three or four plate bands that moved on pivots.

Since the salett itself only covered the upper part of the fighter's face, it acquired a plate bevor, which protected the chin and throat and formed a sort of shield for the upper part of the breast, thus filling the gap between the helmet and the upper edge of the breastplate (III., Pl. 11, Nos. 2—4). A well-known miniature from the Jena Codex, depicting a fight between the Hussites and the crusaders, gives us a good picture of fighters wearing salett of an advanced type.

During the second half of the 15th century we no longer come across the older types of helmets, and whereas with the foot soldiers the main headgear remains the iron casque, where riders are concerned, especially the heavily-armed cavalry, we find the older type of basinet making way for the armet. But side by side with this, even as a part of the more luxurious suit of armour, we often come across the use of the salett and bevor or beaver.

To make the helmet sit a little more comfortably on the head, the inside was lined with cloth or leather, and in the case of examples belonging to lords and knights, this was a silk lining padded with cotton, which was supposed to soften the possible blows or thrusts of the enemy.

A good helmet that protected the head of the fighter in battle meant a great deal, though it could not guarantee complete safety. But not even the best helmets made of steel and fitted with every kind of gadget could protect the ruling lords, from home or abroad, from the crushing blows of the heavy flails and other weapons of the soldiers of the Hussite armies.

1] Prague City Library, 2096, fol. F., p. 7.

3. SHIELDS

The shield was an important accessory to the armour. The fighter carried it on his left arm and tried to ward off the enemy's blows with it before they actually hit his armour, thus defending the left side of his body. The older type of shield in the shape of a "heater" is only to be met with in individual cases in the period with which we are dealing (IV., Pl. 1, No. 2) and its function was by then hardly military; it was there more for decorative purposes on certain kinds of ceremonial occasions. Already by the 13th century this type of shield had evolved into one that was fundamentally triangular with rounded shoulders, and during the 14th century we often come across it in the shape of an equilateral triangle. The leading fighters are equipped with such shields in that beautiful manuscript of Czech origin dating from the first half of the 14th century, known as the *Liber Depictus*;[1] they also appear much later, however, in the 15th century in the Krumlov Manuscript (IV., Pl. 2, Nos. 5, 7, 9) and in the Kyeser Bellifortis manuscript (II, Pl. 32).

Meanwhile the shape of the shield in Bohemia had also undergone some change. In pictures by Master Theodoricus from the sixties of the 14th century, we find shields where the basically triangular form is still obvious but where the corners are curved and the top edge, which was originally straight or curving outwards, now curves slightly into the centre. The whole shield forms a slight arch and the left or *sinister* side (i. e. heraldically as seen by the wearer of the shield; as seen by an observer the right side) is visibly larger or higher than the right-hand side (IV., Pl. 2, Nos. 1, 2).

Other changes took place in the last quarter of the 14th century. There appeared the shield that was basically still triangular in shape and curved, but with a notch or bouche on the right-hand or *dexter* side (King Wenceslas Bible; IV., Pl. 2, No. 8), in which the equestrian knight balanced the shaft of his lance (V., Pl. 25). Another shield, from the same source, that is fundamentally oblong in shape but with a curved lower edge, has a similar notch (IV., Pl. 2, No. 3). Similar types can also be traced abroad (IV., Pl. 3, Nos. 1, 2). The shields of the fighters in the Bellifortis manuscript are also like these in shape, including the oblong notch, but are curved so that the lower and upper edges protrude somewhat forward (II., Pl. 30, Nos. 2, 5). Then there is the shield which, in addition to the arched horizontal curve, has a vertical joint down the middle of the panel (IV., Pl. 3, No. 3), like those carried by the arquebusiers in the famous miniatures of the Viennese manuscript of the second third of the 15th century, depicting a battle between the Hussites and the crusaders. A shield that is again similar in shape is the one dating from the 15th century, composed of four curved bands bent inwards (IV., Pl. 3, No. 4), as are the Florentine shield from the middle of the same century (IV., Pl. 3, No. 5) and the German Degendorf shield from the first half of the 15th century (IV., Pl. 3, Nos. 7, 8). The Hungarian riders' shields of this time differ chiefly in the fact that they are somewhat trapezoid in shape (IV., Pl. 5, Nos. 3—5).

Foot soldiers, of course, also used shields for protection. It was usually a round shield bulging out in the centre into a riveted iron spike, like the one held by the soldier in the panel painting of the Resurrection by the Master of the Třeboň altar-piece dating from about the year 1380 (II., Pl. 3). Here one should probably also mention the oval or oblong rounded shields carried by the infantry in the miniatures of the King Wenceslas Bible, dating from the end of the 14th and the beginning of the 15th centuries (II., Pl. 14, Nos. 1, 5), and perhaps also the great bulging triangular shields which appear so often in the

1] Manuscript in the Vienna State Library.

Krumlov Mirror of Redemption manuscript in the Prague National Museum (II., Pl. 19; Pl. 20), of which one has a riveted spike in the centre similar to that of the buckler painted by the Master of Třeboň.

With the gradual growth of the importance of shooting, at first with merely the arbalest or the crossbow, but later also the arquebus, there came the necessity to protect the crossbowman when tensing the bow or the shooter when loading the arquebus, which operations exposed them to danger for quite a considerable time. This requirement was met by the large shields, mostly oblong, which were known in Bohemia for some time before the commencement of the Hussite wars as the pavise or *pavézy*.

The pavise was a large almost oblong shield, slightly wider and rounded at the top, and strengthened perpendicularly down the centre by a strong ridge or rib. They were made of wooden panels, covered with skin and painted or richly decorated in various ways (IV., Pl. 6—9). Although the examples that have been preserved in Czechoslovakia only date from the second half of the 15th century, they nevertheless hardly differ in basic outlines from the pavise used by the Hussites.[1] They do not even differ in shape very much from those known to have originated in neighbouring Hungary and Austria, where Bohemian arms were imitated, just as they were in all other neighbouring countries.

In contrast to the large pavises which were as much as 130 cm high, there were also the small pavises, which were oblong in shape too and were probably used by the mounted soldiers. These were probably also the kind of small pavises required for the "baggage-boys with skulls and bucklers", in keeping with the so-called Hodětín military regulations, and the Václav Vlček of Čenov's Instructions for the lining up of carts for battle.[2] We come across these small pavises in Czech documentary sources as early as the first half of the 15th century. In later years the difference between the large and small pavises was always made clear.

Even larger were the great pavises which protected the entire body of the warrior when standing. We know what they looked like from the Konrad Kyeser Bellifortis manuscript (IV., Pl. 11, Nos. 1, 2). They were great oblong shields, fitted with a spike for fixing them in the ground and poles against which they could be leant and balanced. Some of them were also made with a notch so that a lance or crossbow could be used from cover. In the 15th century these were sometimes known by the term *taras*.

1] See B. Matějka, "Pavézy české", *Památky archeologické* XX, p. 81.

2] *Staročeské vojenské řády*, Prague, 1952, p. 40 (Hodětín) and p. 50 (Vlček).

CUT AND THRUST AND HAFT WEAPONS

The chief weapons in medieval warfare were those used in close combat, such as the cut and thrust weapons and those used for dealing direct blows.

For the first encounter, while there was still sufficient room between the combatants, use was made of the lance. But as soon as the opponents were in direct contact with one another, it was no longer possible to manipulate the lance with its long shaft. Then it was the turn of the shorter weapons, such as the sword, the knife (the dagger), the club hammer and the battle-axe known as the broad-axe. That was at the beginning of the 14th century. A century later Master Jan Hus enumerated the weapons as used by the knight as follows: the lance, the dagger, the arbalest, the bow, the cudgel, the basilard, the hatchet or hurlbat, the mace and the fist-like spiked club.[1]

For the time being let us leave aside the arbalest and the bow, as these will be dealt with in a later part of the work. From Huss's account, it is clear that the main types of arms had not changed. There remained the lance (the sword had been mentioned in the previous sentence) and the knife (here dagger) or basilard; the martel had probably been transformed into the Hussite spiked club or possibly the mace. There remained only the cudgel which was probably more suitable for use by the infantry than the cavalry, and the hatchet. To explain this last term is not easy; most likely it is here a question of the equestrians' hurlbat or hurling hatchet (*Wurfbeil*), which took the place of the older broad-axe, a weapon which had completely disappeared from the list.

Let us, however, now return to the individual types of weapons. The first we shall deal with in somewhat greater detail is the sword. In the first half of the 14th century swords were often still of an oldish type, a broad blade with short straight, cross-guard or quillons and not very long hilt. We often come across this type in the Velislav Bible and the *Liber Depictus*. One of these is a sword with a crescent-shaped pommel and a straight guard (V., Pl. 2, No. 4) from the Velislav Bible and swords of a similar archaic shape are those in the panel paintings by the Master of the Vyšší Brod Cycle, with very short cross-guards and crescent- or trefoil-shaped pommels (V., Pl. 2, Nos. 1,2). But already in the Velislav Bible, an outstanding example of Czech drawing from the beginning of the 14th century, one sees the changes that were taking place in the shapes of Czech swords. Often one comes across the rounded flat pommel with projections on each side (V., Pl. 1, Nos. 2, 7), the circular surface being ornamented with a cross (V., Pl. 1, Nos. 3, 9). For the time being the quillons remain straight, only the ends being broadened out (V., Pl. 1, No. 3) or drooping sharply downwards (V., Pl. 1, No. 9); occasionally there are also ornamental cross-guards of a different shape, mostly arched with a two-leaf or trefoil at each end (V., Pl. Nos. 1, 7). The hilts are either simple hafts, usually covered with leather (V., Pl. 1, Nos. 4, 7), or wound with thong probably also of leather (V., Pl. 1, Nos. 2, 3, 9).

As late as the sixties and seventies of the 14th century the basic form of the sword remained unchanged, as we see from the miniatures of the Jan of Středa *Liber Viaticus* manuscript and the Emmaus Monastery panel painting (V., Pl. 3, Nos. 1—3). The fine ornamental decoration of the pommel, cross-guard and sheath of the sword depicted in a panel painting by Master Theodoricus is an exception to the usual type (V,. Pl. 2, No. 6). Another type of sword by the same Master (V., Pl. 2, No. 7), which with its ellipsoid pommel is somewhat similar to the Italian sword of Donatello's David, has an equivalent in a panel

---

1] Master Jan Huss, *Sebrané spisy (Complete Works)*, Czech ed. by K. J. Erben, 1865, I, p. 176.

44

painting of Bohemian origin of a slightly later date – namely the Mulhouse altar-piece (V., Pl. 3, No. 4).

In Bohemian art sources, dating from the last quarter of the 14th century, we begin to come across changes in the shape of the sword, which in fact must have undoubtedly been in use at an earlier date. The blades, which in section were still mostly rhomboid, but with a groove running down each side, were still fairly broad (3.5—5 cm), but gradually growing longer. At the same time the hilt also began to be longer, in the case of the equestrian sword as much as one and a half hands. During the eighties, about halfway up the hilt – which gradually acquired a double conic or diamond-shaped form – or sometimes even higher, there would be a dividing ring (V., Pl. 3, Nos. 9, 10) and the quillons, till now still straight and unornamented, more and more frequently acquire a curve and ornamental ends, sometimes curving downwards, elsewhere even with the ends curled round towards the blade (V., Pl. 5, Nos. 8, 9). Likewise the pommels, which so far had mostly been round in shape, began to change. The round pommel was certainly fairly frequent, even into the 15th century, but in addition there sometimes appeared the pommel that was basically square with sliced-off corners and two small blunt pyramidal projections at the front and the back (V., Pl. 5, No. 4), or a pommel with a hectagonal cross-section, and broader and blunter pyramidal projection (V., Pl. 5, No. 1). In the King Wenceslas Bible from the turn of the 14th and 15th centuries we also find a sword with slightly curved quillons and a pommel in trefoil cross-section (V., Pl. 5, No. 3).

In the first third of the 15th century we still find swords of a similar type, but with numerous variations of the details of the pommel and cross-guard (for example, V., Pl. 9, Nos. 1, 4, 7). However quite new forms also appear. Already by the 14th century there had been examples of swords with much thinner blades than the normal and ending in a very sharp point, indicating clearly their use as thrust rather than cutting weapons. Whether it is quite correct to link this type of sword with the term *kord* or *estoc*, which we come across in official documents in Bohemia shortly before the outbreak of the Hussite revolutionary movement, is not quite certain, but it is very likely to be.

That the *estoc*, at this period, was something very typically Czech is proved not only by the fact that we only come across the term in Bohemian sources, but also that in 1432 a Czech *estoc* would be sent abroad as a rare kind of present. This we can see from the letter written by the Rožmberk's commercial agent, Martínek of Bavorov, who was living at the Italian court of the Emperor Sigismund in Piacenza. In this he asks Oldřich of Rožmberk to send him an *estoc (kord)* to Italy as a present for Sigismund's courtier, Michael Ország, with the explanation that the influence of this Hungarian noble was steadily growing at the court.[1] It is obviously a question of some sort of bribe, for which an ordinary object would not have been suitable.

Apart from the *estoc* for thrusting and the ordinary equestrian's sword, there began to be a new type of sword, namely that of the infantry, that to all appearances seems to have had a longish, broad blade with a long hilt, that later in all probability developed into the so-called "two-handed" sword.

As with all other parts of the armour and weapons, one can also find substantial differences in the way swords were made, according to the person for whom they were intended. Apart from simple, ordinary, inexpensive swords, there were also expensive ones, with richly decorated pommels, hilts and cross-guards and they fitted into richly embossed scabbards. The wealthy feudal lords often had their coats-of-arms emblazoned on the pommel (e. g. the sword of the Emperor Albrecht, dating from the 'thirties of the 15th century;

1] A letter printed in *Archiv český* (Bohemian Archives), III, p. 10.

V., Pl. 8); the hilt itself was also often ornamentally decorated (V., Pl. 6, No. 7), at other times both the pommel and the cross-guard (V., Pl. 2, No. 6). Sometimes certain parts would be gilded or plated with silver. Not even the blades remained unadorned. There were also both simple and ornamental scabbards. Apart from the normal scabbard, made usually of dark, stretched leather, and suited to the means of the simple craftsman or mercenary, there were also scabbards covered with precious velvets and richly embossed with gold or silver (V., Pl. 2, No. 6).

Swords, however, were not the only cutting weapons in use during the 14th and 15th centuries. Throughout the period with which we are dealing we frequently find documentary and pictorial references and actual examples of the falchion (tesák). The simplest weapon of this type is like the example found in the excavations made at Badry Castle (V., Pl. 9, No. 10). It is a single-bladed weapon, with a straight blade, about 40—50 mm wide and about 50 cm or more long. The hilt of the Badry falchion is set in line with the blunt edge of the blade. These falchions do not have cross-guards or quillons.

Of course, not all falchions had such simple forms; the simple weapons of this type are usually to be found where the painter wished to indicate an armed peasant, as in the Bellifortis manuscript. From written documentary sources, however, we know of "a falchion with silver shields"[1] and pictorial documentary sources depict many diverse types of such falchions, often very finely adorned.

By the end of the 14th and the beginning of the following century and later, we come across similar types of falchions with curved blades, often broadening out or dividing off at the lower end into two points (V., Pl. 12, Nos. 1, 3, 4, 6, 8). Apart from the hafted hilt with ornamental Gothic quatrefoils on the rivets, we also come across hilts similar to those found on swords, with curved or ellipsoid pommels (V., Pl. 12, Nos. 3, 4, 8). A rare example is the pommel of a falchion, dating from the last decade of the 14th century, in the shape of a hat (V., Pl. 12, Nos. 1, 2); a falchion from the King Wenceslas Bible even has the archaic crescent-shaped pommel (V., Pl. 13, No. 4). Quite frequently one also comes across short, straight, or only slightly curved quillons (V., Pl. 12, Nos. 3, 6, 8), both plain and ornamented (V., Pl. 12, No. 1). The original type from which these curved blades developed was probably the straight falchion with a blade that broadened out at the end into a triangle (V., Pl. 7, No. 2).

These falchions, especially the curved ones, were such a specifically Czech weapon that the Czech term for it, tesák, directly or indirectly in a somewhat garbled form (Dusack, Düsack, Duseghe, Disack) was taken over during and following the Hussite Wars into the language of the neighbouring German-speaking countries,[2] and by the middle of the 15th century the term "Prague falchion" was already known in France.[3]

From the curved blade of the "Prague falchion" it was, of course, only a short step to another type of cutting weapon, the sabre. In pictorial documentary sources we already come across the sabre at the turn of the 14th and 15th centuries. In the Wenceslas Bible we often find a sabre with a straight hilt, a round pommel and a short, straight cross-guard, either slung by a strap over the shoulder (V., Pl. 14, No. 4) or hung from the belt (V., Pl. 14, Nos. 5, 6). The sabre with a cross-guard curving upwards, which is also to be found in this manuscript, is similar to the one worn by the mercenary soldier in the Skalice Crucifixion painting, dating from the end of the first third of the 15th century (V., Pl. 9, No. 8).

An indispensable part of the equipment of the medieval knight, apart from other weapons, was the short knife or dagger. In early sources the Czech term for dagger was

1] Prague, Městská knihovna 992, fol. 147v (1432).   also Zíbrt and Winter, op. cit., I, p. 187.
2] See Titz, Ohlasy husitského válečnictví v Evropě, p. 61;   3] Titz, op. cit., p. 86.

usually concealed in the ambiguous Latin term *cultellus*, which the author of the Alexandrines unhesitatingly literally translated into the term "knife". It was a thrusting weapon which was fairly short – the entire length, including hilt and blade, scarcely ever exceeded 50 cm – and had a variety of forms. The blades were either flat, with rhomboid profile, or else three-edged with triangular cross-section. Daggers were carried in scabbards; in the case of expensive examples, these were often magnificently wrought and ornamented (V., Pl. 2, Nos. 2, 5, 7; Pl. 11, Nos. 1, 14) and the hilts were usually outstanding works of medieval craftsmanship.

For instance the dagger in a picture by the Master of Vyšší Brod, dating from about 1350 (V., Pl. 2, No. 2), has a plate-shaped gilded pommel with a small knob in the centre and similar quillons, arching downwards at the front and the back. The hilt is most probably cut from bone and ornamented with a gold band. The scabbard, which is covered with black leather or possibly velvet, has gold wrought work round the centre and at the point.

A type of dagger hilt to be found frequently in Bohemian Gothic paintings is the hilt that ends in a two-leafed pommel and has a plate-shaped cross-guard curving down at each end (V., Pl. 2, No. 3; Pl. 3, No. 5). Quite often, however, one also comes across the type of hilt that has quillons formed from two hemispheres, that broadens out slightly at the top and is probably cut from ivory, like the dagger worn by the soldier in the Emmaus Monastery panel painting (prior to 1380; V., Pl. 3, No. 6). Similar daggers were to be found in the 14th century, not only in Bohemia (V., Pl. 11, No. 2) but also in most other parts of Europe (V., Pl. 11, Nos. 1, 3—6). Further one finds daggers with a plate-shaped cross-guard and the same kind of pommel, with either a straight hilt (V., Pl. 2, No. 5; Pl. 3, No. 8), or with a variety of other forms of ornamentation (V., Pl. 12, Nos. 10—12). Such a wealth of forms can naturally not be adequately dealt with in just a simple descriptive account.

Daggers were carried at the waist, either slung on straps or on a chain at the right side, so that they hung vertically, as we find them in the Wenceslas Bible (II., Pl. 12, No. 5); or else the scabbard was fixed to a strap so that it hung aslant at the front (II., Pl. 1, No. 1; V., Pl. 2, No. 7), in certain cases adjoining the pouch which was fastened to the belt (V., Pl. 2, Nos. 2, 5). In addition to the expensive examples with magnificient hilts and scabbards, there were, of course, also the weapons of the common soldiers, which were naturally plain daggers with simple, haftlike hilts and unpretentious pommels and cross-guards (II., Pl. 1, No. 3 and others).

The martel and war-hammer were also part of the knight's equipment, in some cases known as the hurlbat. But in both cases the terms signify nothing other than a type of club or mace. It seems that the oldest type of mace was really the shape of a club. The hammer maces or war-hammers, with their pointed spikes running straight upwards and horizontally–placed hammer with a mallet head (often split into short spikes) at one end and a gradual curved point at the other, are often to be found in Bohemian Gothic paintings (V., Pl. 16, Nos. 1—3). The dagger mace is made on the same principle, though it does not have the perpendicular point and the hammer becomes a dagger with the flat surface created by the handle of the dagger at one end and the blade at the other. These maces usually looked like an outstretched arm holding a dagger in its hand (V., Pl. 17). Hence the Czech term "mace in the fist".

The type of mace described above must have been fairly common in Bohemia; a miniature in the Jena Codex depicts Jan Žižka of Trocnov with a similar "club-fist" but without the dagger, and in an illustration to the Konáč's translation of the Silvius Chronicle, dating from the beginning of the 16th century, Žižka also has a similar dagger mace in his hand.

A different type of mace is depicted in the illuminations to the Wenceslas Bible. This is the star-headed mace, which consists of a spherical ball stuck with spikes, held in a socket fixed on the end of a shaft (II., Pl. 16, No. 1). A similar mace is depicted by Kyeser in his Bellifortis manuscript, dating from the beginning of the 15th century. Frequently maces were six- or eight-bladed, with six or eight blades set in asteroid horizontal section round a socket fixed to a shaft (V., Pl. 18). Such maces were apparently in quite common use in Bohemia just at the time of the Hussite wars; we know of them from various excavations, and from similar weapons discovered at Tábor.

The drawings in the Velislav Bible and in the *Liber Depictus* manuscript provide us with good examples of the soldier's hatchet or broad-axe of the first half of the 15th century. A special hatchet, with a straight upper edge and a sharp, slightly curved lower side ending in a point, was firmly fixed into a short shaft (V., Pl. 19, Nos. 5-6). This was the mounted soldier's battle-axe. Hatchets or axes for foot soldiers were probably not fundamentally different, merely having a longer shaft. At the beginning of the 15th century we begin to find a greater variety of shapes and forms. The sharp edge of the hatchet is often lengthened out upwards into a point, whereas the lower projection is substantially shorter and sometimes bluntly bent back (V., Pl. 19, No. 9). Other hatchets or axes of this period have a curved sharp blade, the upper end of which curves slightly inwards and backwards, the lower edge ending off straight (V., Pl. 19, No. 7). In many cases, especially among actual historical finds, it is difficult to tell the fighter's axe from that used by the workman. However it is very probable that those used for fighting had a short arm and a long knife in the shape of a fairly narrow blade which extended evenly and quite considerably in both directions (V., Pl. 19, No. 11; Pl. 21, No. 1).

Already during the 14th century a special type of hatchet, the hurlbat, intended for hurling, was used in cavalry charges. Not even in this case can one really speak of any unity of form, although one can indicate the basic shape. The blade usually had a curved edge extending either equally in both directions, or else somewhat more towards the top. Either it was fixed to the shaft in a socket, and in this case the arm at the back formed a short hammer, or else it was driven into the shaft and held by a wedge. Plate 20 shows various examples of this type of weapon, dating from the 14th and the beginning of the 15th century.

The lance, which was an important weapon in both cavalry and infantry warfare, consisted of a shaft and a spike. From documentary material found so far it is not possible to determine the chronological evolution of the various lance forms, which are concerned primarily, of course, with the shape of the spike. In pictorial sources dating from the first half of the 14th century (e. g. the *Liber Depictus*), we come across lances that have a plain shaft, the lower part of which is ornamented with two double bands, and a spike with a very short socket and a broad rhomboidal blade. Similar lances with pennons are often to be seen in Czech paintings from the beginning of the 15th century (and the Krumlov manuscript (V., Pl. 22, Nos. 4, 10). In the same source we also come across a lance with a socket that is distinctly separate from the spike, which is based very low and has a long point (V., Pl. 22, No. 5). The lance with a pennon, dating from the same time, in the *Knihy o anatomii* (Books on Anatomy), in the Prague Chapter Library, has a very long socket and a slender spike (II., Pl. 34, No. 1). Amongst preserved treasures we more often find the lance with a long socket and a spike that is comparatively small and rhomboid in form. The lance of this kind in the Prague City Museum has a socket 18 cm long and a spike only 8 cm long (V., Pl. 23, No. 1). Probably the commonest type of lance used by the cavalry in the 15th century was a similar lance but with a flatter, though short, spike (V., Pl. 23, No. 3) and it was usually set in a plain shaft, which had a metal support ring, which was fastened to the hook on the breastplate (V., Pl. 24, No. 4; its use, V.,

Pl. 25), or in a shaft with a special place for holding the weapon that was turned on a lathe (V., Pl. 24., No. 1).

The expensive lances of the feudal knights, like their other weapons and armour, were ornamented in various ways. We have proof of such ornamentation in the actual examples that have been preserved. In the National Museum in Prague there is a spike to a lance, dating from the 15th century, with a low rhomboid-shaped blade, which is gilded with clear Gothic miniscules. The neck, where the socket holds the spike, is encircled by two double gold bands filled in with covered scale-like ornamentation.[1]

The foot soldiers' lances had plain smooth staves and a visibly larger pike. Usually the blade was the shape of a leaf or an uneven rhombus, which at the lower end had a shorter edge. The socket was usually spherical, with circular cross-section, but there are some examples where the socket had a hexagonal outline. Lances with blades in the shape of a rhombus are frequently to be met with in manuscripts dating from the beginning of the 15th century (e. g. the Krumlov manuscript, fol. 58, II., Pl. 23; the Bible of the Prague Cathedral Chapter Library, ref. No. A 10, II, Pl. 35, No. 2); these leaf-bladed lances also appear frequently in the Wenceslas Bible (II., Pl. 14).

Another of the foot soldiers' weapons was the "lance and hook", a type of boar-pike, which first appears as early as the turn of the 14th and 15th centuries, in the Wenceslas Bible. The hook is set just beneath the actual blade, sometimes with a mounting (V., Pl. 21, No. 4); in other cases it comes straight out of the socket (V., Pl. 26, No. 3). The javelin, which is frequently mentioned in old writings, had a definitely shorter stave than the lance and a lighter blade. In some accounts, however, it seems as though this term was used synonymously with that of the word lance.

The awl spiess was also one of the long thrusting weapons. It had a long narrow spike, most frequently with a circular cross-section, and always had a plate-shaped ring at the lower end where it was set in a fairly short wooden stave. We come across it in Czech documentary material, dating from the beginning of the 15th century, in the Krumlov manuscript and again later than the middle of the same century, in the Hussite Göttingen Codex (V., Pl. 27, Nos. 1-2).

The lance, the javelin and the spiess were not the only weapons carried by foot soldiers. In addition to these one often finds mention of one remarkable weapon made famous by the Hussite armies – namely the halbard. It would be a mistake, however, to think that the halbard dates only from this time. It was a much older weapon. As early as the first half of the 14th century one finds instances of the halbard in the miniatures of Bohemian manuscripts. In the Velislav Bible there is, on the one hand, a lance with a hatchet attached that has a curved blade (V., Pl. 28, No. 7), then there is one that is probably a halbard forged in one piece with the pike of a lance, on one side a hatchet with the blade cut away and on the other a sharply-curved hook (V., Pl. 28, No. 5). A soldier in mail shirt, from the *Liber Depictus* manuscript, is also carrying a similar weapon. This halbard, however, has only a narrow thrusting spike (not the blade of a lance) and a hatchet with a strong bar and blade that is only slightly curved. The hook on the other side projects slightly lower than the upper edge of the hatchet (V., Pl. 28, No. 2).

In one of the works of the Master of Vyšší Brod we find an interesting type of halbard or gisarme, in which the spike is curved like a hook and the hatchet has a broad blade with a curved edge and sharp projections at the top and the bottom set in a single broad mounting. We also know of a similar weapon, dating from the 14th century, coming from Scotland (V., Pl. 28, No. 3).

1] *Památky archeologické* XX, 1910, pp. 53–4.

Dating from the sixties of the 14th century we find a pole-axe in the *Liber Viaticus* MS, which is really only a hatchet with a prolonged upper end to the curved blade and set with a double mounting on a long stave (V., Pl. 28, No. 4). The illuminator of the King Wenceslas Bible, dating from the turn of the 14th and 15th centuries, indicated a weapon of a similar kind (V., Pl. 21, No. 3). Another almost identical one, though with the difference that it is set in the socket of a spike of the rhomboid type, is a pole-axe type halbard dating from about 1380 (V., Pl. 28, Nos. 6, 8).

This does not have either a hook or a spike on the other side; these began to appear at about this time (V., Pl. 28, No. 9) and later became the normal thing. Halbards with lance pikes, a hatchet on one side and a hook or spike on the other, are to be found frequently in the Wenceslas Bible (V., Pl. 26, Nos. 7, 12) and in panel paintings of the first third of the 15th century (V., Pl. 28, Nos. 10, 12, 14, 15), and indeed even in the Jena Codex, dating from the end of the 15th century (V., Pl. 28, No. 16). In a picture by the Master of the Rajhrad altar-piece, apart from this type of halbard, we also find one with a hatchet and hammer, which splits into two spikes (V., Pl. 28, No. 11). A different type of halbard is that introduced in the Kyeser Bellifortis manuscript, dating from between 1402—1405. It has a lance head with a rhomboid blade and on each side there is a similar hatchet with a curved blade and cut-away inside edge, somewhat like a partizan (V., Pl. 35, No. 7).

It is interesting to note in what ways the Bohemian halbards of the 14th and 15th centuries differed fundamentally from the contemporary foreign weapons of a similar type. The German and Swiss type halbards, whose development is to be found in V., Pl. 29—31, for a very long time preserved the form of a hatchet in which the upper point of the blade was drawn out into a spike. This spike, however, remained part of the hatchet. The only Bohemian weapon of a similar kind is that to be found in the *Liber Viaticus* manuscript, dating from shortly after the middle of the 14th century (V., Pl. 26, No. 4) and a single example in the Wenceslas Bible (V., Pl. 21, No. 3). It is not until the end of the first third of the 15th century in Bavaria and by the middle of the century elsewhere that we come across examples of the Bohemian halbard with the spike separated from the hatchet (V., Pl. 32, No. 8) or with a spike (V., Pl. 31, No. 11). Undoubtedly this was due to the influence of the Bohemian Hussite warriors, who took these Bohemian halbards with them on their famous expeditions into neighbouring countries; there they acquired the general term halbards, and were later known in Bohemia as *hallaparta*.

Equally typical was another type of spear, known in German literature as the *Böhmische Ohrlöffel* and in English as the "Bohemian ear-spoon". It was a weapon with the leaf- or rhomboid-shaped blade of a lance, from the lower end of which there projected either sharply bent hooks, one on either side (V., Pl. 26, No. 1), or else straight spikes (V., Pl. 26, No. 4). Both these types of halbard are to be found in the miniatures of the Wenceslas Bible, dating from the turn of the 14th and 15th centuries. And the type maintained itself for some time. For instance it appears in the Bellifortis manuscript (V., Pl. 35, No. 3); it still appeared after the middle of the century (V., Pl. 27, No. 4), and was known even later, also abroad.

The peculiar type of halbard or bill, with the appearance of a long knife ending in a point, which usually had two triangular-shaped projections at the join of the socket and the pike, and which had a sickle-like hook on one side of the blade and on the other a straight triangular spike (V., Pl. 33, Nos. 1—6; Pl. 34), never really seemed to take root in Bohemia. The origin of this type of weapon was probably the sickle set at the end of a stave (see V., Pl. 33, Nos. 9, 10) or a knife bent like a sickle (V., Pl. 33, No. 11). As a primitive form in the development of this halbard we could probably take the gisarme-type weapon in the Velislav Bible, which has the above-mentioned sickle-like bent knife blade with a small projection jutting out from its edge (V., Pl. 33, No. 8). A plain sickle such as this is also mentioned in the Bellifortis manuscript as being a Bohemian weapon of the time (V., Pl. 35, No. 6).

In the Hus text mentioned above, apart from the weapons we have already discussed, there is also reference to the club or cudgel. It seems as though by the term *řemdih* one has to include not only the cudgel on a long stave (V., Pl. 36), but also various types of battering weapons, hanging on chains either from a long stave in the case of foot soldiers, or from a short one in the case of the cavalry. A club of this kind with a short stave was depicted by the illuminator of the Wenceslas Bible (V., Pl. 26, No. 2) and it seems as though these kinds of weapons were very common especially in the 15th century. There were, for instance, iron or wooden spherical balls stuck all round with spikes – in England they were known as the "great holy-water sprinklers" from the way they spattered blood around (V., Pl. 37, No. 7); elsewhere there was just an iron ball without spikes, like the one preserved in the Prague Military History Museum (V., Pl. 37, No. 3). Sometimes there would be a sword head hanging from a chain (V., Pl. 37, No. 2).

These cudgels were very common weapons and were prepared for battle in various ways. Often it was considered quite sufficient to drive spikes into a completely plain rough wooden cudgel – the so-called "morning stars" (V., Pl. 36, Nos. 4, 5). This simple type of cudgel can be seen among Žižka's followers in a drawing in the Göttingen Codex. The better cudgels or clubs, however, had a head nicely rounded into a sphere or other convenient shape, and fitted firmly to the stave and stuck evenly with spikes (V., Pl. 36, Nos. 2, 3, 5, 9). We even find a club like this in the Wenceslas Bible (V., Pl. 21, No. 6).

The club or cudgel was a weapon which the common Hussite soldier knew how to make use of, as it was very similar to the everyday work tools of the common people.[1] Equally suitable for these armies, which to a great extent were composed of country people, was the famous Hussite flail; the soldiers, armed with these flails, acquired such skill with them that they struck terror into the hearts of the native and foreign feudal lords. The oldest drawing of a war flail in Bohemia, however, dates back to the pre-Hussite period, to the early years of the 15th century. A flail, whose bat was covered with iron bands held in place by spikes, which did not extend beyond the surface of the bands, was recommended as a good military weapon by Konrad Kyeser, who was living in Bohemia at the time (V., Pl. 35, No. 8). It seems that it was in Bohemia that he learnt of the military uses of the flail, which were carried into battle by the serfs pressed into military service for their feudal lords.

But the real fame of the battle flail belongs to the time of the revolutionary Hussite movement. The Hussite infantry had detachments of "flailers", who, together with the archers and halbardiers, carried out important tasks in various victorious battles. At the beginning of the revolutionary movement flails carried into battle were hardly to be distinguished from tools used in agricultural work. The flail depicted in the Viennese manuscript has a plain wooden head with dangling ironwork. The spikes are simply driven into the wooden head (V., Pl. 38, No. 3). As time passed, however, the flail acquired a different appearance. Flails preserved in Czech museums have wooden bats spirally bound round with between four and six twisted bands which are held at regular intervals by three or four transverse bands from which projected powerful battering spikes (V., Pl. 38, Nos. 1, 4). The flail head was hung on iron rings, which gave it flexibility. A flail such as this in the hands of the country peasants, who were accustomed to using it, must have been a terri-

---

1] Demmin, p. 794, calls such a club a *Žižka star*.

fying weapon, which could bash the finest helmets and plate armour of the crusaders to smithereens.

It is quite clear that many of those who had the misfortune to meet with a flail in the hands of a Hussite succumbed completely. So it is not surprising that their fame soon spread beyond the borders of the country. Bohemian flails (*behemisch Drischel*) are to be found listed one hundred years later in the arms inventories of the German Emperor Maximilian and elsewhere in the neighbouring lands.[1]

We have tried to give a picture of the wealth of types and varieties of cutting, thrusting and battering weapons known to us from documentary and other sources dating from the fourteenth and the first half of the fifteenth centuries. In some cases we were able to give an outline of the development of the various types and varieties, in others there was much that we could only surmise. Nevertheless in conclusion, it is necessary to emphasise the great significance of Bohemia in the development of weapons during this period. Above all there were the Bohemian *estocs* (*kordy*), which were much in demand abroad, and there were the Bohemian falchions, halbards and flails, which were made famous throughout Central and Western Europe by the great Hussite victories. They therefore marked important steps forward in the evolution of the various weapons, and the labour of Bohemian craftsmen thus contributed to the general development.

1] See Titz, *op. cit.*, p. 56; Winter, 1. c., p. 278.

PROJECTILE WEAPONS AND SIEGE MACHINES

Mechanically-firing weapons include those where the missile (an arrow, stone, bolt, etc.) is set in motion by a mechanical force, resulting either from the elasticity of the throwing mechanism (bow, cross-bow or arbalest) or from the lever principle (ballistas or catapults).

The bow, an ancient hunting and fighting weapon, remained as part of the soldier's equipment right through the period with which we are dealing. In illustrated documentary material at our disposal, we find it comprising part of the armour of both foot and mounted soldiers as late as the time of the Wenceslas Bible (II., Pl. 6, Nos. 1,2). In most cases it is the long bow consisting of a bow made of pliant wood and a cord tied to each end of the bow (VI., Pl. 1, No. 1). Arrows that were used for shooting with a bow usually had a long shaft and a flat head, either leaf-shaped (VI., Pl. 1, No. 2) or barbed (VI., Pl. 3, No. 3). The bows carried by mounted soldiers from the East, such as those with which the light Kuman cavalry was probably armed, were considerably shorter. The arms equipment of an archer also included a case for the bow (VI., Pl. 1, No. 6) and a quiver for the arrows (VI., Pl. 1, No. 7; II., Pl. 6, No. 1).

By the 14th century, however, the more frequent weapon in Bohemia was the cross-bow. The cross-bow had a powerful bow made of pliant wood or horn – from the second third of the 15th century, even of iron – a bowstring and a wooden shaft, which was fixed to the centre of the bow, with a notch for holding the cord and an iron trigger or release mechanism (VI., Pl. 3; Pl. 4, Nos. 1, 3; Pl. 5, No. 1; the mechanism of the trigger VI., Pl. 5, No. 5).

The purpose of this short, powerful bow was to give the missile greater initial speed and thus to increase the range of the shot and its power of penetration. It was not possible, however, to obtain increased tension when drawing the bow merely by hand. In order to set the arbalest ready for shooting, it was necessary to use various devices. The simplest of all was the method of creating tension by treading. For this purpose the crossbow had a small stirrup at the front, into which the archer placed his foot, he held the bowstring with hooks from his archer's belt and by treading down on the stirrup, applied tension to the bow till the cord was caught in the groove of the notch (VI., Pl. 2, No. 4; a variety of belt hooks, VI., Pl. 8).

In order to simplify this difficult task various kinds of device were invented. One of them was a windlass, which wound the cord to which the hook was attached by means of a rack and pinion (VI., Pl. 2, No. 2). As early as the beginning of the 15th century, in the Kyeser Bellifortis manuscript, we come across a windlass fitted with a set of pulleys (VI., Pl. 3, No. 7; Pl. 4, No. 6). The most frequent device, however, for tensing the cross-bow, was the lever method. This device consisted of a cog-wheel turned by a handle which moved an iron-toothed rod with a hook on the end; this caught hold of and stretched the cord (VI., Pl. 4, No. 4; Pl. 9, No. 1). With this device it was possible to tense the bow while kneeling, so that the archer did not provide such an obvious target for the enemy, as in the case of the archer working the winch or tensing it by foot. The lever could even be used by a mounted archer on horseback. Other methods of tensing the bow were also used, such as devices using the principle of the catapult (VI., Pl. 9, No. 3; Pl. 10). In the Kyeser Bellifortis manuscript we find screw devices (VI., Pl. 3, No. 6) and a system of small wheels (VI., Pl. 3, No. 2), but of course it is not clear whether these were ever actually used in practice.

Arrows with short wooden shafts and an arrowhead were shot from these crossbows. The arrow-heads sometimes preserved the shapes which we have already described above,

i. e. either leaf-shaped or barbed, but the main type of arrow used with crossbows consisted of arrows that were penetrating, with a head that had a square or rhomboid cross-section (VI., Pl. 5, No. 7). During the 15th century we find that ornamental arrows and arrows with other kinds of decoration were in use, but these were probably mostly arrows used for hunting or on special occasions. In addition to plain iron arrows, by the 15th century we know that there were also arrows made of steel and inflammable missiles, which were wound with cloth below the arrow-head, this being set alight with some inflammable substance, usually sulphur.

At the other end of the shaft there was a "vane" made of real feathers (VI., Pl. 5, No. 4), of parchment or of paper, which served to keep the missile on the course given it by the archer. The archer kept his arrow in a quiver, which was a leather case hung from his belt. According to a miniature in a Vienna manuscript, dating from the second third of the 15th century, this was cylindrical and covered with fur on the outer side (VI., Pl. 5, No. 2).

Apart from the crossbow and other weapons, the Hussite soldiers also used the ancient weapon of the common people, the sling, or modern catapult. The Hussite slingers, young lads not fully grown, probably used simple slings consisting of a leather thong broadened out in the centre to form a pouch in which they placed a stone (VI., Pl. 16, Nos. 1, 2). There is a similar sling to be seen in the Jan of Středa *Liber Viaticus* manuscript, dating from soon after the middle of the 14th century; there is also one in the Bellifortis manuscript dating from the first years of the following century.

Apart from hand-manipulated mechanical shooting weapons, during the Middle Ages there were also large machines used for besieging fortresses. For instance there were complicated devices for hurling great missiles with spikes for war-heads, rocks and barrels, filled with incendiary substances, and the like into the enemy's fortresses. Then there were the catapults and ballistas. The ballista was really a large mechanically-tensed crossbow, placed on a fixed or wheel-like base, that hurled enormous arrows, like javelins, into the air (VI., Pl. 21). The great arrow-machine, depicted in VI., Pl. 22, was, however, worked on quite a different principle. A powerful spring was stretched backwards by means of a windlass and when this was released, it propelled a gigantic arrow into motion.

The giant slings and catapults, designed for hurling great rocks and so on, looked quite different. They were still very common in Bohemia during the 15th century and were also used during the Hussite wars in conjunction with cannons, which were at that time still in their very earliest stage of development.

Smaller machines for the hurling of stones and rocks were designed on the principle of the spring. The rock placed in the leather pouch was hurled out by the force of a pliant, bent piece of wood that was suddenly released (VI., Pl. 24, No. 1). But the chief type of mechanical weapon of this kind was the catapult using the lever principle, known as the trebuchet. A long beam, hanging from a peg on a wooden construction, was heavily weighted down at one end – the shorter end. From the other, the longer end, of the beam hung a pouch on ropes. By the help of the pulleys and a windlass the operator hauled the longer arm down to the ground, so that the weight was lifted up, and placed the missile into the sling. As soon as the rope holding down the longer arm of the beam was released, the falling weight suddenly jerked the other arm up and the rocky missile was hurled from the opening pouch, over the top of the construction itself, describing a great arc into the air.

Catapults of this kind were either small and generally fairly simple, like the one depicted in VI., Pl. 24, No. 2, or great, powerful complicated constructions designed for hurling heavy boulders greater distances as in VI., Pl. 27.

The disadvantage of all types of catapults was the fact that the missile described a great arc and only fell on the target with the force of its own weight; so it was really only something that harassed the besieged rather than did them damage. The catapults were not capable of direct, destructive shots that would create a sufficiently large gap in the besieged town's or castle's walls to enable the hordes of foot soldiers to storm them. Thus it happened, during the second half of the the 15th century, that when heavy siege artillery began to be developed further, catapults and similar machines disappeared from military use fairly quickly.

The shortage of suitable incendiary materials or their lack of perfection had to be compensated for by various means. In order to break down gates or possibly even walls, all kinds of battering rams were invented. Basically these consisted of heavy beams of hard wood, studded with iron at the front end and suitably slung so that they could be set in motion by rocking. Those operating them tried to break through by making a number of successive blows. As machines such as these had to be brought into the direct proximity of the enemy fortress, the operators had to be protected against shots. Battering rams were therefore concealed in mobile wheeled wooden constructions, the sides of which – made of strong boards – were covered with skins. Those operating the machines, being under cover, were able to haul them to the required proximity and get to work under the protection of the archery of their own archers (VI., Pl. 27, Nos. 1, 2; Pl. 29, No. 2).

In addition to battering rams, all kinds of machines and devices were used to facilitate the approach to the ramparts and their storming, even without the aid of a breach in the walls. For this purpose there were the so-called *belfreys* or *sentina* (VI., Pl. 29, No. 1). The Kyeser Bellifortis manuscript, dating from the beginning of the 15th century, depicts a number of such breaching towers which were wooden constructions on wheels studded with wooden boards, protected by skins, and often even including little drawbridges by means of which the fighters could reach the parapet on the ramparts of the besieged fortress (VI., Pl. 28, Nos. 3, 4).

In addition to these big machines, there were a number of other lesser means, during the Middle Ages, by which soldiers approaching the walls of a besieged fortress were protected against the archery of the enemy. The commonest were the mobile shields or *testudos* – originally consisting of interlocking shields and later made of faggots woven together or of boards and beams nailed together, and fixed on wheels, which were hauled by soldiers up to their target (VI., Pl. 30). The increasing significance of shooting in military undertakings at the start of the 15th century made it more and more necessary to think of new and better ways of protecting the masses of the infantry and of enabling them to penetrate the enemy's ranks with as few losses as possible. These deliberations resulted in a great variety of proposals, often quite fantastic, for the construction of the most varied kinds of military machines and carts, many of which remained merely the product of the imagination of medieval "military engineers", such as Kyeser, with his manuscript Bellifortis.[1] But, of course, nothing of this kind could really solve the problem. The solution could only come from a fundamental change in the social composition, organisation and tactics of the armies, such as was provided by the creation of the new type of revolutionary peasant armies of the Hussites.

1] See "K vojensko-technickým problémům na počátku 15. století", *Historie a vojenství*, No. 3, 1953, p. 29 ff.

FIREARMS

The first written records of firearms in Bohemia date from the last quarter of the 14th century. In 1383 the author of the somewhat legend-like biography of the Prague archbishop Jan of Jenštejn noted the fact that, during the plundering of the archbishop's estate in Kyje, near Prague, a "weapon, known as a *puška* (gun)" exploded in the hands of one of the archers, inflicting severe wounds on him, to which he soon succumbed.[1] In 1412 when Jan Ptáček of Pirkštejn and his guardian Hanuš of Lípa were making an agreement on the ceding of the inheritance, it was specially stated that the "guns" which belonged to Ptáček's father were to be kept by the guardian at the castle of Rataje.[2] Since Jan Ptáček's father had died some time before 1395[3], these guns must have been procured even before that year and therefore, at the very latest, they date from the last quarter of the 14th century.

It would, however, be a mistake to think that the first written accounts in documentary material also indicate the first appearance of such firearms in Bohemia altogether. The fact, alone, that the author of the Jenštejn biography uses the Czech term for a firearm in a Latin text shows that the weapon was already generally known and that the Czech term was in current usage. In actual fact the first gunsmith appears among the names of the Prague burghers already ten years prior to the events in 1383 in Kyje. And again, since we know that during the 15th century gunsmiths were still normally employees of the towns and only became burghers in very exceptional cases, the granting to Master Jindřich of the rights of a burgher cannot be accepted as a proof that he had only just arrived in Prague at that time. In fact we shall not be mistaken if we assume that the first gunsmiths and firearms appeared in Bohemia shortly after the middle of the 14th century.

The words of Engels apply to Bohemia and Moravia just as they applied elsewhere: "The introduction of gunpowder and firearms was not at all an act of force, but a step forward in industry, that is an economic advance. The provision of powder and firearms required industry and money, and both of these were in the hands of the burghers of the towns. From the outset, therefore, firearms were the weapons of the towns, and of the rising monarchy drawing support from the towns, against the feudal nobility."[4] And indeed, both in Bohemia and Moravia there are towns – in the 14th century it was Prague, Stříbro, Chrudim and others, and in the first third of the 15th century Znojmo, Brno, Jihlava, Bělá pod Bezdězem, Louny, Tábor and so on – from which we have records of gunsmiths and guns.

The Czech term *puška* (gun) in the 14th and 15th century does not clearly determine which kind of weapon was implied; whether it was a hand gun or an artillery weapon. From the contents of the report of the events in Kyje, in 1383, it is clear that in this case it was a question of a hand gun, and a light hand gun at that, which the gunner fired in such a way that an extension of the wooden butt of the hand gun rested on his shoulder. It seems that it is very probable that the production and development of firearms started with the smaller arms. There is no doubt that from the technical production point of view it was easier to forge a barrel from plate metal and then weld it together by forge hammering, when the measurements were small. It was only with the experience gained in this work that it was possible to work on the forging of big gun barrels. And the same certainly also applied to rifles cast in copper or bronze.

1] *FRB* I, p. 467: "...*quidam, dum se prepareret ad iaciendum de instrumento, quod puška dicitur, mox illa fracta et scissa iacere volentis unam aurem amputavit et sequenti die ... per mortis sublacionem vulneri ... finem imposuit.*"

2] *AČ* VI, p. 25.
3] A. Sedláček, *Hrady, zámky a tvrze...*, XII, p. 54.
4] F. Engels, *Anti-Dühring*, p. 188.

One of the oldest iron guns, or rather hand-gun, in Czechoslovakia is undoubtedly the one in the museum in Moravská Třebová, which is so far not known in technical literature, dealing with the subject.[1] It has an octagonal-shaped welded barrel forged from an iron plate, which is 376 mm long, and each side 23 mm wide. At the nozzle end of the barrel there is a circular collar that is 15 mm thick and roughly 107 mm in diameter, the purpose of which is to prevent the splitting of the rim of the nozzle as a result of gas-pressure produced in firing. The other end of the barrel, the chamber (*komora*), is obviously strengthened by a mantel, fitted round it, so that here the sides on their outer perimeter measure 37 mm. The bore of the barrel, in view of the size of the gun and the strength of the walls, is small – only 32 mm. The vent is 50 mm from the rear end and is a simple vertical round opening, in front of which is a cross engraved on the surface with a firm groove, obviously a means of providing a rough aim. It is, indeed, an extremely primitive gun, but the fact that it is marked by the maker – the marks (a ring inscribed with crossed hammers) are in a band along the back rim – show that it is a gun produced by a craftsman, an expert. This also speaks for the age of the gun, which probably originated as early as the second third of the 14th century.

As a type and as regards form this weapon is closely related to the gun preserved in Hungary, which probably originated in Steyr (VII., Pl. 11, No. 1). The barrel corresponds in length (the Hungarian hand-gun is 370 mm long), but there is a basic difference in calibre (55 mm) and the strengthening of the rim of the barrel in the Hungarian gun is different; it is also octagonal. This gun, dating vaguely from some time during the 14th century, bears no maker's mark.

The oldest bronze gun preserved in Czechoslovakia probably also dates from about the same time. It is a gun with a smooth barrel, with four not very prominent bands, and at the back there is a socket for attaching it to the stock; in shape it almost exactly corresponds to the hand gun of German origin, dating, according to Rathgen, from about the middle of the 14th century (VII., Pl. 1, No. 1).[2] A hand-gun similar to this one in type but polygonal in shape is the one set in a stock, which is being fired by a gunner in a drawing in the Bellifortis manuscript dating from the years 1402—1405 (VII., Pl. 5, No. 1).

Certain other Czech hand-guns also undoubtedly originated still in the 14th century. For instance there is the hand-gun in the Prague National Museum (VII., Pl. 4, No. 1) with an octagonal barrel 295 mm long which is strengthened at the nozzle and has a calibre of 33 mm; it is fixed to a wooden support equipped with a hook for absorbing the recoil when firing (hence the term arquebus, *Hakenbüchse*); this weapon is also fitted with a ramrod. The oldest gun of this type in Plzeň Museum is probably the hectagonal hand-gun, which is 315 mm long, has a straight muzzle and it is more slender (VII., Pl. 3, No. 1). In Plzeň there is also another gun dating from the 14th century, which has an octagonal barrel 290 mm long, strengthened at the muzzle and round the chamber at the rear; it is placed in a rough wooden stock without a hook, but in its place there is a metal-plated ridge on the underside of the stock (VII., Pl. 2, No. 1).

By the turn of the 14th and 15th centuries there began to be various distinctive differences in the types of hand-gun. On the one hand there was the evolution of the short light gun, which in Bohemia acquired the name *píšťala* (a pipe or whistle), and was widely used during and after the Hussite wars, spreading in various forms throughout almost the whole of central and western Europe; then there were the longer and heavier guns which could not be fired without a support and which were therefore equipped with a hook, to lessen the effects of the recoil.

1] Moravská Třebová Town Museum, cat. no. 21118.   2] B. Rathgen, *Das Geschütz im Mittelalter*, plate IX.

The Tábor *pišťala* is an example of the first type. It has a barrel altogether 423 mm in length, of which, however, 143 mm are the socket alone. The barrel is cylindrical, forged from iron, and narrowing slightly towards the muzzle, which is strengthened; it is an 18 mm calibre gun (VII., Pl. 3, No. 3). It possibly dates from as early as the beginning of the 15th century. It is a light-weight type of hand gun that is probably of Czech origin. This is not altered by the fact that the Czech term does not appear in Czech written sources until the thirties of that century and that then it became very common. Already in the twenties Silesian and Lusatian sources (dating from 1427) make fairly frequent references to a small firearm, using terms which are undoubtedly a garbled version of the Czech *pišťala* (namely Pischolu, Pischullen, Pyscheln). The term and the weapon became well-known throughout Germany, and even reached Italy, from whence it finally returned in the form of the gun known as a *pistole*, which we know to this day. The *pišťala* also spread direct to Poland and the Ukraine.

An example of the older type of arquebus is the Plzeň gun with an octagonal barrel 415 mm long and a strengthened muzzle, which has a small indent on the rim, for sighting. It is about a 29 mm calibre gun. The rim of the muzzle is decorated with a band marked with crossed lines; similar bands are repeated twice round the barrel. The gun bears the mark of a cross on a Gothic shield. The barrel rests on a trestle to which it is tied by two iron bands, the front one ending in a hook at the bottom (VII., Pl. 3, No. 2).

A typical feature of the development of the arquebus is the lengthening of the barrel. Thus an arquebus in the Plzeň museum (VII., Pl. 7, No. 8) has a barrel over 870 mm long. It is an octagonal-shaped gun with a strengthened muzzle and a hook welded to the barrel, the back part of which is strengthened with a mantel in such a manner that the edge of the back part points towards the surface of the front part. We also find other weapons like this elsewhere. There is an arquebus preserved in the Znojmo Town museum, which is 90 cm long and is strengthened at the back in a similar way. The above-mentioned arquebuses from Plzeň and Znojmo date, at the latest, from the thirties, possibly even ten years earlier. A much more advanced type, however, is the arquebus in Plzeň, the barrel of which is strengthened twice over in the direction of the chamber, and which, by its shape and execution, probably dates from somewhere in the second half of the 15th century (VII., Pl. 7, Nos. 5, 6).

The transition stage to artillery weapons was provided by heavy hand-guns with large calibres, though the existence of the hook would still justify their being called arquebuses. As an example there is the gun, dating from the first decade of the 15th century, with a narrower chamber and a barrel of iron plate, strengthened by oblique bands (VII., Pl. 1, No. 3); the length of the barrel, together with the chamber (76 cm) and the calibre (120 mm) clearly indicate that in this case it is not a hand gun but a large gun, really a cannon, which is shown working in VII., Pl. 12.

Long before people began to differentiate between the terms hand-gun and cannon we come across differences in the hand-guns themselves. As early as the 14th century gunsmiths produced large guns designed for shooting stone balls and also enormous "great guns", known as bombards, used as siege guns for demolishing the walls of beleaguered fortresses. These were usually guns with a rather narrow chamber and a broad barrel, which in the early stages was very short; the shot was placed right at the end of the muzzle, and this had to be tilted, so that the ball would not fall out when firing (VII., Pl. 8, Nos. 2, 3, 5, 7). These bombards, with calibres of about 50 cm and often even larger, were usually forged from oblong iron bands and strengthened by transverse rings; but even during the 14th and 15th centuries there appeared the first, though smaller, examples cast from iron (VII., Pl. 8, Nos. 8, 9). The barrels of these enormous guns were gradually lengthened until they reached three calibres, later even more. The tremendous weight – a bombard in Vienna, dating from the first half of the 15th century, weighs 10 tons – their clumsiness in transport and the comparatively small effect of their fire at great distances constituted their chief shortcomings.

Such bombards were also produced and used in Bohemia. In the pre-Hussite period there was a great gun known as the *Chmelík* – once the property of King Václav (Wenceslas) – which was won by the victorious Hussite armies when they took Tachov in 1427.[1] Bombards were also used by the Prague armies in 1422 at the siege of Karlštejn Castle, and in other parts of Bohemia and Moravia.[2] We know, therefore, that such bombards existed in the Czech lands, but we do not know what these Czech guns looked like. Certainly they would not have been very different from the types common to other European countries of that time. The preparation of the bombard for firing involved the construction of a mighty wooden trestle (see VII., Pl. 23, 24), and in order to mitigate the recoil complicated devices of various kinds were attached to the trestle made of brushwood and boards. So that the gun could be as effective as possible, the gun's operators had to approach as near as possible to their target and had to defend themselves against the fire of the enemy's crossbows, hand guns and smaller cannon. This was achieved by means of protective folding shields which were lowered while the gun was being loaded and raised at the moment of firing (VII., Pl. 25—28).

The use of such heavy guns, however, was not a typical feature of the Hussite armies. The greatest significance of Hussite warfare and its influence on the development of fire-arms, particularly of artillery, was its experimenting with smaller guns and the creation and development of field artillery.

There is no doubt that guns with calibres and of types something between the light hand-guns and the great bombards were well-known as early as the 14th century. For instance there was the gun with a hook and 120 mm calibre already mentioned and there were the guns on supports with dispart sights, dating from about the year 1400 (VII., Pl. 13). In addition to the firearms with a rather narrow chamber and broader barrel (VII., Pl. 13, No. 1), there were also guns with the same inside diameter in the chamber as in the barrel. Stone balls were shot from these; in the case of smaller calibres, lead bullets were also used. The main task of these weapons lies in their use as weapons of defence and in the beleaguering of the enemy's strong points. Until the time of the Hussite wars the use of the guns in field warfare was the exception. It could not have been otherwise, so long as the one decisive type of military force, employed and relied on by the feudal lords, was that of the privileged cavalry of the knights-at-arms. It was the Hussite commanders that first solved the problem of co-operation between various types of armies and the tactical direction of the individual sections during the course of the battle, thus creating the pre-conditions for the emergence of the first real field artillery in the history of warfare.

The basic type of Hussite field gun was the howitzer (*houfnice*). It was a gun that fired cannon balls and had a calibre of between 150—250 mm and a chamber with a smaller diameter. In Vienna a howitzer has been preserved that dates from the first half of the 15th century. The barrel, with a calibre of 160 mm, is forged out of oblong iron rods, held together by a number of transverse rings (VII., Pl. 14; Pl. 15, Nos. 1, 2). This gun is very similar to the howitzer in the Berlin Museum (VII., Pl. 15, Nos. 3, 4).

The howitzer (*houfnice*) was in fact the field gun used by the Hussite armies where large groups of soldiers were involved – (*houf* = a crowd) – from whence it undoubtedly gets its name.

1] *Staré letopisy české*, Charvat ed., p. 77.

2] Brno City Archives, collection of documents, No. 249 (1420).

In Czech sources of an official nature they are mentioned during the forties, but there are documents telling of their use in the year 1426 at the Battle of Ústí. The origin of the word, however, and the weapon were older. Already in the twenties of that century the Bohemian howitzer was in common use in the neighbouring region of Silesia and later also elsewhere, especially in those parts of Germany which adjoin Bohemia; however the howitzer spread also to Hungary and Rumania and took root in the various military terminologies of these countries so that in many languages, to this day, the original Czech term, somewhat corrupted, still indicates a specific type of gun.[1] It is hard to believe that merely a new method of using the old "stone-throwing guns" (bombards) was sufficient reason for the acceptance of the Czech term abroad. It is more probable that the older guns of this kind were adapted in some way. Concerning this the documentary sources tell us nothing, but it is fair to assume that it was the greater mobility of these guns – an advantage which was acquired by laying them on two-wheeled gun-carriages – which served to differentiate them most of all from the older guns.[2]

Evidence of the fact that the laying of guns on two-wheeled gun-carriages became a common phenomena during the course of the Hussite wars comes from a number of accounts from Görlitz, dating from the twenties and thirties of the 15th century. They speak not only of "two wheels to the gun"[3], but also of "firing waggons for guns" (*Schisswogen*).[4]

It was probably a similar process that took place somewhat later in connection with another type of gun of smaller calibre, namely the *tarasnice* or *palissade* gun. This was originally a kind of fortress gun, which was used above all in advanced defence posts, made of logs and known as a *tarras* or blockhouse. All it needed was a firm base and a trestle fitted with a device for sighting, just as we know it from the traditional drawing and the gun, which is preserved in the museum at Tábor (VII., Pl. 16, No. 1). Judging from the account in the *Staré letopisy* (Ancient Chronicles) it is quite clear that the Hussite armies also used to take these guns into the field of battle. Originally on fixed platforms they were guns that were probably transported en masse in large waggons, as seen in a miniature of a Vienna manuscript, but later also on two-wheeled gun-carriages. As proof of this there is the "*tarasnice* on wheels" dating from the year 1430, mentioned in the Točník Castle inventory. The transformation of the *tarasnice* into a field gun, which began in the Hussite wars, still, however, took quite a long time.

And now let us examine one of these *tarasnice* guns more closely. A gun of the same type as the *tarasnice* we mentioned, from the Tábor Museum in VII., Pl. 16, No. 1., has a barrel 113.5 cm long; this is octagonal and doubly strengthened in the direction of the chamber. It has a flaring muzzle. At the back the gun has a socket 160 mm long into which the gunstock is set. The fixture for the barrel, likewise the actual pedestal itself and the gunstock, are modern. The bore of this gun, 53 mm, approximately correspond to the average diameter of the lead shot found during archaeological research and excavation of the Hussite siege camp outside Kunratice (60 mm). The majority of such guns as have been preserved in Czechoslovakia, however, have a smaller bore (41—46 mm).

The oldest of these is obviously the *tarasnice* in the Plzeň Museum (originally in Horšov Týn, ref. no. HT 2), which has a cylindrical barrel 108 cm long (23 calibre), with the back section strengthened with a mantel and the muzzle slightly raised. The outer diameter of the muzzle is 106 mm, the bore 46 mm (VII., Pl. 17, No. 1). There is a similar

1] See Titz, *op. cit.*, p. 41; "Doplňky ke spisu Ohlasy", *VHS* VII/1, pp. 28–9.
2] *Žižkův sborník*, R. Urbánek, *Žižka a husitské válečnictví*, p. 49.
3] *CDLS* II/1, p. 218 (1425); CDLS II/2, pp. 328, 345, 356 (1432).
4] *CDLS* II/2, p. 44 (1429): "*vor zwu schisswogen zu den bochsin…*"

tarasnice in the Military History Museum in Prague, but this betrays much rougher work than the above-mentioned one. Again it is a 23-calibre gun, but the walls of the barrel are much thicker.

In contrast to the two guns just mentioned, the Znojmo *tarasnice* (ref. no. Zb 512), and similar other guns in Plzeň, have octagonal barrels, doubly strengthened in such a way that the edge of the strengthening always alternates with a section of the surface of the barrel. The barrel, with a diameter of 92 mm at the muzzle, is 108.5 cm long (24 calibre) and has a bore of 41 mm. A similar Plzeň *tarasnice* (ref. no. Ht 1) is even longer and measures 133 cm (30 calibre). Its bore is 45 mm. All these guns are made from iron plate welded round a rod; the welding seam is usually quite visible.

It is known, however, that these *tarasnice* guns were also cast in bronze. We have a number of documentary proofs from Görlitz and probably part of the Znojmo account dealing with the casting of these guns concerns the *tarasnice*, though this is not expressly stated. The great Görlitz *tarasnice*, dating from the year 1423, and other accounts prove that guns with long barrels and even larger bores were also considered to be pallisade guns. A pallisade gun like this is shown in VII., Pl. 17.

There is still one more type of gun, fairly common during the 15th century, which should be mentioned. These are the so-called breech-block or chamber guns. In contrast to other guns already described, which were muzzle-loaded, these guns had a chamber separate from the barrel, which could be taken out and filled with powder. This made it possible to fire much more frequently than had been the case with muzzle-loaders, for the gunner could have several such interchangeable breech-blocks for each gun, which were prepared by his assistants while he was firing. It was, of course, necessary to fix the breech-block very firmly at the back part of the barrel, and to wedge it (VII., Pl. 19, Pl. 20). But in spite of its advantages this type of gun disappeared from use at a fairly early stage during the 16th century. The reason for this probably lay in the fact that even the finest wedged chamber, with what was after all rather rough usage, inevitably produced a considerable loss of energy.

Such breech-block guns were also known in Bohemia. For instance the "quick-firer" used in 1422 at the siege of Karlštejn, which apparently could fire thirty times a day, where others could only fire six or seven times, was probably one of these breechblock guns.[1]

The ammunition for firearms with large bores consisted of cannon balls; in the case of smaller guns it was shot made of lead or forged from iron. In addition to cannon balls, even as early as during the Hussite Wars, we find that grapeshot was also probably used. In order to pack the powder, handfuls of small pieces of scrap iron were shaken on to the powder and these were then held down with a layer of wood. There is apparently proof of this in the registry entry from Znojmo dated 1425, which speaks of payment for "one hundred pieces of scrap for the guns".[2] A special type of ammunition used by these pallisade guns consisted of the type of cylindrical shot found during the archaeological investigation of the Kunratice camp. They were lead cylinders with a diameter of 60 mm and weighed 2 kilogrammes. They were probably used on purpose by the defenders of the castle, who increased the weight of the shot (as opposed to cannon balls of the same calibre) in an effort to destroy the great catapult used by the men of Prague, which was situated at about half the distance of the supposed effective range of the pallisade gun. In addition, as early as the first third of the 15th century, use was made of incendiary ammunition.

1] *Staré letopisy české*, Charvat ed., p. 64.
2] Znojmo Town Library, 240, fol. 43v (1422); a similar account from Görlitz, *CDLS* II, p. 198 (1431):
"*70 sch. schroteling zu geloten.*"

Konrad Kyeser speaks of this in his Bellifortis manuscript; but it is also mentioned in other documentary sources under the name "fireballs".

Bullets for hand-guns and gunpowder, produced by gunsmiths from saltpetre, sulphur and charcoal, were carried by the gunners in leather pouches. The equipment of the gunner also included a ramrod and a measure for the gunpowder. The firing of the gun was carried out either by means of an iron hook, the bent end of which was made red-hot in a pan of glowing charcoal, or by means of a fuse (VII., Pl. 21).

The peculiar characteristics of the Hussite revolutionary armies made it possible to introduce a bold, new tactical use of hand firearms as well as artillery, which also had an important influence on changes in tactics and the art of warfare in general. The concentration of material and human forces and above all the support of a great number of Czech towns made it possible to equip the armies with such a quantity of the most modern weapons of the time that it aroused fear and amazement in the hearts of the foreigners taking part in the wars. In each field army, and for every 6,000 foot soldiers, there were about 360 hand firearms, about 36 field guns and about 10 larger guns,[1] and when the two armies combined together with local troops and the Prague militia, as they did for the great and "glorious raids" in the winter of 1429—1430 in 2,500 waggons, the entire force had about 300 field guns, 60 larger guns and possibly even 5 bombards to every 3,000 hand-guns.

The important position acquired by firearms in Bohemian warfare during the Hussite wars continued to be maintained. The great progress made in these arms in Bohemia depended on the development that had been going on in Bohemian towns, and was encouraged by the great efforts of the people in their struggles against their own and foreign reactionary feudal lords; this progress placed Bohemia, during the period of the revolutionary Hussite movement, in the forefront of Europe in that field. The Bohemian arquebus and *pišťala*, and the Hussite howitzer and *tarasnice* on gun-carriages became well-known not only in the countries immediately neighbouring the Bohemian border, but even in far more distant lands. This position of supremacy was maintained by Bohemia for a greater part of the 15th century.

1] See Durdík, *Husitské vojenství*, 1954, p. 74.

FLAGS AND BANNERS

Flags and banners played an important part in medieval methods of warfare. Sooner or later, during the course of each battle, every clash between two enemy armies ended in a fight between individuals; the cause, apart from other things, lay primarily in the nature of the weapons and armour in use at that time. It was a question of dispersing the crowds of mounted knights and men-at-arms, which had gathered together for the battle or which came together during the course of the fight. In the immense confusion of fighters of both sides, equipped very often with smaller arms and armour, the flag or pennon upraised on a lance stave became an important point of orientation and a mark of identification.

In the Hussite army, where it was considered particularly important to maintain the unity and cohesion of the various individual parts of the army, flags and banners fulfilled a similar function. For this reason each company in Žižka's army had its own banner, behind which it was arrayed and with which it went into battle. Apart from the smaller, and probably tactical, units, the great, many thousand strong groups of the army were also distinguishable by their own particular standards and banners.

There is scarcely any doubt that each of the Hussite armies, whether home guard or field forces, had its own standard by which it was known. We find proof of this in the words of the *Very Beautiful Chronicle* about Jan Žižka, which relates that after the death of their great leader, the Hradec fighters "had Žižka himself emblazoned on their banner, riding a white horse and wearing his knightly armour, and brandishing a fist-dagger mace as was his wont . . ."[1]

As far as the shapes of the standards and banners was concerned, one should point out that here there was not the slightest sign of uniformity. By the end of the 14th and the beginning of the 15th century the most common shape for a pennon was probably that of a long narrow triangle, similar to the one on a stave held by Prince Wenceslas in the Mulhouse altar-piece, dating from the eighties of the 14th century (II., Pl. 4), or the youth with a banner in the Chapter Library manuscript *Knihy o anatomii* (Books on Anatomy) (II., Pl. 35). But one also finds warriors with similar banners as late as the thirties, in fact even after the middle, of the 15th century (VIII., Pl. 3, Nos. 1, 3).

During the first half of the 15th century standards were often oblong, hanging downwards from the width, or square (VIII., Pl. 3, Nos. 2, 4, 5, 7), but right at the very beginning of the century we come across banners with a long triangular piece running out from the upper corner of the oblong or square. We find such banners in the Kyeser Bellifortis manuscript dating from the years 1402—1405 (II., Pl. 31) and later they became more and more common. These "banners with a long tail" as they were known at the time,[2] are also to be found in the Prague University Library manuscript known under ref. no. XVII A 34, dating from about the year 1430 (Fol. 115 v; II., Pl. 39), i. e. right at the end of the Hussite wars; there is also just such a banner bearing the symbol of a goose, in one of the miniatures of a Viennese manuscript, dating from between 1437 and 1450, which depicts a phalanx of fortified waggons (VIII., Pl. 2, No. 3); a similar banner, bearing the symbol of the chalice and the inscription *Veritas vincit* was used by the Hussite cavalry when going into battle, as we know from an illumination to the Jena Codex (VIII., Pl. 2, No. 1). In the same manuscript the Hussite infantry, like those in the Göttingen Codex, have a great triangular-shaped flag with the same symbol but without inscription (VIII., Pl. 2, No. 2).

The banners and flags were probably usually made of coloured cloth or silk and the

---

1] *Staročeské vojenské řády*, p. 35.   2] Bohemian Archives IX; p. 163 (1437).

symbols were painted on to them. In the case of the feudal armies, these symbols were the hereditary bearings of the individual feudal lords, with their own heraldic colours (VIII., Pl. 6, Nos. 1, 3—5). As far as the colours of the Hussite flags and banners were concerned, it is necessary to point out that there is no direct evidence of the existence of the supposedly traditional black or white banner with the red chalice. It seems clear that this is a question of mistaking the colour proposed for the "signalling banner" by Václav Vlček of Čenov in his aforementioned *Instructions*, dating from the third quarter of the 15th century.[1] Where we can really see the colour, for example, in the Jena Codex, the flags and banners are red with a yellow (gold) chalice and one can assume that these were the most common colours used by the Hussites.

In order to facilitate the carrying of a heavy lance and banner, riders used to have special saddles fitted with a metal holder, into which they inserted the lower end of the shaft; in some cases this holder, of leather or metal, was tied to the stirrup (VIII., Pl. 8, No. 2). Infantry standard bearers probably carried their banners with a special strap and fixture that was worn over the shoulder (VIII., Pl. 9).

One should however differentiate between the great standards and banners and the small pennons flown mainly by horsemen from their lances. These were usually triangular or oblong shaped, and the free end was often dagged (II., Pl. 20, No. 2; VIII., Pl. 3, No. 6).

Mention of these "signalling banners" brings us to one of the most important means of signalling that was used when on the march and for the arraying of the waggon phalanx. Another means of signalling in those days — though mostly only on the field of battle – was that of sound, using trumpets and drums (VIII., Pl. 8, Nos. 1, 3; Pl. 10, Nos. 1, 2). How this was done we can discover from the military regulations set down by Václav Vlček, where he states: "... instruct them that they listen carefully, so that when the trumpets sound, they attack with gusto, and when the drums play they should come to a halt as quickly as possible and cease chasing the enemy..."[2] Thus the trumpets gave the sign to attack, whereas the beating of the drums called for a halt. And this regulation of Vlček's – even though the regulations as such were more recent – is certainly of ancient origin. That trumpeting was also a sign for attack for the Hussite armies is made quite clear in an account of the Battle of Lipany which maintains that when the Brothers saw the enemy retreating (feigning retreat), "They blew on their trumpets and shouted: they're running, they're running! and ran out from their encampment in order to give chase."[3] Thus the participation of trumpeters in military expeditions was not without significance.

1] *Staročeské vojenské řády*, p. 52: "Item. Eight indicative or signalling banners should be included, the best colours being black and white."

2] *Staročeské vojenské řády*, p. 46.

3] Palacký, *Urkundliche Beitrage* II, p. 414.

THE HORSE'S HARNESS AND BARDINGS

Medieval riding saddles were mostly rather high and by no means uniform in shape. They obviously varied according to the purposes for which they were required. A common feature was the markedly high front saddle bow, which forced the rider to hold the reigns fairly high. In the case of travelling or hunting saddles it was somewhat lower than that of the battle or jousting saddle, where it ran out into pommels of various shapes, often broadening into a shield, to protect the uncovered parts of the rider against thrusts directed at him straight from the front (IX., Pl. 3, Nos. 4,5; Pl. 5, Nos. 2, 4).

The rear saddle-tree or cantle tended to become a back-rest, in the case of the travelling saddle not a very high one, which either followed the line of the horse's back or split down the middle in a heart shape (IX., Pl. 4, No. 1; Pl. 5, Nos. 1, 3; Pl. 7, No. 3). Battle saddles had a higher back-rest. Very often these were almost like a small arm-chair with arms on each side enveloping the rider's hips. The high back of the cantle helped the armoured rider to remain in the saddle when rammed by an enemy lance, whose thrust he would catch on his shield or breastplate. Hence it was typical of the battle or jousting saddle. We come across it most frequently during the second half of the 14th and the first half of the 15th centuries; later it slowly disappears and is only to be found as a jousting saddle (IX., Pl. 2, No. 1; Pl. 4, Nos. 3—6; Pl. 5, Nos. 2, 4, 5; Pl. 6, Nos. 1, 4, 5; Pl. 11, No. 1; Pl. 12).

The sides of the saddle were usually ornamented and the edges often dagged, the burr and cantle plates – especially in the case of luxuriously made battle saddles – often being studded with nails and decorated with small metal discs and larger rosettes and quatrefoils or other Gothic forms of ornamentation (the saddle of St. George at the Prague Castle, IX., Pl. 3).

The saddle was held in place by one or two girths, which usually seem to have been striped. To prevent the saddle from slipping forwards or backwards with the movement of the horse, the saddle was usually fitted with a crupper and breast-straps, which were held in place horizontally by a whole system of large and small straps, some of which were very ornamental. The trappings were often embossed in various ways and ornamented with metal tacks and discs; in colour they nearly always harmonized with the colours of the saddle, just occasionally they were in contrast (IX., Pl. 1, 8, 11, 12 – various types of ornamental trappings – IX., Pl. 2, No. 1; Pl. 10, No. 2).

Beneath the saddle there was sometimes a caparison, or richly made saddle cloth; this was already customary in the 13th century. By the turn of the 14th and 15th centuries, in the miniatures of the Wenceslas Bible, we come across it fairly frequently (IX., Pl. 6, Nos. 1, 2, 4, 5). These caparisons were usually made in the heraldic colours of the bearings of the knight-at-arms, or were actually emblazoned with armorial bearings themselves (IX., Pl. 14). They were probably used most frequently when jousting. The side pieces of the battle saddle were sometimes so long that they reached down to the fetlocks and were decorated in a variety of ways and dagged or perforated in various shapes and patterns. (IX., Pl. 4, Nos. 3, 6; Pl. 6, No. 3). In this case the saddle was covered with material, usually velvet.

The horse was guided either on a curb or snaffle-bit (IX., Pl. 32, No. 1), or on a combination, which we know to-day as the Pelham bit (IX., Pl. 32, No. 2). The bit was usually in two parts, in the case of a curb bit, sometimes even three, and the centre piece was known as the port. In the case of curbs, the bit was usually fairly strong and fitted with strong rings, so as not to tear the gums or the flesh at the corners of the mouth of the horse, especially as the lower lever of the bit was usually fairly long.

In Czech drawings and paintings from the Gothic period snaffle-bits were the exception (IX., Pl. 34). In the St. George altar-piece, dating from about 1470 (IX., Pl. 8) there is a horse depicted with a curb bit (IX., Pl. 33). It does not mean, however, that this type of bit was not in use in our country until this date.

A simple bridle consisted of the right and left cheek-pieces, the throat-latch and the brow band. Sometimes the bridle would be fitted with a nose strap sewn to the cheek-pieces. Sometimes there was also a straight front strap joining the brow band, front and nose straps, in other cases the bridle was fitted with cross straps, or face pieces, which ran from the front strap, crossed between the eyes and were fixed to the cheek-pieces at the bit. The forked or semi-forked strap was similar (types of bridles IX., Pl. 26; Pl. 28).

As protection for the head the charger sometimes had a protective metal plate attached to the bridle, known as a chanfron. In Czech Gothic painting this part of the bardings is rarely to be seen; it was much more common in France (IX., Pl. 15, No. 1). Sometimes, however, one comes across mail protection for the horse. In a picture dating from about 1420 the head and the upper part of the neck of the horse on which the English King Henry IV is riding is protected by plate armour, whereas the lower part of the neck, the breast and the back have mail protection. Although such protection for the horse is not to be found in Czech pictorial documentary sources, nevertheless it was undoubtedly known here. Of this we have proof in an entry in the Brno City Accounts Books, where amongst forfeits listed for unpaid dues for the year 1338, there is one for "the armour for a horse".[1]

From the end of the 15th century, in pictures by Hans Memling, we also come across saddle bags. They consist of a cylindrical pouch which is fixed to the saddle at the back, and at the top is fastened with straps (IX., Pl. 16, No. 2). Saddle bags, however, were in use at a much earlier date. We have an account of them from Görlitz as early as the first third of the 15th century. They were probably of a different kind from those depicted by Memling, for in this case it speaks of a pair of saddle bags, and they were probably more like the modern saddle pouch in shape. But it seems that they were only part of the equipment of the traveller's saddle, for they are not found in connection with the equipment of the battle charger.

The stirrup basically kept its triangular shape, or rather that of a trapeze, with a loop for attaching it to the stirrup leather at the short upper side. It enabled the rider to mount more easily and to maintain his position on the horse when riding. The medieval rider put his foot right into the stirrup, and for this reason the lower bar or tread was often quite wide. The stirrups, like all other parts of the medieval equestrian fighter's equipment, differed in finish and ornamentation according to the wealth of the owner. The arches of the stirrup were either plain (IX., Pl. 9, No. 12) or decorated ornamentally (IX., Pl. 36, No. 1); in some cases they were even done in beautiful filigree (IX., Pl. 36, No. 10).

To goad the horse into action or to guide its course when moving fast or turning quickly, the rider was equipped with spurs, which were fixed firmly to the foot by means of two straps. The arches of the spurs were bent in such a way that they circumvented the ankle. The weight of the neck of the spur, which in the course of its development grew longer and longer, was balanced by buckle rings, set so far apart that they formed a two-armed lever, which kept the spur in a horizontal position (IX., Pl. 37). Older types of spur, dating from

1] Brno City Account Books, ed. B. Mendl, p. 83: "Pancirium pro equo."

the 14th century, had a short shank; the fairly narrow arch usually ended in a sharp pointed rowel (IX., Pl. 38; Pl. 39, No. 3). Further development was chiefly characterized by the lengthening of the shank and the broadening of the arch to fit the ankles (IX., Pl. 40). Luxury spurs were also richly adorned and worked in filigree, thus displaying the wealth and position of their owners.

If we consider the long neck of the spur and the long lever of the curb bit, we come to the conclusion that the knight's horse had to be swift and agile, in order to fulfil the tasks demanded of it by equestrian battle, in which a number of combats between armoured knights were taking place simultaneously on the field of battle.

Pictures of medieval battles usually show us horses charging. We have to assume therefore that cavalry charges were made at the gallop, in order to make full use of the speed and strength of the horse. Attacks at the trot or at walking pace would certainly not have achieved any positive results and the infantry soldiers would easily have been able to defend themselves against them.

WAGGONS

No army, not even a medieval army, could manage without means of transport for its supplies, fodder, tents and various other needs. For this purpose all kinds of waggons were used, from the great team-drawn waggons (X., Pl. 2, No. 1) and the smaller waggons, whose sides were made of plaited withies and wood, and the common peasant hay-waggons (X., Pl. 1, No. 2), to the ordinary two-wheeled carts such as the illuminator depicted in Kyeser's Bellifortis manuscript (X., Pl. 1, No. 1). The task of providing these waggons and other means of transport, together with a corresponding load of stores, seems, in the 14th century in Bohemia, to have been left to the monasteries and their representatives.

Even in very ancient times it seems to have been the custom, when pitching camp for the night, for the resting army to use their means of transport for creating a protective enclosure, and during the 13th, 14th and the beginning of the 15th centuries such camps surrounded by waggons often became a place of refuge for the defeated armies when fleeing from the field of battle.

The period with which we are dealing, namely the 14th and 15th centuries, was one, as has been stated several times already, in which the infantry groups of archers and artillery men and others gained steadily in importance at the expense of the mounted knights-at-arms. F. Engels rightly considered that it was during this period that the new urban infantry came into being and he called it the "rebirth of the infantry."[1] For a long time, however, this new infantry was still unable to compare in importance with the heavy cavalry which, in spite of serious shortcomings, was still the decisive force in times of war. Certain shortcomings – above all the weak firing power of the archers with their cross-bows and their primitive firearms – prevented them from gaining permanent predominance over the heavy cavalry. It was essential to find a way of enabling the hordes of foot soldiers to withstand the first attack of the riders, because then it was easier to overcome the undisciplined knights, who soon scattered. In Flanders and in Switzerland they were very clever at making good use of natural and artificial barriers and suitable mountain terrain, but this could not guarantee lasting predominance for the infantry over the heavy cavalry. It was necessary to find a means which would guarantee the ability to hold the cavalry at any given place.

Already by the beginning of the 15th century the first attempts were made to use an artificial barricade for this purpose composed of waggons. The solution of this problem could only have been brought about by such a revolutionary upheaval in the development of the art of warfare as that produced by the birth of the revolutionary Hussite armies. These armies, in which the mass of fighters were the common people from the towns and the country, were largely infantry armies. It was an infantry that had attained a far higher level of battle-readiness than the old feudal infantry and the newer urban units, primarily because the conviction of the justice of their struggle, stirred them with an unbreakable spirit of devotion and gave them great moral superiority. Since these armies were armed with the power of the revolutionary movement, which had set out to attack the feudal order, they could not be satisfied with the occasional natural barrier as their defence. It was necessary to seek out the enemy and destroy him, at the same time, however, it was also necessary to provide such conditions that the army, which was largely composed of infantry, could at all times be assured of victory. And one of the

1] F. Engels, *Pěchota, historie vojenství*, I, 1954, p. 16.

important elements in the conduct of the struggles waged by the Hussite armies, was the use of the waggon phalanx.

At the commencement of the revolutionary movement, in the autumn of 1419, the waggons used did not differ very much from the normal means of transport, the common peasant or town carts. But just as the simple peasant flail was soon improved to become an effective weapon of war, so the ordinary carts soon became "battle waggons".

It is true that the battle waggon did not differ very much from the common means of transport, except perhaps in the fact that it was a little larger and better made. However, when prepared for battle, the outer sides of the waggons were strengthened by boards which were suspended round them. The pictures (X., Pl. 2, Nos. 2, 3) show clearly how one of these waggons appeared to the artist of the 15th century. The construction and details of such a waggon are shown in pictures X., Pl. 3—7.

These battle waggons were well equipped with tools and implements, mostly of the kind necessary for clearing the roads when on the march and for making trenches for camps. According to a contemporary account each waggon had "two axes, two spades, two pickaxes, two hoes, two shovels . . .; (Types of tools: XI., Pl. 2, Nos. 1—4, axes; Pl. 1, Nos. 1—3, hoes; Pl. 1, Nos. 4, 5, pickaxes; Pl. 3, Nos. 1, 2, 5, 8 spades; Pl. 3, Nos. 4, 6, 7, shovels.) Apart from these, each waggon had a fairly long chain with a hook and ring, which was used for coupling the waggons together in battle order.

The battle waggon in the Hussite armies became the basic organisational unit around which the foot soldiers were concentrated. This also soon became the case wherever Hussite tactics were imitated. Hence each waggon also had two arquebusiers (they either had arquebusses or *pištaly*), about six crossbowmen, four fighters with flails, four halbardiers, two bucklers and finally two well-armed drivers, who had to be good team-drivers when on the march and at the same time well-versed in the art of forming a phalanx of waggons when in battle.[1] In addition to all this, each waggon also had a pallisade of staves, which was used to fill in the gap between the waggons when in phalanx, and one or two lances with hooks.

The unit naturally also had to take sufficient ammunition for the hand-guns and crossbows and also certain foodstuffs as emergency supplies, an account of which is to be found in an Austrian regulation dating from the year 1431.

For the transport of supplies, fodder for the animals and other necessities, there were special waggons known as "place" waggons, so called because in camp they were situated in the centre, in the "place" or central square. In appearance they were not very different from the waggons round the perimeter of the camp, only they probably did not have defence boards suspended on their outer sides and they also probably did not carry all the implements prescribed for battle waggons (X., Pl. 7).

In between the "place" waggons round the central square and in the lanes between the rows of carts in the camp there were tents (types of tents, XI., Pl. 5, Pl. 6), in some instances also penthouses and huts (XI., Pl. 4), which in those days were usually built over shallow, oblong ditches, especially when it was a case of a more permanent camp – for example, when besieging an enemy castle – and protected on the enemy side by low earthworks.

The battle waggons and the waggon phalanx were perhaps the chief things that, at first sight, differentiated the Hussite armies from the crusading feudal mercenary armies. Although it was only one of the elements that enabled the peasant armies of the Hussite revolutionary movement to overcome the superior strength of their enemies, who were

1] See Durdík, *Husitské vojenství*, 1954, p. 118.

experienced in battle, it was certainly primarily the waggons which the defeated might of Europe considered to be the main cause of its lack of success. Hence the first attempts at imitating the new Hussite methods of fighting usually consisted of imitating the waggon phalanx. But just because this was merely a part of the entire tactics of the Hussites, these attempts at imitation were not successful for a long time. It was not until the main supporters of the movement, namely the field armies, had been defeated, when their scattered remnants sought means of existence in the mercenary armies of neighbouring lands, that they brought with them not only the art of using these waggons and the waggon phalanx, but also the other elements of Hussite tactics, together with Czech arms such as the flails, halbards, sabres, arquebusses, *píšťaly*, *howitzers* and *tarasnice* guns and spread their fame throughout almost the whole of Europe. The Hussite art of warfare had an important influence on contemporary warfare for a long time to come and it was not until a further step in the development of hand and artillery guns, namely the improvement in their fire power, had such an effect on the art of warfare at the beginning and during the course of the 16th century, that certain of its elements were gradually discarded. Others, and, in fact, the most important, namely the co-ordination of the various sections of the army and the direction of the troops in battle, constituted the lasting contribution of the Hussite art of warfare to the development of European warfare in general.

LIST OF SOURCES AND BIBLIOGRAPHY

A. UNPUBLISHED SOURCES

Konrad Kyeser's *Bellifortis* (1402—1405), Göttingen State University Library; ref. no. 63. (Photo-copy in the Prague Military History Institute Archives).

Abbess Kunhuta's Passional. Prague University Library; ref. no. XIV A 17.

Velislav Bible (1st half of 14th century). Prague University Library; ref no. XXIII C 24.

King Wenceslas IV Bible, Staatsbibliotek, Vienna (Photo-copy in the State Documentary Centre, Prague).

Latin Bible (*circa* 1430). University Library, Prague; ref. no. XVII I 34. Latin Bible (15th century), Prague Cathedral Chapter Library; ref. no. A 10.

De moribus et officiis viventium (1st half of 15th century), Prague Chapter Library; ref. no. G 42.

Jena Codex (turn of 15th and 16th centuries), National Museum Library, Prague; ref. no. IV A 29a.

Jan of Středa *Liber Viaticus* (3rd quarter of 14th century), National Museum Library, Prague; ref. no. XIII A 12.

Libri XX de anatomia humani corporis et aliis naturalibus Joannis de Parma (1404), Prague Chapter Library; ref. no. L 11.

Novum testamentum (1418), Prague Chapter Library; ref. no. A LIX 3.

Petri de Crescentiis Ruralium commodorum libri XII, Prague University Library; ref. no. VII C 8.

The Mirror of Redemption (Krumlov MSS – beginning of 15th century), National Museum Library, Prague; ref. no. III B 10.

B. PUBLISHED SOURCES

Bohemian Archives; Vols. I, III, VI, VII, IX, XV, XXI. Prague, 1840 onwards.

Codex diplomaticus Lusatiae Superioris, II, III, Zhořelec, 1910.

Codex juris Bohemici, Jireček, II, 3—4; Prague 1889, 1898.

Fontes Bohemicarum, Vols, I, III, IV, V.

Flajšhans, Václav, *Klaret a jeho družina*, I, II, Prague, 1926, 1928.

Huss John, Selected Writings, ed. K. J. Erben, Prague 1865.

Palacký F., *Urkundliche Beitrage zur Geschichte des Hussitenkrieges, Vols.* I and II, Prague 1872.

Staré letopisy české, ed. F. Palacký, Prague 1829.

Staročeské vojenské řády, pub. F. Svejkovský, Prague 1952.

C. BIBLIOGRAPHY

Alteneck, *Trachten.*

Bock F., *Geschichte der liturgischen Gewänder.*

Boeheim W., *Handbuch der Waffenkunde*, Leipzig 1890.

v. Boehm, *Die Mode, Menschen und Mode im Mittelalter vom Untergang der alten Welt bis zur Renaissance*, Munich 1925.

Bouchet H., *L'epopée du costume militaire français*, Paris, s. a.

Bruhn W. – Tilke M., *Das Kostümwerk*, Berlin 1941.

Bruhn W. – Skarbina H., *Kostüm und Mode*, Leipzig 1938.

Burger – Schmitz – Beth, *Die deutsche Malerei der Renaissance*, Vol. II, Berlin 1917.

Buss G., *Das Kostüm in Vergangenheit und Gegenwart*, Leipzig 1906.

Dehio G., *Geschichte der deutschen Kunst. Der Abbildungen zweiter Band*, Second Ed., Berlin-Leipzig 1923.

Demmin A., *Die Kriegswaffen in ihrer geschichtlichen Entwickelung*, Leipzig 1895.

Diener – Schönberg A., *Die Waffen der Wartburg*, Berlin 1912.

Dreger M., *Waffensammlung Dreger, Mit einer Einführung in die Systematik der Waffen*, Berlin-Leipzig 1926.

Drobná Z., *Les trésors de la broderie religieuse en Tchécoslovaquie*, Prague 1950.

Enlart C., *Manuel d'archéologie française, III Le costume*, Paris 1916.

Essenwein A., *Quellen zur Geschichte der Feuerwaffen*, Leipzig 1872.

Estruch y Cumella J., *Museo Armeria*, Barcelona 1896.

Ffoulkes Ch. J., *Inventory and Survey of the Armouries of the Tower of London*, London 1916.

Forrer R., *Die Waffensammlung des ... R. Zschille*, I—II, Berlin.

Glaser C., *Die altdeutsche Malerei*, Munich 1924.

Gollerová-Plachá J., *Látky z pražské královské hrobky*, Prague 1937.

Graus F., *Chudina městská v době předhusitské*, Prague 1949.

Graus F., *Český obchod suknem ve 14. a počátkem 15. století*, Prague 1950.

Grossmann O., *Die deutsche Soldatenkunde, II Bilderatlas*, Leipzig 1937.

Gumbel H., *Deutsche Kultur vom Zeitalter der Mystik bis zur Gegen-reformation*, Potsdam 1936.

Haenal E., *Alte Waffen*, Berlin 1913.

Has W., *Geschichte des I. Kurhessischen Feldartillerie-Regiments Nr. 11*, Marburg i. H. 1913.

Hassenstein W., *Das Feuerwerkbuch von 1420*, Munich 1940.

Henne am Rhyn O., *Kulturgeschichte des deutschen Volkes II*, Berlin 1886.

Hergsell G., *Talhoffers Fechtbuch (Gothaer Codex) aus dem J. 1443*, Prague 1889.
Ambrasser Codex aus dem J. 1458, Prague 1889.
Ambrasser Codex aus dem J. 1467, Prague 1887.

Jähns M., *Atlas zur Geschichte des Kriegswesens von der Urzeit bis zum Ende des 16. Jhdts.*, Berlin 1878.

Kropáček P., *Malířství doby husitské – česká desková malba prvé poloviny XV. století*, Prague 1946.

Lacroix P., *Moeurs, usages et costumes au moyen âge et a l'epoque de la renaissance*, Paris 1871.
  Vie militaire et religieuse au moyen âge et a l'epoque de la renaissance, Paris 1873.
Laking F. G., *A Record of European Armour and Arms through Seven Centuries, I—IV*, London 1920.
Lauts J., *Alte deutsche Waffen*, Burg b. M., 1938.
Leclère R., *Histoire du costume*, Lausanne 1949.
Léderrey E. M. G., *L'armée suisse, ses origines et traditions, son état présent, sa raison d'être*, Geneva 1929.
Lejsková M., *Dvojí šat královen z hrobky českých králů v chrámě sv. Víta v Praze*, Pam. arch. skupina hist., XXXVII, Prague 1931.
Matějček A., *Česká malba gotická. Deskové malířství 1350—1450*, Prague 1938.
  Velislavova bible a její místo ve vývoji knižní ilustrace gotické, Prague 1926.
Mützel H., *Kostümkunde für Sammler*, Berlin 1919.
Naumann H., *Deutsche Kultur zur Modetracht*, Berlin 1923.
Nejedlý Z., *Dějiny husitského zpěvu za válek husitských*, Prague 1913.
Novotný V., *Postavy českých dějin v umění výtvarném*, Prague 1939.
  500 łat malarstwa polskiego, Warsaw 1950.
Quincke W., *Handbuch der Kostümkunde*, Third Ed., Leipzig 1908.
Racinet O., *Le costume historique*, III, Paris.
Radnor J., *It All Happened Before. The Home Guard through the Centuries*, London 1945.
Rathgen B., *Das Geschütz im Mittelalter*, Berlin 1928.
de la Ronciere Ch., *Histoire de la Marine française, illustrée*, Paris 1934.
Seeger K., *Marschallstab und Kesselpauke*, Stuttgart 1939.
v. Schlosser J., *Die Bilderhandschriften Königs Wenzel I*,

  Jhrb. der kunsthist. Sammlungen der AK, Vienna 1893.
Schoenbeck R., *Das Pferd und seine Darstellung in der bildenden Kunst*, Leipzig 1892.
Schultz A., *Deutsches Leben im XIV. und XV. Jhdt.*, Vienna, Prague, Leipzig 1892.
Schultz H., *Blut und Eisen, Krieg und Kriegertum in alter und neuer Zeit*, II, Berlin, s. a.
Stone G. C., *A Glossary of the Construction, Decoration and Use of Arms and Armor*, Portland 1934.
Szendrei J., *Ungarische Kriegsgeschichtliche Denkmäler...*, Budapest 1896.
Terlinden Ch., *Historie militaire des Belges*, Brussels 1931.
Titz K., *Ohlasy husitského válečnictví v Evropě*, Prague 1922.
  Dodatky ke spisu Ohlasy . ., Vojenský historický sborník, VII-i, Prague 1937.
Trapp O., *The Armoury of the Castle of Churburg*, London 1929.
Unger W., *Meister der Reitkunst*, Leipzig 1926.
Viollet le Duc M., *Dictionnaire raisonné du mobilier français I-VI*, Paris 1858—1875.
  Dictionnaire raisonné de l'architecture française I-X, Paris 1858—1868.
Waffen und Kunstsammlung Karl Gimbel, Baden-Baden, Berlin 1904.
Weese A., *Skulptur und Malerei in Frankreich im XV. und XVI. Jhdt.*, Potsdam 1927.
Weiss H., *Die Kostümkunde*, Bd. 3/1, Stuttgart 1873.
Weygand, *Die Geschichte der französischen Armee*, Berlin.
Winter Z. – Zíbrt Č., *Dějiny kroje v zemích českých I-II*, Prague 1892—1893.
Zeitschrift für historische Waffenkunde, I-VIII, Dresden 1897—1920.
Zeitschrift für historische Waffen- und Kostümkunde, 9 Bd., Dresden 1921—1942.

PLATE 1

Noble women from the Abbess Kunhuta's Passional, dating from about 1320, fol. 3v (1), and the Velislav Bible, fol. 126 (2)

PLATE 2

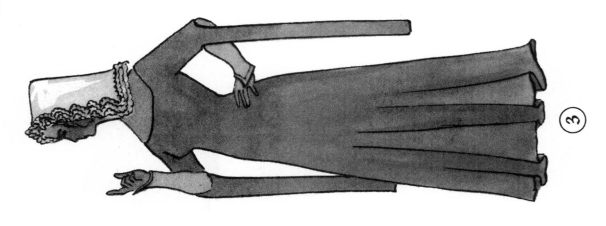

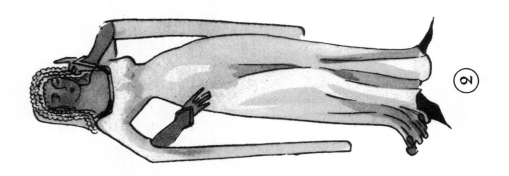

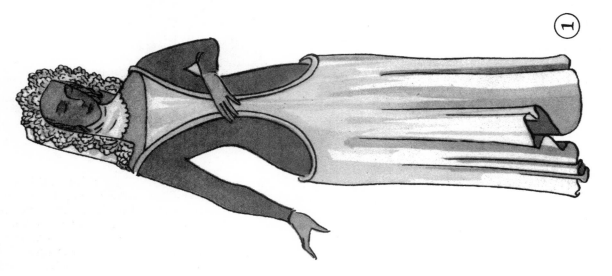

Noble women from the Velislav Bible: (1) fol. 13. (2) fol. 7. (3) fol. 10.

PLATE 3   PART I

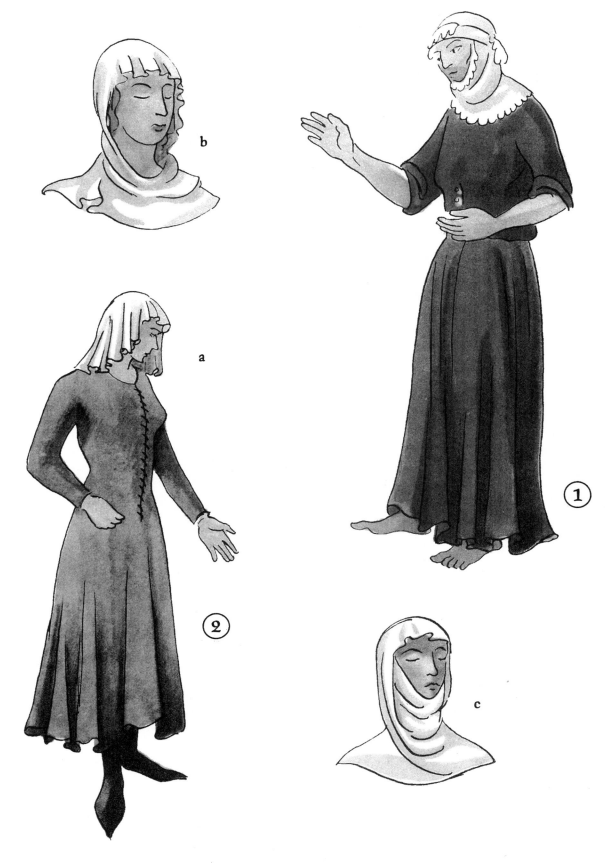

Married women wearing wimples and veils. (1) Peasant woman of about 1350: skirt and blouse with fastening in the centre above the waist; her head-veil is bound like a wimple covering the neck and chin and falling over the shoulders. From the painting "The Birth of Our Lord" by the Vyšší Brod Master, dating from about 1350. (Matějček, *Gothic Painting in Bohemia*, pl. 5.) (2) A middle-class woman from an illustration in the Krumlov MS, National Museum, ref. no. III B 10, fol. 47. dating from the beginning of the 15th century. She wears a tunic with closely fitting bodice, fastened with lacing down the front from the neck to below the waist, and with a fairly high neckline and long sleeves; the lower half of the tunic, which reaches almost to the ankles, falls in voluminous folds. (3) Various types of headdress: (a) a loosely flowing veil, (b) the head-veil of St. Mary Magdalen in the Třeboň altar-piece, dating from about 1380, draped to give the appearance of a wimple covering the shoulders like a cape, but leaving the neck and chin free (Matějček, pl. 93), (c) wimple and head-veil covering chin, neck and shoulders from the portrait of St. Clare by Master Theodoricus, about 1360 (*ibid.*, pl. 63).

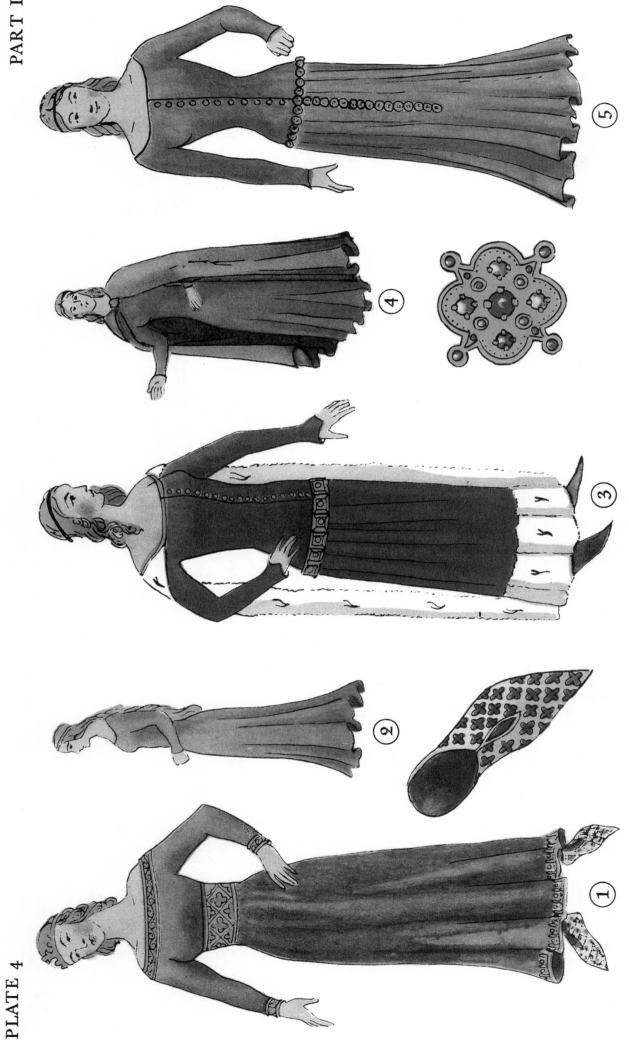

PLATE 4

PART I

(1) A maiden of noble birth, depicted as an angel, in the painting of the Resurrection by the Vyšší Brod Master, dating from about 1350 (Matějček, pl. 17), and a detail of her shoes. This dress was already old-fashioned for the period, originating in a Byzantine style of costume. (2) The daughter of a rich peasant of about 1376. A fashionable hairstyle: loose curly hair with fillet (the Tomáš of Štítný illuminated MS, Prague University Library, ref. no. XVII A 6, fol. 36). (3) A noble woman of about 1376. The dress is made in two parts: a closely fitting bodice with low neckline, fastened down the front with buttons, and long narrow sleeves ending in points over the back of the hand; a full skirt with wide ermine border. The girdle is worn low over the hips; long ermine tippets flow from the shoulders. (4) A young lady of noble birth in a long cloak fastened at the neck with a clasp (Štítný MS, fol. 36). Below it is an enlargement of the cape clasp. (5) A young lady of well-to-do family (*ibid*, fol. 44). Style of dress as in (3).

PLATE 5

PART I

(1) Noble women with caps and dresses bordered with fur; broad oval necklines, narrow sleeves slightly broader and trumpet-shaped at the wrist. The dresses fit closely at the waist, but then flare to fall in folds to the ground. The brocade circular cloak has a low oval neckline bordered with ermine. (2) Women of noble birth from the miniatures in the King Wenceslas Bible. They wear the fashionable dress with low oval neckline, long narrow sleeves and long fur tippets (in this case ermine), which hang from wide cuffs above the elbow.

PLATE 6

(1) A queen from an illustration in the Krumlov MS, fol. 7. (2) A queen (*ibid.*, fol. 13). The dress is laced down the front. (3) A young lady (*ibid.*, fol. 254). A change of fashion is noticeable: the overtunic or kirtle is now drawn in at the waist, and no longer below it; it has long, full, sack-like hanging sleeves, and the full sleeves of the undertunic are drawn into a band at the wrist. (4) A woman with belted tunic and cloak, which fastens with a chain and two clasps across the breast (*ibid.*, fol. 66). (5) The costume of a well-to-do woman (*ibid.*, fol. 239). The overtunic or dress, belted at the waist. has full, open, half-length sleeves ending in long, flowing tippets bordered with fur. The undersleeve, of different materiai and colour, is full and drawn in at the wrist. The overtunic is also lined with a material of contrasting colour. On her

PLATE 7   PART I

A noble woman of about the year 1405, dressed in German fashion: the figure of the Queen of Sheba from an illustration in the Bellifortis MS, reproduced from *Deutsches Leben*, pl. XXVI. The dress, an overtunic, is made in two pieces: a long, close-fitting bodice laced down the front, with a low oval neckline exposing the shoulders, and sleeves slit at the elbow, with wide, flowing, open tippets reaching almost to the ground; the lower part of the garment falls in heavy folds from the hips and has a wide ermine border. The wide, scalloped edging to the neckline and the lining for the tippets of the oversleeves are also of ermine. The dress is completed by a broad belt, ornamented with little bells, worn below the waist. The narrow undersleeves are in contrasting material and of a different colour. Left of the queen is a detail of the necklace, the tunic lacing, and part of the belt.

head is an ornamental circlet and a fine veil. (6) A woman from an illustration in the Latin Bible, preserved in the Chapter Library of St. Vitus's Cathedral, Prague, ref. no. A–10, fol. 198. Noteworthy are the sleeves, with two buttons and cuffs, also the fastening of the dress, with buttons at the rather high neckline.

PLATE 8

PART I

(1) The wimple and veil of a married woman, dating from about 1350, covering the head, neck, chin and shoulders, from the head of the Madonna in the "Resurrection" by the Vyšší Brod Master (Matějček, pl. 17). (2) A young woman of burgher or rich peasant family wearing a flowing veil, dating from about 1404, from *Libri XX de anatomia*, Prague Cathedral Chapter Library, ref. no. L 11, fol. 51.

PLATE 9

(1) A family travelling, dating from the first half of the 15th century. The child wears a shortish tunic reaching just below the knee, girdled at the waist and with long, tight sleeves. The woman wears a tunic or dress, with close-fitting bodice and long, narrow sleeves, belted at the waist and with a full skirt; she also has a cloak, fastened at the neck. The man is in a belted tunic reaching below the knees, also a full cloak of the same length, fastened at the neck with two buttons. The woman wears a wimple, the man a straw hat. From the Latin Bible, fol. 23. Details: the man's satchel and another pouch from the Velislav Bible, dating from about 1340.

PLATE 10   PART I

A bath attendant in her working clothes: a long white tunic of linen or other thin material, supported by narrow shoulder straps and drawn in at the waist by a belt or sash. The shoulder straps and belt were sometimes of braid, which also trims the neckline. (1) From the time of King Wenceslas IV (King Wenceslas Bible). (2) About the year 1500 (Jena Codex).

PLATE 11   PART I

French women's fashions of the second half of the 14th century. The dress – overtunic – is cut in one piece. An interesting point are the vertical slits resembling pocket openings in the front of the dress below the waist, also the long ermine tippets hanging above the elbow from the cuffs of the sleeves of the overtunic. (1) A woman's costume of the 14th century (Viollet le Duc, *Dictionnaire raisonné du mobilier Français*, IV, p. 88). (2) A costume of about 1352 (*ibid.*, III, pp. 275–6). (2a) A pattern of the same. (3) A costume of about 1370 (*ibid.*, III).

PLATE 12

(1) The dress of a noble lady of about 1370: undertunic or kirtle, with close-fitting bodice and long, narrow sleeves, and girdle at hip level; also the typical French overtunic, known as the surcoat, with armholes so deeply cut that the ermine border is all that holds the front and back together. (Viollet le Duc, IV, pp. 358, 359.) (2) The same surcoat from the back. (3) A French-Burgundian surcoat of about 1430. The same type as in (1), but in the process of development it has lost all the material in the front, and only the lower part and back remain, held in position by a strip of fur over the shoulders and across the breast. The same surcoat from the back. (Viollet le Duc, IV, 387, 390.)

Burgundian and French fashions of about 1430. (1–4) The tall cornet-shaped headdresses of the women were sometimes as much as one metre high, and from them a fine veil hanging in folds was draped in various ways, sometimes shading the face. (5) Complicated and ingenious arrangement of a veil of heavy starched linen fixed to an inside frame, forming a "butterfly" headdress. (6) A more modest cornet-shaped headdress of smaller size. (7–8) Simpler hoods and wimples (Viollet le Duc, *passim*).

PLATE 14   PART I

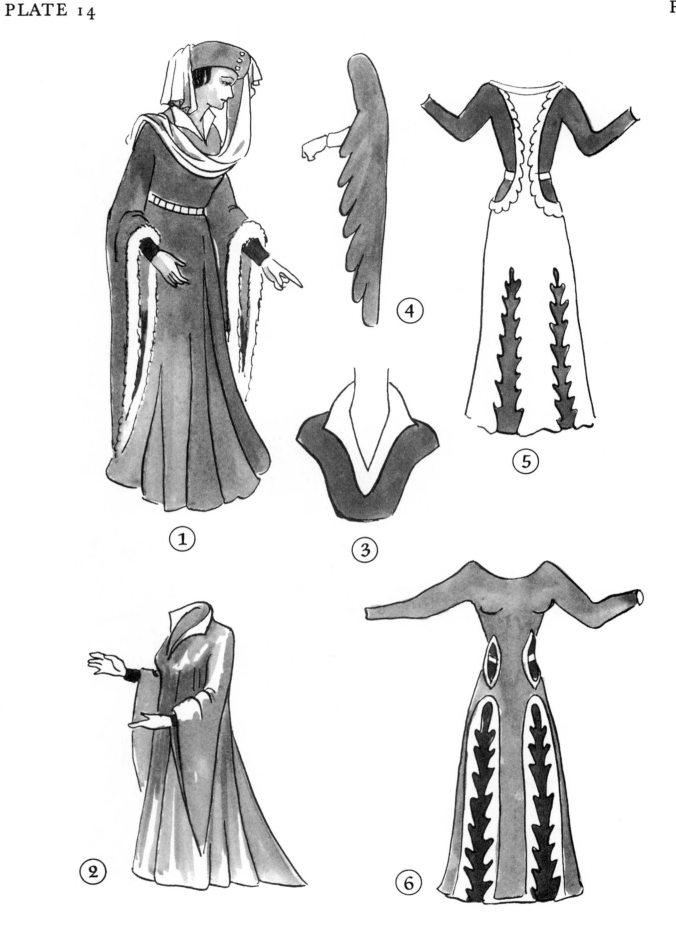

Women's fashions in Germany during the late 14th and early 15th centuries. Noteworthy are the wide, open sleeves of the overtunic which reaches to the ground; the edges were often dagged (4). There was also a new neckline and an unusual hat, with a veil thrown loosely over it. French influence is to be seen in the double slits at the waist resembling pocket openings. The dagged trimming in the front of the tunic is another echo of French-Burgundian fashions. (1–4) Women's fashions of about the year 1410 (*Deutsches Leben*, p. 300). (5–6) Women's fashions of the 14th century (*Deutsches Leben*, p. 267).

PLATE 15   PART I

Hungarian woman's costume from the end of the 15th century. The dress is cut in two pieces: a close-fitting waist-length bodice, and a full skirt. An ornamental belt is worn slantwise across the hips. The long, circular gown has wide, open sleeves bordered with ermine, which also forms the collar and the narrow trimming round the hem of the cloak. The turban-type headdress indicates Eastern influence (Mihály Némes, p. 73).

PLATE 16

③

②

①

Male figures from the Abbess Kunhuta Passional (1320). (1) Fol. 22 v, (2) A nobleman, Fol. 3 v, (3) Fol. IV.

PLATE 17   PART I

Figures from the Kaufmann Crucifixion, dating from after 1350. The man on the right wears a knee-length tunic. The man on the left wears a shorter tunic with a belt at the waist and with a slit down the front of the skirt; it has half-sleeves with short tippets, lined inside – like the rest of the tunic – with a contrasting material. The undersleeves are narrow and of a different material, fastened with a row of small buttons from the elbow to the wrist. On his head he wears a hood which covers his shoulders, and over it a hat with a curved brim. He also wears woollen hose. Three different types of male felt hats (Matějček, pl. 33).

PLATE 18

Male Czech costumes from the years 1350–60 depicted in Jan of Středa's *Liber Viaticus*, National Museum, ref. no. XIII A 12. Woollen hose and knee-length tunics of various types: either full and gathered in at the waist, fitted to the waist with or without a belt, or with a belt worn over the hips. The head is covered by a hood or a felt cap or hat with a curved brim. The use of two colours, popular for tunic and cloak, is also to be noted in the hats. Here we already note the upstanding collar, which became common later.

PLATE 19

PART I

Czech male costumes of the lesser nobility, dating from 1376, from the Štítný MS. (1) Fol. 58. A knee-length tunic close-fitting to the hips, the belt at hip level; a hood rolled down over the shoulders. (2) Fol. 24. Woollen parti-coloured hose (mi-parti); a shorter close-fitting tunic, with narrow sleeves fastened at the wrist with small buttons; a leather belt round the hips; a hood rolled down over the shoulders. (3) Fol. 36. Woollen parti-coloured hose worn, apparently, with a short close-fitting tunic with narrow sleeves, which are just visible; also a circular cape, which is fastened with buttons down the front; it is lined with contrasting material. In these examples we have caught just the moment in the development of a man's tunic when it was transformed into the gipon or doublet, more closely fitting and with the opening down the centre front.

PLATE 20

PART I

Male Czech costume dating from the end of the 14th century: figures from a tympanum in the Týn Church in Prague. Woollen hose, a short close-fitting tunic, fitted at the waist, which we find gets gradually shorter, with a purely ornamental belt below the hips and another for carrying the sword. A hood draped in turban form with a twisted scarf hanging down the back, or a hat.

PLATE 21

Male Czech costume from the end of the 14th century: figures from a tympanum in the Týn Church in Prague. Hose, close-fitting padded tunics with narrow sleeves, fastened with small buttons to the elbow or even as far as the armpit; in various styles, i. e. pleated (2) or scalloped round the lower edge (4). It is interesting to note the uses made of the belt and the position in which it lies. On their heads they wear hoods, parti-coloured caps with turned-up brims, or hats.

PLATE 22

PART I

Figure from a tympanum in the Týn Church in Prague: tight-fitting fashionable tunic with belt placed low. Details: the trimming of the tunic, parts of other girdles and belts, and a rosette used for trimming a belt.

PLATE 23   PART I

Male Czech costumes prior to the year 1400: figures from the miniatures in the King Wenceslas Bible. (1, 3) Figures with hoods twisted turban fashion, wearing close-fitting tunics, dagged at the lower edge. (2) Close-fitting, knee-length tunic, the right half of one colour, the left half striped. (4) Tunic, fitted over the chest, flaring from the waist, and with a slit over the hips. (5) Man wearing a long cloak, fastened at the neck in front; over it he wears a hood pulled down over the shoulders. (6) Short, full tunic gathered in at the waist, with broad, loose, elbow-length sleeves, worn over narrow undersleeves. (7) Rolled-down top boots.

PLATE 24   PART I

Male Czech costumes of the common people of about 1400, from the miniatures in the King Wenceslas Bible. (1) A trumpeter. Short tunic with belt worn round the hips. (2–3) Men in tunics, their hoods with long tippets, pushed back. They wear shoes or high boots. (4–5) Hoods and caps with lobe-shaped dags. (6) A hood with a short shoulder cape, bordered with a contrasting colour. (7) Long gown, the folds gathered in at the waist – a sedate, "respectable" form of dress. (8) A figure with rolled-down hose. He wears shoes and a close-fitting tunic, which is slit up the centre front.

PLATE 25   PART I

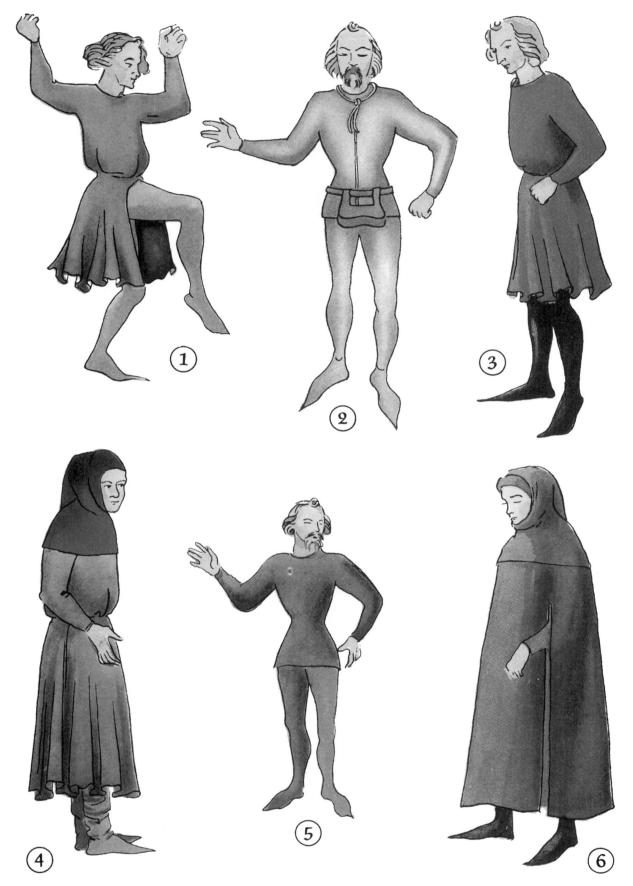

Czech men's and women's costumes of the early 15th century, from the miniatures in the Krumlov MS. (1) A young lad in hose and a knee-length tunic, flared, belted at the waist and slit from the waist down (fol. 44). (2) A man in fashionable costume: hose, an exaggeratedly short, tight-fitting tunic, belted at the hips, fastening down the centre with hooks and an ornamental knot (a love knot?) at the neck (fol. 219). (3) The figure of Shimei begging to King David (fol. 50). A plain, full, knee-length tunic gathered in at the waist. (4) A man in long, full tunic gathered in at the waist, wearing a hood over his shoulders and high boots (fol. 51). (5) A fashionable dandy: a short close-fitting tunic and parti-coloured hose. (6) A woman in a long, closed cloak, slit down the left side and lined with a contrasting colour. She wears a hood over her shoulders. Beneath the cloak she wears a dress with long, narrow sleeves (fol. 149).

PLATE 26   PART I

Male Czech costumes of the early 15th century, from the miniatures in the Krumlov MS dating from the beginning of the 15th century. (1) A figure from "The Sacrifice of Geza and Tobias" (fol. 14). (2) The figure of a priest carrying a chest (fol. 29). (3) The figure of a prophet (fol. 34). (4) A figure from the illumination depicting "The Disgracing of David's Messenger" (fol. 50). (5) Fol. 50. (6) The figure of Abel (fol. 43). (7) Fol. 40. These figures wear various types of tunics: a long, flared tunic reaching to below or just above the calf, girded at the waist, and with long narrow sleeves or somewhat more fully cut sleeves; or a knee-length or somewhat shorter tunic, girded at the waist or with an ornamental belt over the hips, with narrow sleeves or the full, half-length oversleeve, either finished off straight or with dags showing the narrow undersleeve. Various caps.

PLATE 27

PART I

Male Czech costume of the early 15th century. The travelling apparel of an elderly man: a longish, full tunic with long, full sleeves, tapering at the wrist; a shorter travelling cloak fastened in the centre front with one button; he also wears a hat (Balaam, from the Krumlov MS, fol. 8).

PLATE 28

Male Czech costume of the year 1432. A cote-hardi that is close-fitting down to the hips, but more fully cut below and reaching almost to the knees; a wide ornamental belt is worn well below the waist. Sleeves are either long and narrow or full; sometimes they are full to the elbow and then slit, forming a long, hanging tippet of material which reaches almost down to the ground, lined with another material of a contrasting colour. Narrow undersleeves are worn beneath the latter type. The neckline is high and round or else shaped like a "V", under which one can see the undertunic fastened right up to the throat. One tunic has button fastenings from the neck to the waist. Tight hose, sometimes with shoes or rolled-down high boots. (From a MS in the Prague University Library, ref. no. XVII A-3.)

PLATE 29

PART I

Male Czech costume about 1360. Old man in parti-coloured *chausses* and parti-coloured tunic, belted at the waist, the lower hem being scalloped; the tunic also has a hood. The drummer wears a knee-length tunic with hood and shoulder cape. (Illuminations in Jan of Středa's *Liber Viaticus*, dating from about 1364.)

PLATE 30

PART I

(1) Czech paupers' dress from about 1360. A barefooted shepherd wearing a torn tunic, with a long, hooded cape covering his arms and reaching down to his waist and with a wide straw hat on his head. A vintner, carrying a vat on his back, wearing a long tunic girded at the waist, a wide-brimmed straw hat and hose and boots. Another shepherd in hose and boots, wearing a tunic gathered at the waist by a belt, also a hood with a short lipipe (from Jan of Středa's *Liber Viaticus*). (2) A poor shepherd of about 1350 with torn stockings, a knee-length tunic and a waist-length cape; he also wears a cap with a rolled-up brim (from the painting by the Master of the Vyšší Brod Cycle, "The Birth of Our Lord", Matějček, pl. 5,6).

PLATE 31

PART I

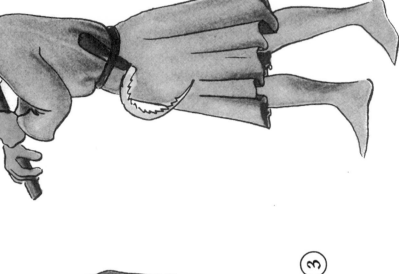
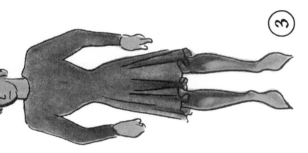

Czech workingmen's costumes from the end of the 14th century to the first half of the 15th century. (1) A woodcutter in full, knee-length tunic gathered in at the waist, wearing a hood with a scalloped lower edge; end of the 14th century. (2) A peasant in a straw hat, wearing a long linen tunic, drawn in at the waist by a belt, with fairly full, long sleeves. Both figures are taken from an illumination in a MS in Prague University Library (ref. no. C 1 a.) and date from the end of the 14th century. (3) A bricklayer with hose and tight-fitting tunic flared from the hips to just above the knee (from an illumination in the Latin Bible, fol. 167).

PLATE 32

(1) An old man from the year 1350, in a long flowing surcoat, with wide half-sleeves to the elbow; the garment is fastened at the neck with two buttons, the sleeves are lined with a contrasting coloured material; under them show the long, narrow tunic sleeves. He also wears a cap with a fur border. (From the painting by the Master of the Vyšší Brod Cycle, "The Lament for Christ", Matějček, pl. 15). (2) An old man, dating from about 1380, in a long, full gown reaching to below the ankle, girded at the waist and complete with matching cape-hood and long, narrow sleeves (from "The Laying in the Sepulchre" by the Master of the Třeboň altar-piece, Matějček, pl. 105. (3) A man wearing a long, full over-garment with long, narrow sleeves, which is fastened by several buttons at the neck and has slit openings at the waist for the hands. A cap with a turned-up edge. (From the King Wenceslas Bible). All the men wear pointed shoes with "pikes".

PLATE 33

Czech peasant dress about 1405. Tight hose; one of the tunics is gathered in at the waist and has long, full, open sleeves, dagged at the edges in the same manner as the hem of the tunic itself; the other two are short, tight-fitting tunics buttoned to the waist. One has short, the other long, fairly wide sleeves, with pleated folds in the tunic skirt. One of the men wears a wide-brimmed straw country hat. From pictures of country-folk in an illustration in the Bellifortis MS.

PLATE 34

PART I

Bohemian costume of the 14th and 15th centuries. (1) The long sheepskin fur coat of the poor peasant, early 15th century (Krumlov MS: Adam). (2) The fur jacket worn by a day labourer working out-of-doors in winter, end of 15th century (from the frescoes in St. Barbara Cathedral, Kutná Hora). (3) A Wallachian archer of 1330, wearing a rough, knee-length fur coat and a fur cap (*Ungarisches Soldatentum*, pp. 56, 57).

PLATE 35

Czech male costume of the early 15th century. Workingmen of the middle of the 15th century. Three gardeners in tunics, smocks, gathered in at the waist and reaching to below the knees; a high neckline and long, narrow or fairly full sleeves; tight hose. One of them wears a cap with the brim turned up and slit over the forehead. Details: a belt, also a pouch hanging from the belt.

PLATE 36

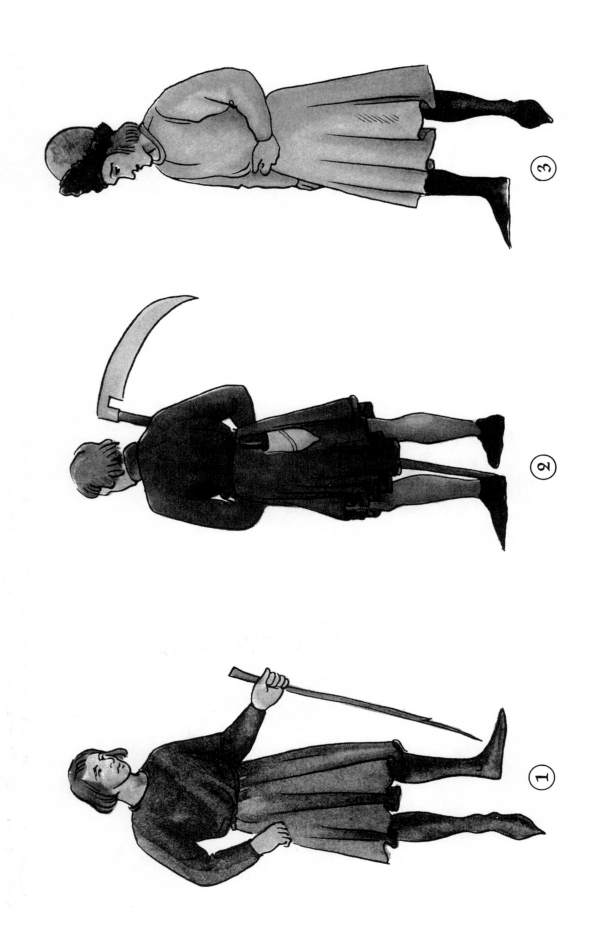

Czech male costume of the early 15th century. Figures of workers from *Ruralium commodorum Libri XII.* (1) A ploughman in dark smock and hose. (2) A reaper in a smock reaching just to the knees, also hose and shoes. (3) A peasant in hose, a coarse tunic and a fur cap.

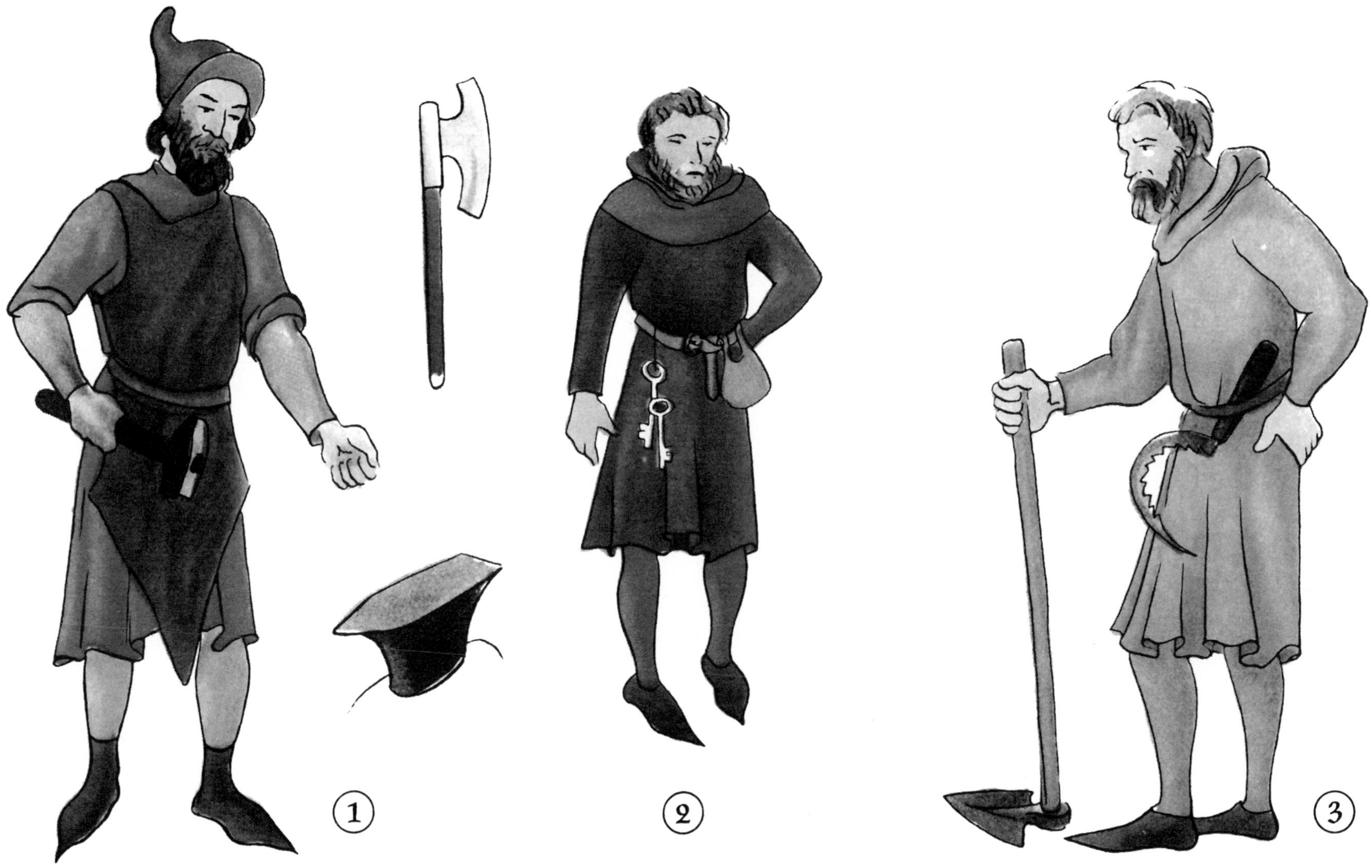

PLATE 37

Costumes of the first half of the 15th century from the MS *De moribus et officiis viventium* in Prague Cathedral Chapter Library, ref. no. G. 42. (1) A blacksmith – part of the anvil is shown – wearing hose and boots, a tunic with elbow-length sleeves (beneath these he has long, narrow undersleeves); he also wears a leather apron and cloth cap. (2) An innkeeper with a neat tunic gathered in by a belt, wearing a cape-hood; also hose and shoes. (3) A peasant with hoe and sickle, wearing a coarse tunic with a hood and shoes.

PLATE 38

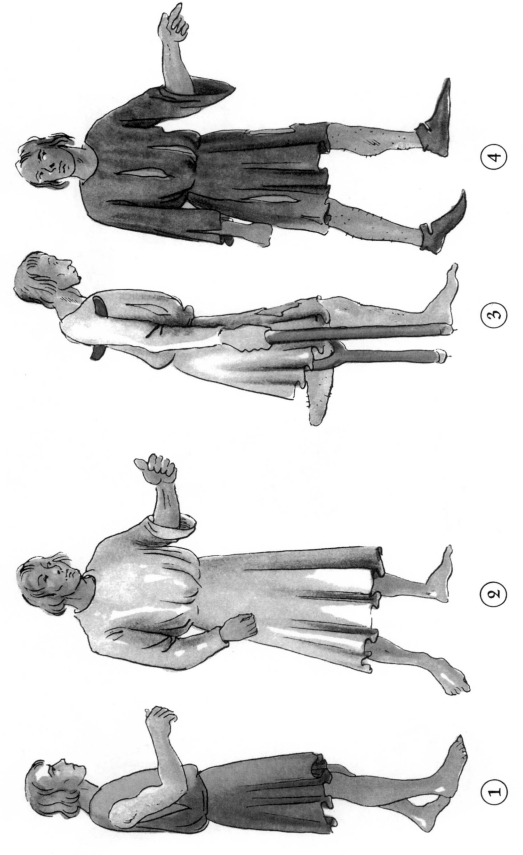

Czech poor at the beginning of the 15th century. (1–2) Fishermen in smocks and tunics, early 15th century (Krumlov MS, fol. 12). (3–4) Poor folk in torn tunics, their only garment (Krumlov MS, fol. 316).

PLATE 39

PART I

Beggars, about 1390–1410, wearing tunics; one wears a longish cape-hood. From the miniatures in the King Wenceslas Bible. (Photographic reproductions from the State Documentary Centre, formerly the State Photometric Institute.)

PLATE 40

PART I

The costumes of Czech labourers of the late 14th and early 15th centuries. (1) A blacksmith from the King Wenceslas Bible. (2) A labourer of about 1405 from the Bellifortis MS. Both wear tunics and aprons; the labourer also wears a hood. (3) A Czech miner in his ceremonial white smock with decorative stripes and a hood with a decorative border. From the end of the 15th century. The white smock was sometimes worn plain without the stripes. (From the frescoes in the gallery of St. Barbara Cathedral, Kutná Hora.)

PLATE 41

PART I

Czech male costumes from the early 15th century. Craftsmen from the miniatures in *Ruralium commodorum libri XII*.
Two of the men are dressed in knee-length tunics, the lower hems of which are dagged in various ways; the carpenter
wears a grey tunic gathered in at the waist and a cap with a turned-up brim.

PLATE 42

PART I

Male Czech costumes of the early 15th century. (1) The costume of a labourer: hose, girded knee-length tunic and hat (Krumlov MS, fol. 217). (2) The figure of Adam in long white smock (*ibid.*, fol. 6). (3) A blacksmith in a full tunic, gathered in at the waist (*ibid.*, fol. 533). Detail: his anvil. (4) A workingman, dating from about 1420, dressed in chausses and rolled-down top boots; also a long overgarment slit down the centre front from the hips, with long sleeves and wide turned-back cuffs. It also has a V-shaped neckline with revers. A broad-brimmed hat. (From the Rajhrad altar-piece, "The Finding and Testing of the Holy Cross", Matějček, pl. 192.)

PLATE 43

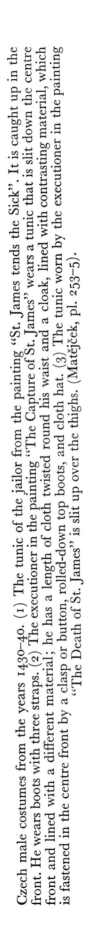

Czech male costumes from the years 1430–40. (1) The tunic of the jailor from the painting "St. James tends the Sick". It is caught up in the front. He wears boots with three straps. (2) The executioner in the painting "The Capture of St. James" wears a tunic that is slit down the centre front and lined with a different material; he has a length of cloth twisted round his waist and a cloak, lined with contrasting material, which is fastened in the centre front by a clasp or button, rolled-down top boots, and cloth hat. (3) The tunic worn by the executioner in the painting "The Death of St. James" is slit up over the thighs. (Matějček, pl. 253–5).

PLATE 44

PART I

Czech costumes of the first half of the 15th century. (From a picture in the St. James altar-piece dating from between 1430–40. (1) The executioner wearing a tunic slit up the centre front; a length of twisted cloth is wound double round his waist. He wears a hat. (Matějček, pl. 253.) (2) An executioner wearing an apron over his tunic from a painting of the Crucifixion by a Bavarian master dating from the middle of the 15th century (Glaser, *Die alt-deutsche Malerei*, pl. 73). (3) An executioner wearing his working apron. In (1) it is probably this apron which the executioner is wearing twisted round his waist. The apron is clearly visible in the Náměšt panel "The Martyrdom of St. Apollonia" (Matějček, pl. 215).

PLATE 45   PART I

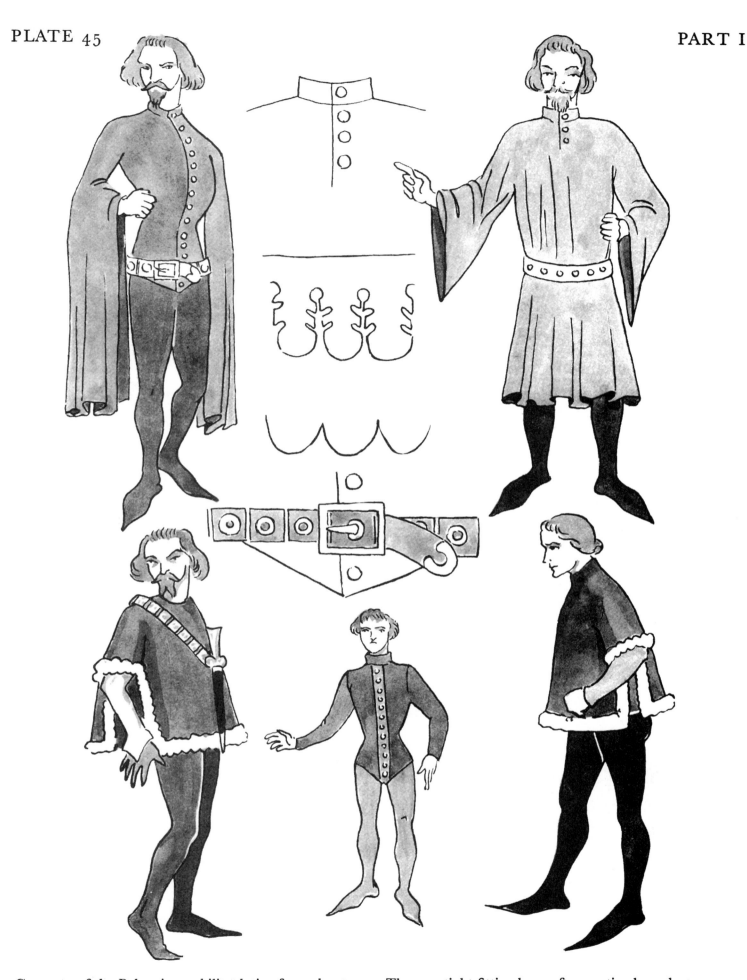

Costumes of the Bohemian nobility dating from about 1400. The very tight-fitting hose, often parti-coloured, are a some-what striking feature, as is the close-fitting doublet or *gipon*, which is well padded over the chest, shoulders and back, and short, just covering the waist and hips and ending in a point. The doublet is buttoned up the front and has a stiff stand-up collar; often an ornamental belt is worn at hip level. The sleeves are either narrow, sometimes ending in a point over the back of the hand, or are slit up and fall in a long flowing tippet. Over this doublet the fashionable man wore a short circular cape, slit up above the hips, with open sides and bordered with fur. Alternatively, he wore a loose, calf-length tunic, fastened at the neck in the front with a few buttons, belted at the hips and with long, full, open sleeves. From the miniatures in the King Wenceslas Bible. Details: a tunic collar, the dagged tunic hem and a belt buckle.

PLATE 46   PART I

Male Czech costume of the 14th and early 15th centuries. (1) A tight-fitting tunic from "The Murder of Eglon", a miniature in the Krumlov MS, fol. 65, early 15th century. (2) A tunic with gold-bordered neckline dating from the early 15th century (Krumlov MS, fol. 29). (3) A close-fitting tunic with short sleeves and belted at the hip, from the early 15th century (*ibid.*, fol. 236). (4) A long cloak and hood lined with contrasting material, slit up at the lower centre front, dating from the year 1376 (Štítný MS, fol. 4). (5) An unusual figure in a garment thought to be a peculiar kind of priestly vestment (Zíbrt and Winter, *Dějiny kroje v zemích českých (The History of Costume in the Czech Lands)*, II, p. 200, pl. 110). The man has a cinique tonsure, a double fringe of hair, and carries a cudgel over his shoulder. The garment

PLATE 47   PART I

Czech male costume of the early 15th century. Two noblemen wearing tunics which are gathered in at the waist and have decorative belts at the hips. They have long, full sleeves, close-fitting at the wrist. One of the tunics is slit up the centre front. From the Krumlov MS, fol. 101, 235.

is long and parti-coloured, and has full, open sleeves ending in tippets. The original is in the Latin Bible, fol. 217. (6) A cloak thrown back over the shoulders dating from about 1376 (Štítný MS, fol. 23). (7) A full circular cloak from the painting "Elias being taken to Heaven", early 15th century (Latin Bible, fol. 127). (8) A nobleman's costume: a close-fitting tunic pleated from the waist, with hood to match and belted below the hips (Krumlov MS, fol. 77). (9) A man's or woman's cloak with two slits up the front, lined in contrasting colour (*ibid.*, fol. 333).

PLATE 48   PART I

Upper-class Czech male costumes dating from the early 15th century. (1) A man in tight-fitting surcoat, from the shoulder of which there hang long, dagged lappets reaching to the lower hem of the tunic, which is trimmed in a similar manner. His long, narrow undersleeves are in a contrasting colour. He wears an ornamental belt over the hips with a pouch, also tight hose. (Krumlov MS, fol. 46.) (2) The figure of Joab in a full tunic gathered in at the waist, with wide, open sleeves, beneath which are long, narrow undersleeves. He has an ermine cape over his shoulders. (*ibid.*, fol. 42.)

PLATE 49   PART I

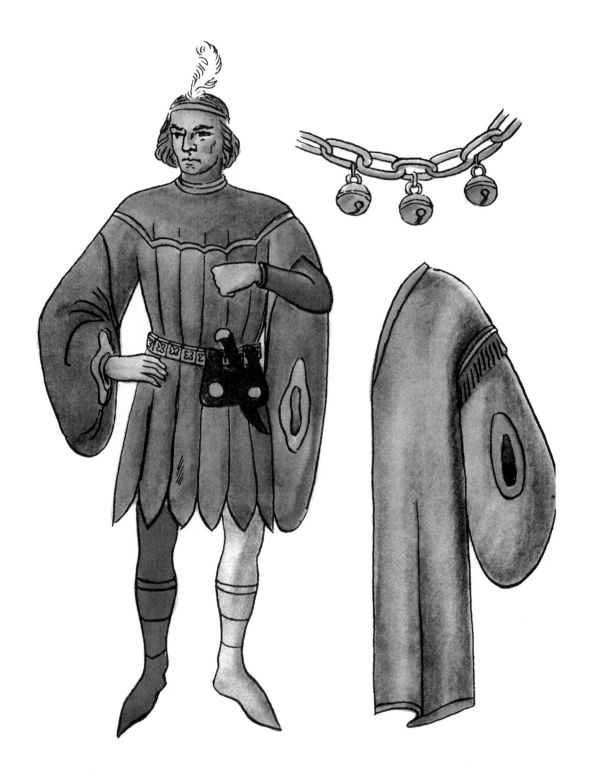

The costume of a Czech nobleman of rank from the beginning of the 15th century. Tight, parti-coloured hose, a thickly padded tunic sewn from several pieces, which reaches to just above his knees and ends in a dagged border; it has a high neck and exaggeratedly full sleeves. They are long and baglike, with two openings for the arms: one is below the shoulder and if this is the one used, the rest of the sleeve falls in a long, bag-shaped lappet; the other is normally placed and if this one is used, the sleeve becomes a long, full and bagpipe sleeve. From the Krumlov MS, fol. 337. In addition there is another type of sleeve shown, similar but with only one opening (*ibid.*, fol. 88). Detail: a necklace with tiny bells.

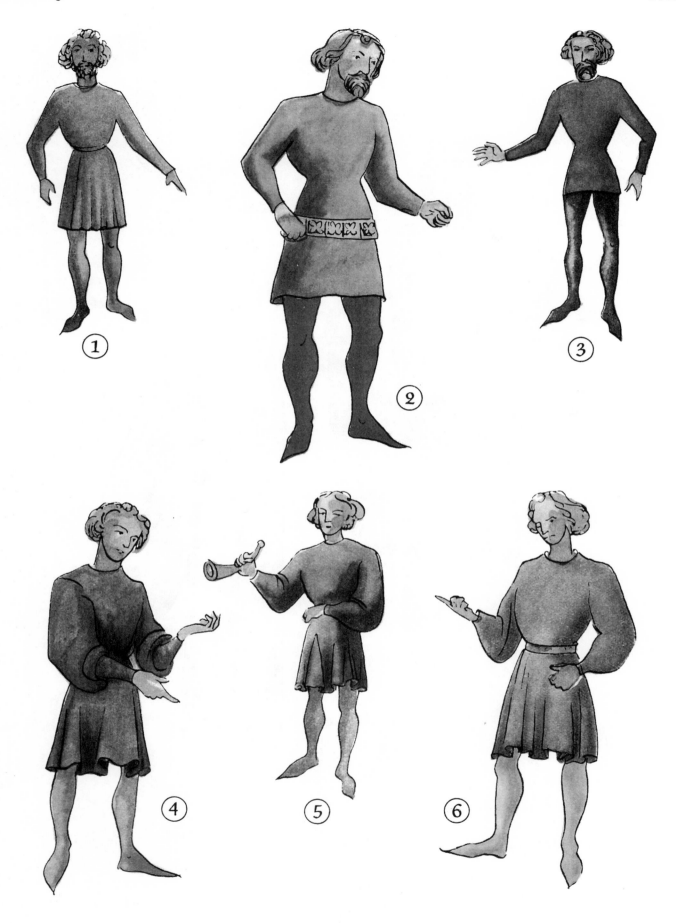

Bohemian male costume from the beginning of the 15th century. (1) Figure from the MS of the Chapter library in Prague, L 11, fol. 51, from 1404. (2) Figure of nobleman from 1379—1417 (Chapter library missal, P 1). (3) Costume from the period 1379—1417 (*ibid.*) (4), (6) Figures from the Prague Chapter library MS, -L 11, fol. 53. (5) Figure from the same MS, fol. 61.

PLATE 69

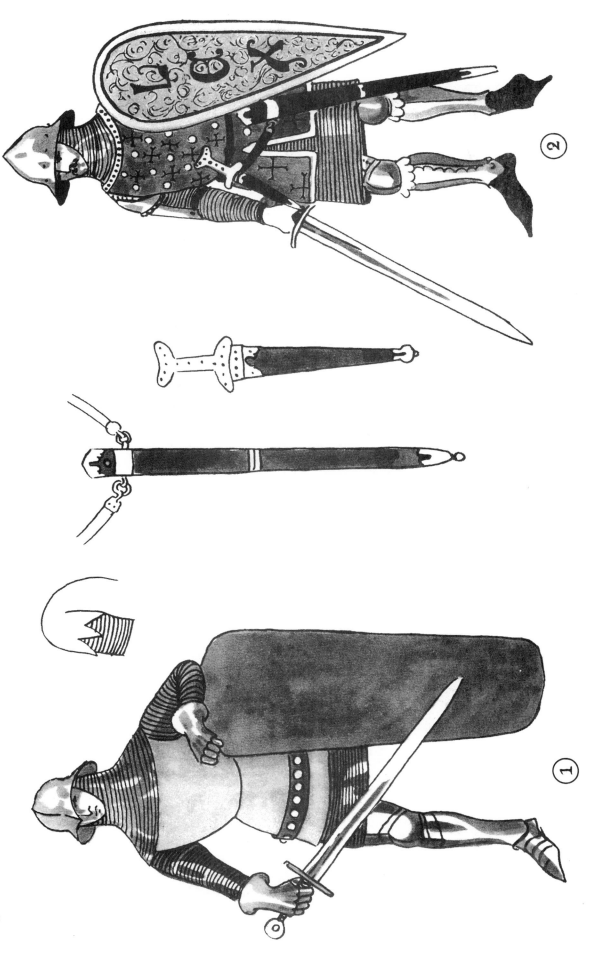

(1) A Parisian soldier of the 14th century (*Die Geschichte der französischen Armee*, p. 84). (2) A soldier, 1340 (*European Armour*, II, p. 60, pl. 414). Details: a dagged sleeve, an alternative to that worn in (1), the sword attachment, also the dagger from (2).

PLATE 70

(1) An armour bearer of the 15th century (*Zeitschrift für historische Waffenkunde*, VI, p. 385). (2) An armour bearer dating from after 1430 (*Geschichte der deutschen Kunst*, p. 178, pl. 257), (2a) The breastplate, (2b) Iron casques. (3) An armour bearer, from the "Stations of the Cross" in Lorch am Rhein, dated 1430 (*Geschichte der deutschen Kunst*, p. 178, pl. 257). (4) A mounted soldier, dated 1443 (Thalhofer's *Fechtbuch* of 1443; pl. XI).

PLATE 71

PART II

(1) An archer, from the painting "The Martyrdom of St. Ursula" (Hans Memling, 1435–94). (2) A foot soldier carrying a spear, from the same painting.

PLATE 72

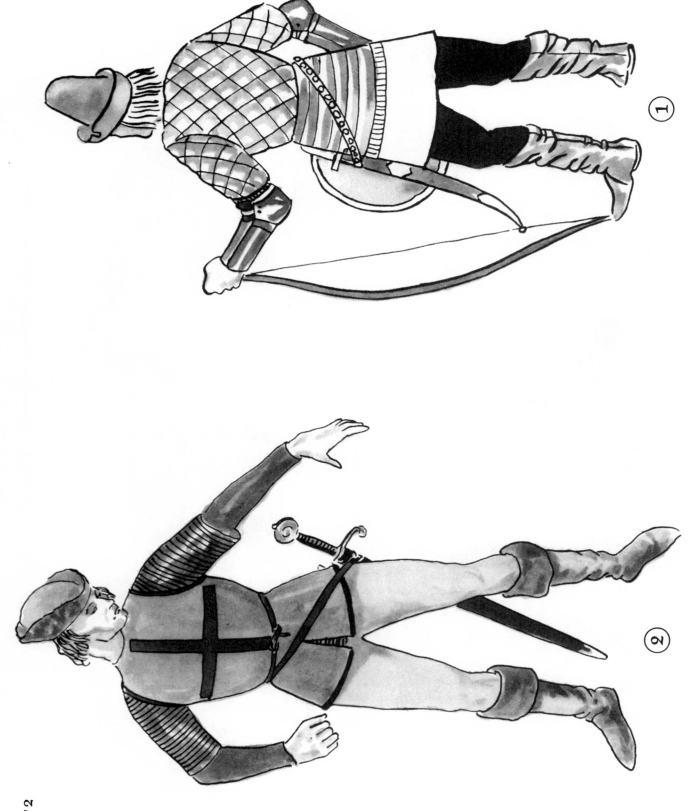

(1) An archer, dating from 1430, taken from a picture by Jan van Eyck. (2) A mercenary soldier, from a contemporary painting "The Burning of the Maid of Orleans" (*Die Geschichte der französischen Armee*, p. 95).

PLATE 73

Soldiers, first half of the 15th century (reconstructed by E. Wagner).

PLATE 74   PART II

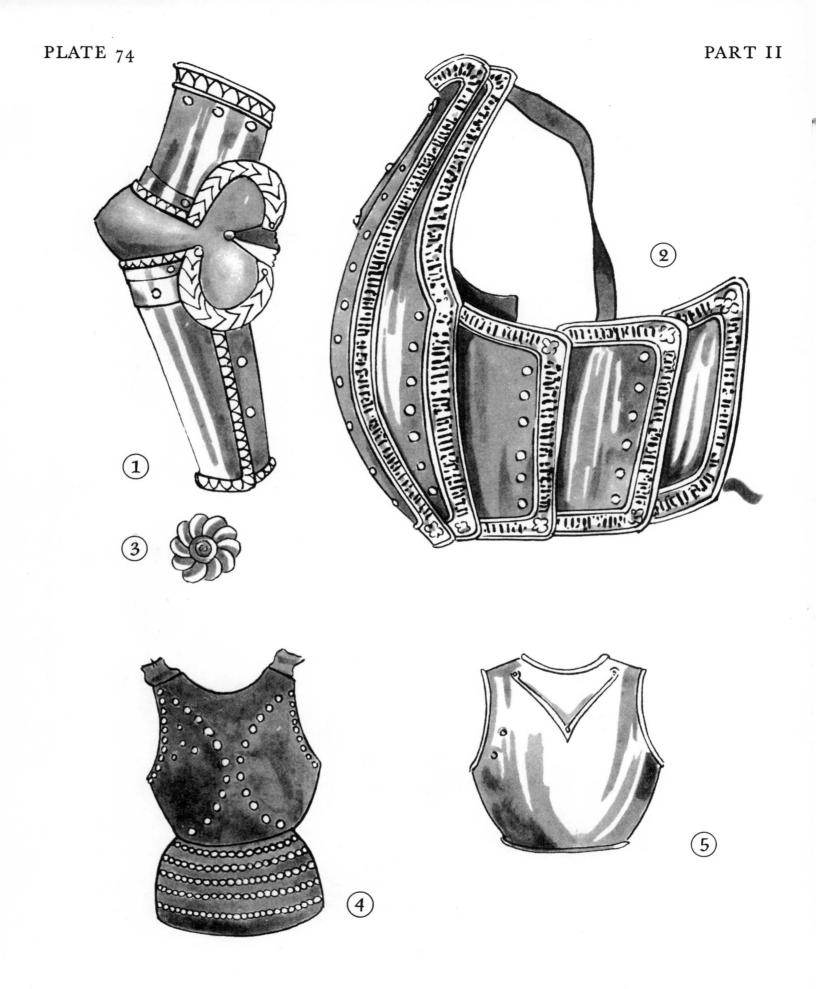

(1) A plate-mail vambrace, dated 1390. (2) Cuirass composed of plates, about 1390: height 34.5 cm., circumference 54 cm., weight 2.65 kilograms. (3) Detail: the head of a rivet. The cuirass and sleeve belong together (*The Armoury of the Castle of Churburg*, pl. X, XI, XII). (4) A breastplate covered with material, about 1380 (*Zeitschrift für historische Waffenkunde*, 1940/1942, p. 230, pl. 7). (5) A breastplate, about 1410 (*The Armoury of the Castle of Churburg*, pl. XVI).

PLATE 75

PART II

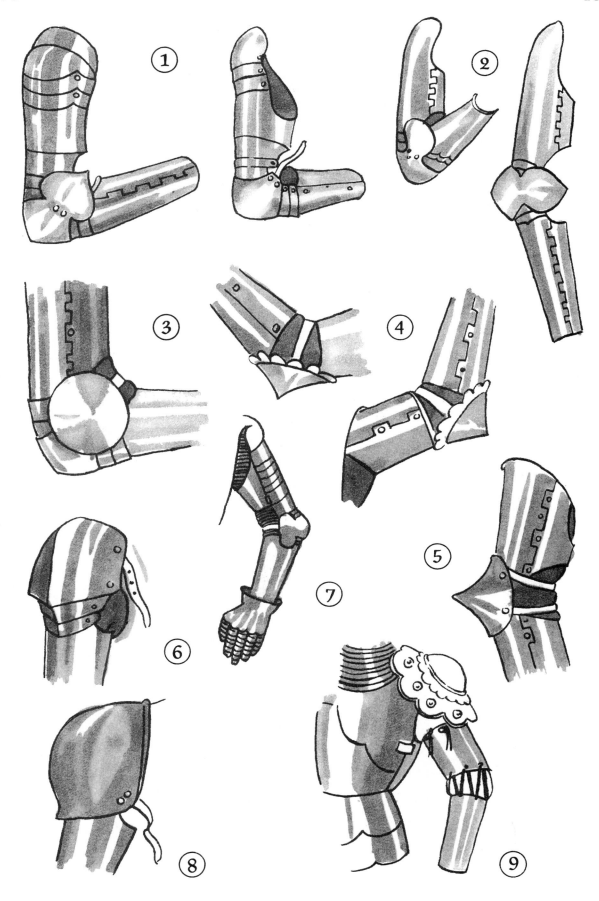

Plate vambraces from Viollet le Duc. (1) Circa 1402. (2) From the monument to the Duke of Alençon, who fell at the Battle of Crécy (1346). (3) 1390–1400. (4) Circa 1300. (5) Circa 1300. (6) Circa 1370. (7) Second half of the 14th century. (8) Mid-14th century. (9) Probably 1430.

PLATE 76   PART II

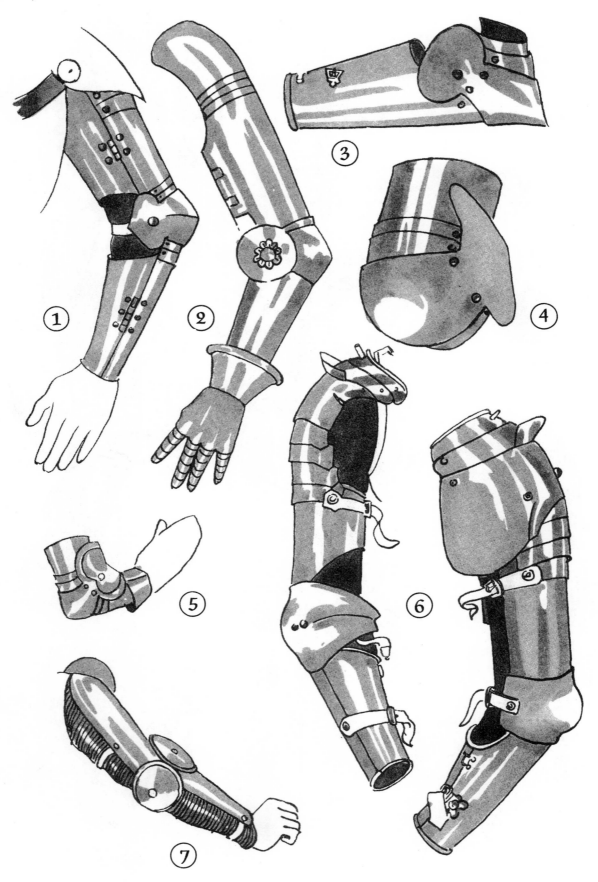

Plate vambraces of the 14th–15th centuries. (1) From the tomb of Břetislav I in St. Vitus's Cathedral, Prague, second half of the 14th century. (2) 14th century (*European Armour* I, p. 157, pl. 195). (3) A cowter. (4) A right-arm cowter of the early 15th century (*European Armour* I, p. 161, pl. 196). (5) First half of the 15th century (*European Armour*, I). (6) Plates, tied over mail sleeves, about 1300 (*Viollet le Duc*). (7) The right-arm armour of Ferdinand of Aragon, Italian work dating from about 1480 (Boeheim, p. 69, pl. 67, a, b).

PLATE 77   PART II

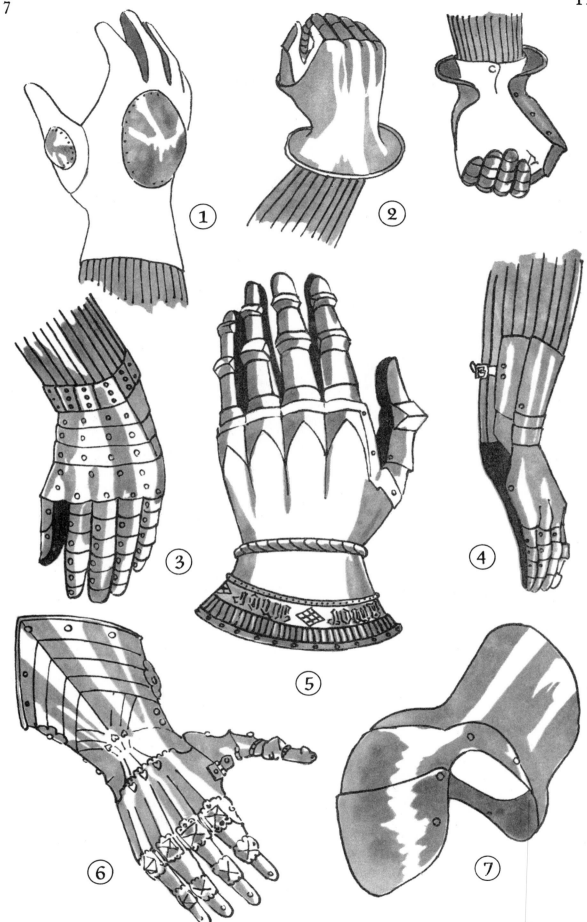

(1) Leather gauntlet with small convex metal plates, from about 1300 (Viollet le Duc; also Jähns, p. 41, pl. 13, but dated about 1250). (2) A metal gauntlet of the 14th century (Viollet le Duc, V, p. 454). (3) A plate gauntlet of the first half of the 14th century (*ibid.*, V, p. 454). (4) A metal gauntlet of 1325 (*ibid.*). (5) A metal gauntlet with a wide cuff ornamented with the inscription *Amor*, dating from between 1350–60 (*ibid.*, V, p. 456). (6) A plate gauntlet dating from 1440, according to Viollet le Duc, V, p. 457. This type is more common between 1470–90. (7) A metal gauntlet dating from 1460 (*European Armour*, II, p. 216, pl. 513).

PLATE 78

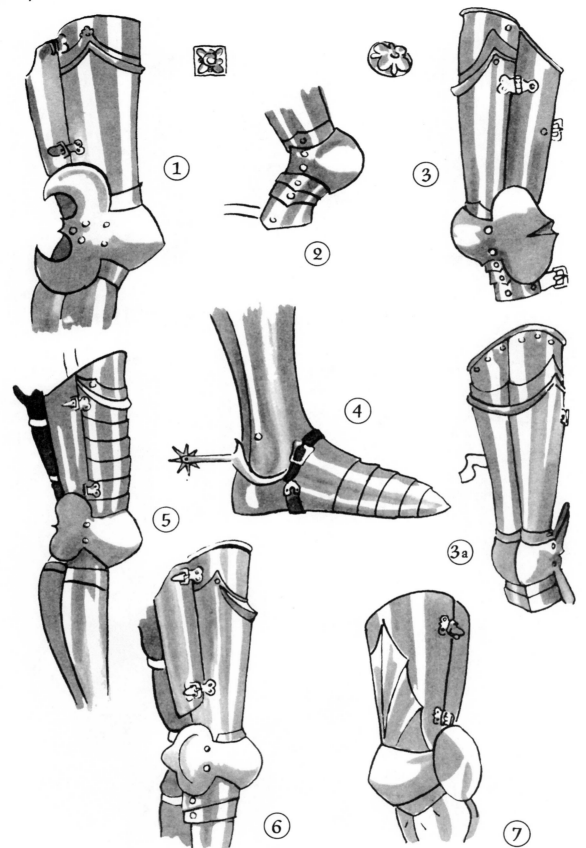

The various metal plates protecting the legs, according to Viollet le Duc, V. (1) Plate armour dating from about 1450. (2) Detail of a poleyn, dating from 1390. (3–3a) The cuisses and poleyn, seen from the front and side. (4) The sabbaton, or plates covering the foot, dating from 1397. (5) Plate armour dating from 1440. (6) Plate armour dating from 1390. (7) Plate armour dating from 1450.

PLATE 51

(1) The costume of an upper-class dandy: a close-fitting padded doublet with long, sacklike sleeves and an ornamental belt over the hips; parti-coloured hose. (2) The costume of a wealthy German nobleman of the year 1405 from the Bellifortis MS: an outer garment developed from the overtunic (probably a type of houppelande) which acquired various shapes, lengths and sleeve styles. Beneath the garment one sees the under-sleeves, which are full but close-fitting at the wrist. The dags at the lower hem and the dagged ornamentation at the shoulders are reminiscent of Franco-Burgundian fashions. A Bohemian and German male costume of the year 1405. (3) The costume of a nobleman or university teacher: another type of houppelande, a long, circular, cloak-style garment with trailing, open sleeves, bordered with fur. The use of little bells as orna-ments was very popular at this time especially in Germany. Detail: an ornamental chain with its tiny bells. From the Bellifortis MS with colours according to a reproduction in *Deutsches Leben.*

PLATE 52   PART I

A Czech male costume of the early 15th century. A royal ambassador from the first half of the 15th century, on horse-back and wearing a tunic and cloak, which – like the brim of the hat – is trimmed with ermine and is in the shape of a cape covering his shoulders and upper arms.

PLATE 53

Bohemia from the 13th to the 15th centuries. Examples of monks' tunics, cowls, cloaks, and hoods; the tunics are usually gathered in at the waist by a cingulum: see (2) and (5). (1) A monk of the early 15th century (Krumlov MS). (2) A monk of the 13th century (Prague University Library MS, ref. no. XIV 3). (3) A church dignitary of the late 15th or early 16th centuries (Jena Codex). (4) The figure of St. Giles from the frame of the Vyšší Brod Madonna, dating from the first quarter of the 15th century (Matějček, pl. 205). (5) A monk (Jena Codex).

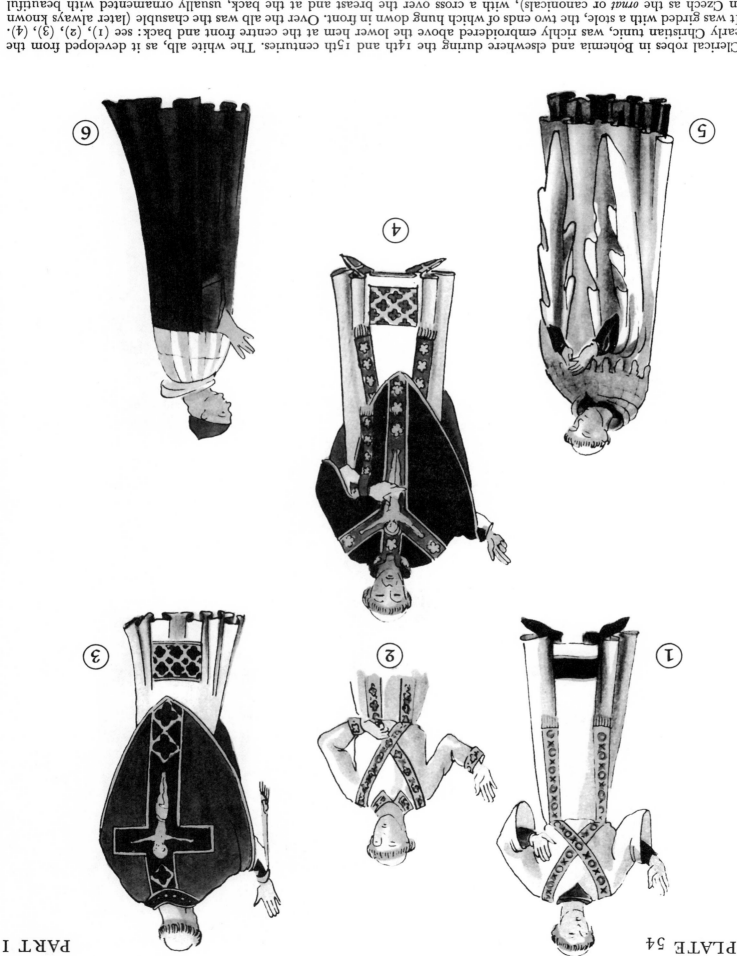

PLATE 54   PART I

Clerical robes in Bohemia and elsewhere during the 14th and 15th centuries. The white alb, as it developed from the early Christian tunic, was richly embroidered above the lower hem at the centre front and back: see (1), (2), (3), (4). It was girded with a stole, the two ends of which hung down in front. Over the alb was the chasuble (later always known in Czech as the *ornat* or canonicals), with a cross over the breast and at the back, usually ornamented with beautiful embroidery: see (3) and (4). During this period the chasuble was circular in cut. A full cloak (really more of a secular addition to the dress) was worn with an ermine hood: see (5) and (6). A priest from an illumination in Jan of Středa's MS, *Liber Viaticus*, dating from about 1360. (2) A priest from a painting by Master Theodoricus, dating from about 1360 (Matějček, pl. 59). (3–4) A priest in liturgical vestments (Racinet). (5) A priest, a high dignitary of the early 15th century, as depicted in the frame of the Vyšší Brod Madonna (the figure of St. Simon, the donor, Matějček, pl. 207). (6) An ecclesiastical dignitary from the Jena Codex.

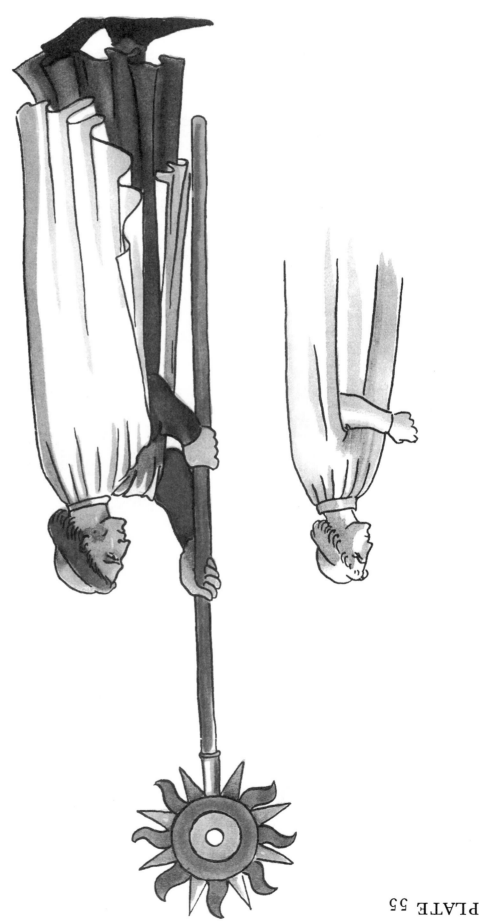

A Hussite priest with monstrance, dressed in a blue tunic and white surplice, from the Jena Codex. Late 15th or early 16th century.

PLATE 55

PLATE 56

Clerical vestments in Bohemia in the second half of the 14th and the early 15th centuries. (1) A bishop, from the end of the 14th century, from an illumination in a MS in Prague University Library, ref. no. XIII C 1a. He is dressed in an alb, ornamented at the bottom of the centre front; over this he wears a dalmatic, slit at the sides, and finally the chasuble or canonicals. On his head he wears a mitre and he holds a bishop's crozier in his hand. (2) A priest from the year 1376 (Štítný MS, fol. 127), wearing an undertunic, a white dalmatic and a fur hood. (3) A cardinal in a purple robe, cloak and cardinal's hat, from the early 15th century. (4) A deacon in tunic and dalmatic (Štítný MS, fol. 110). (5) A church chorister in tunic and white surplice (Latin Bible, fol. 225). (6) A bishop in an alb, with a stole over his shoulders, wearing a mitre (Krumlov MS, fol. 251).

PLATE 57

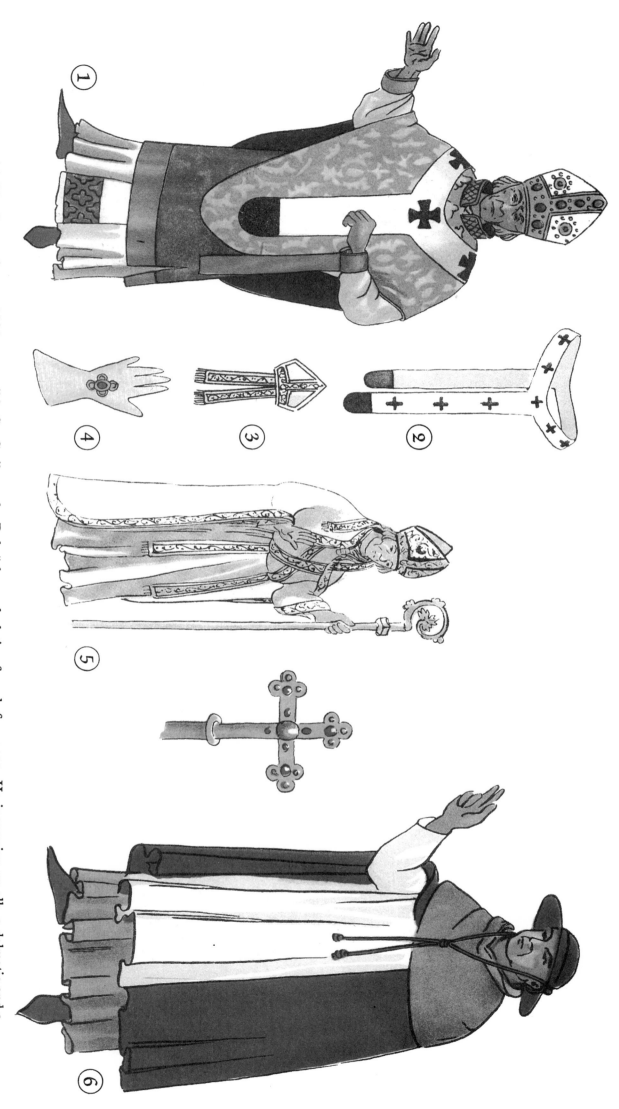

(1) The figure of an archbishop, possibly St. Cyril, on the Dubeček panel, dating from before 1400. He is wearing an alb, a dalmatic and a chasuble; over his left wrist is wrapped the maniple, and he wears a mitre. Over his shoulders and resting on the chasuble is the pallium, the insignia of an archbishop. (2) The pallium. (3) A mitre (with infula), as seen from the back. (4) The left glove, ornamented at the back. (5) A bishop wearing an alb and stole; the ceremonial cloak (pluvial) is fastened over his breast with a clasp, he wears a mitre and holds a bishop's crozier in his hand. Dating from about the middle of the 15th century. (Die alt-deutsche Malerei, p. 112, pl. 75.) (6) A high ecclesiastical dignitary from the painted border to the Krumlov Madonna, dating from about 1450. A cardinal wearing a white surplice over a tunic, also a cloak and hood over his shoulders; he wears a cardinal's hat. (Prague National Gallery, no. 162.)

PLATE 58   PART I

The young Wenceslas IV, on the votive picture of Jan Očko of Vlašim, about 1370 (Prague National Gallery.) He is dressed in hose and a close-fitting brocade surcoat, padded over the chest, which is exceptionally close-fitting, and has long tight sleeves: over his hips he wears an ornamental belt with a short sword. From his shoulders there flow long ermine tippets, and an ornamental chain hangs across his shoulders (Matějček, Pl. 75).

PLATE 59   PART I

Bohemian court costume of about 1400. King Wenceslas IV as a fashionable dandy in piked hose ending in a point, which are often parti-coloured. He wears short, closely fitted, padded surcoats in plain coloured or gay brocaded material, either unbelted or with the belt round the hips, and love knots wound at the waist or above the elbow; the surcoats have various types of sleeves: either broad at the shoulder and narrow at the wrist, or long and bell-shaped with dags cut at the edge and sometimes parti-coloured. From the miniatures of the King Wenceslas Bible.

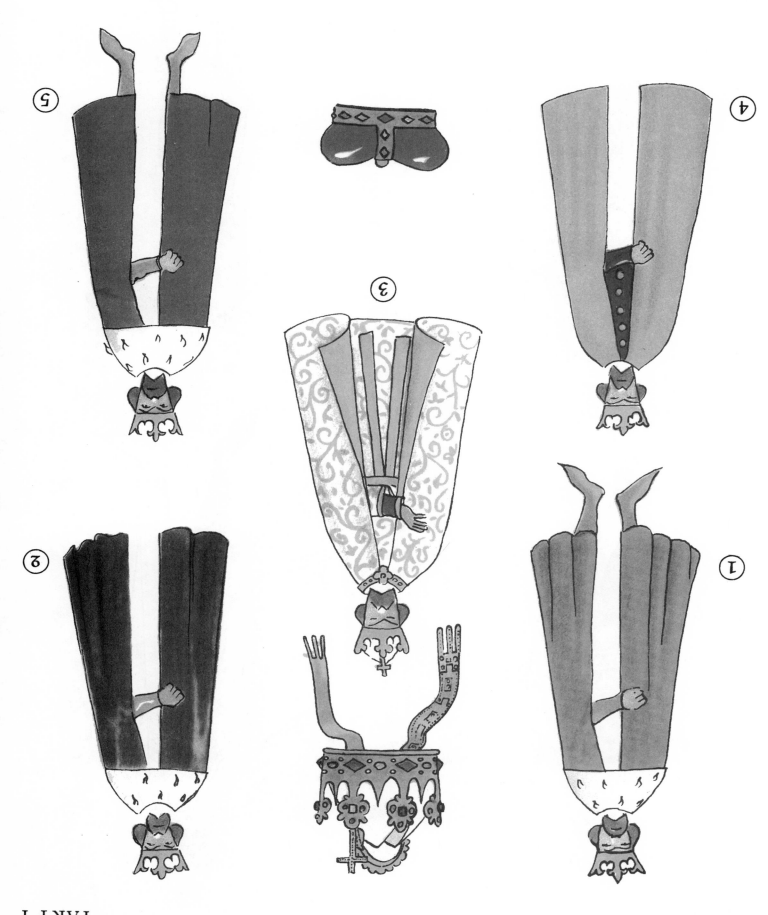

Royal schemes: the colour cloaks. These cloaks were similar to the cloaks worn at that time by other classes of society; basically they were still the full, circular cloak fastening over the breast or at the neck. The royal cloak only differed from the others in the richness of the material, the embroidery, the decoration and the ermine cape over the shoulders.
(1) King Solomon from the Latin Bible, fol. 208 and 245. (2) A king from the Latin Bible, fol. 233. (3) The ceremonial vestment of the Emperor Charles IV from the Jan Očko of Vlašim votive painting. Above him is the Imperial crown from the same picture (Matějček, pl. 75). (4) A king wearing a simple cloak with no ermine (Latin Bible, fol. 246).
(5) A king from the Latin Bible, fol. 252. In the centre the prince's crown from the Jan Očko of Vlašim votive painting.

PLATE 60

Royal apparel in Bohemia at the beginning of the 15th century. (1) King David from the Latin Bible, fol 190, in a fashionable tight-fitting surcoat with low belt, tippets hanging from the shoulder and a matching hood. (2) The figure of a king in full houppelande – probable slit up over the left thigh – and wearing above it an ermine cape (*ibid.*, fol. 222); the picture of a king in fol. 227 is similar, though the cloak is green. (3) A king in full cloak fastened at the neck; over it is an ermine cape (*ibid.*, fol. 215). (4) King Solomon consulting with the elders (*ibid.*, fol. 151). He wears fashionable hose and a close-fitting padded short surcoat, with low belt and a slit up the left side. (5) A king in short cloak without sleeves, completely open and slit up both sides – probably a type of tabard. (From the Krumlov MS, fol. 57). Details: the royal crown from the Jan Očko of Vlašim votive painting. The head of St. Wenceslas's sceptre, according to Master Theodoricus. The imperial orb from from the painting of the Kladsko Madonna (Matějček, pl. 28).

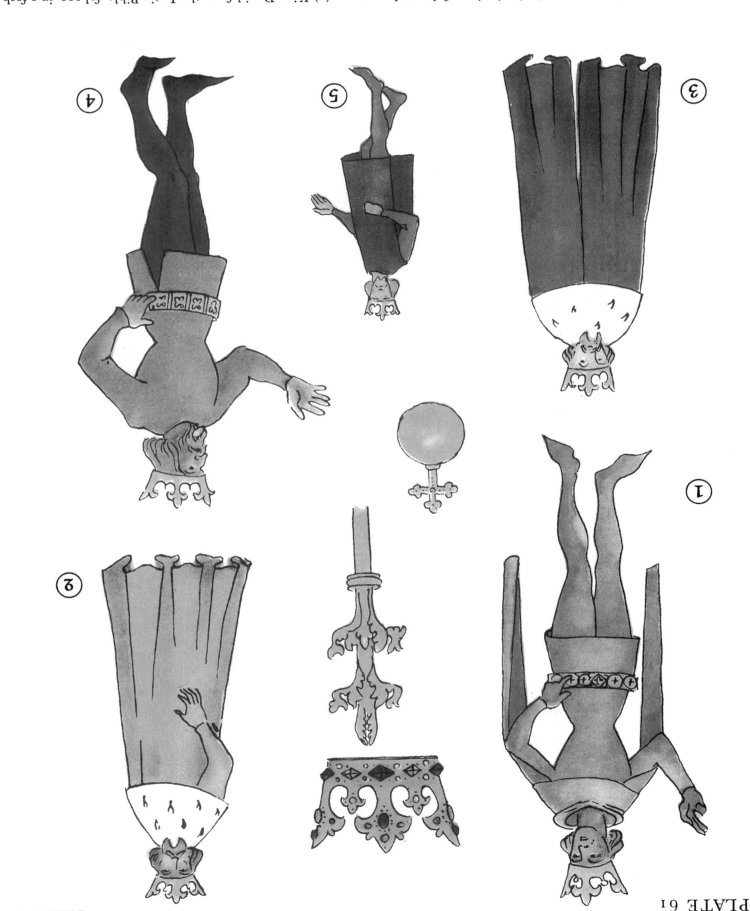

PLATE 61

PLATE 62

German court apparel at the beginning of the 15th century. (1) A king in parti-coloured chausses, wearing a short, close-fitting tunic with long sleeves, over which is a short cloak trimmed with dagging and open at the sides, a type of tabard. From the Kyeser Bellifortis MS, based on reproductions published in *Deutsches Leben*, pl. XXVI. (2) A king wearing parti-coloured chausses and a padded, close-fitting surcoat, which has dagged ornamentation at the shoulders: there are also full flowing slit sleeves, beneath which can be seen the under-sleeves. (From an illustration in the J. de Cessolis MS reproduced in *Deutsches Leben*, pl. XXIV).

Belts and other details of costumes from the second half of the 14th century and the 15th century. (1, 3, 9) The knightly girdle as worn over armour (Viollet le Duc, *passim*). (2) The fastening of a knightly girdle, if it has a buckle (Viollet le Duc). (4) The knightly girdle on the tomb of Přemysl Otakar II, in St. Vitus's Cathedral, Prague; late 14th century. (5) A knightly girdle dating from about 1405 (*European Armour*, III, p. 768). (6) The knightly girdle from the tomb of Břetislav I, in St. Vitus's Cathedral, Prague; late 14th century. (7) The knightly girdle from the tomb of Břetislav II, in St. Vitus's Cathedral, Prague. (8) A knightly girdle from St. George's Chapel, Prague; second half of the 15th century. (10) How the knightly girdle was worn over the surcoat.

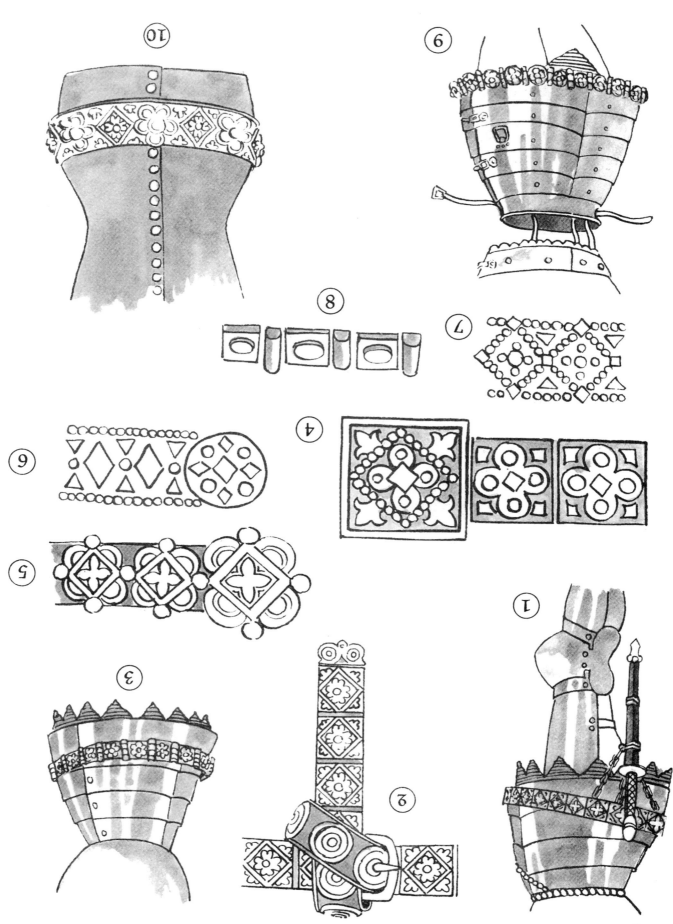

PLATE 63

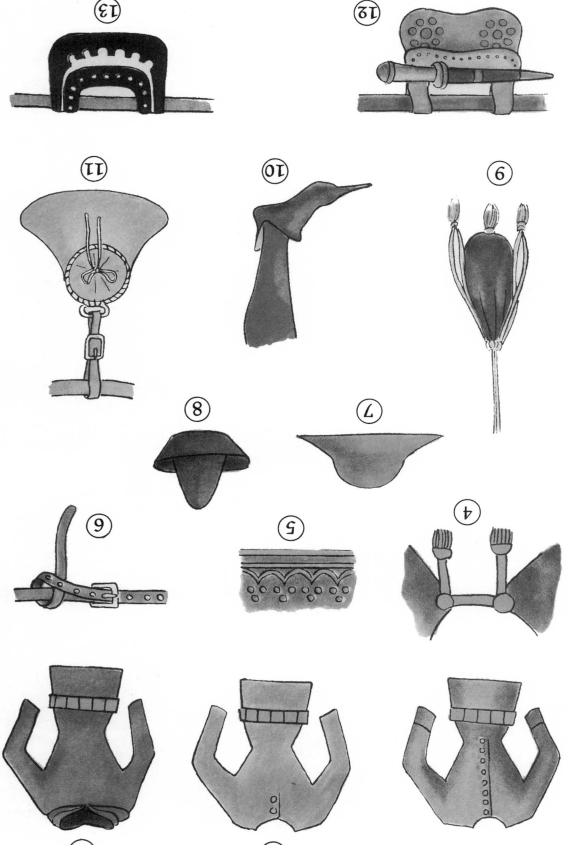

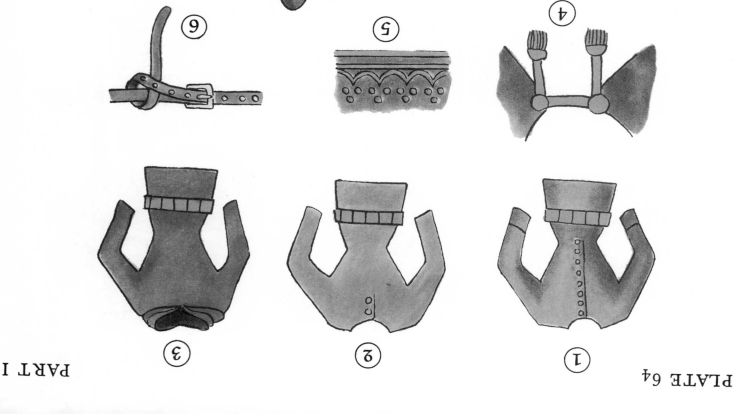

Details and accessories to the Bohemian costumes of the 14th and 15th centuries. (1–2) The surcoats of great noblemen at the bed of King David, from the miniatures in the Latin Bible dating from the early 15th century. (3) The surcoat of a great nobleman at the enthronement of the king, also from the Latin Bible; early 15th century. (4) A method of fastening the cloak, from the painting of the Madonna between St. Catherine and St. Margaret, dating from about 1360 (Matějček, pl. 42). (5) The border of the Madonna's cloak, in the Doudleby Madonna, dating from the year 1340 (Matějček, pl. 243). (6) The clasp of a belt, from a miniature in the Krumlov MS, fol. 193; early 15th century. (7–8) Two hats (ibid., fol. 348, 100); early 15th century. (9) A pouch, from a miniature in the Krumlov MS, fol. 100); early 15th century. (9) A pouch, from the painting "The Visitation of the Virgin Mary" in the St. James altar-piece, dating from 1430–40 (Matějček, pl. 248). (10) A shoe, from a miniature in the Sttný MS, dating from the year 1376, fol. 127. (11) A "gicpelere" from the painting "The Laying in the Sepulchre" by the Master of the Třeboň altar-piece, dating from about 1380 (Matějček, pl. 105). (12) A pouch, from a miniature in the Krumlov MS, fol. 239; early 15th century. (13) The executioner's satchel, from the painting "The Beheading of St. John the Baptist" from the Zátoň altar-piece, dating from about 1430 (Matějček, pl. 227).

PLATE 64 PART I

PLATE 65

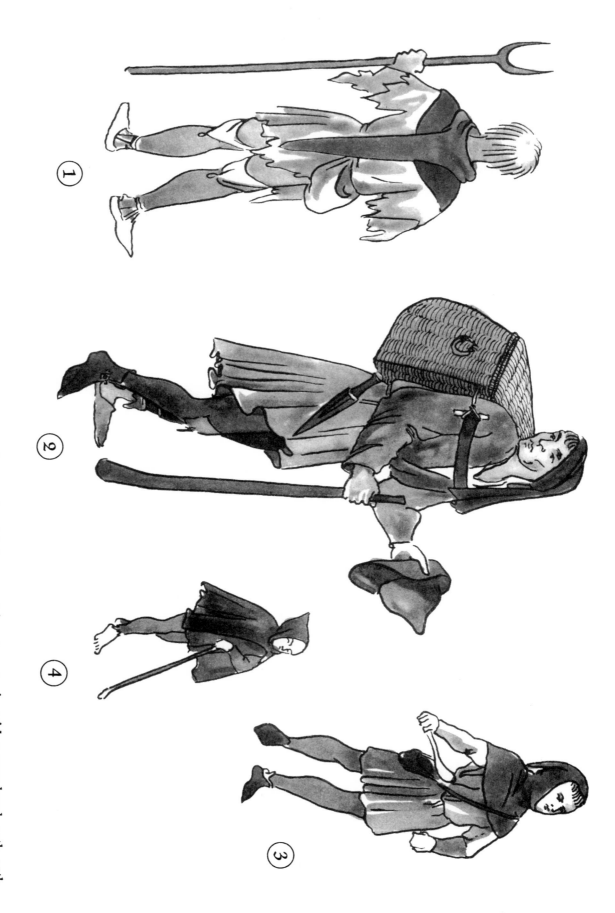

French and Netherlands costumes of the common people, 14th and 15th centuries. (1) A peasant in a torn tunic, with a cape-hood, 14th–15th century. (Viollet le Duc, IV, p. 383). (2) The prodigal son, from a picture by Hieronymus Bosch (1460–1516). He wears torn hose and odd shoes, a shirt with a short tunic over it, tucked up at the waist; a twisted cloth hood, rolled turban-wise, over which he wears a hat (now carried in his hand). (3) A well-dressed peasant: stockings and shoes and a short tunic, gathered in at the waist, and a cape-hood (Viollet le Duc, IV, p. 210.) (4) A bare-footed shepherd in torn hose, a short tunic, and hip-length hooded cloak.

PLATE 66

The German common people, early 15th century. Shepherds from the Bavarian Legend altar-piece. (*Die alt-deutsche Malerei*, P. 74, pl. 52). One wears a tunic, rolled-down hood and a hat; the other a short, full cloak and a headcloth. They both wear hose and laced boots.

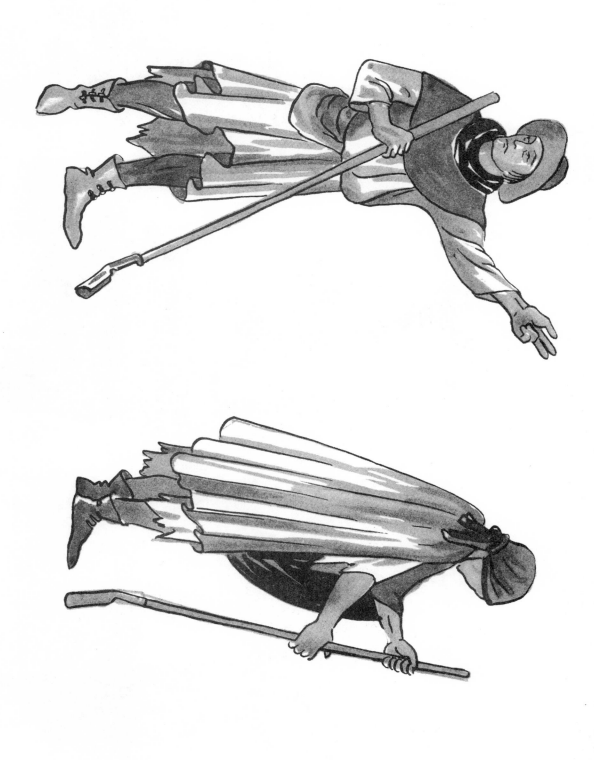

PLATE 67

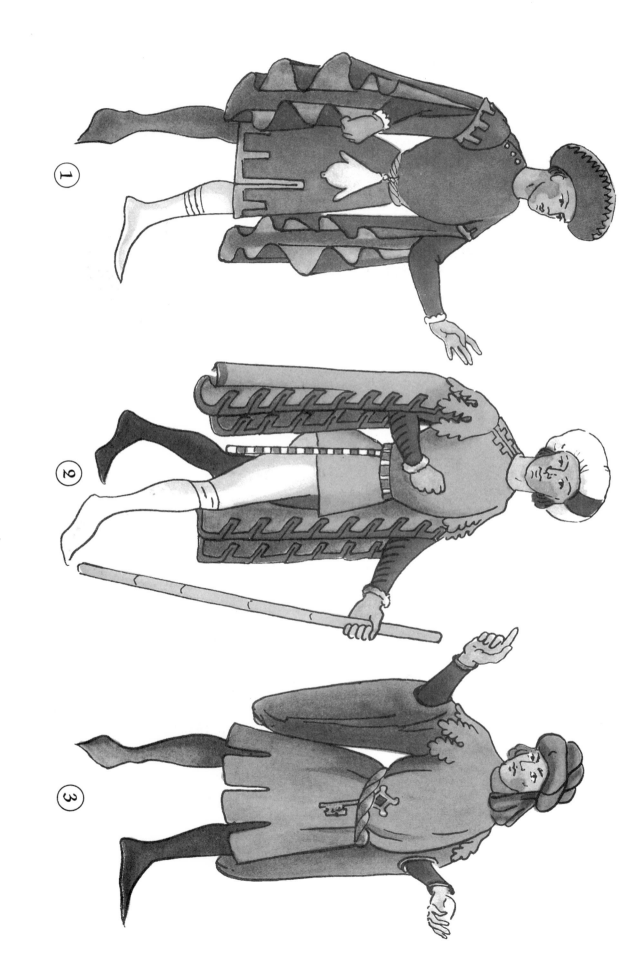

The costumes of well-to-do German burghers, dating from about 1407 (*Deutsches Leben*, pl. XXV). (1) A tailor in close-fitting surcoat with open sleeves, falling loosely in cascades; beneath them can be seen the long, narrow undersleeves. Parti-coloured hose. (2) A merchant in close-fitting short surcoat with dagged ornamentation at the shoulders and open tippet sleeves with dagged border; beneath these are the long undersleeves; parti-coloured hose. (3) An innkeeper in girded overtunic with bagpipe sleeves; parti-coloured chausses and a twisted cloth cap.

PLATE 68

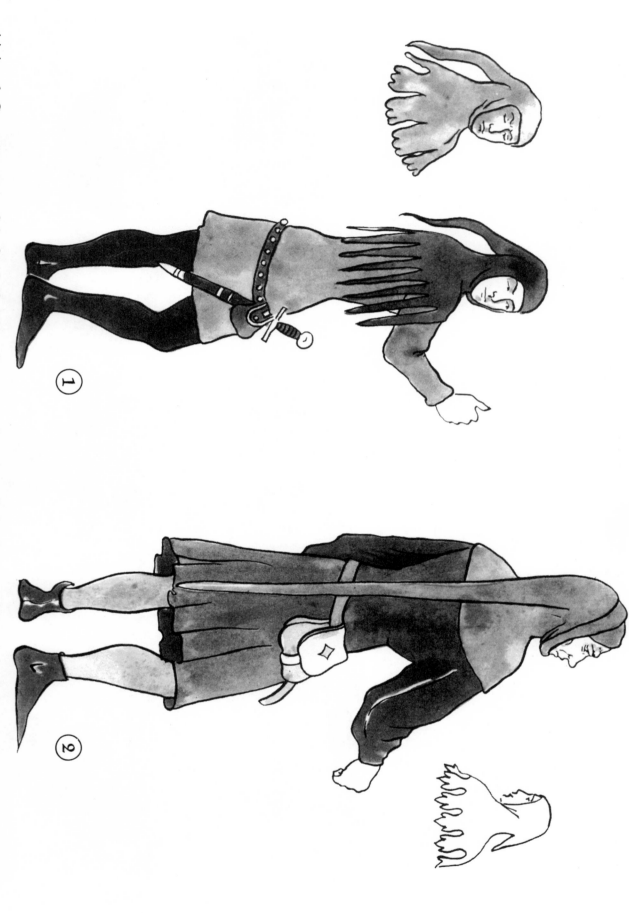

(2) A male German costume of the first half of the 15th century. A costume dating from 1430. A man from the Lorch am Rhein "Procession of the Cross" wearing a long tunic with a low belt, a hood with long tippet, and boots. (*Geschichte der deutschen Kunst*, p. 178, pl. 257.) (1) Male costume from the Netherlands, example of a hood from the middle of the 14th century (*Kulturgeschichte des deutschen Volkes*, I, p. 247.) Another example of a hood from the early 15th century. A man in fairly long straight tunic, wearing a cape-hood with tippet, which is dagged round the lower edge over the shoulders. Detail: other examples of the various forms of dagging round the lower edge of a hood. (From a painting by Jan van Eyck, dating from between 1415–17.)

PLATE 69

German male costume of the 15th century. (1) A German costume of the mid-15th century. (*Kulturgeschichte des deutschen Volkes*, I, p. 290.) (2) A German mayor of the 15th century (*Das Kostümwerk*). Examples of overgarments: two types of tabard, a shorter, full tunic with a border of fur at the lower edge and girded, also one that is longer, reaching to the calves, open up to the armpits and bordered with fur. Both types are worn with a cap or a hat. (3) A German costume of the year 1468: a young man in a close-fitting short surcoat, slit up over the left thigh; he wears parti-coloured hose (*Kulturgeschichte des deutschen Volkes*, I, p. 283).

PLATE 70

(1) Jewish costume of the late 13th century. (Albert Kretschmer, *Die Trachten der Völker*, pl. 36). A longish tunic with full tabard open at the sides; also the characteristic yellow Jewish hat. (2) Jewish costume of the 15th century, from the same source. It is a long gown with narrow sleeves and is hemmed with a narrow fur border; again the typical yellow Jewish hat. The costume has no particular characteristics; it is similar to the contemporary costumes of other burgher classes of society.

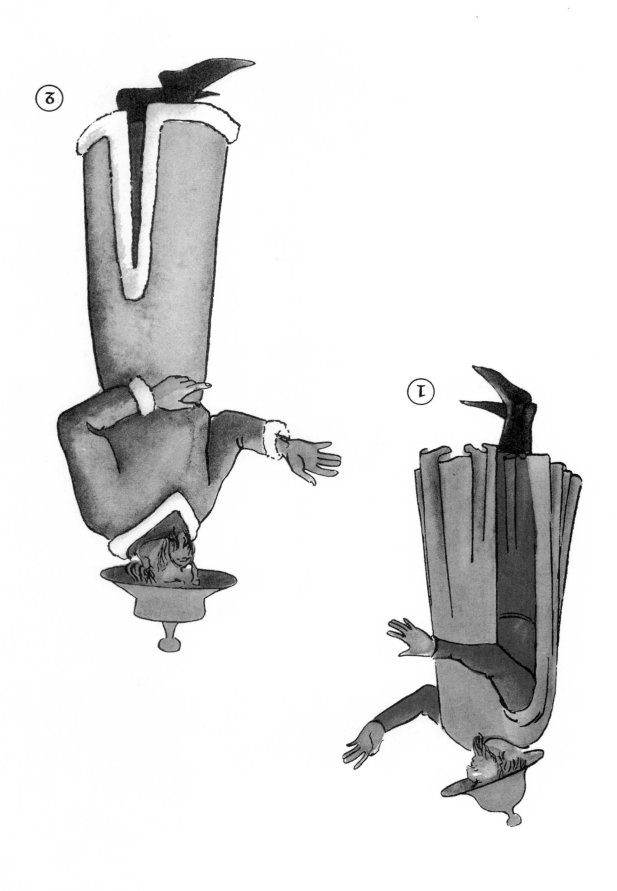

PLATE 71

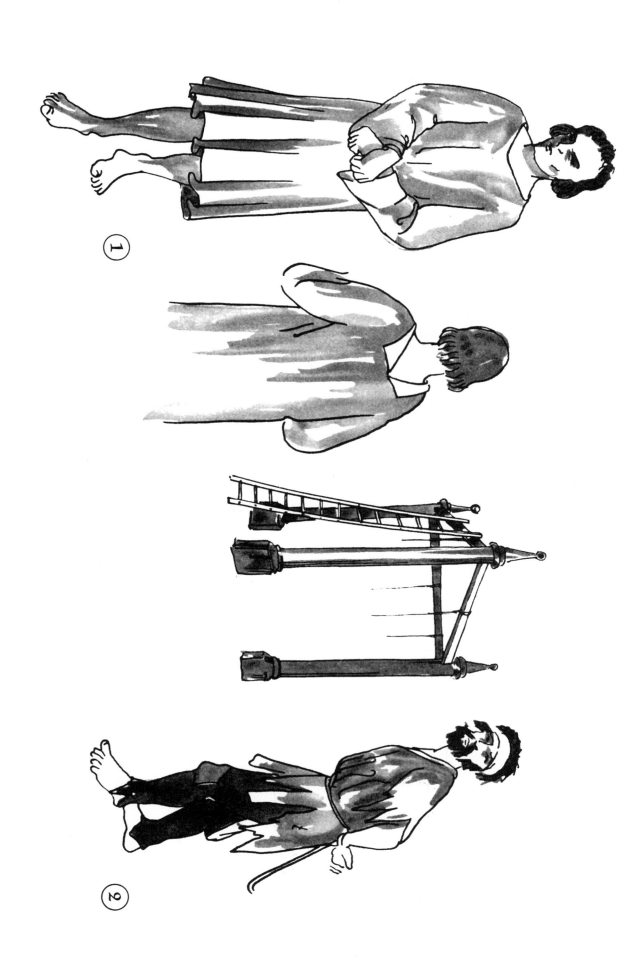

Netherlands and German costumes, first half of the 15th century. (1) The condemned man dressed for execution, from a painting by Dirk Bouts. (2) The gallows and the condemned man in torn patched stockings and tunic. From drawings in the German MS, *Mittelalterliches Hausbuch.*

PLATE 72

(1) French costume dating from 1430–45 (*Zeitschrift für Waffenkunde*, 1923/1925, p. 43, pl. 5). A simple tunic slit up over the left thigh, also a hat with long flowing scarf. (2) Another French costume from the years 1430–45 (*ibid.*, p. 43, pl. 5). A long tunic open at the front, with a narrow belt at the waist. A full circular cloak fastened at the front neck; also a hood, over which the man wears a hat with a rolled-up brim.

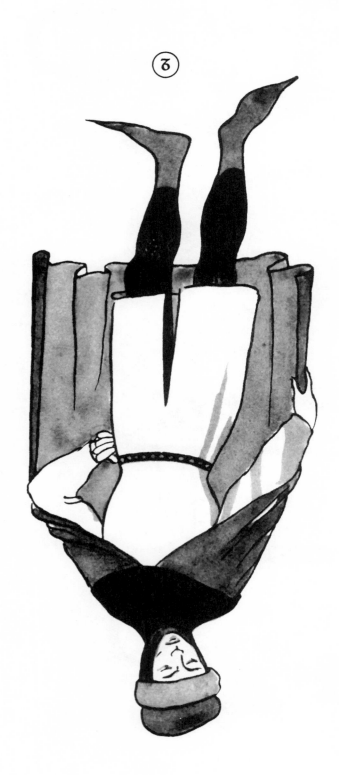

PLATE 73

German costumes from 1380–1430 (Alteneck, *Trachten*). (1) An overgarment with baglike sleeves, beneath which are to be seen the narrow long, contrasting undersleeves. (2) A short, close-fitting surcoat, buttoned down the front, with a small high collar, and a dagged border to the lower edge of the tunic and to the edges of the half-sleeves, which broaden out into tippets. (3) Short, close-fitting surcoat worn with a dagged hood and a hat.

PLATE 74

PART I

Male German costumes about the year 1419. Examples of overtunics and surcoats, with various types of sleeves: see (2), (4), (5), (6). Also a short, completely circular cloak. (1) A longish overgarment, bordered with fur – a type of houppelande. (3) A warm overtunic with a fur border. (7) Various types of men's hats. (*Deutsches Leben, Kulturgeschichte des deutschen Volkes* I: (1) no. 292, (2) no. 302, 310, (3) no. 293, (4) no. 294, (5) no. 298, (6) no. 298, (7) no. 292.)

PLATE 75

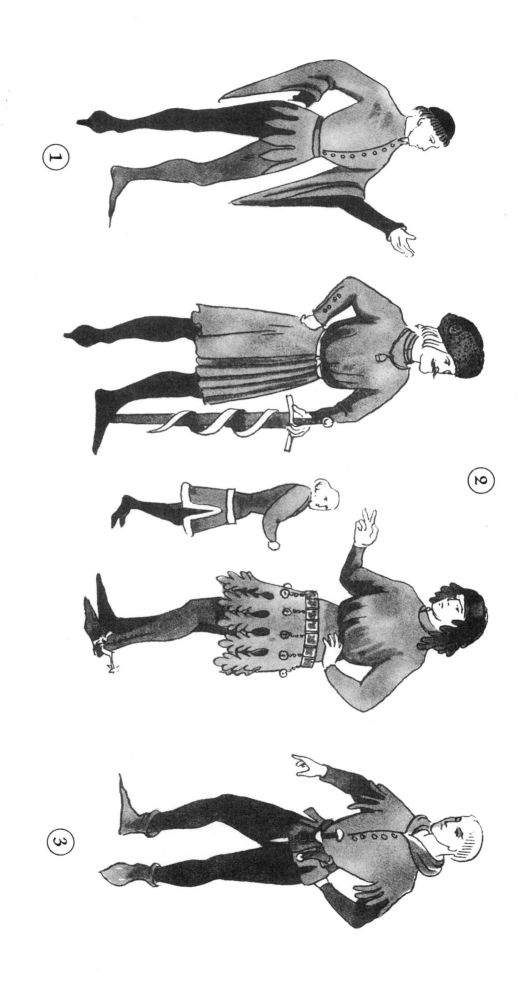

German costumes of the 14th and 15th centuries. Examples of surcoats and gipons, with dagged ornamentation and buttons down the front, long sleeves or open half-sleeves and hoods. Also a longish tunic with oak-leaf patterned dags round the lower hem and a low belt hung with little bells. Two types of hat. (1) A German costume from a Gobelin tapestry, dating from between 1380–1400. (*Kulturgeschichte des deutschen Volkes*, plate between pp. 262 and 263.) (2) Costumes from Thalhofer's *Fechtbuch*, dating from about 1443, pl. 8, 30. (3) A 15th century costume (*Kulturgeschichte des deutschen Volkes*, I, p. 292).

PLATE 76

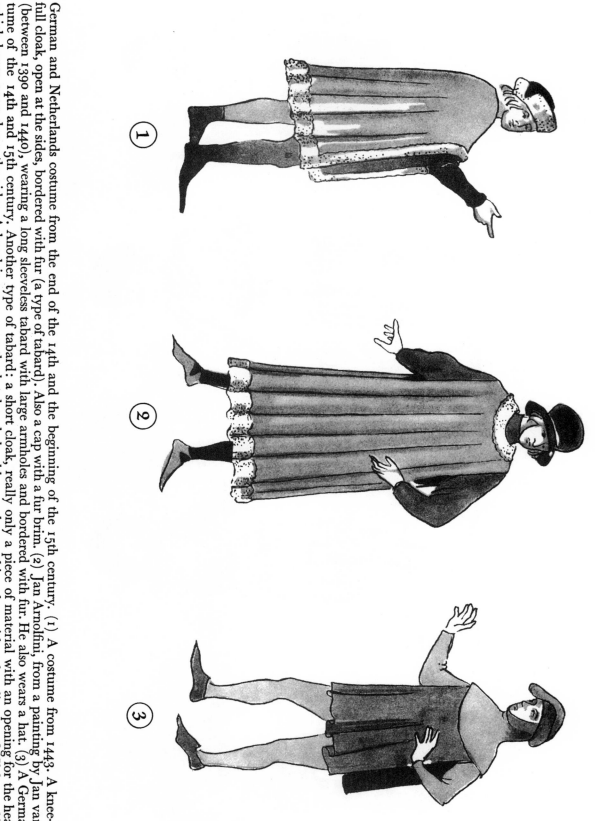

German and Netherlands costume from the end of the 14th and the beginning of the 15th century. (1) A costume from 1443: A knee-length full cloak, open at the sides, bordered with fur (a type of tabard). Also a cap with a fur brim. (2) Jan Arnolfini, from a painting by Jan van Eyck (between 1390 and 1440), wearing a long sleeveless tabard with large armholes and bordered with fur. He also wears a hat. (3) A German costume of the 14th and 15th century. Another type of tabard: a short cloak, really only a piece of material with an opening for the head and which hangs open down the sides. A hood is worn over the head and shoulders and over this a hat with a dangling scarf (*kulturgeschichte des deutschen Volkes*, I, p. 283).

PLATE 77

Germany: a mounted courier of about 1468, wearing a short travelling cloak and a hat with a broad brim (*Kultur-geschichte des deutschen Volkes*, I, p. 283).

PLATE 78   PART I

①   ②

(1) A French nobleman from the year 1410. Of special note is the overtunic, a pleated doublet which flares out below the waist and has open sleeves with lobe-shaped dags. It is lined with a contrasting material and hemmed with fur. (*Meyers Konversations-Lexikon*, XI, plate between pp. 536 and 537.) (2) The costume of a French nobleman in 1440. He wears tight, soled hose, with long pointed toes and has a short close-fitting surcoat, probably of brocade, which flares out below the waist and is bordered with fur; he has a long, full cloak. He also wears a fur-trimmed hat with a coloured scarf (*Larousse Universel*, p. 538).

PLATE 79

(1) German male costume from the end of the 14th century: a figure from the tomb of Johann von Holzhausen – who died in 1391 – in the cathedral at Frankfurt. A longish, knee-length tunic fastened with small buttons sewn close together down the whole length from top to bottom, belted at the waist and with a second belt with pouch and dagger at the hip. He also has an interesting circular cloak and hood, which is fastened over the right shoulder with a row of several small buttons. The cloak has a hood. (Dehio, *Geschichte der deutschen Kunst*, pl. 259, 383.)

(2) A male costume in the Franco-Burgundian fashion of the 15th century. The typical short, well-padded tunic or doublet, shaped to fit closely at the waist, with open sleeves heavily padded at the shoulder, with the so-called "mahoîtres" (Tilke).

PLATE 80

German male costume of the first half of the 15th century. (1) The costume of a nobleman of about the year 1429. An over-tunic with short sleeves, bordered with fur; a hat with fur trimming (*Die deutsche Malerei der Renaissance*, pl. XXII). (2) A short cloak and hood and tippet, dating from the first half of the 15th century (*ibid.*, p. 326, pl. 405). (3-5) Costumes from the years 1420-60. Fitted shortish tunics or doublets, sacklike baggy sleeves and dagged hoods; one has long tippets with oak-leaf dags which are repeated on the skirt border and the hood. (Alteneck, pp. 272, 256).

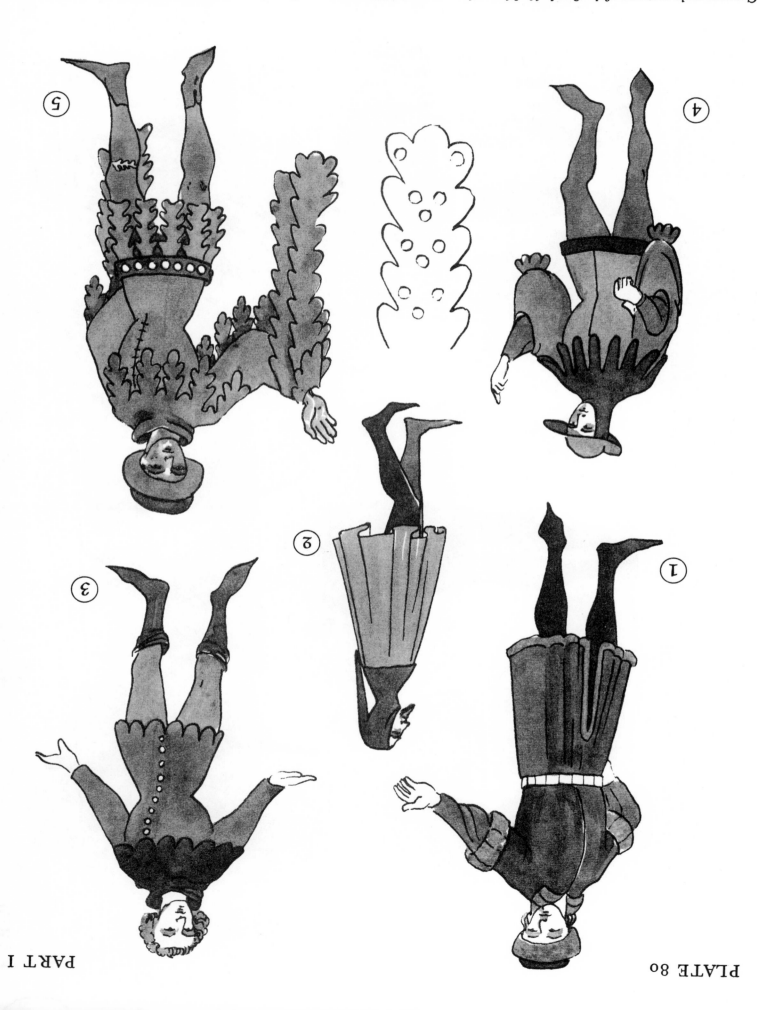

PLATE 81

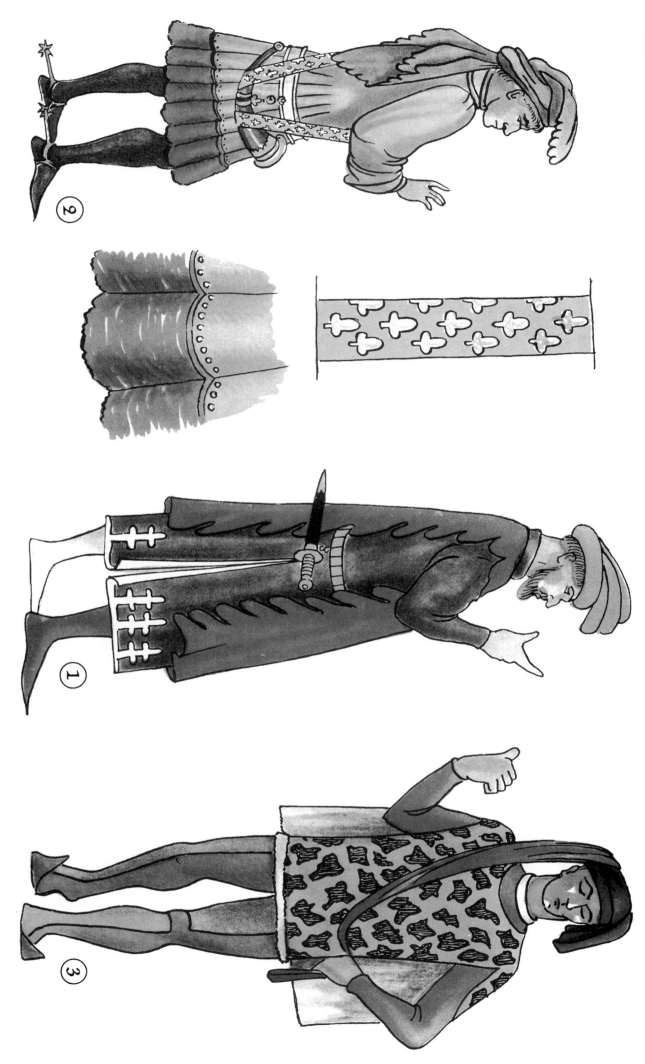

(1) The costume of an English nobleman of the 15th century. A longish tunic reaching to the knees, belted and slit at the sides: long; full sleeves. Over this he wears a knee-length tabard with lobe-shaped dags. He wears a chaperon, a hat of cloth trimmed with folded material. (Tilke, I, pl. 36, p. 54.) (2) Italian male costume: St. Hubert, from a picture by S. Pisanello. He wears a houppelande with a wide hem of fur and a soft cloth hat with dagged scarf; over his left shoulder he carries a hunting horn on an ornamental strap. (3) A Florentine nobleman of the 15th century, wearing fashionable parti-coloured chausses, a tight-fitting undertunic with long sleeves and a short, straight tabard-type cloak. The hat with its long scarf is also typical. *Meyers Konversations-Lexikon*, XI, plate between pp. 536 and 537.

PLATE 82

(1) The figure of a prince in French costume: a sleeveless surcoat trimmed with fur and flowing tippets from the shoulders. A hat with a fur border and a long scarf (Tilke, pl. 46; Rosenberg dates it from the 14th century). (2) The costume of a German nobleman, end of the 14th century. The German fashions tended to exaggerate certain features of the basic European fashions, for example, the very wide exaggerated open sleeves of the well-fitting doublet, that we have already come across; also the trumpet-shaped end of the undersleeves, the white collar beneath the stiff stand-up collar of the doublet. A great deal of decoration was also very popular at this period, for example, belts hung with tiny bells which also ornament the decorative chain worn across the shoulders. (From the portrait of Herman von Vertherst who died in 1395, in *Deutsches Leben*.)

PLATE 83

French and Netherlands costumes of the 15th century. Figures from the paintings of the Adoration of the Magi. Their garments are heavily ornamented in these paintings. (1) One of the three kings by Jaques Daret (a master painter in 1432) wears a bell-shaped overtunic drawn in at the waist and trimmed with fur. (2) One of the three kings in a painting by Rogier van der Weyden (1400–64, a master-painter in 1432) has long oversleeves ending in broad, flowing tippets. Details: a hat with a crown, a turban with a crown and the border of a tunic trimmed with ermine.

PLATE 84

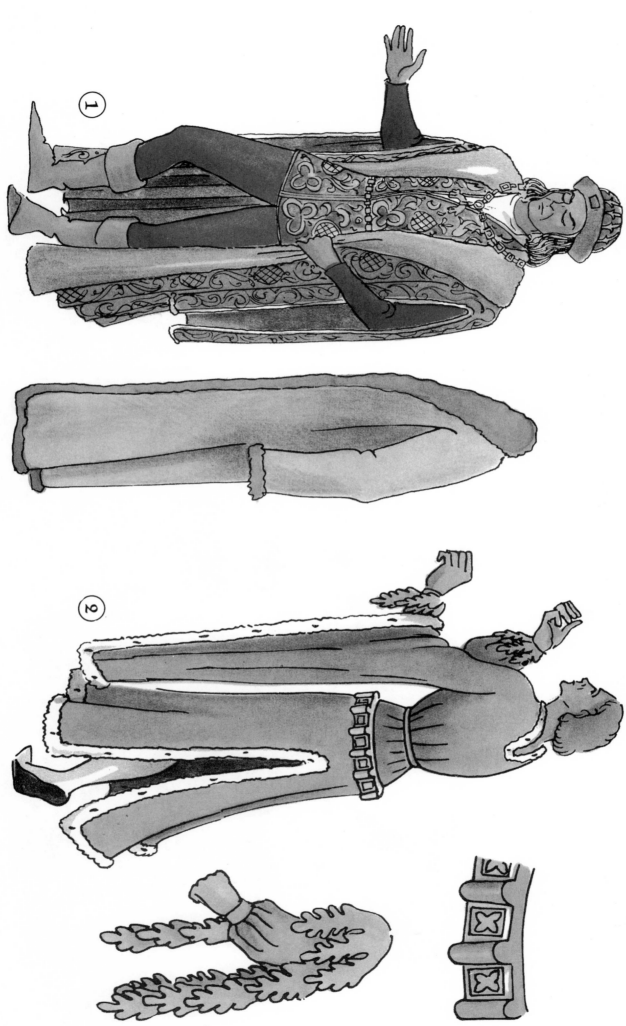

(1). Charles, Duke of Burgundy (1433–77), with hose and turned-down top boots, a close-fitting doublet or surcoat with undersleeves (Paul La-croix, *Vie militaire et religieuse au Moyen âge*, p. 72). (2) The figure of one of the three kings from the Ortenberg altar-piece, dating from the beginning of the 15th century; he is wearing a long, bizarre outer garment in the German fashion, with long tippets to the sleeves and slits at the back for walking. Details of the belt and undertunic.

PLATE 85

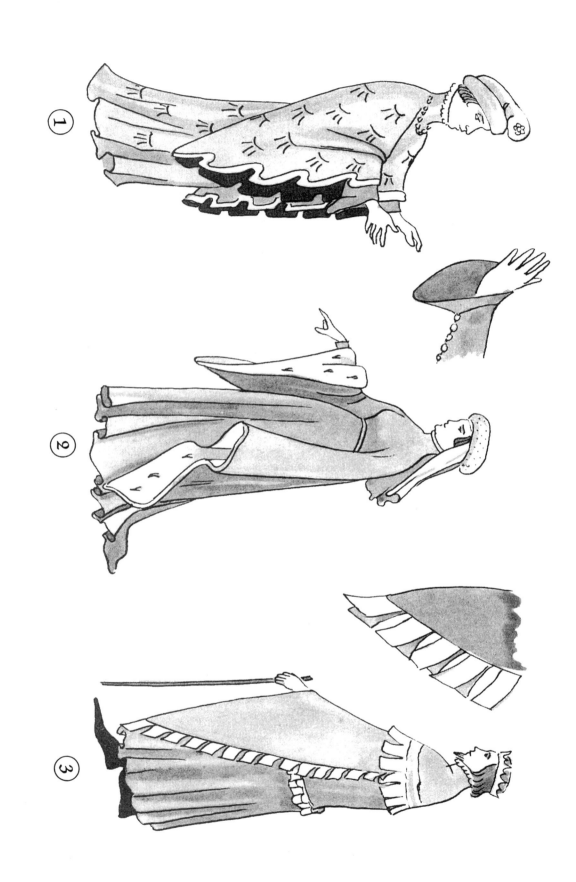

Full, open sleeves and their trimmings in French and German costumes of the 15th century; long and pointed, lined with expensive furs and edged with castellated dags of contrasting materials. (1) The figure of a nobleman from the painting of the Crucifixion by Konrad von Soest, dating from 1404 (*Die alt-deutsche Malerei*, p. 61, pl. 41). The costume is completely covered with decoration. Detail: the trumpet-shaped ends to the undersleeves, which are fastened with tiny buttons. (2) The costume of a noble woman from the middle of the 15th century (Viollet le Duc, III, p. 476). (3) Viollet le Duc, III, p. 465.

PLATE 86

Head coverings of the 14th and 15th centuries. Hoods with tippets, their cut and how they are worn; felt hats; hats with long flowing streamers made of material, plain and with dagged edges. (Viollet le Duc, III, pp. 132, 136, 137, 128, 129, 139: IV, p. 451.)

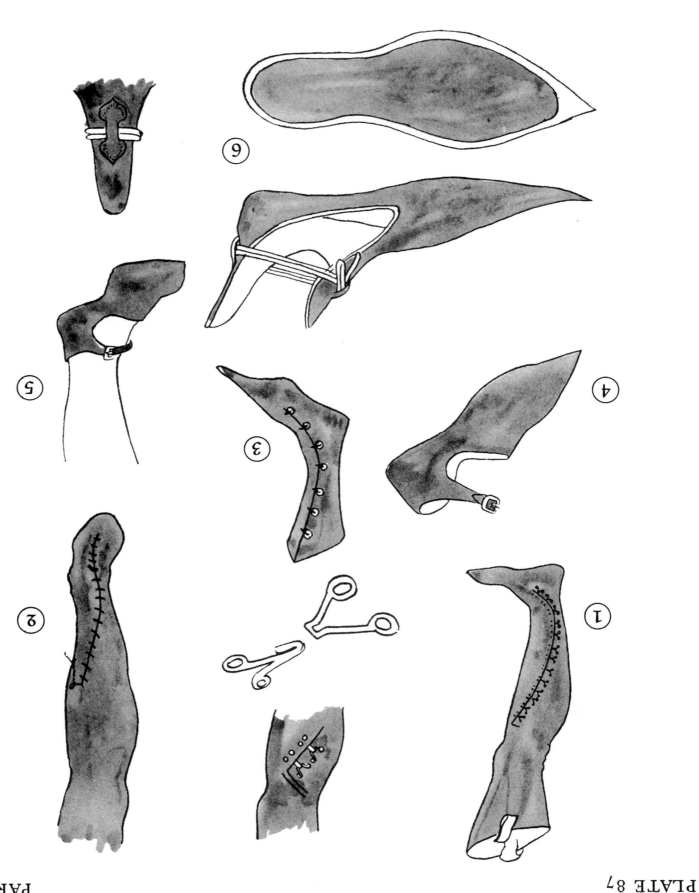

Footwear of the 13th and 14th centuries (Viollet le Duc). (1) Thigh boot for riding (14th century): detail of the boot and the hooks for fastening it. (2) Buskins as worn by a huntsman on foot, laced up. They date from the end of the 14th century. (3) A half-boot, about 1370. (4) A shoe, about 1245 (IV, p. 161; III, pl. 793, p. 32). (5) A shoe, same period (IV, p. 336). (6) A shoe, 14th century, with details (IV, p. 337).

PLATE 87

PLATE 88   PART I

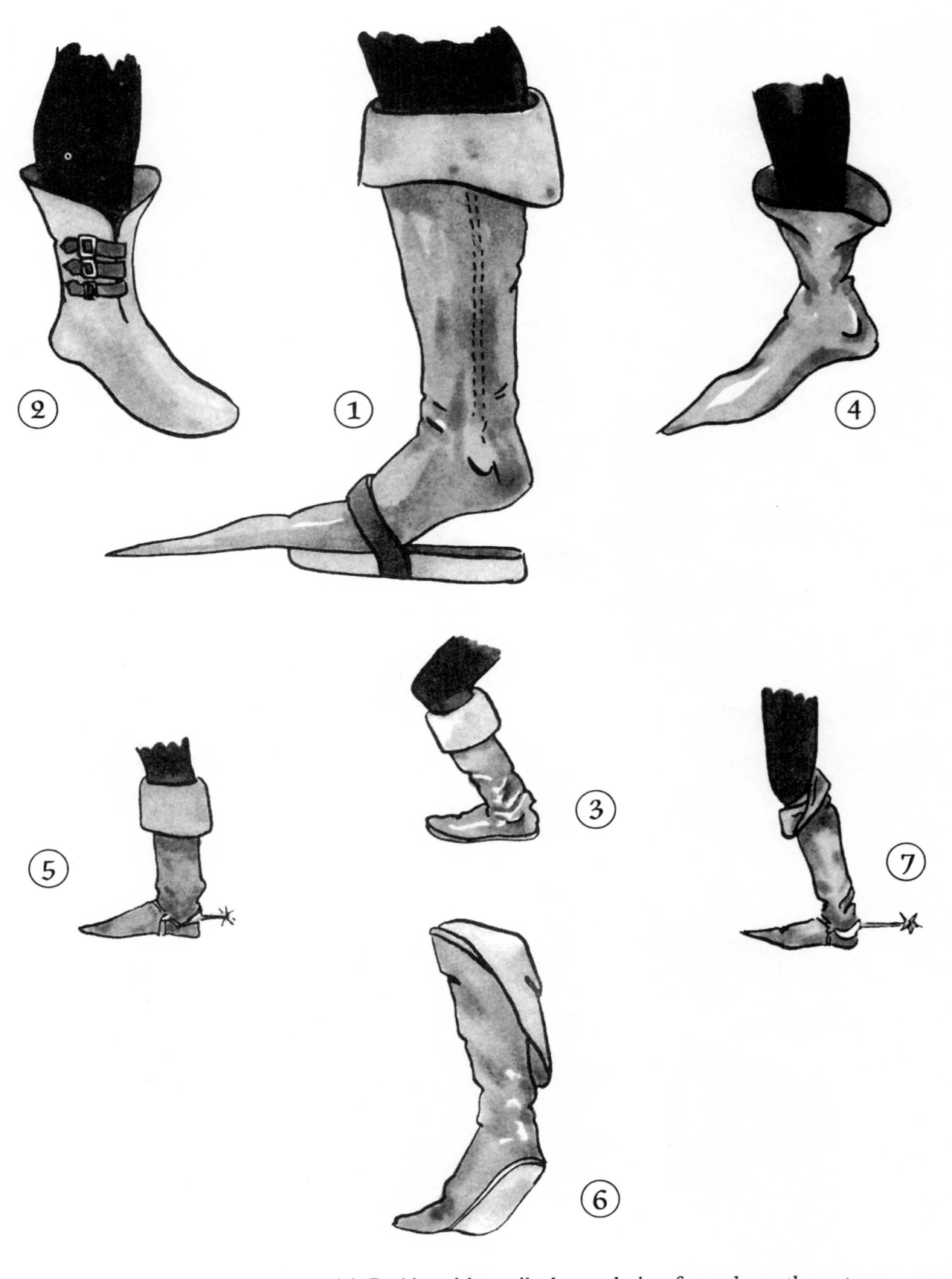

Examples of footwear from the 15th century. (1) Buskin with a piked toe, dating from the 15th century, worn with a wooden patten. (Wolfgang Bruhn and Max Tilke, *Das Kostümwerk*, Berlin, 1941.) (2) A buskin fastened with straps as worn by the jailor in the painting "St. James healing the Sick" in the St. James altar-piece, 1430–40 (Matějček, pl. 254). (3) A thigh boot with turned down top, 1495. The Littoral School: "The Descent from the Cross". (*500 lat maliarstwa polskiego*, pl. 23, p. 172.) (4) Pointed buskin as worn by the executioner in the painting "The Capture of St. James" in the St. James altar-piece, dating from between 1430 and 1440 (Matějček, pl. 253). (5) A boot with a spur, from the painting "The Adoration of the Magi" by the Master of the Brabant gem (Heindrich Ernst, *Alt-Niederländische Malerei*, Jena, 1910, pl. 62). (6) A boot as worn by the executioner from the picture "The Martyrdom of St. Apollonia (the Náměšť Panel, dating from about 1430, Matějček, pl. 215). (7) A high boot with spur, from a painting "The Adoration of the Magi" (*Alt-Niederländische Malerei*, pl. 62.)

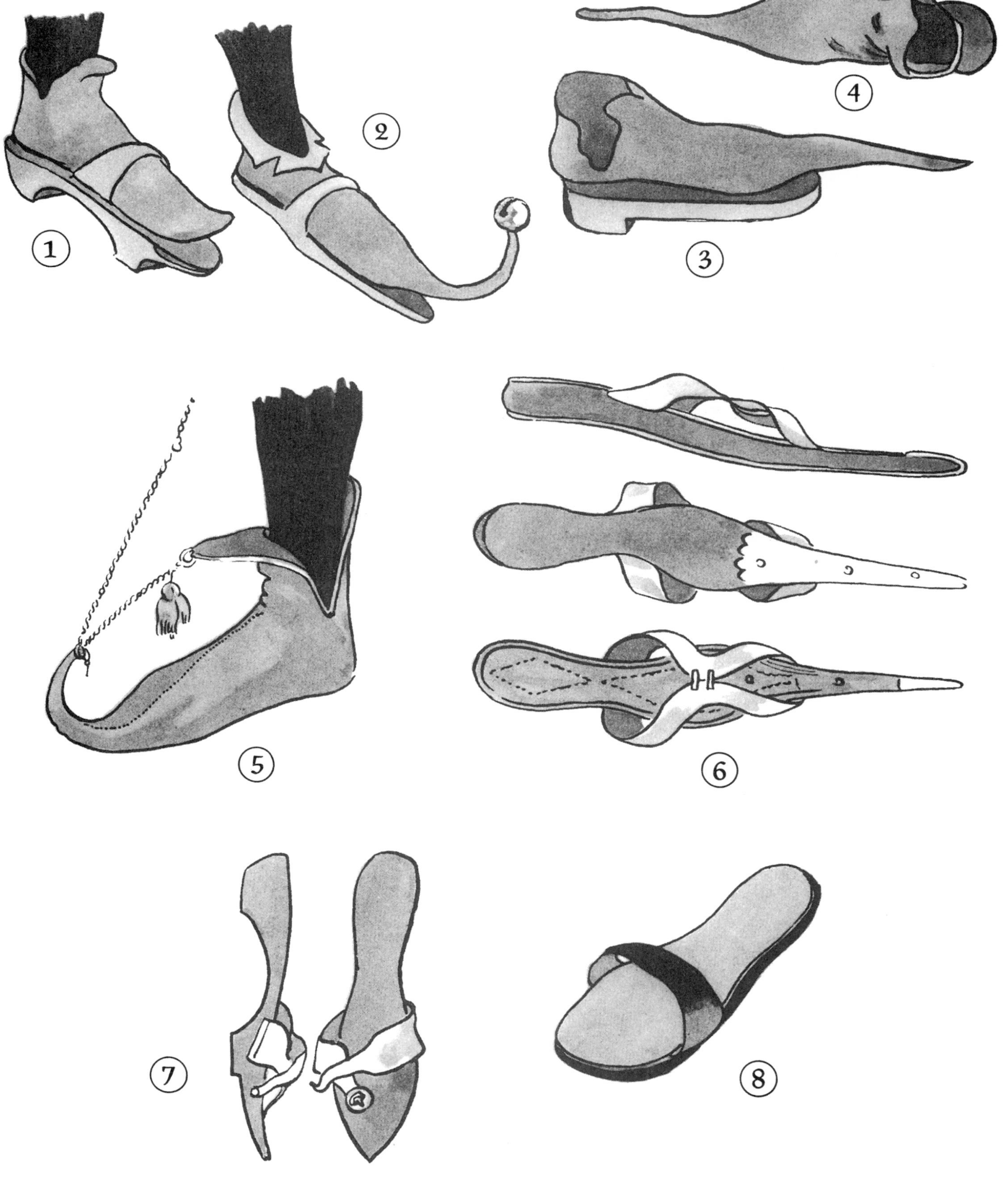

PLATE 89

Footwear of the 14th and 15th centuries from *Das Kostümwerk*. (1) A cloth buskin with a wooden patten. (2) A shoe with a long piked toe tipped by a little bell and a wooden patten. (3–4) Shoes dating from 1460, from the Kolmar Museum. (5) A shoe which belonged to the Scottish King James I. (6) Pattens from the second half of the 15th century. (7) Ordinary wooden pattens. (8) A monk's sandal.

PLATE 90

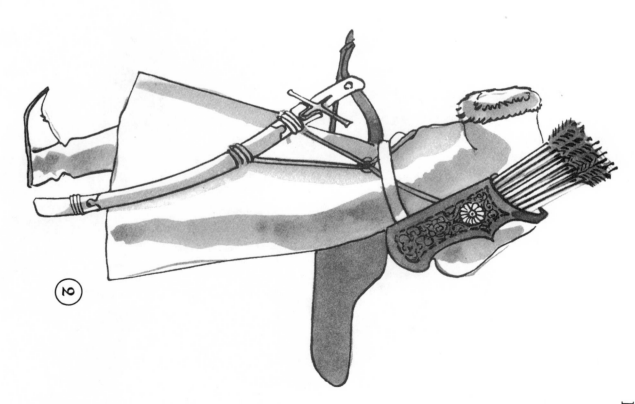

Methods of carrying a quiver and case for a bow, as depicted in drawings by Just Aman (*Das Pferd und seine Darstellung in der bildenden Kunst*:
(1) p. 173, pl. 277. (2) p. 174, pl. 278).

PLATE 91

(1) A Hungarian hussar, from the painting by Albrecht Dürer "*Die Nürnberger Feldschlange*" (*Kulturgeschichte des deutschen Volkes*, I, p. 273). (2) The costume of a Hungarian nobleman of the 13th century (Némes Mihály, p. 46). Detail: a plait of hair entwined with a chain of pearls. (3) A Hungarian costume of the 14th century (Némes Mihály, p. 63). (4) A Hungarian nobleman of the first half of the 15th century (Némes Mihály, p. 69).

PLATE 92

(1) A Hungarian costume, dating from the time of János Hunyadi, i. e. first half of the 15th century (Némes Mihály, p. 69). (2) The costume of a Hungarian nobleman, dating from the middle of the 15th century (Némes Mihály, p. 69).

PLATE 93

(1–2). Hungarian costumes of the time of the Jagellons, 1490–1526 (Némes Mihály, p. 75). Details: a clasp and a button. (3) A Hungarian warrior, dating from the end of the 15th century (Kosina, *Dějiny světové*, II, p. 569). He has a mace in his hand and is leaning on a pavise or large shield. Detail: the ornamental decoration of a tunic.

PLATE 94

(1–2) Kuman noblemen of the 14th century (Némes Mihály, *A. magyar jelmez*, p. 54: *Tudományos zsebkönyvtár*). In (1) the costume is obviously influenced by the western European mode.

PLATE 1

PART II

Soldiers of about 1350. From the picture of the Resurrection, by the Master of the Vyšší Brod cycle.
Part of a sword, an iron war-hat, an early form of knight's helmet and details of the metal-work
of two belts.

The armour of a knight-at-arms, dating from 1373 (the equestrian statue of St. George at Prague Castle). The details of (1), (2) and (3) (the belt clasp and the body armour from front and back) are drawn from a picture in *Zeitschrift für historische Waffenkunde*, 1940/1942, p. 229, pl. 5). (4) The arms and legs are protected by scale armour, but it is possible that these scales are a conventional representation of mail mesh. (5) A gauntlet. (6) The leg and foot, with plate jamb and spur. (7) The metal cuisse, covering the thigh.

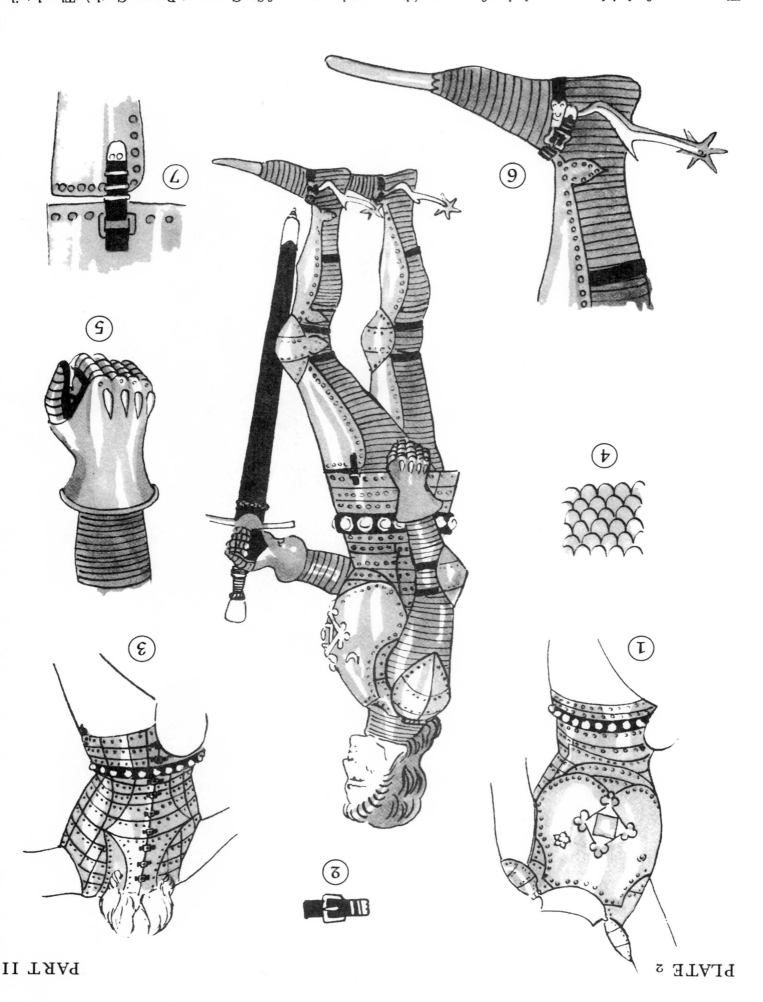

PLATE 2

PLATE 3 PART II

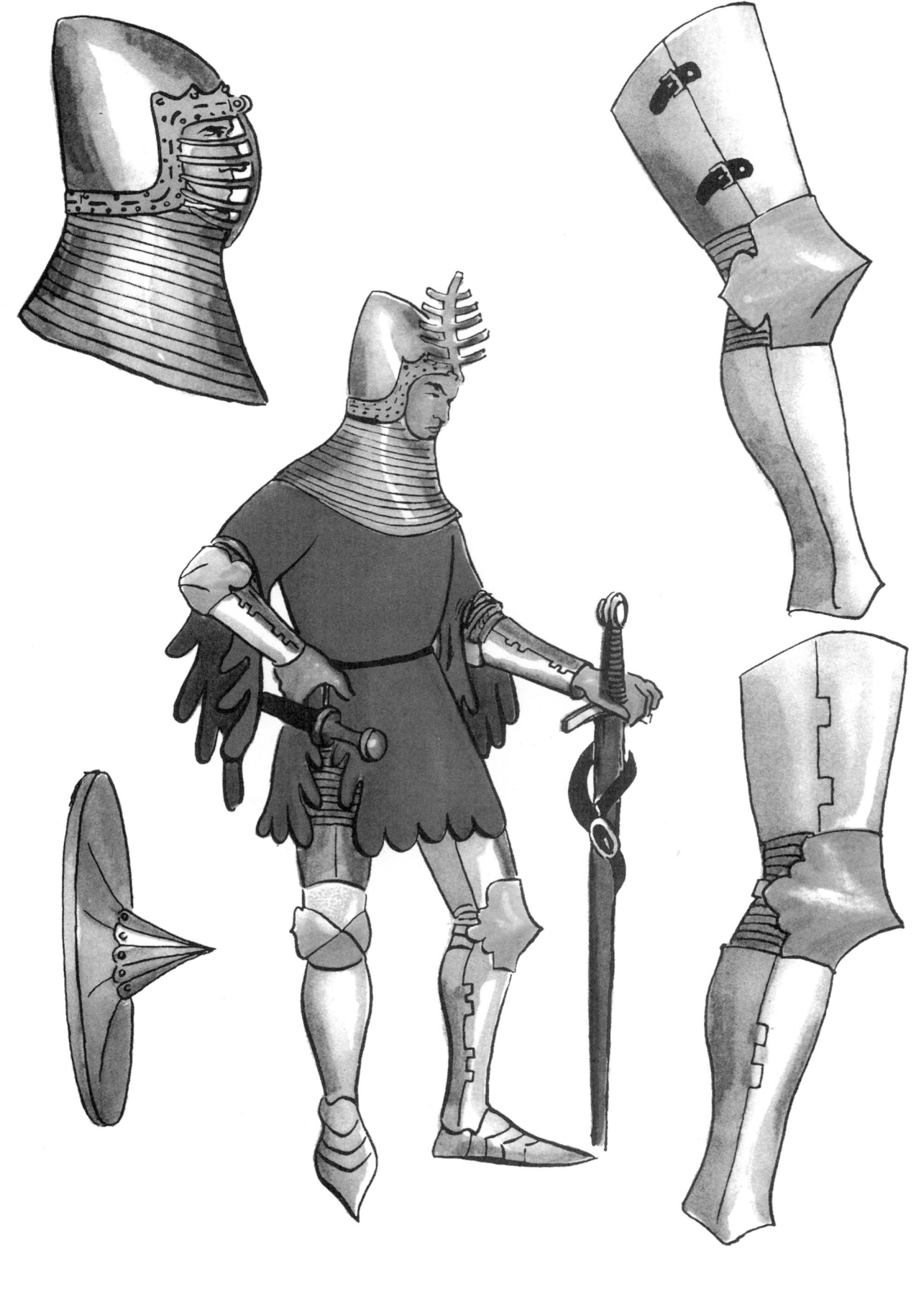

Man at arms about 1380. From the picture of the Resurrection, by the Master of the Třeboň altar-
piece (Matějček, Pl. 96).

PLATE 4 PART II

St. Wenceslas, from the Mulhouse altar-piece 1385 (Matějček Pl. 87).

PLATE 5

PART II

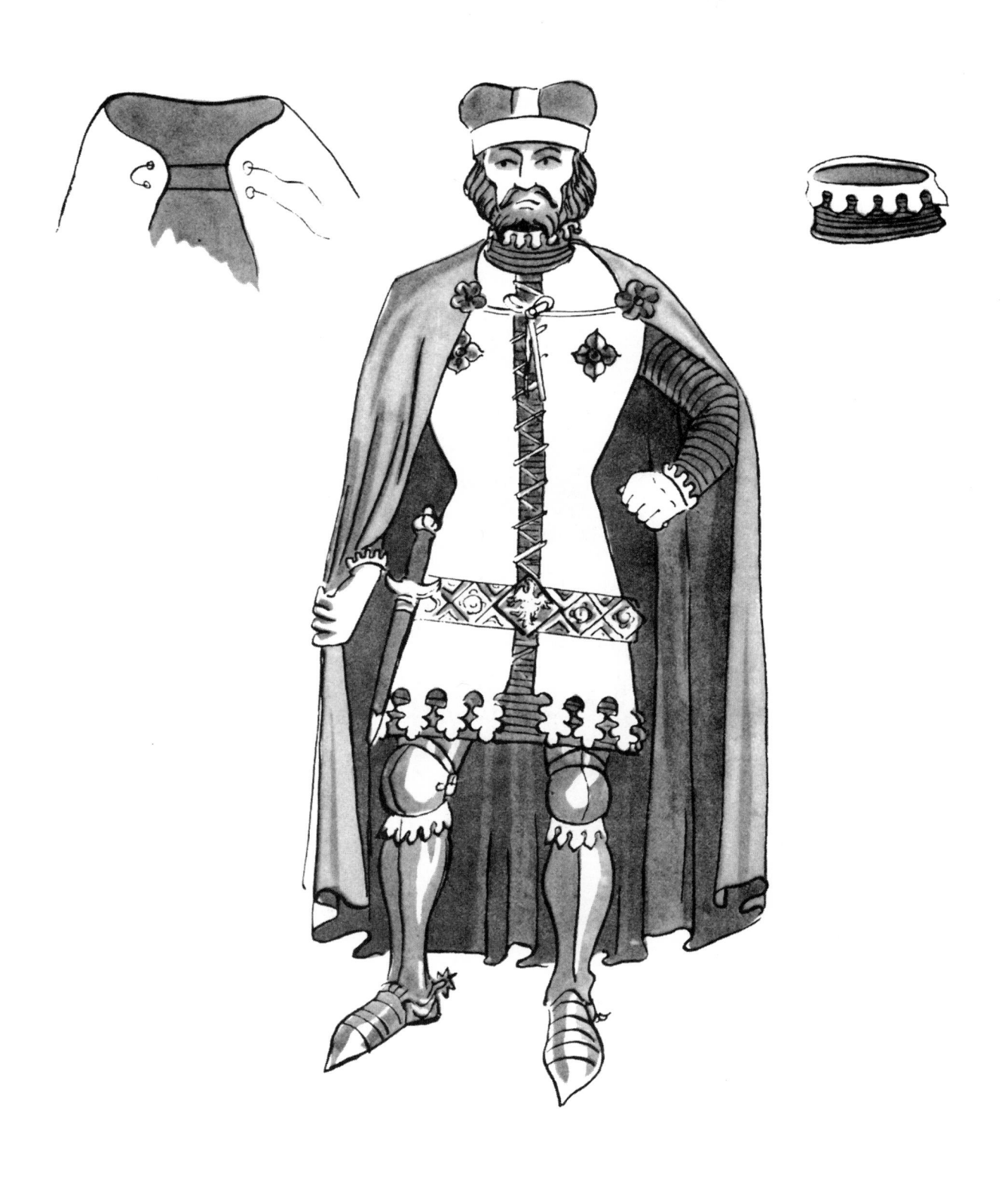

A knight's armour, from the second half of the 14th century (Statue of St. Wenceslas in St. Vitus's Cathedral, Prague). Detail: the fastening of the cloak, and the collar of his mail shirt.

PLATE 6

① ② ③

Archers from illuminations in the King Wenceslas Bible (Photographic reproductions in the State Documentary Centre, Prague). (1) An archer accompanying a prince. (2) A mounted archer. (3) A crossbowman.

PLATE 7　　　　　　　　　　　　　　　　　　PART II

Soldiers as depicted in illuminations in the King Wenceslas Bible.

Armour from the illuminations in the King Wenceslas Bible. (1) A soldier in quilted tunic or gambeson, wearing a breast-plate. (2) The left arm protected by plate. (3) Tilting helm. (4) A doublet with quilted skirt. (5) Lower part of a quilted tunic or gambeson. (6) A sword.

PLATE 9

Costumes from illuminations in the King Wenceslas Bible. (1–2) Town dress. (3–5) Peasant costumes. (6) A pouch and belt. (7) A buskin, with detail of its fastening.

PLATE 10

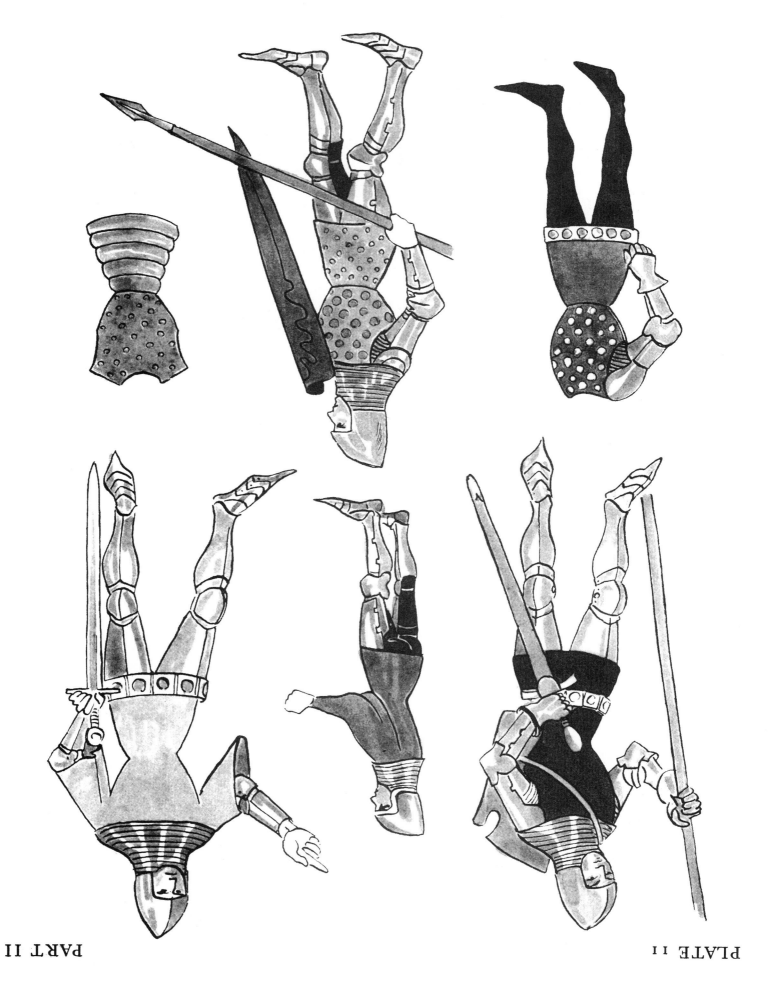

PLATE 11

PLATE 12

Armour of knights-at-arms, from illuminations in the King Wenceslas Bible.

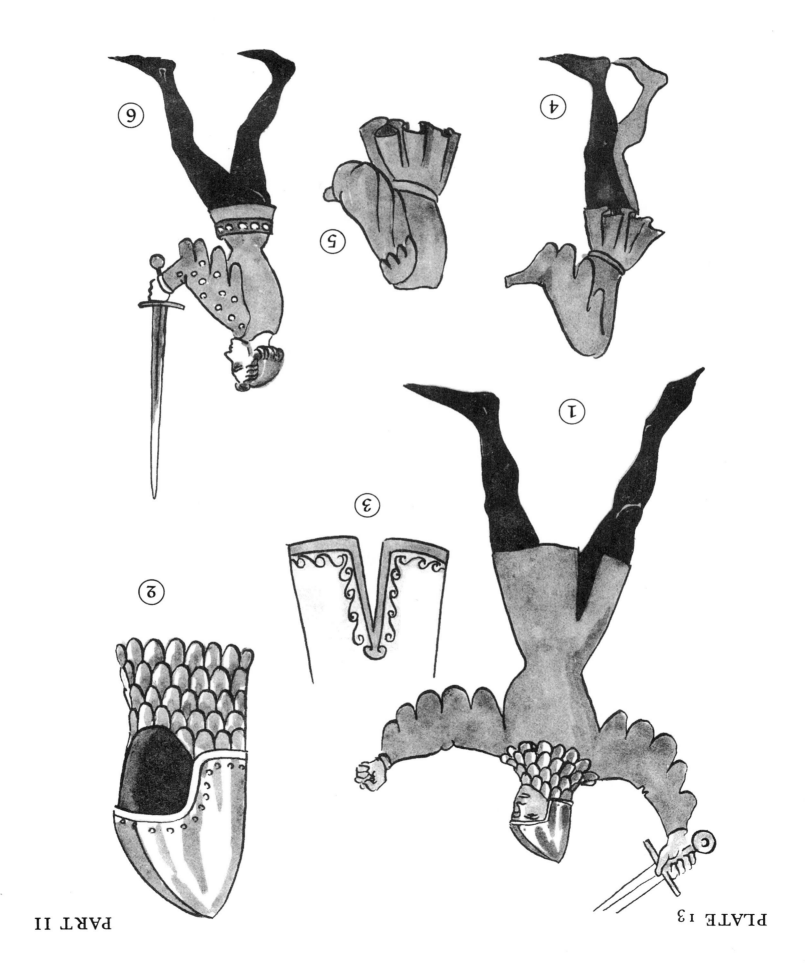

From the illuminations in the King Wenceslas Bible. (1) A soldier with a helmet and camail, a scale ventail. (2) An enlargement of the helmet from the preceding picture. (3) The side slit to the tunic. (4) An everyday civilian costume. (5) A doublet with dagged epaulet. (6) A man in doublet, carrying a sword.

PLATE 13

PLATE 14

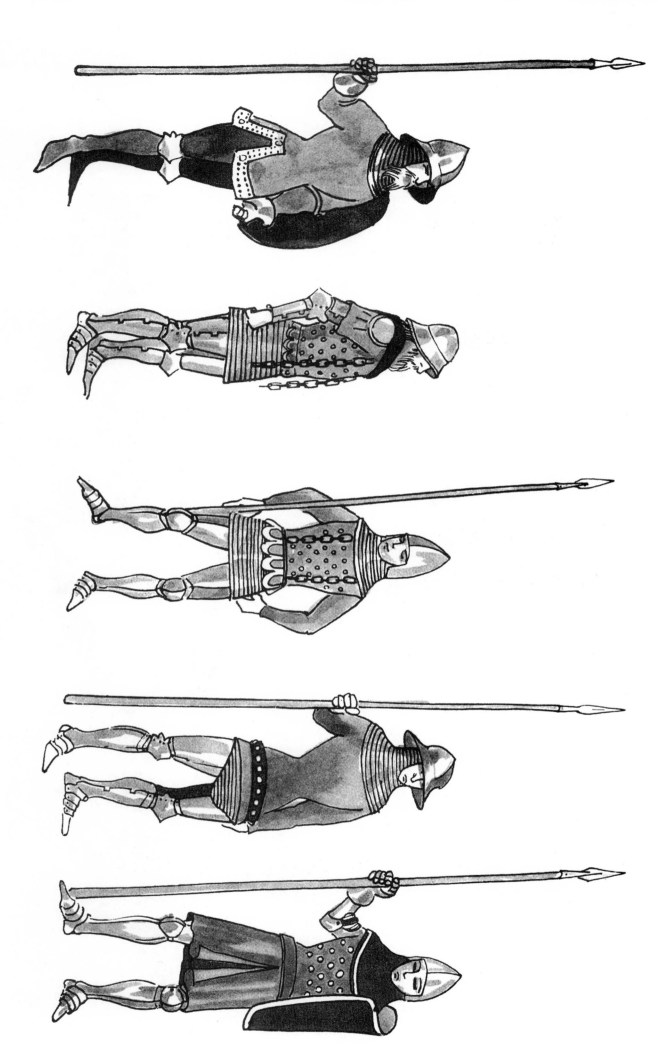

Squires from illuminations in the King Wenceslas Bible. The second and third squires are probably wearing the coat of plates, a canvas garment lined with metal plates, which is fitted with two short chains for catching the blows of the enemies' sword-cuts.

PLATE 15

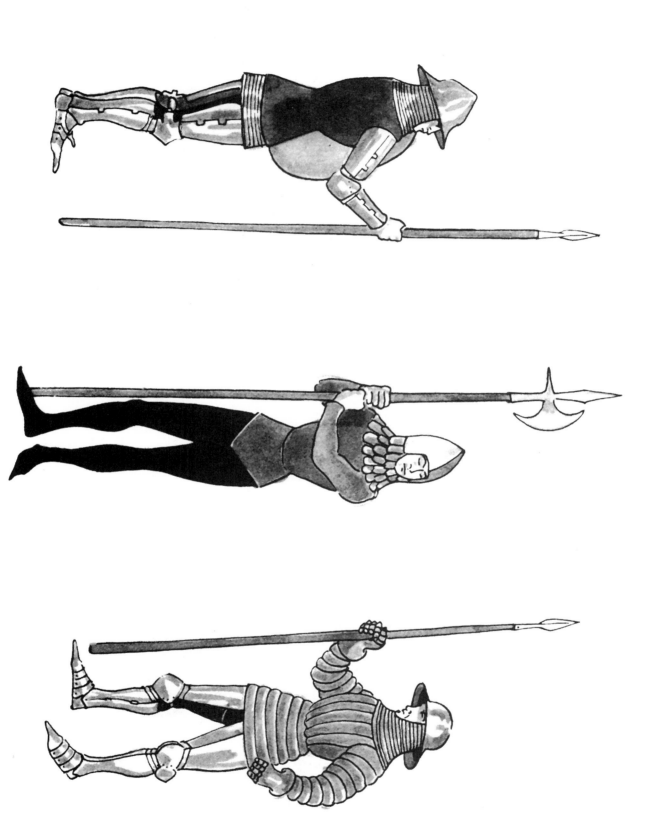

Soldiers from illuminations in the King Wenceslas Bible. The one on the right is wearing a gambeson.

PLATE 16   PART II

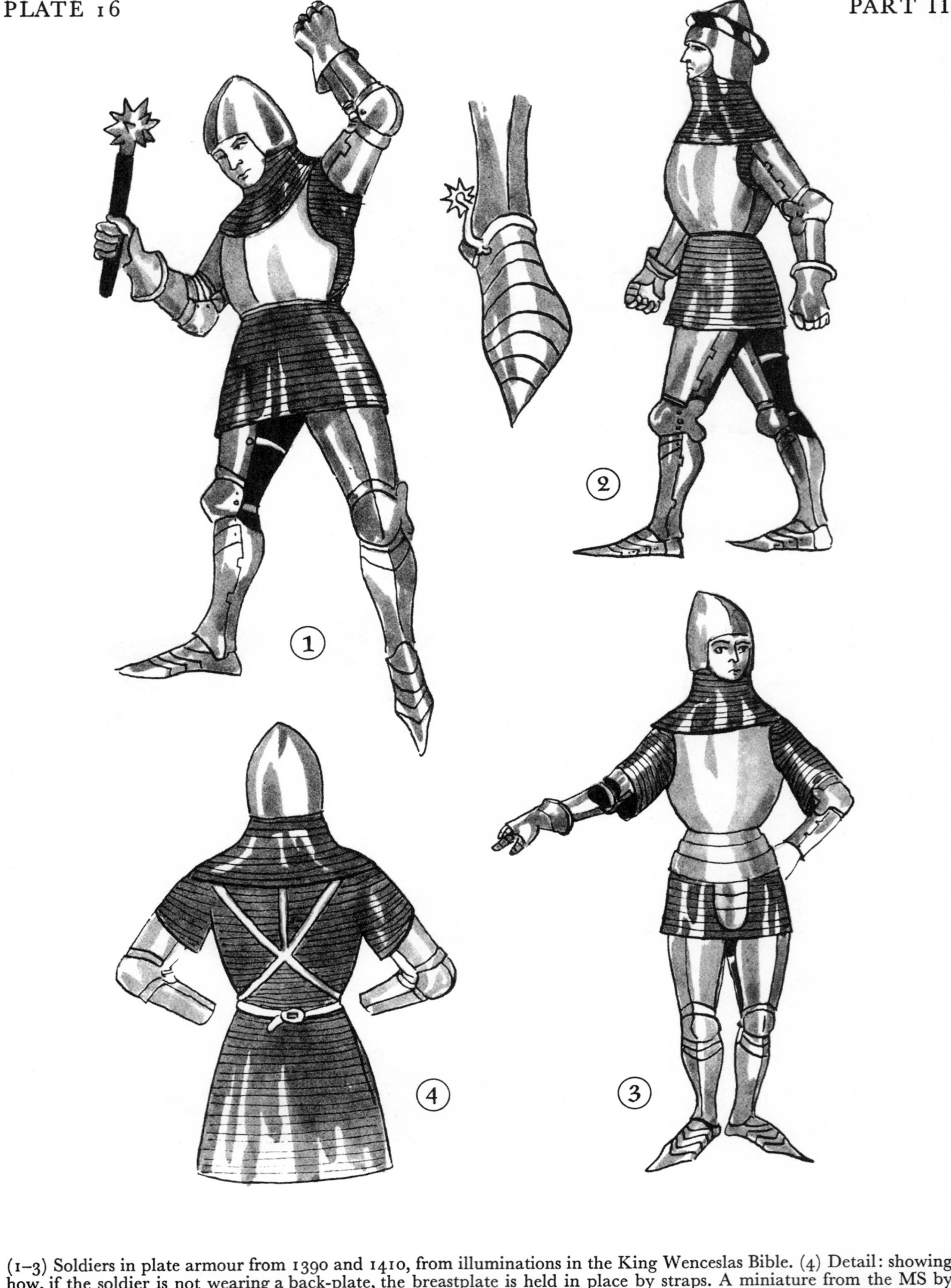

(1–3) Soldiers in plate armour from 1390 and 1410, from illuminations in the King Wenceslas Bible. (4) Detail: showing how, if the soldier is not wearing a back-plate, the breastplate is held in place by straps. A miniature from the MS by R. von Hohenems, dated 1385, reproduced in Kosina, *Světové dějiny*, II, p. 477. Above: a detail of a left foot in armour, with spur.

PLATE 17   PART II

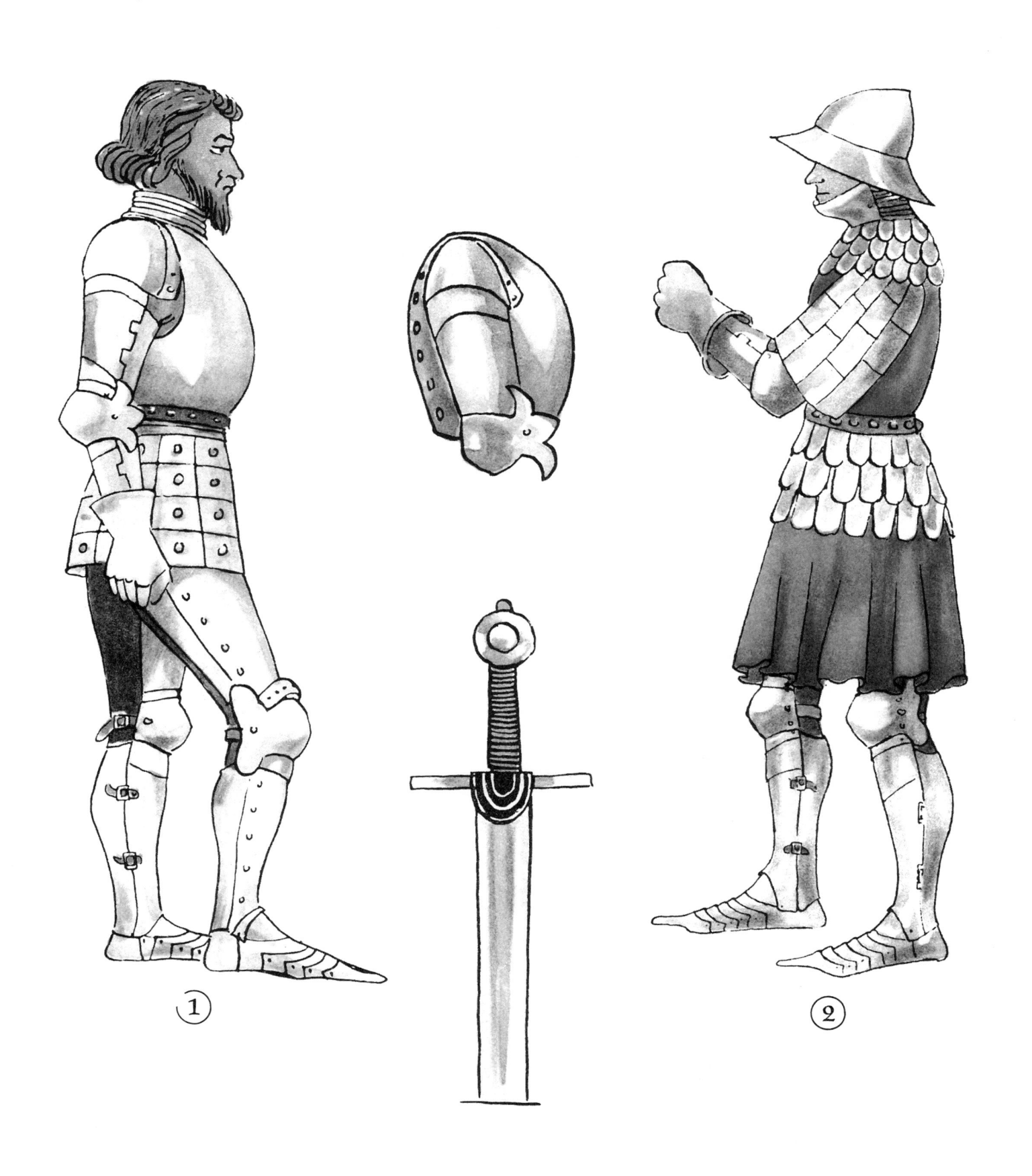

(1) The figure of Goliath, attired as a knight in complete suit of plate armour, dating from the early 15th century. (Krumlov MS, fol. 31.) (2) A soldier of the early 15th century, fol. 38, "Melchisedech offers Bread and Wine".

PLATE 18

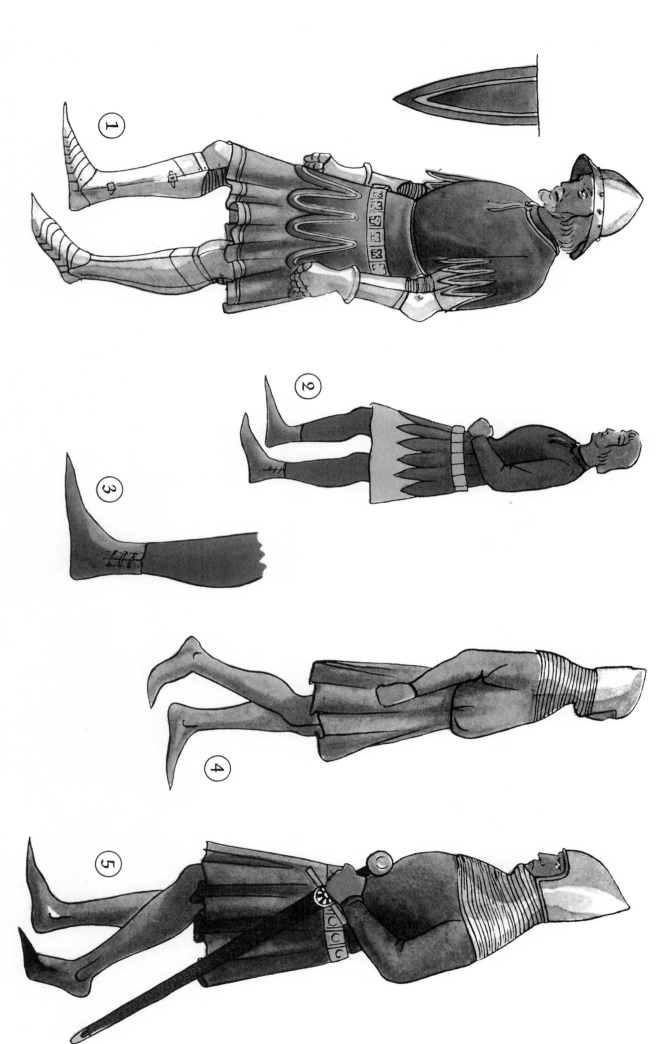

From the Krumlov MS, early 15th century. (1) A soldier from "Christ betrayed by Judas", fol. 42. (2) A figure from "The Scourging of Christ", fol. 46 [with (3)]. (3) Detail: buskin lacing on the outer side. (4) A soldier, fol. 39. (5) The soldier leading Christ before Pilate, fol. 100.

PLATE 19   PART II

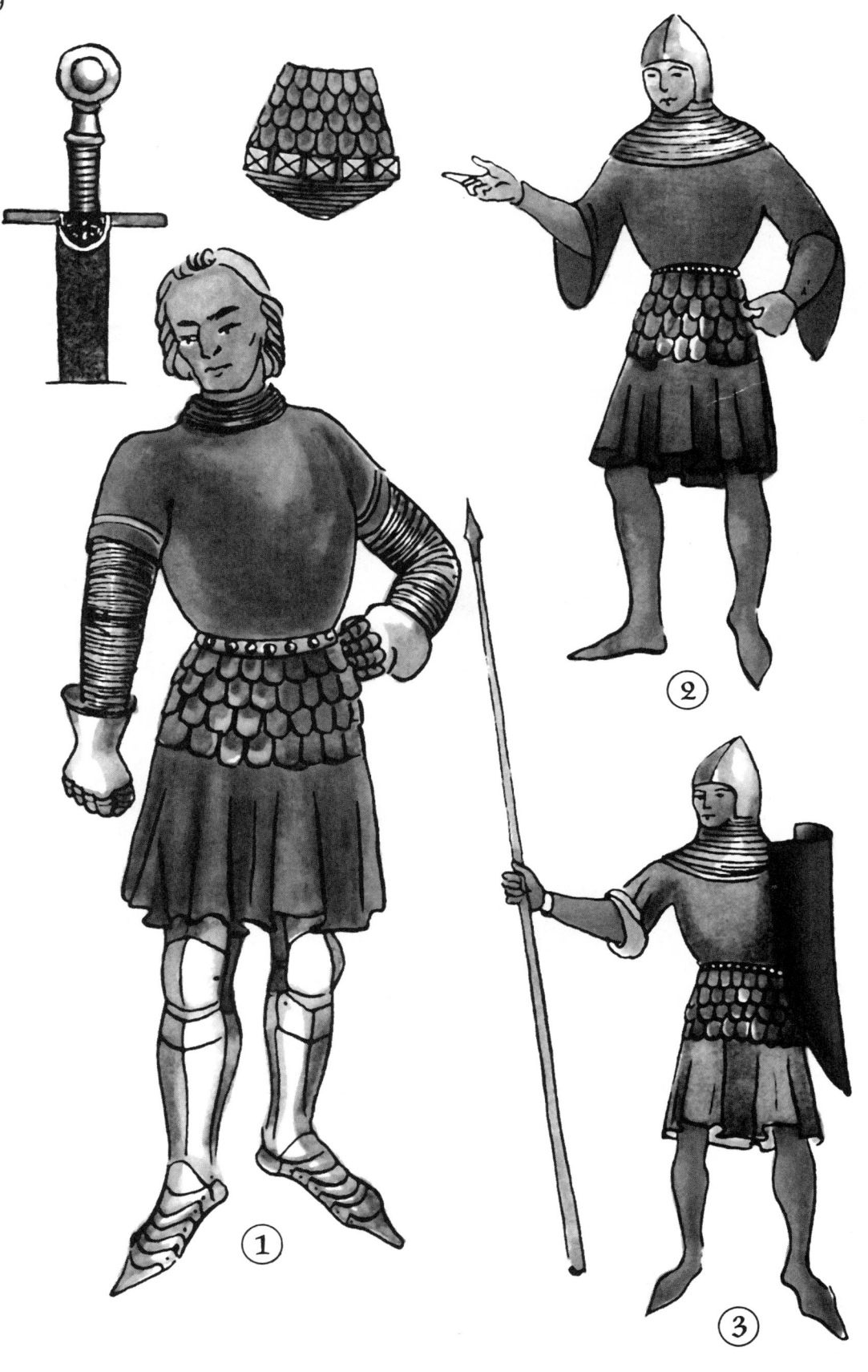

From the Krumlov MS, early 15th century. (1) A nobleman (Sisera), wearing a scale shirt, fol. 67. (2–3) Figures from the illumination, "The Slaying of Absalom", fol. 58. Above: detail of a sword hilt, and the scale shirt and knight's belt over a chain-mail shirt.

PLATE 20

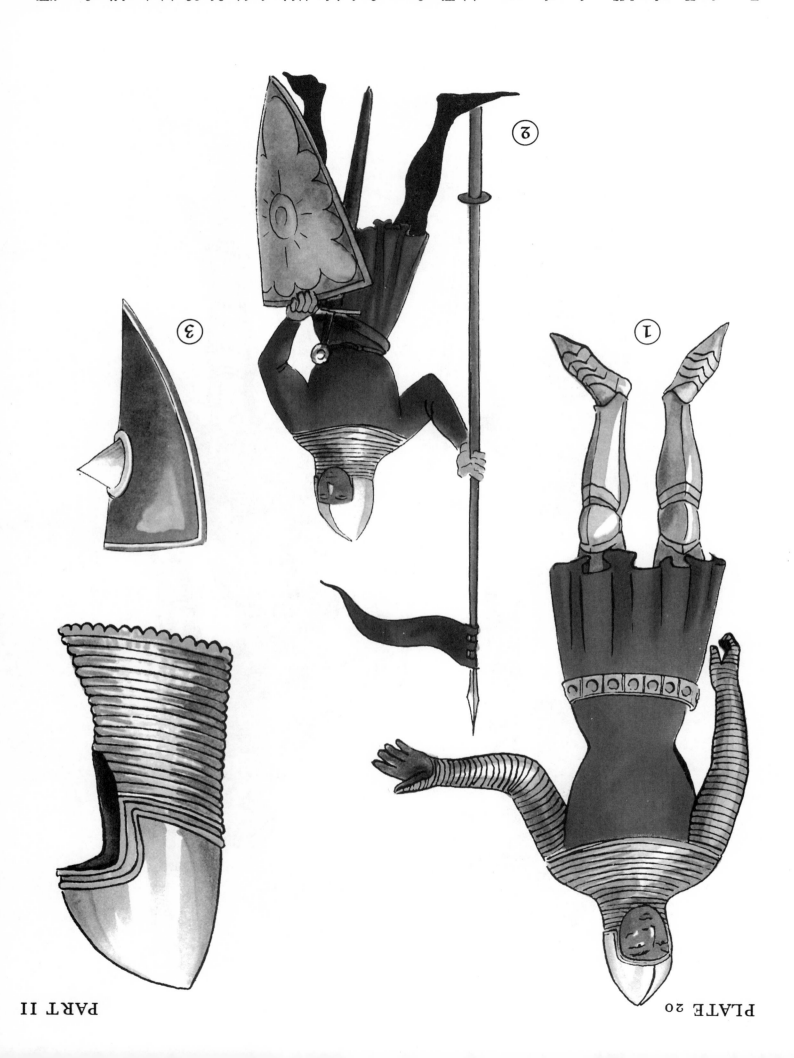

From the Krumlov MS, early 15th century. (1) The figure of a knight (Abimelech), fol. 86. (2) A soldier from "The Slaying of King Godrus", fol. 56. (3) A shield, fol. 15.

PLATE 21   PART II

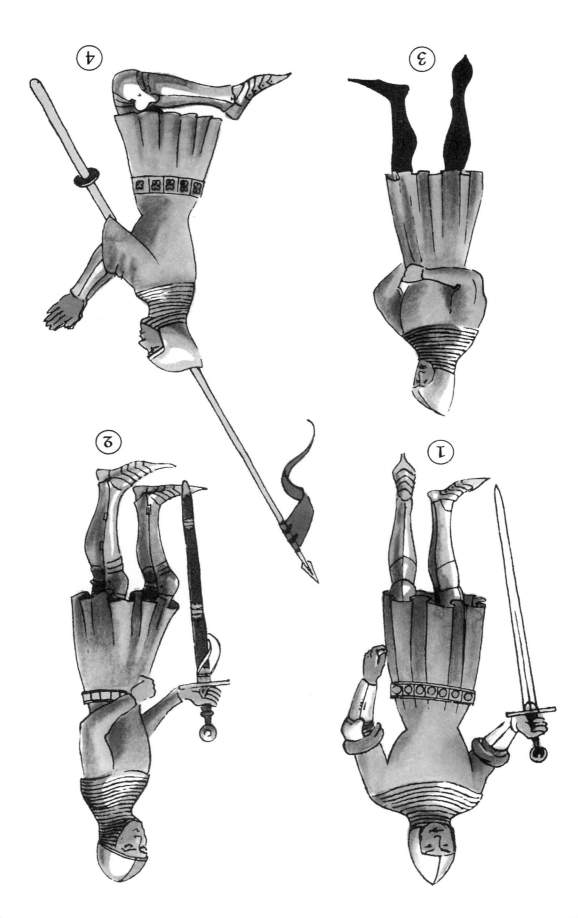

PLATE 22

PART II

From the Krumlov MS, early 15th century. The figure of Eleazar with an awl-pike. "Eleazar confounded the Elephant."
Above: a trumpeter, fol. 56.

PLATE 23

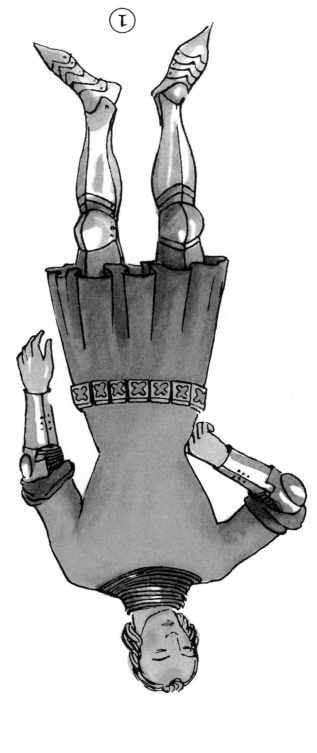

(1) Absalom from the Krumlov MS, fol. 58. (2) Heliodor, *ibid*, fol. 36.

PLATE 24

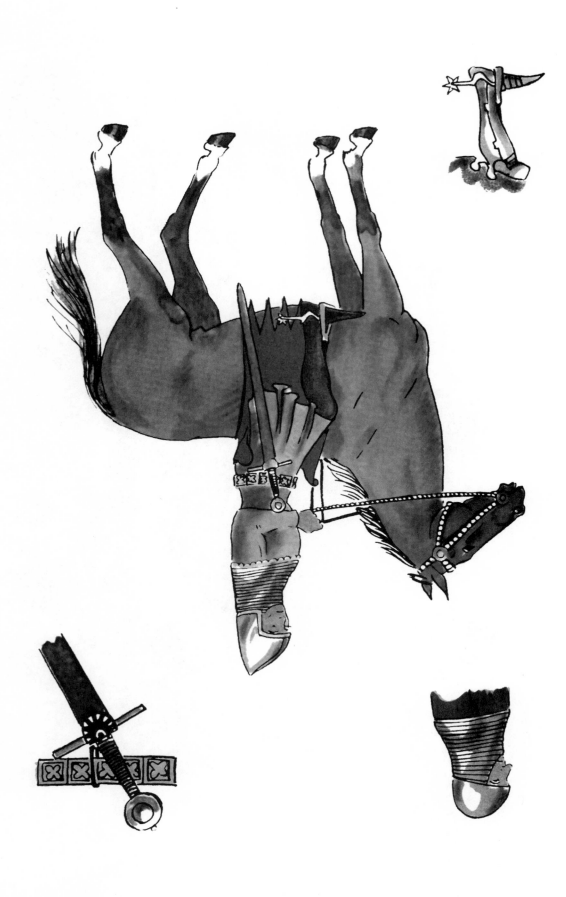

From the Krumlov MS, early 15th century. A mounted soldier, possibly Joab. Details: the head of one of his followers, the girding of the sword, the leg armour.

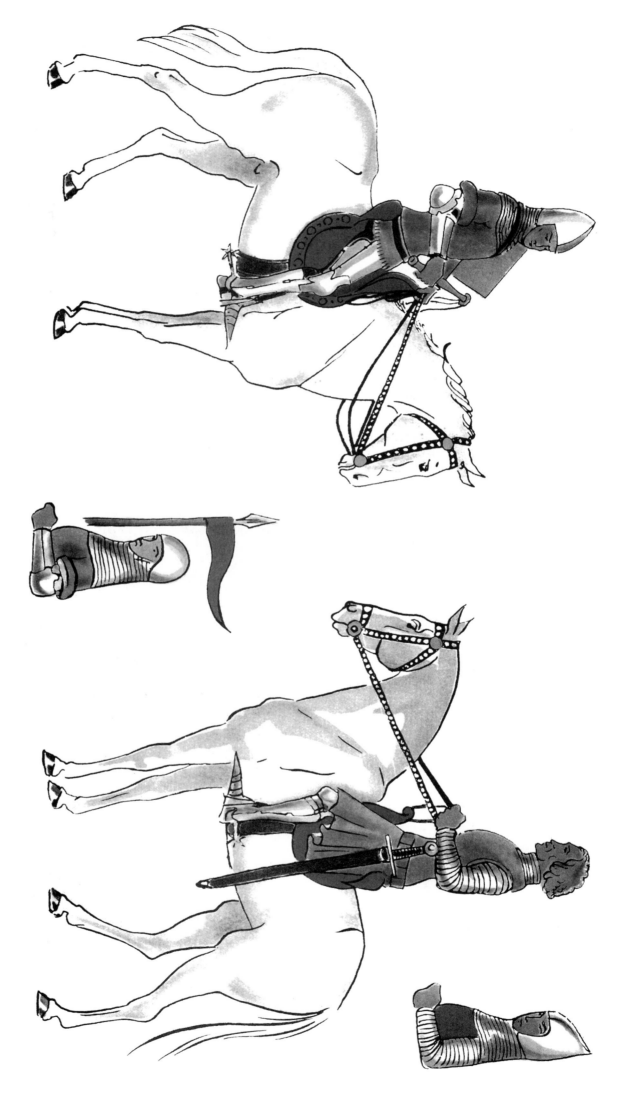

PLATE 25

From the Krumlov MS, early 15th century. (1) A rider in fol. 36. Heliodor being whipped by one of God's Messengers. (2) A knight (Tharbis) and his followers, fol. 86.

From the Krumlov MS, early 15th century. The figure of King David and his armour bearer, fol. 83.

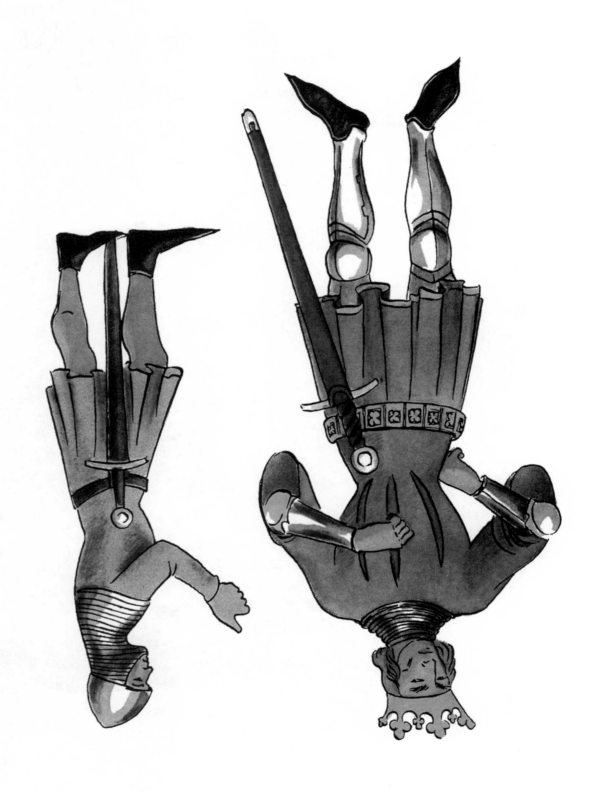

PLATE 26

PLATE 27

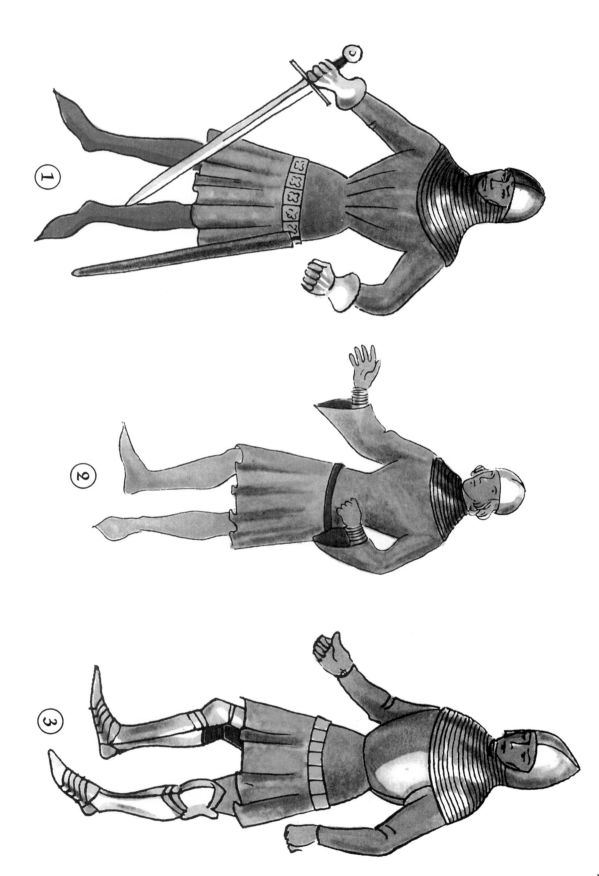

Squires as depicted in the illuminations of the Krumlov MS. (1) Fol. 86. (2) Fol. 51. (3) Fol. 95. (An Egyptian soldier wearing a breastplate and possibly also a back-plate.)

A soldier and a hand-gunner from the Kyeser Bellifortis MS, dating from the year 1405.

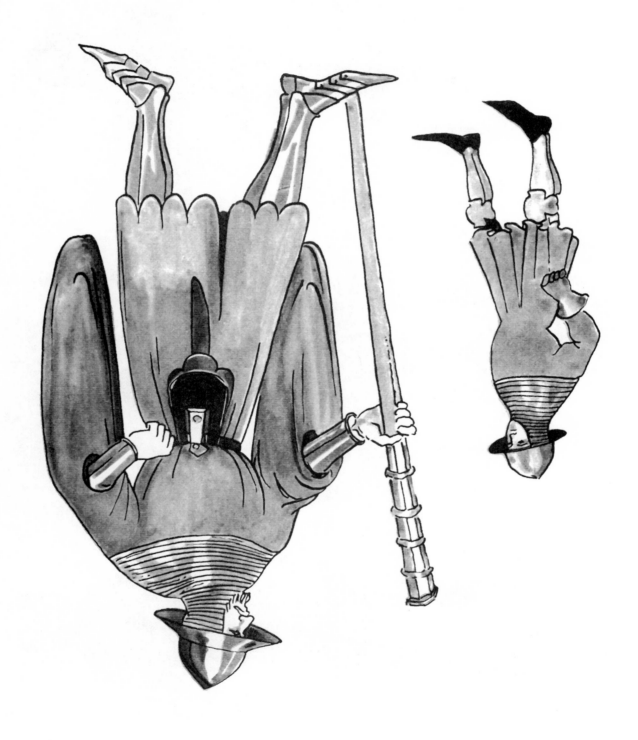

PLATE 28

PLATE 29

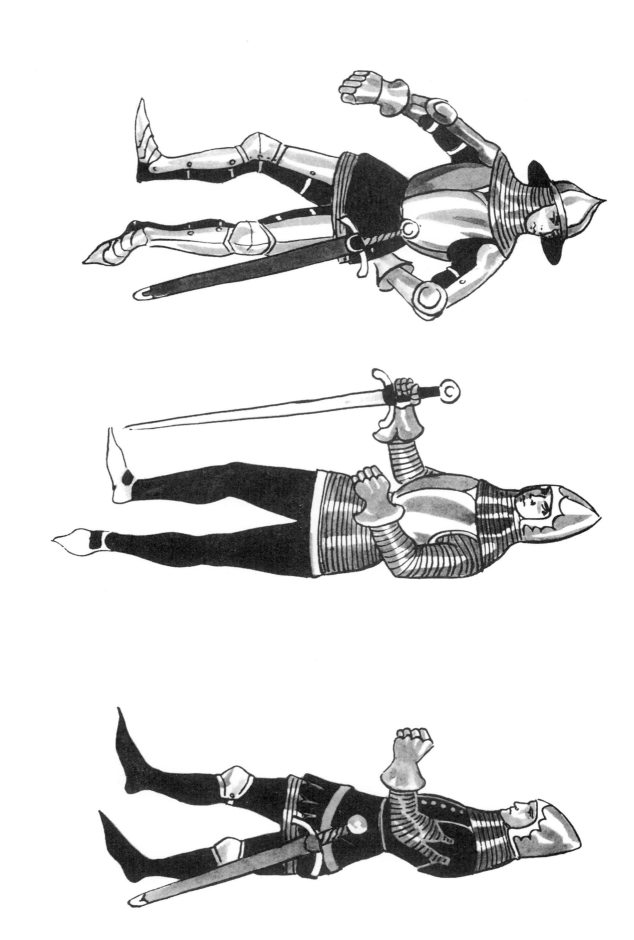

Soldiers dating from 1405, from the picture of the drunken soldiers being attacked by peasants in the Bellifortis MS.

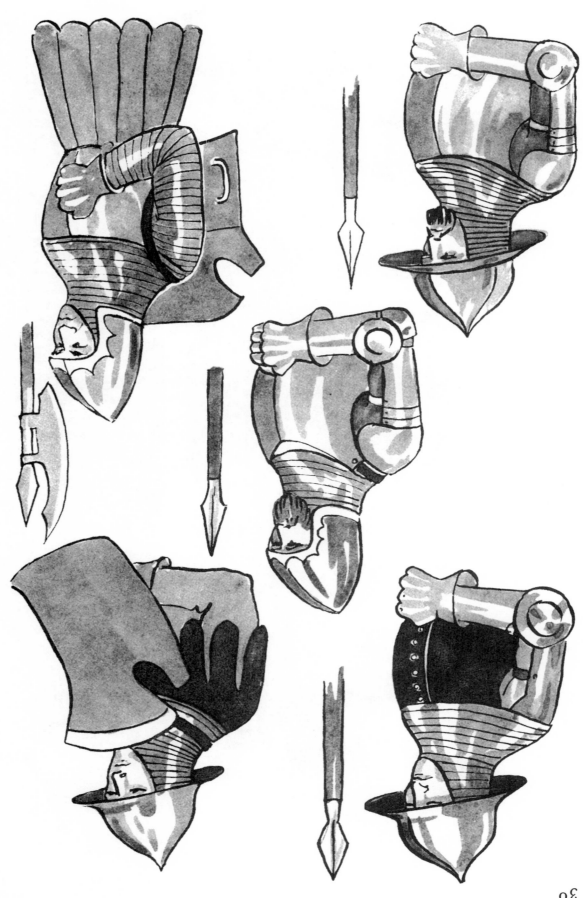

PLATE 30

Soldiers of 1405, from the Bellifortis MS. Picture of a stone-filled wagon being pushed down on attackers in a ravine.

PLATE 31   PART II

A heavily-armed knight, dating from 1405, in long coat of mail, reaching below the knees, wearing a breastplate and a crested jousting helmet or heaume with lambrequin. Bellifortis MS, fol. 128.

PLATE 32   PART II

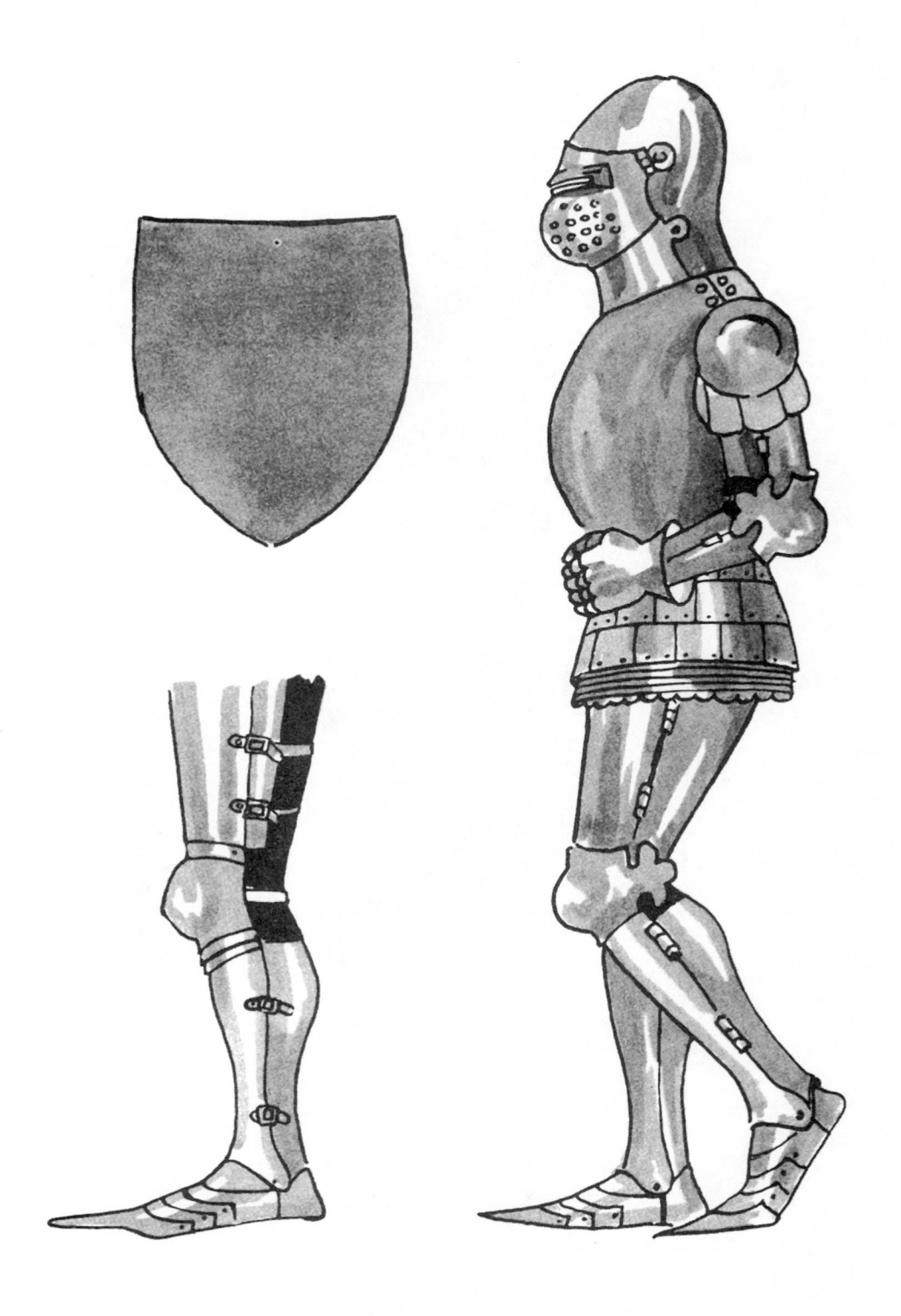

A knight in full suit of plate armour, wearing a vizored helmet, dating from 1405; from the picture of knights jousting, in the Bellifortis MS.

PLATE 33   PART II

Figures depicted in *Libri XX de anatomia*, dating from 1404. (1) Youth with a banner, fol. 53. (2) A man in half armour,
i. e. only the upper part of his body is protected by plate armour, fol. 51. (3) A helmet and shield, fol. 125.

PLATE 34

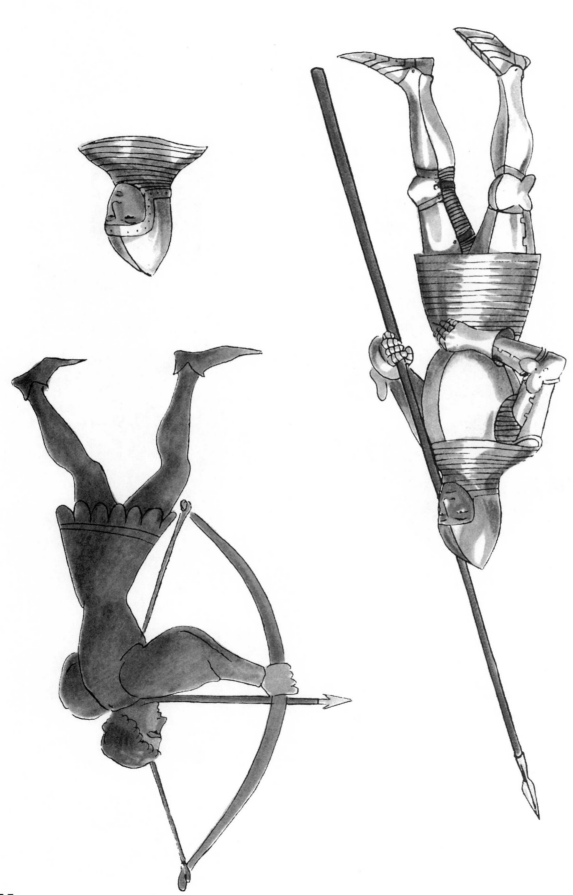

A warrior of 1404, in full suit of armour, from *Libri XX de anatomia*, fol. 101. An archer, *ibid*, fol. 130.

PLATE 35

PART II

The figure of Saul and his armour bearer, from the Latin Bible, fol. 104.

PLATE 36   PART II

(1) A squire as depicted in the painting of the Crucifixion in the Rajhrad altar-piece, dating from prior to 1420. (2) A soldier, in the Rajhrad altar-piece painting "Carrying the Cross" (Matějček, pl. 181–6).

PLATE 37 PART II

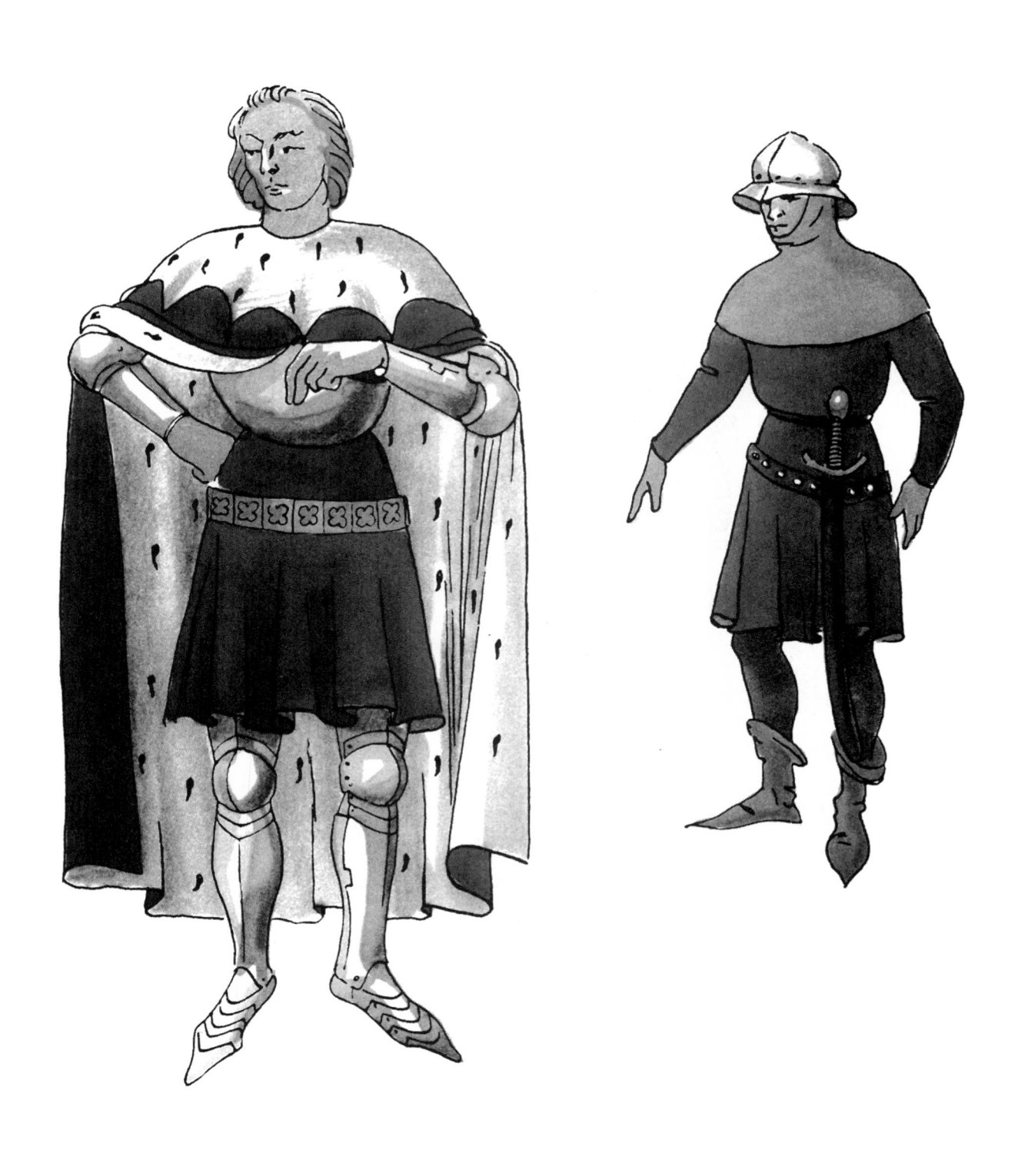

A captain and a soldier, of the first third of the 15th century (the Skalice Crucifixion, Matějček, pl. 239).

PLATE 38   PART II

A mercenary soldier, parts of his armour and details of the belt, dating from about 1420, from the Rajhrad altar-piece painting of the Resurrection (Matějček, pl. 190). He is wearing parts of his ordinary civilian dress.

PLATE 39   PART II

(1) A knight in full suit of plate armour, dating from about 1430, from a MS in Prague University Library, ref. no. XVII-A-34. (2) The figure of a knight in full plate armour from the tomb of Jindřich of Stráž, who died in 1466 (Zíbrt and Winter II, p. 250, pl. 144).

PLATE 40

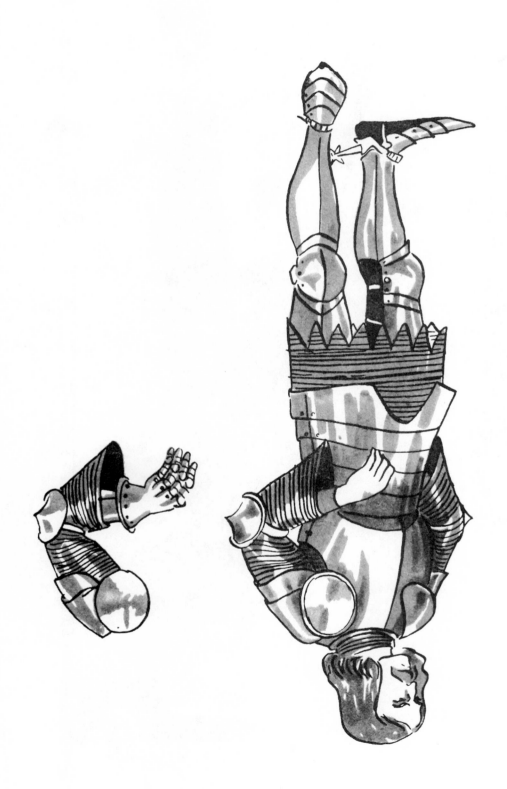

A figure from the tomb of a Polish knight, dating from the mid-15th century. (*Zeitschrift für historische Waffenkunde*).

PLATE 41

Crossbowman carrying his pavise on his back, also various details of his equipment: the pavise, pole-arm, banner, helmet and aventail, breastplate over the tunic. From the MS in Prague University Library, ref. no. XVII-A-34, p. 115a.

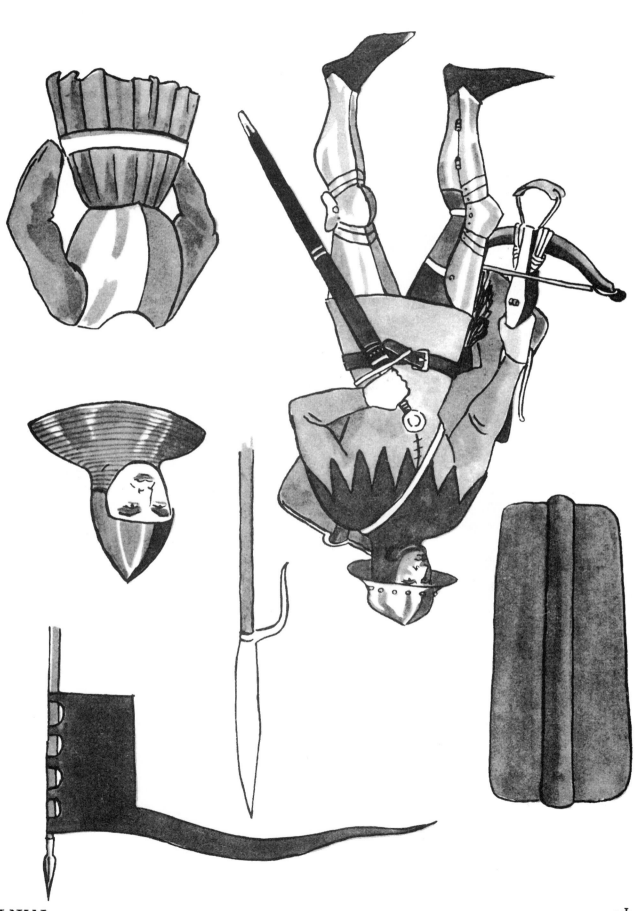

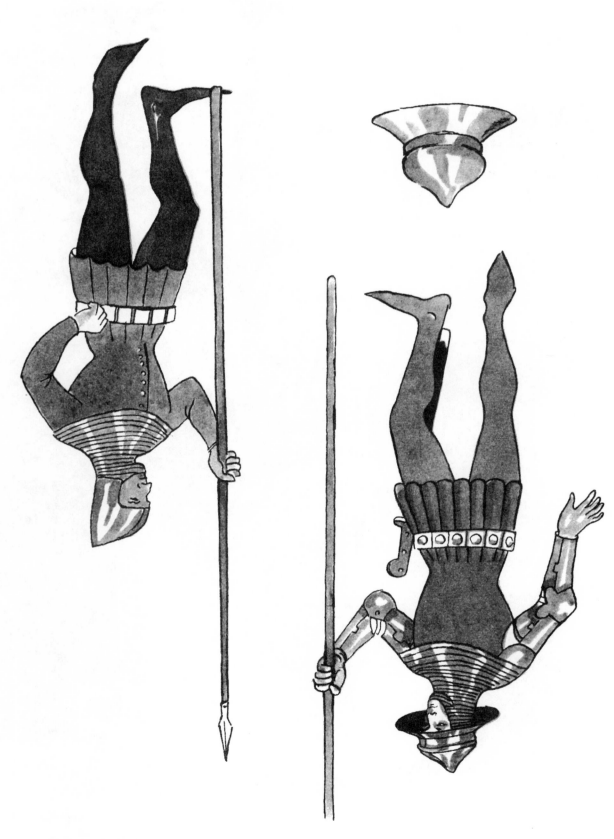

PLATE 42

PLATE 43   PART II

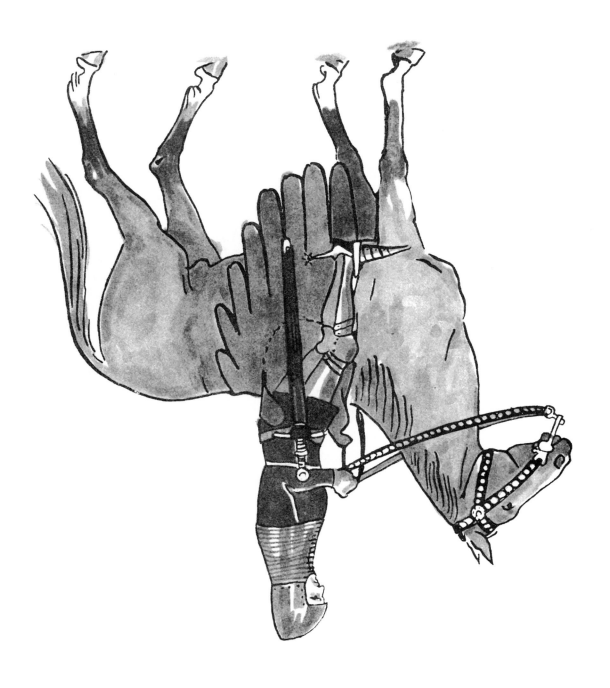

A mounted soldier, from an illumination to the Padeřov Bible, dating from 1433–5. In contrast to other small Gothic paintings, the horse is here painted with a curb instead of a snaffel bit.

PLATE 44

PART II

Jan Žižka's costume. In the Jena Codex Jan Žižka is shown in the following manner at the head of the army: he is beardless, wears a loose grey tunic, a blue hood, over it a flat grey cap; he also has black high boots with spurs, and a white bandage over his eyes. He sits in a red saddle on a white horse, with a red bridle and red rein. Otherwise the horse has no other trappings. In his hand he holds the kind of gold mace which one could assume to be a "dagger-mace" (a fist holding a dagger). The same source depicts Žižka in Heaven, dressed in a blue tunic with a red cloak, with red (fox) fur collar. He has a bandage over his eyes and wears a green cap with a fox fur brim, slit at the front. The head of Žižka depicted in the small Jistebnice hymnal is covered by a mail hood, over which he wears a cap. In his left hand he carries a banner and in the right a mace, which again resembles a hand holding a dagger. The Tábor head of Žižka has a flat cap of uncertain colour, with a fur brim. Over his left eye he has a square protecting pad. All the

PLATE 45

PART II

Hussite soldier from the Jena Codex showing the colour of his hood and tunic.

three heads are bearded, the Tábor one is obviously barbered, the upper part of the chin beneath the lips being bare. A chronicle describes Žižka's battle dress very well in the following extract: "The people of Hradec decided to have Žižka painted on their banner, riding a white horse, in knightly array, with a mace as his weapon, just as he rode when he was alive."

(1) A method of lacing a squire's surcoat at the side under the armpit, dating from between 1350–5 (*Zeitschrift für historische Waffenkunde*, 1940–1942, p. 143, pl. 1). (2) The knight on the tomb of Johann III of Rappolstein, after 1361 (*ibid.*, p. 144, fig. 3). The knight wears his armorial bearings on a small escutcheon on the camail of his helmet and his complete coat-of-arms (in this case three shields) on his gambeson. Detail of the leg-plate fastening.

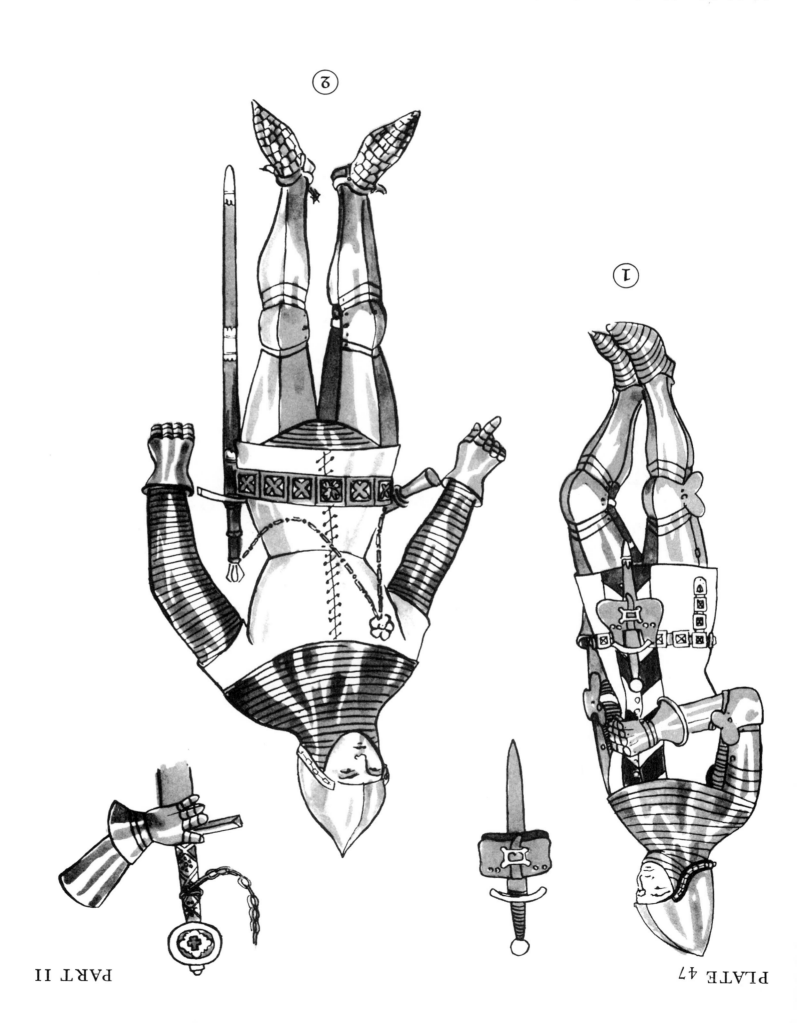

PLATE 47

PART II

(1) A knight with a dagger and pouch attached to his belt (Boeheim, p. 295, pl. 335; the pouch and dagger, Demmin, 762 E). (2) A knight with his tunic laced down the front (Otto von Pienzenau, died 1371; *Deutsches Leben*, p. 338, pl. 528). Detail: a sword hilt with chain fastening, according to a painting by Tommaso da Modena, who worked in Bohemia in 1357.

PLATE 48

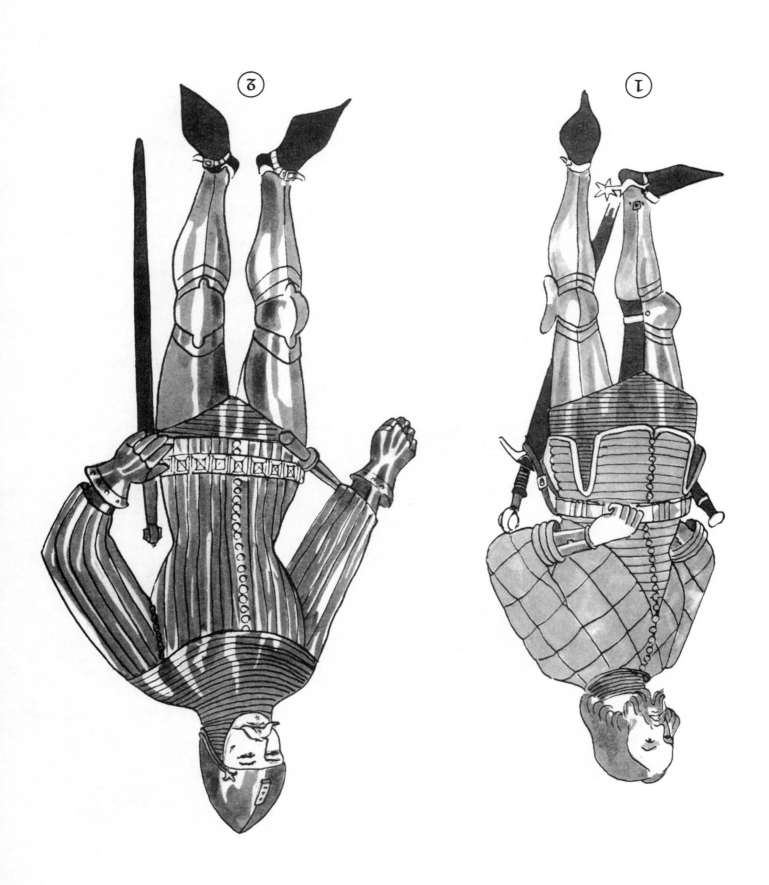

(1) The figure of a knight in a gambeson, from the tomb of Theodorick of Wirzleben, who died 1376 (*Zeitschrift für historische Waffenkunde*, 1935, p. 179, pl. 4, and 1940/1942, p. 238, pl. 7). (2) A knight in a gambeson, wearing a knightly girdle (figure of Peter Kreilinger, died 1365; *ibid.*, 1926/1928, II, p. 156; also Rosenberg, pl. 66).

PLATE 49 PART II

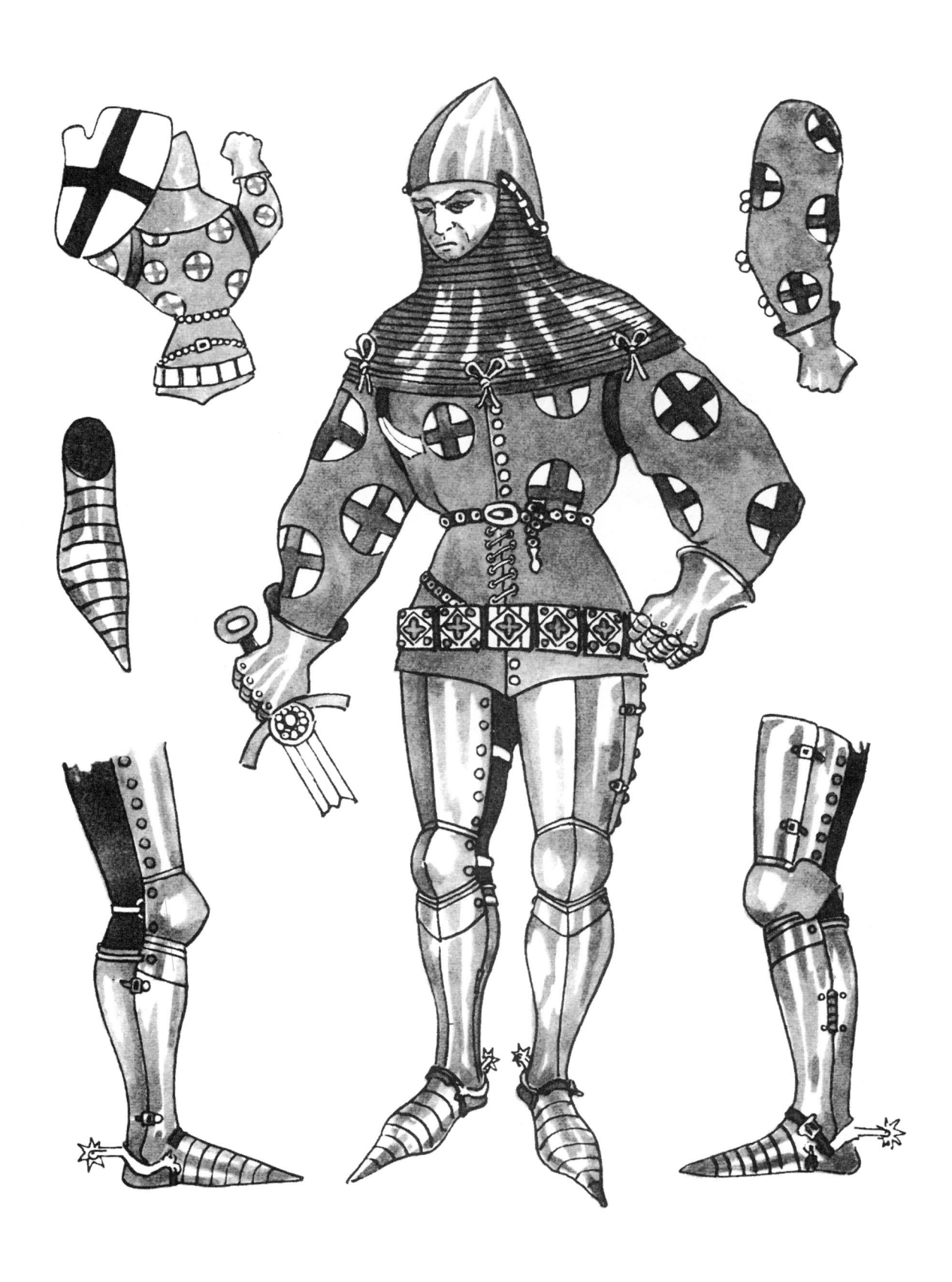

A knight from the Dijon "St. George" (*European Armour* II, p. 70, pl. 424A). The knight's aventail is tied down to the tunic.

PLATE 50

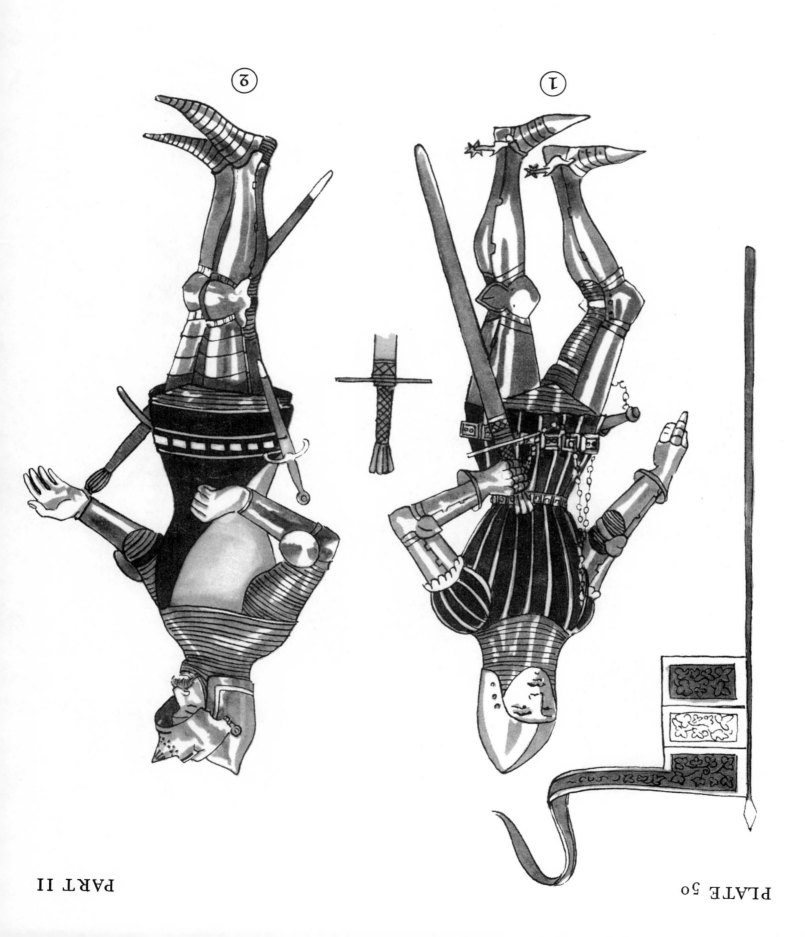

(1) Albert III, Duke of Austria, 1365–95 (*Kulturgeschichte des deutschen Volkes*, I, p. 261). (2) A knight of the 14th century (Lacroix, *L'armée française*, p. 216, pl. 137).

PLATE 51   PART II

(1) An example of heraldic bearings emblazoned on the tunic. Figure of the Black Prince from his tomb (Spamer,
Illustrierte Weltgeschichte, IV, p. 591, pl. 303). (2) A knight (St. George), 1420 (Tilke; also Rosenberg, pl. 68).

PLATE 52

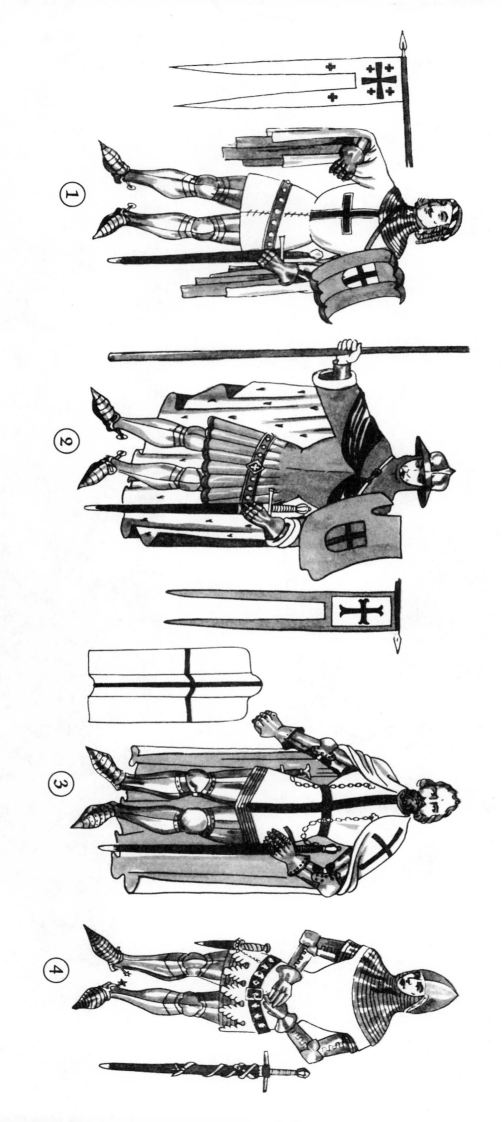

(1) A German knight of the early 15th century (*Zeitschrift für historische Waffenkunde*, IV, p. 119). (2) A German knight of one of the Orders: Kuno von Libensteyn, Commander of Strassburg, 1389–91 (*ibid.*, II, p. 101). (4) An Italian knight from the tomb of Giovanni di Lalata – died 1421 – Italy (*ibid.*, V, p. 161, pl. I).

(3) A German knight of the early 15th century (*ibid.*, IV, p. 120).

PLATE 53

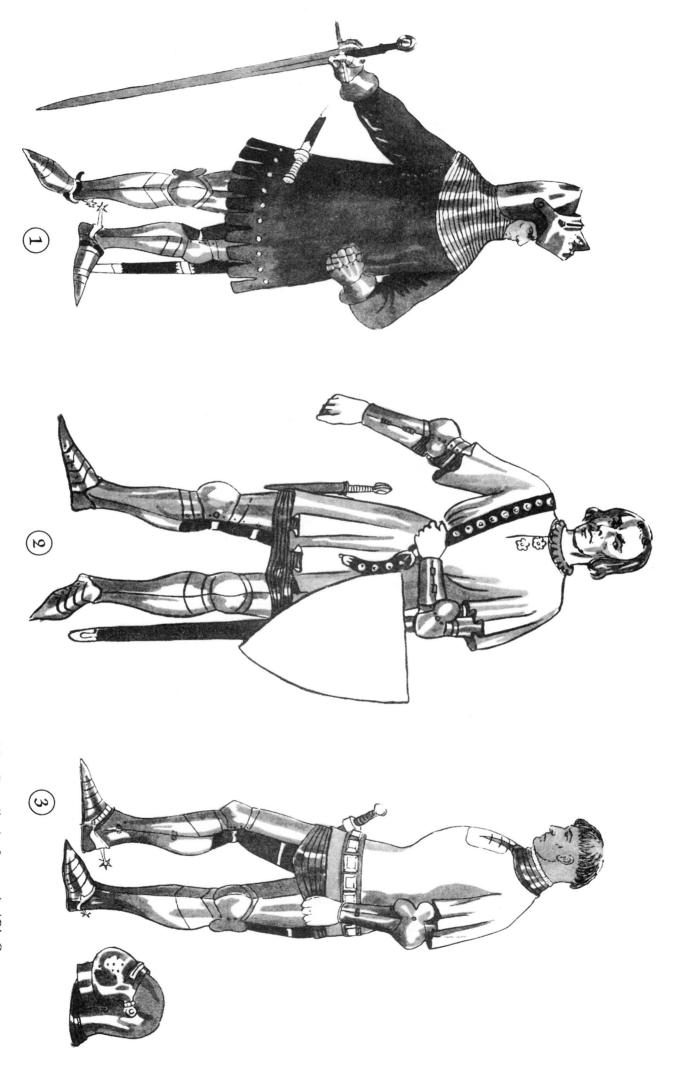

(1) French knight of the late 14th century (*European Armour*, II, p. 152). (2) The knight from the tomb of Du Guesclin (1360–1410). (*Die Geschichte der französischen Armee*, p. 83). (3) The knight from the tomb of Simon de Laval, died 1407 (*Zeitschrift für historische Waffenkunde*, IX, p. 20).

PLATE 54

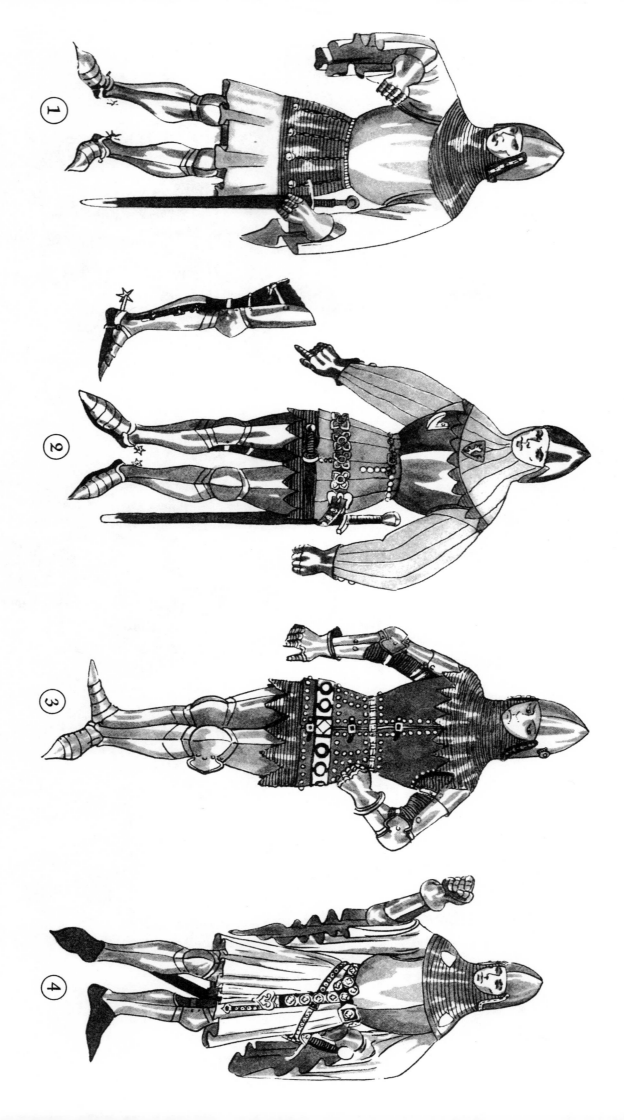

(1) A knight (Ludwig van Hutten, died 1414) from the second half of the 14th century, wearing a breast- and back-plate with mail shirt, and small bells dangling from his belt. (Demmin, p. 393; Alteneck.) (2) A knight wearing gambeson and breast-plate (Herr von Hohenklingen, died 1386 at Sempach). (*Zeitschrift für historische Waffenkunde*, VI, p. 191.) (3) A knight wearing a brigandine, dating from 14th–15th century (Stone, *A Glossary* etc, p. 26, pl. 1). (4) The knight on the tomb of Margrave Rudolph III, died 1428 (*Geschichte der deutschen Kunst*, p. 259, pl. 382). The knight wears a breastplate over his cloth tunic.

PLATE 55   PART II

①

②

(1) A French knight dating from 1405 (Tilke). Viollet le Duc dates this type from 1395. (2) A full suit of plate armour worn with a wide-sleeved tunic. The figure of St. George on Maréchal Boucicault's watch (1366–1421). (*Histoire de la marine française illustrée*, p. 25).

PLATE 56

PART II

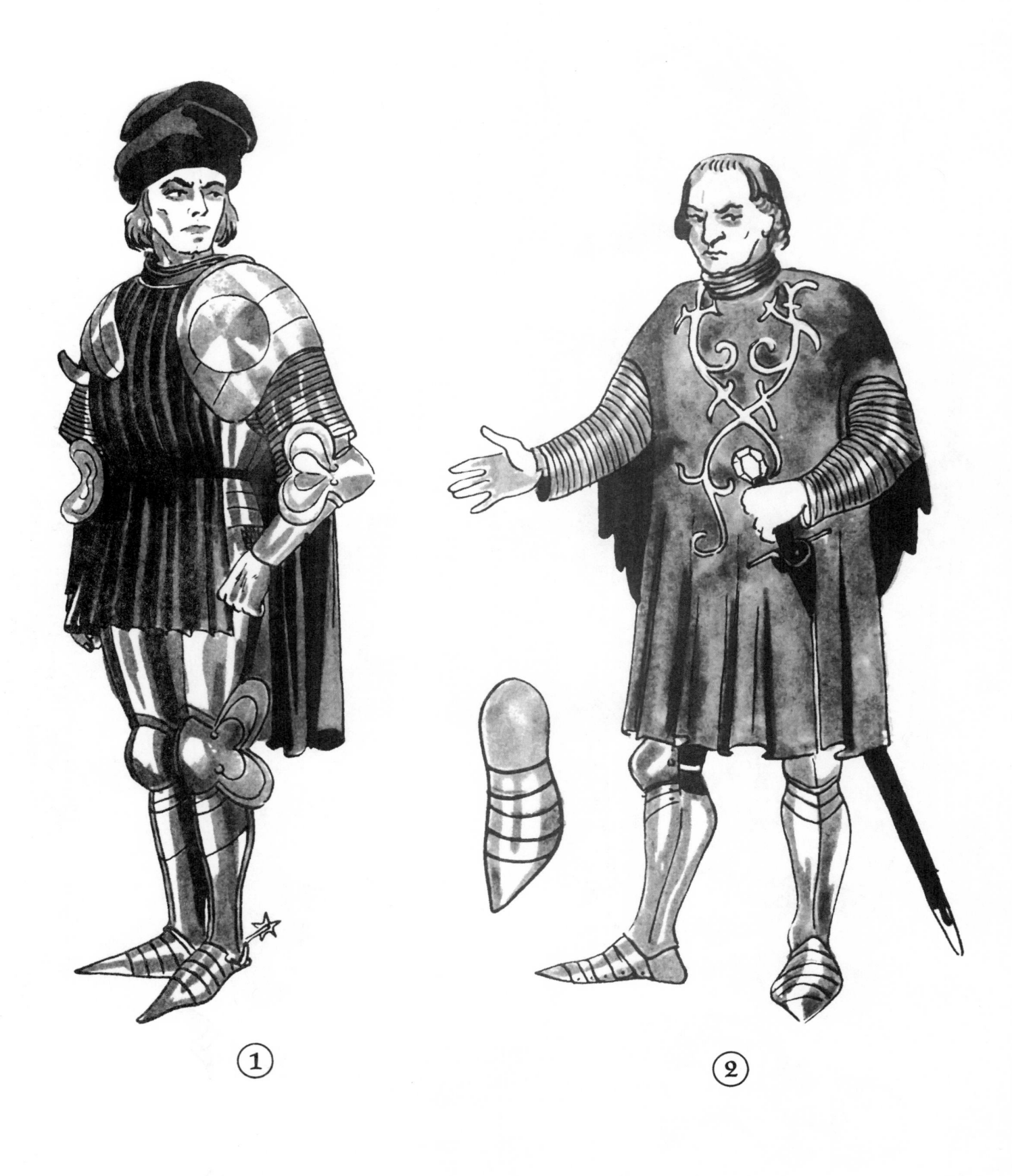

①

②

(1) Italian knight of the early 15th century: Farinata degli Ulberti (*European Armour*, p. 187, pl. 219). (2) The knight from the Basle altar-piece, after 1434 (*Geschichte der deutschen Kunst*, p. 299, pl. 441).

PLATE 57

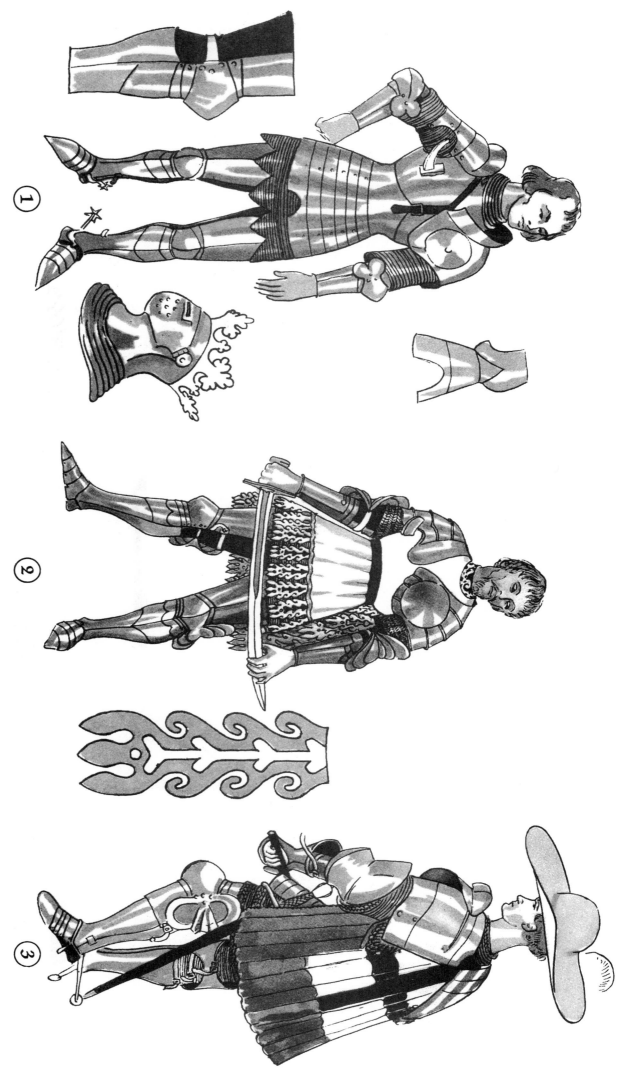

(1) King Henry V (1413–22), in full suit of armour (*European Armour*, p. 188, pl. 221). (2) Pippo Spano of Ozora, Sigismund's commander in the Hussite wars. He has fair hair, beard and eyebrows. Brown eyes. His sword is not curved but bent. From a painting by Andrea del Castagno, 1430 (*Hungarische Kriegsgeschichtliche Denkmäler*, p. 294, pl. 1109). (3) St. George, from Pisanello's painting "The Madonna with St. Anthony and St. George", circa 1437.

PLATE 58

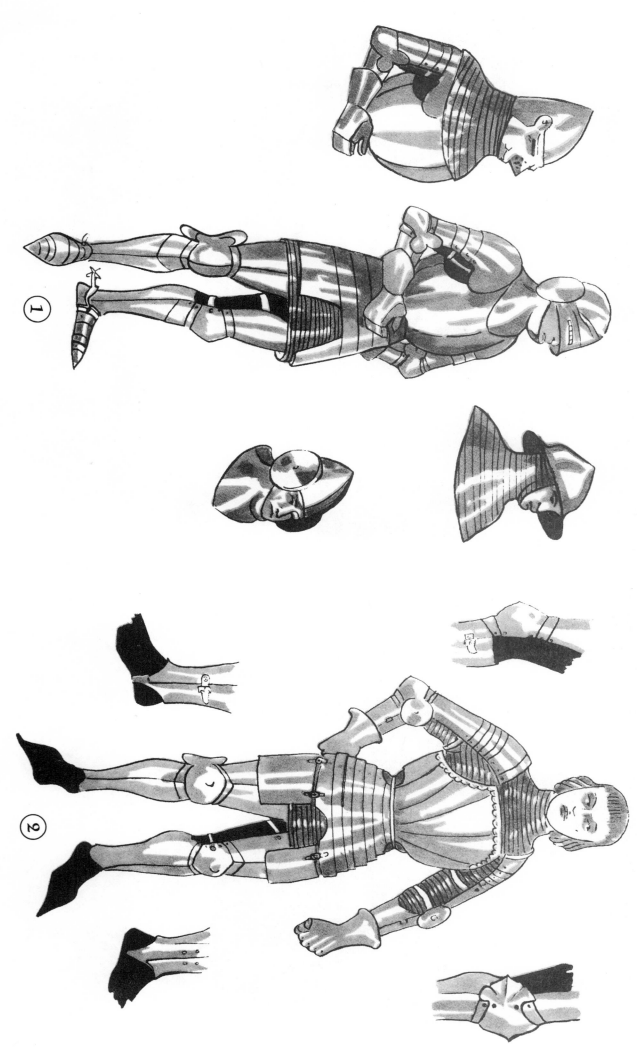

(1) A knight, about 1415–17, from a painting by Jan van Eyck (*Skulptur und Malerei in Frankreich*, p. 85, pl. 109). (2) The knight from the Stettenberg tomb, died 1428 (Alteneck).

PLATE 59

(1) A knight's suit of plate armour, dating from about 1420 (*European Armour*, III, p. 154, pl. 961). (2) Early 15th century knight from a painting of the Crucifixion by a Bavarian master-painter (*Die altdeutsche Malerei*, p. 36, pl. 22). (3) The head of a soldier from the same source. (4) Part of a suit of armour, dating from 1429, as depicted in the Bamberg altar-piece (*Die altdeutsche Malerei*, p. 30, pl. 18). (5) A knight from a painting by Konrad Witz (1400-46). Again the knight has little bells dangling from his belt.

PLATE 60

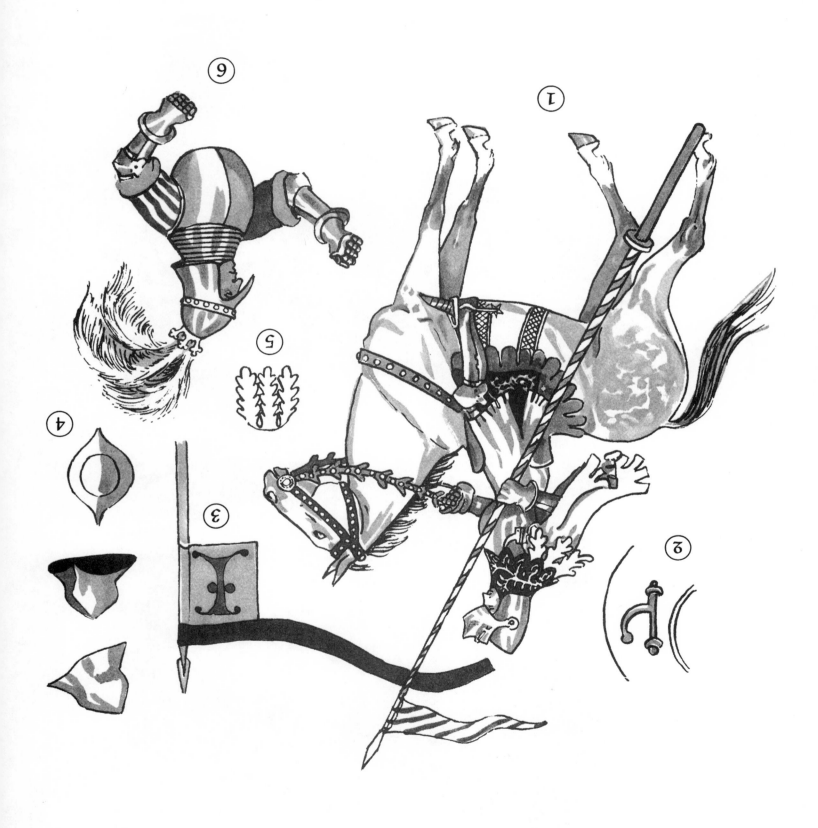

(1) A knight from an illumination in the Togenburg MS.: Joshua and his princes (*Soldatenkunde*, p. 279). (2) A lance rest attached to a breastplate. (3) A pennon inscribed with the initial "I", for Joshua. (4) Various helmets. (5) The dagged decoration at the top of his sleeve. (6) Joshua.

PLATE 61

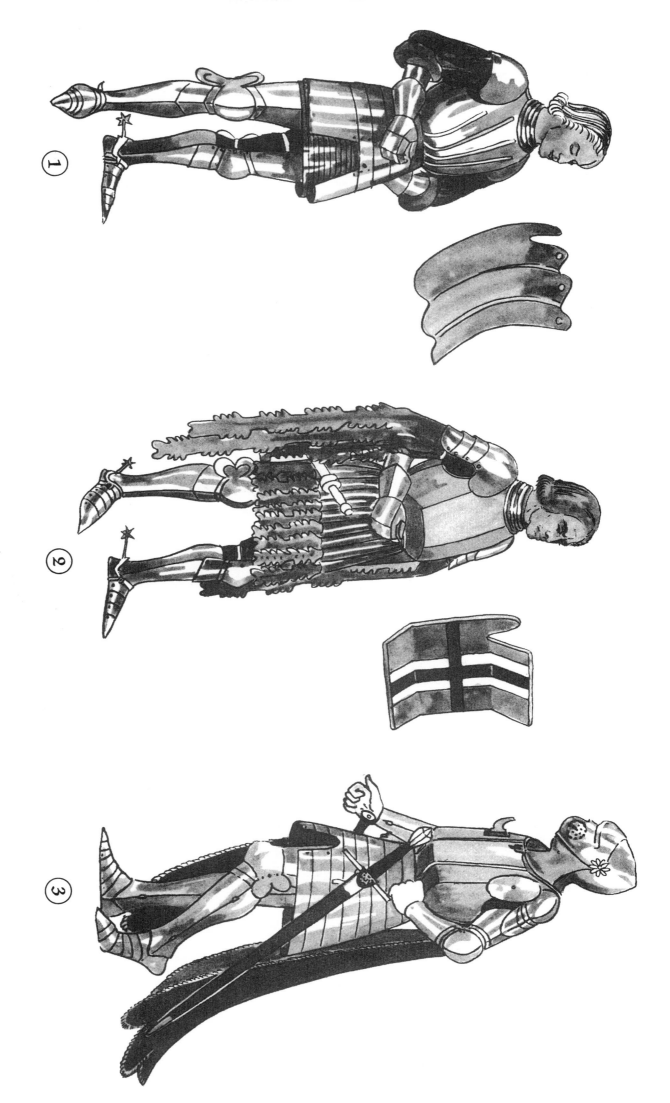

(1) A knight, dating from 1430 (Van Eyck, Ghent altar-piece). (2) A knight, dating from 1430 (*ibid.*). (3) A knight from the Basle altar-piece, dating from after 1434 (*Geschichte der deutschen Kunst*, p. 299, pl. 441).

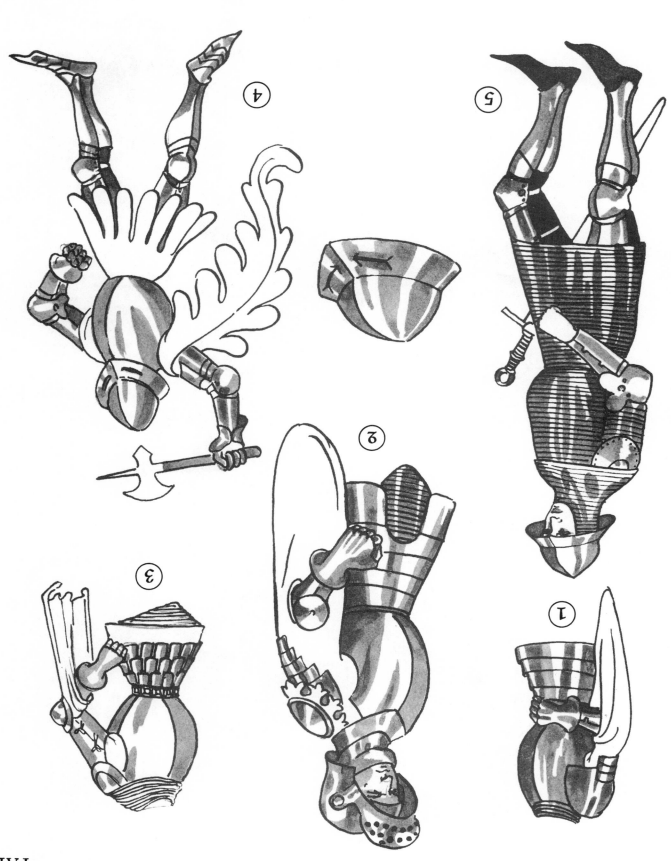

Plate armour worn with long, flowing cloth sleeves. (1) 1390–1430 (Alteneck, p. 242). (2) Detail from the tomb of G. Epstein, 1437 (Alteneck, p. 253). (3) Detail from the tomb of Kunz Haberkorn, 1421 (Alteneck, p. 242). (4) A soldier wearing a basinet, dating from 1419 (*Deutsches Leben*, pl. 531). (5) A marksman in coat of mail, 1390–1400 (Essenwein, pl. A-VII).

PLATE 62

PLATE 63

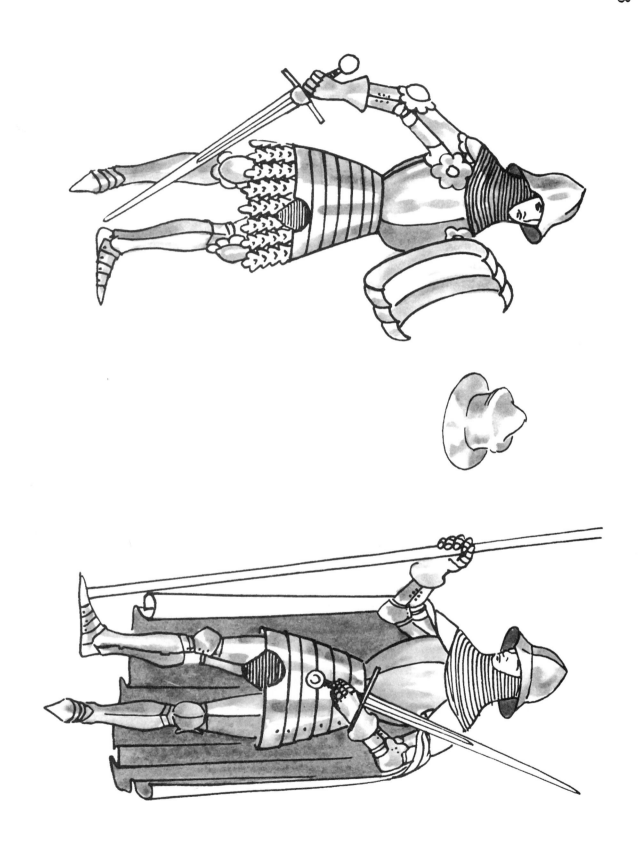

Soldiers dating from 1430, from stained glass in the Castle of Gondorf-on-Moselle (*Die deutsche Malerei der Renaissance*, p. 389, pl. 472). An iron hat, dating from 1400 (*Die deutsche Malerei der Renaissance*, p. 420, pl. 514).

PLATE 64

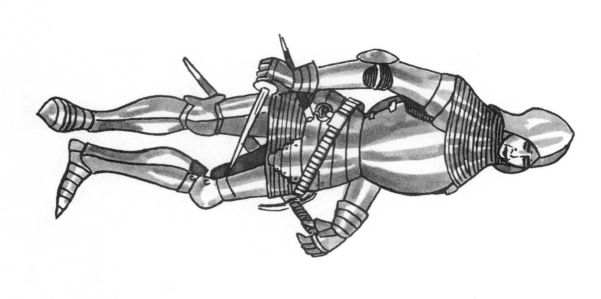

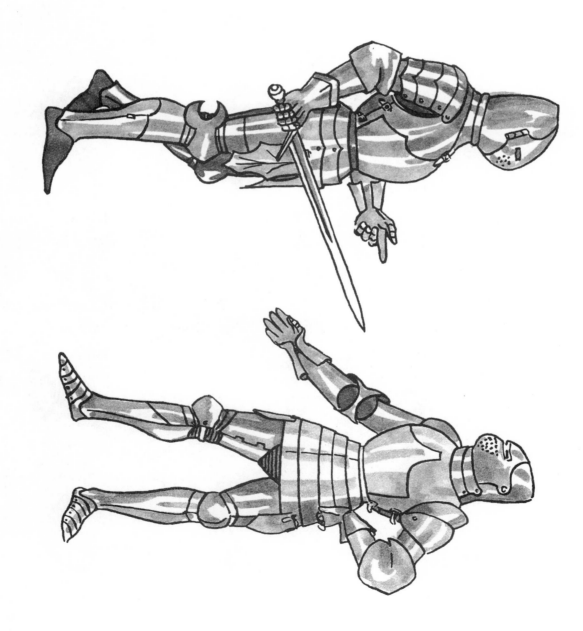

Plate armour of the 15th century (Viollet le Duc).

PLATE 65

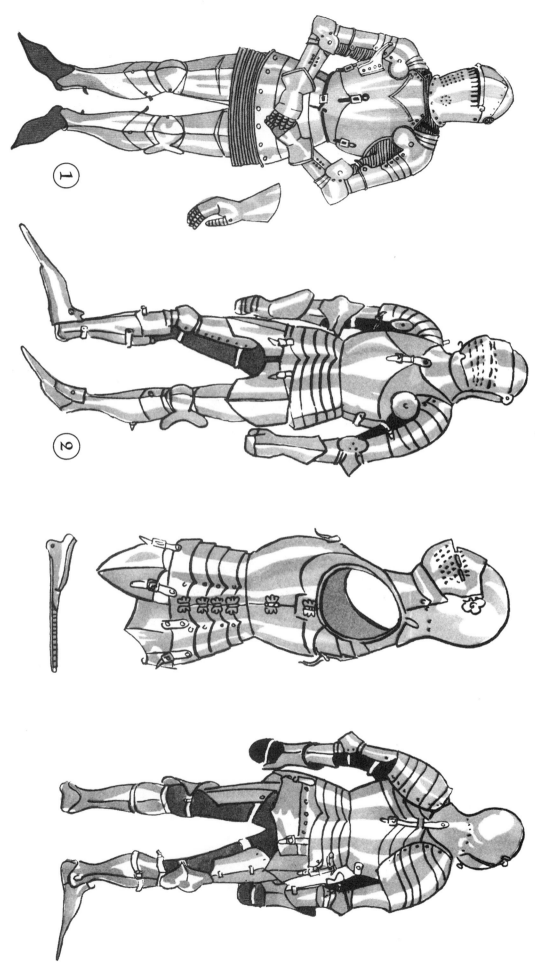

(1) **Plate** armour dating from 1420 (*The Armoury of the Castle of Churburg*, pl. XVIII). (2) Knight's plate armour made in Milan by Tomaso da Missaglia, circa 1450 (Boeheim, pp. 146, 147, pl. 159, 160; also P. 93, pl. 92 and *Armi ed Armaioli*, p. 216).

PLATE 66

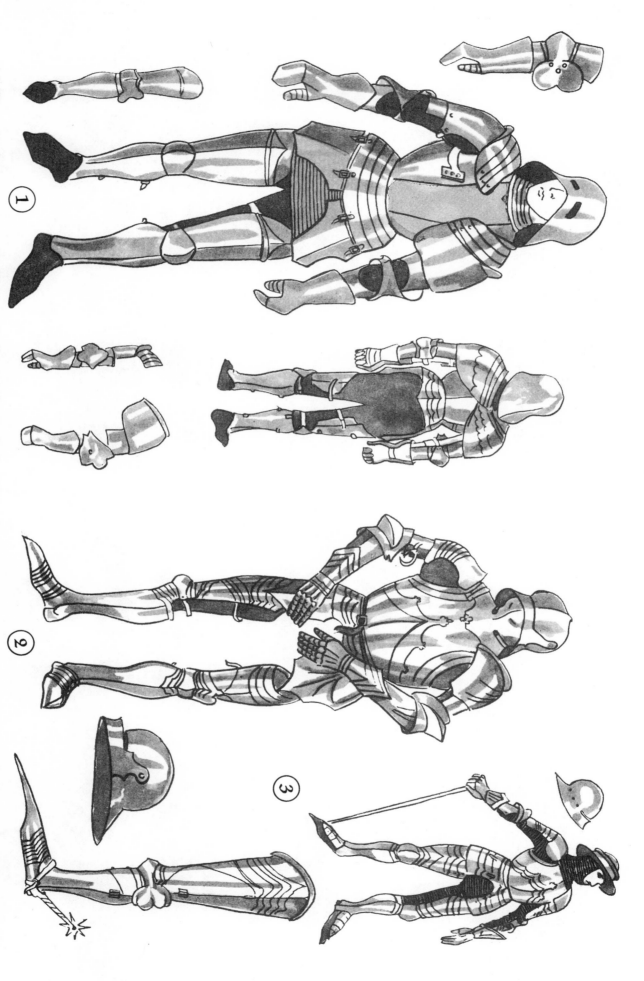

(1) The suit of armour worn by Roberto da Sanseverino – died 1487 – the work of the Milanese armourer, Antonio da Missaglia, 1480 (Boeheim, p. 148, pl. 161-2; also *Zeitschrift für historische Waffenkunde*, 1937/1939, p. 68, pl. 6; dated 1470). (2) A knight's suit of armour dated about 1480 (*Deutsches Leben*, p. 393, pl. 535). Also side view of the plate protecting the left hand and leg; dated about 1480 (Boeheim, p. 111, pl. 121). The validity of this reconstruction is doubtful. (3) A knight of the 15th century (Frankenberger, *Naše velká armáda*, p. 27).

PLATE 67

Various types of armour as depicted in Viollet le Duc, V, pp. 284, 444, 446. (1) A mounted soldier in a long gambeson, about 1390. (2) A foot soldier, with a spiked mall, wearing a long gambeson, about 1395. (3) A mounted soldier in coat of mail, with a low breastplate, from 1400. (4-5) Foot soldiers with low breastplates and chain-mail aprons from 1400.

PLATE 68

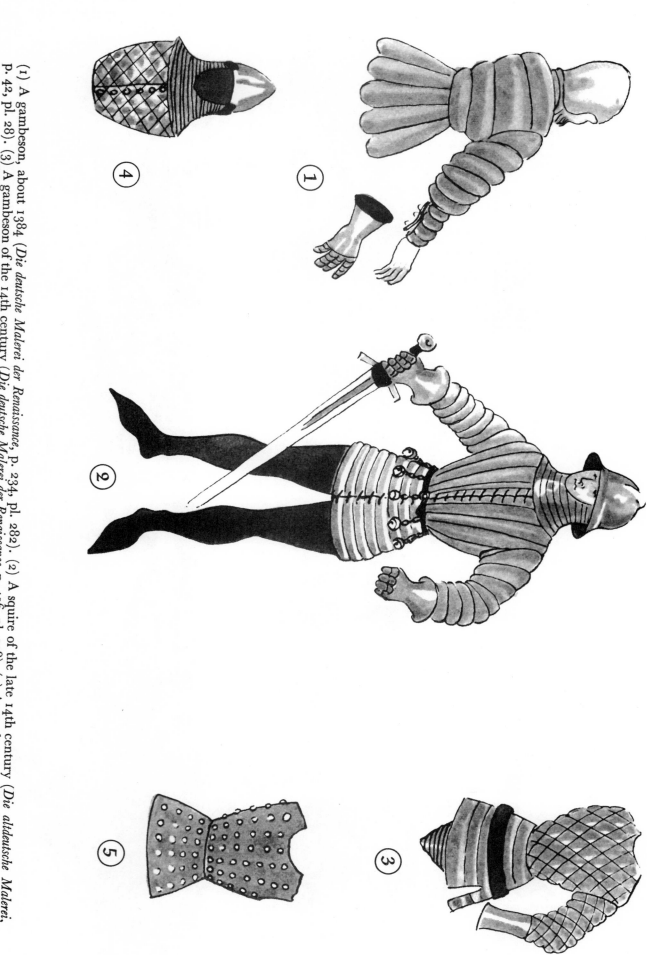

(1) A gambeson, about 1384 (*Die deutsche Malerei der Renaissance*, p. 234, pl. 282). (2) A squire of the late 14th century (*Die altdeutsche Malerei*, p. 42, pl. 28). (3) A gambeson of the 14th century (*Die deutsche Malerei der Renaissance*, p. 416, pl. 508). (4) A gambeson and helmet with aventail (Viollet le Duc). (5) A brigandine from the Runkelstein fresco (*Die deutsche Malerei der Renaissance*, p. 254, pl. 306).

PLATE 79   PART II

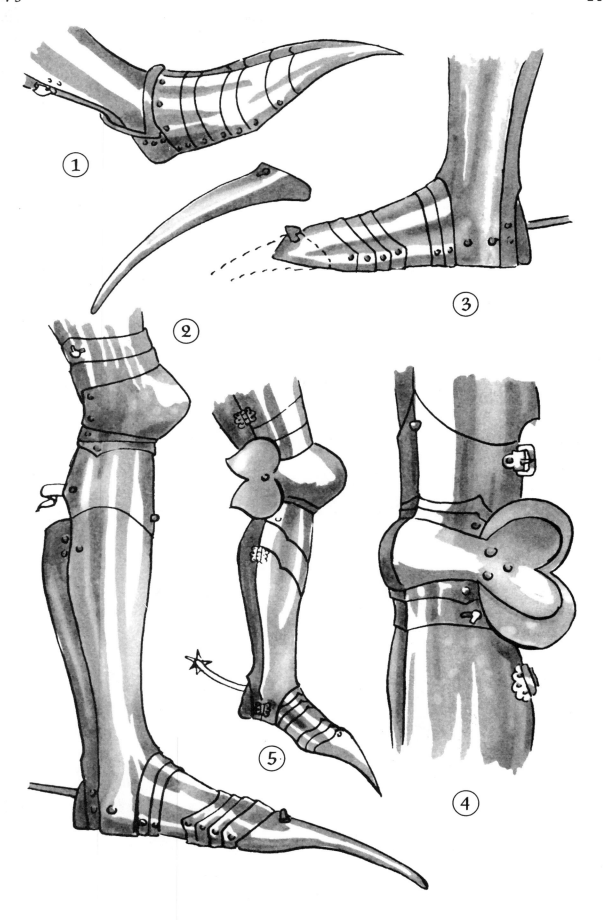

(1) Sabbaton à la Poulaine, dating from 1370 (Viollet le Duc, V). (2) The various plates protecting the leg, seen from the instep side. The sabbaton also includes a removable point or "beak". (Viollet le Duc, p. 488). (3) Detail of (2) with the "beak" removed. (4) The armour for the same leg, seen from the outer side. (5) Leg plate armour dating from 1450, from the outer side.

PLATE 80   PART II

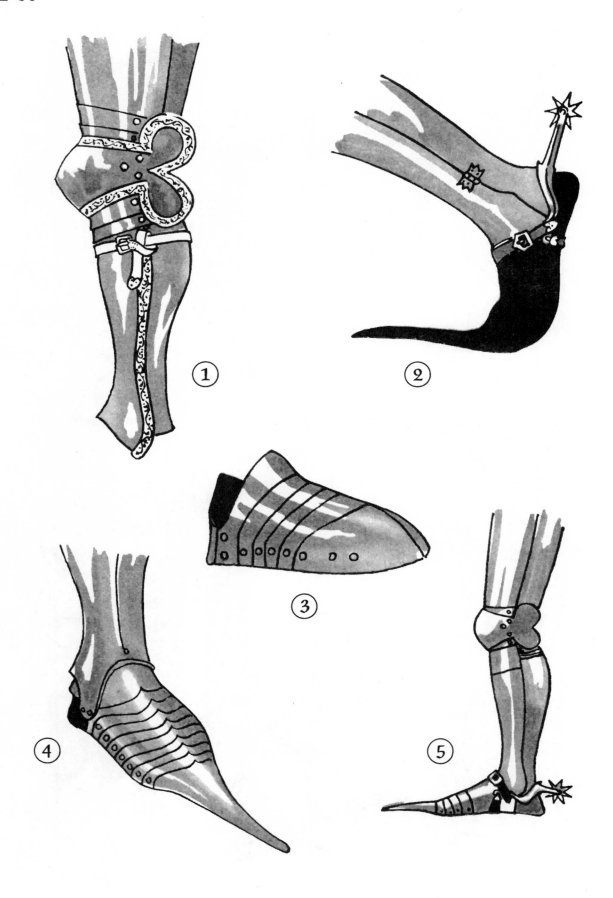

(1) Left-leg armour fastened from the outside. (2) Left-leg plate armour with unprotected foot (Tilke; Rosenberg).
(3) An iron solleret à la Poulaine, from the mid-15th century (Tilke; Rosenberg). (5) Left-leg plate armour, from the
tomb of the Black Prince.

PLATE 81   PART II

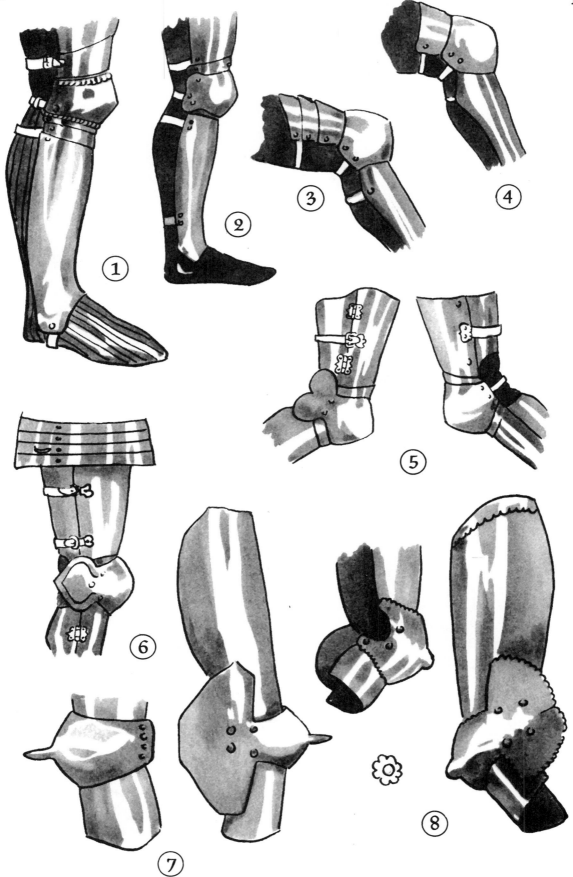

Plate armour as recorded by Viollet le Duc, V, pp. 307, 309, 313, 407. (1–2) Leg plate armour of the early 14th century. (3–4) Leg armour of the mid-14th century. (5) Leg armour of the year 1370, seen from both sides. (6) Leg armour from about 1465. (7–8) Plate protection for the leg, dating from the middle of the 15th century. Seen from both sides. Detail: ornamental rivet.

PLATE 82   PART II

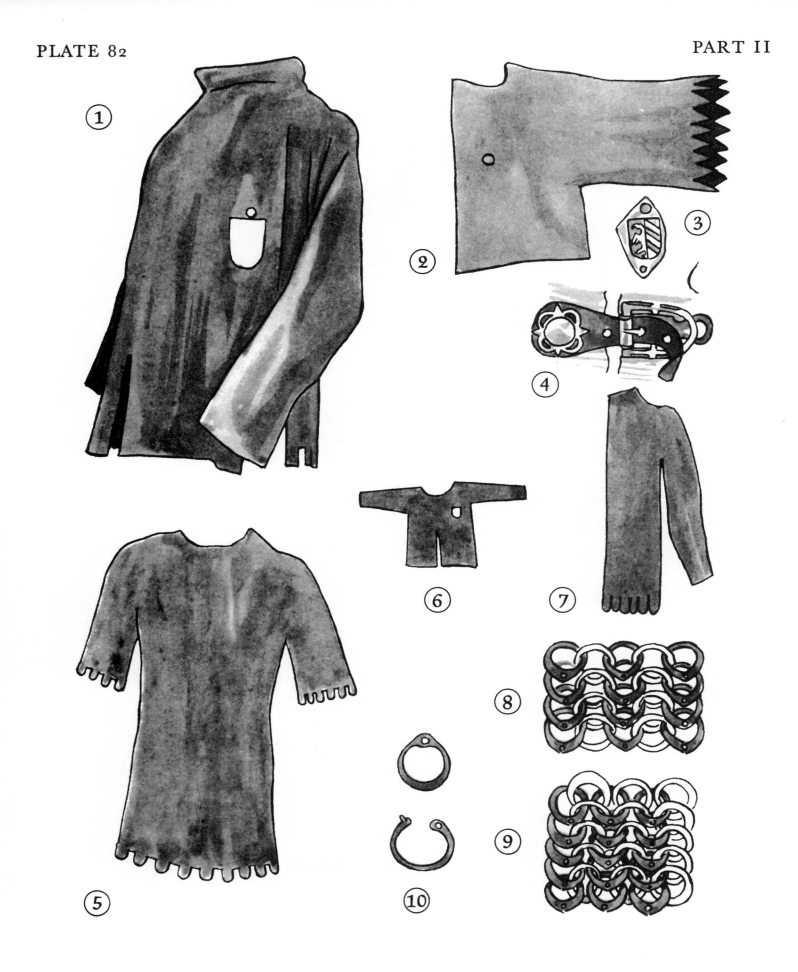

(1) A hauberk or coat of mail (*Zeitschrift für historische Waffenkunde*, 1929/1931, p. 79, pl. 1). (2) The sleeve of a coat of mail (*ibid.*, pl. 8). (3) The Nuremberg town bearings on a coat of mail (*ibid.*, pl. 56). (4) The buckle for fastening a coat of mail (*Zeitschrift*, 1912/1914, p. 192). (5) A coat of mail with half-sleeves, scalloped at the sleeve and lower hem edge (*European Armour*, II, p. 178, pl. 516). (6) The shape of the hauberk in (1). (7) A coat of mail with long sleeves and dags at the lower edge, middle of the 14th century (*European Armour*, II, p. 180, pl. 518). (8) Mail mesh of the 15th century (Boeheim, p. 143, pl. 155). (9) Mail mesh (Italian) from the 15th century (Boeheim, p. 148, pl. 157). (10) Individual links in the mail of a hauberk.

PLATE 83

The surcoats of knight-at-arms, dating from the 14th–15th centuries (*European Armour*, III, pp. 16, 19, pl. 761, 760, 768).

PLATE 84   PART II

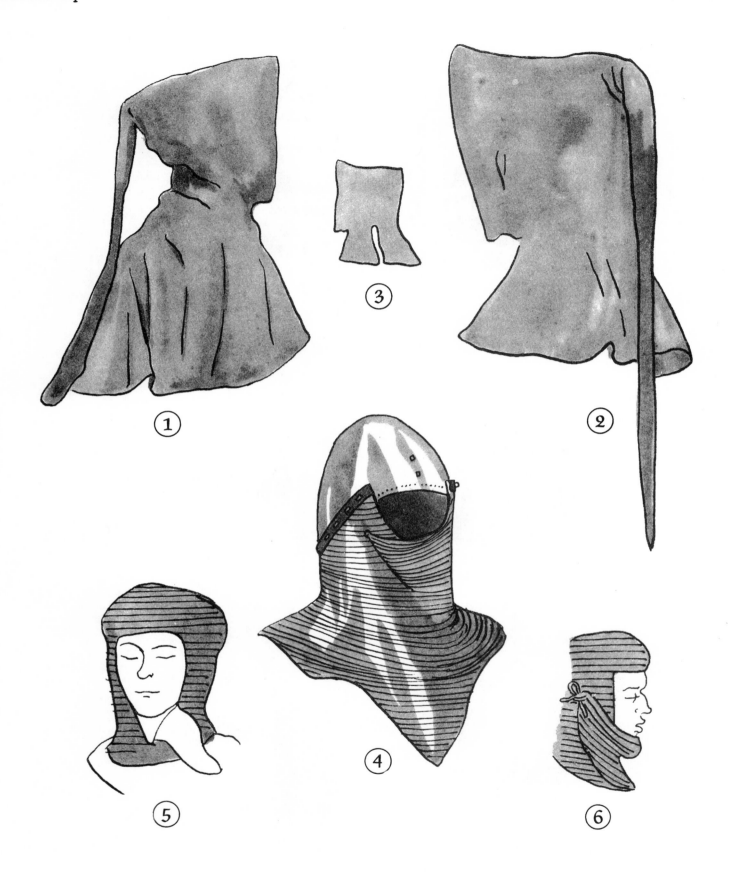

(1–3) Hoods from the second half of the 14th century (*Zeitschrift für historische Waffenkunde*, 1926/1928, II, pp. 256, 257, pl. 1, 2, 3). (4) A helmet with aventail, dating from the 14th century (*Zeitschrift*, 1929/1931, p. 87). (5–6) Method of fastening the aventail in the 13th century (*Zeitschrift*, 1932/1934, p. 106, pl. 3 and 4).

PLATE 85

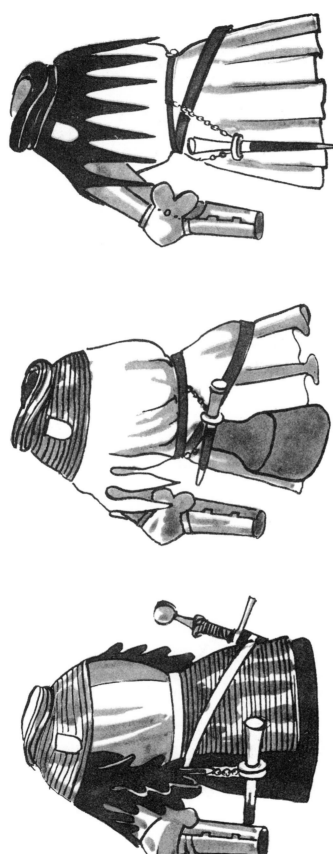

Small escutcheons as worn by German knights of about 1430 (H. Pruss, *Allgemeine Weltgeschichte*, VI).

PLATE 1   PART III

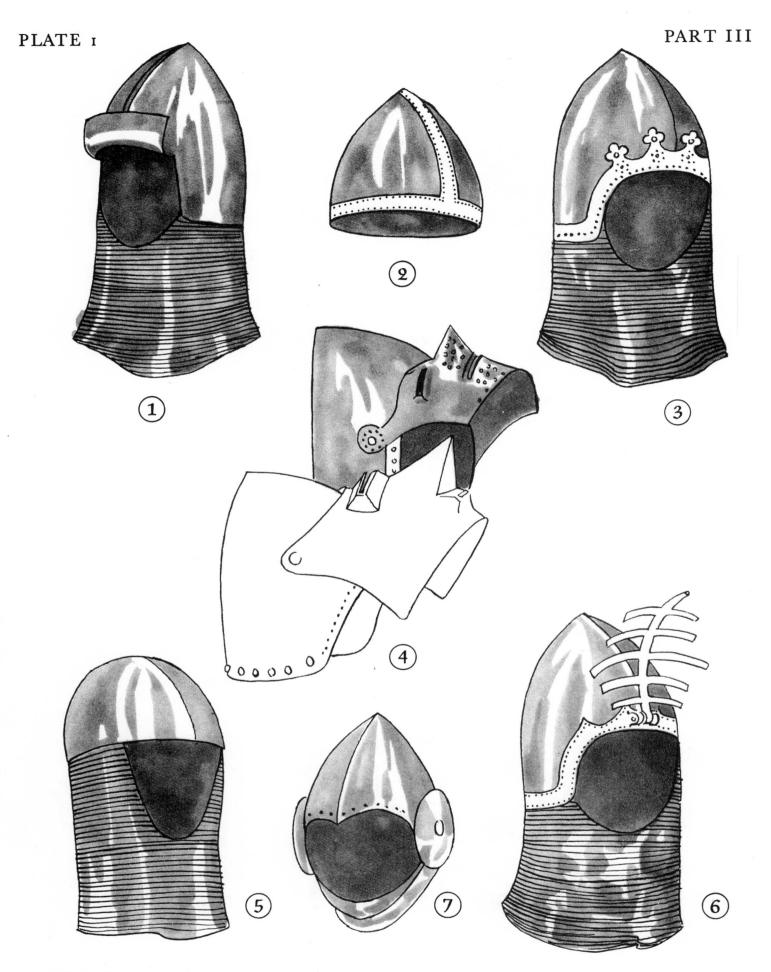

(1) From the Resurrection by the Master of the Vyšší Brod Cycle, about 1350. (2) From the Crucifixion in the Emmaus Monastery, about 1375. (3) The St. Barbara Chapel Crucifixion by the Master of the Třeboň altar-piece, about 1380. (4) A basinet helmet with visor, from the painting by the Master of the Třeboň altar-piece, "Christ on the Mount of Olives" about 1380. The helmet used for comparison is drawn according to *European Armour*, I, p. 236, pl. 280 b. (5) A helmet with camail, from the early 15th century (Krumlov MS). (6) A helmet with lattice visor, from the Resurrection by the Master of the Třeboň altar-piece, about 1380 (Matějček, pl. 96). (7) From the Rajhrad altar-piece, the Resurrection, about 1420 (Matějček, pl. 190).

PLATE 2　　　　　　　　　　　　　　　　　　　　　　　PART III

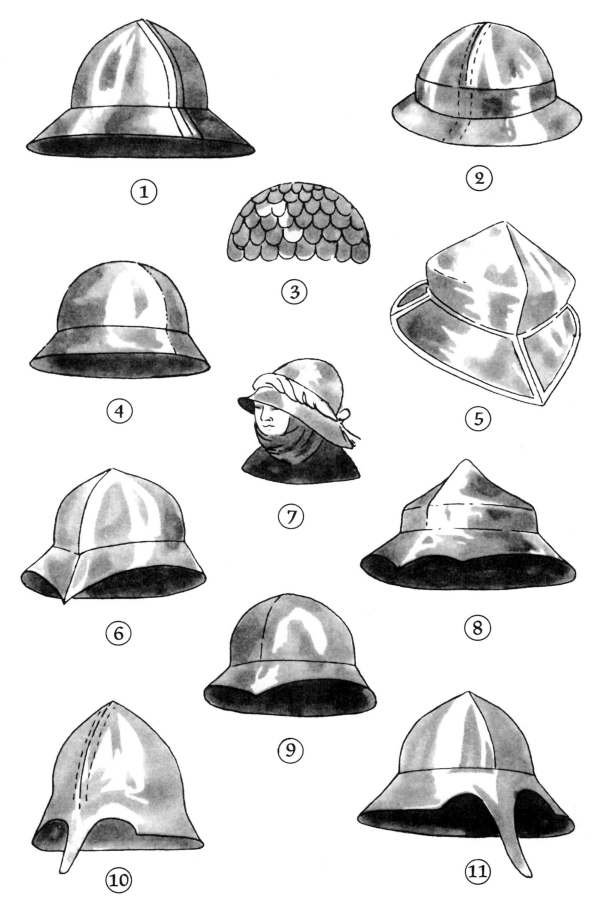

(1) From the Resurrection by the Master of the Vyšší Brod Cycle, about 1350. (2) From the Rajhrad altar-piece, the Crucifixion, found in Nové Sady, dating from about 1420. (3) A scale helmet, from the Resurrection by the Master of the Třeboň altar-piece, dating from about 1380. (4) From the Rajhrad altar-piece, the Crucifixion. (5) From the Rajhrad altar-piece, the Resurrection, about 1420. (6) From the Skalice Crucifixion, about 1430. (7) From the St. James altar-piece, dated between 1430–40. (8) From the Rajhrad altar-piece, the Crucifixion. (9) From the Emmaus Monastery Crucifixion, about 1375. (10) An iron hat with nose-piece, from the painting "Christ on the Mount of Olives" by the Master of the Třeboň altar-piece, about 1380. (11) A helmet with nose-piece, from the Resurrection by the Master of the Třeboň altar-piece, from about 1380 (Matějček).

PLATE 3

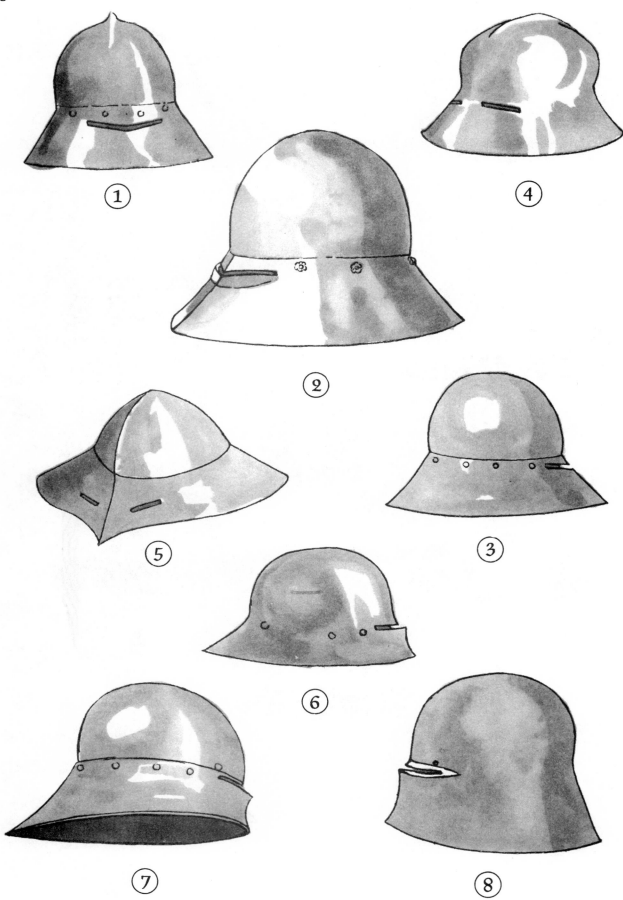

(1, 3) A German salett dating from about 1460 (*European Armour*, II, pl. 4, pl. 333). (2) A salett from about 1400 (*Zeitschrift*, V, p. 38; Haenel, p. 52, pl. 45, dates this salett from 1480). (4) A salett dating from 1440 (*European Armour*, II, p. 3, pl. 331; Viollet le Duc, II, p. 376). (5) Early 15th century salett (Viollet le Duc). A similar salett is mentioned in *Deutsches Leben*, pl. 531, depicting a soldier of the year 1419. (6) A salett dating from 1450 (*European Armour*, II, p. 27, pl. 366). (7) A German salett dating from the middle of the 15th century (Haenel, p. 41, pl. 44). (8) A salett from about 1440 (*European Armour*, II, p. 28, pl. 369).

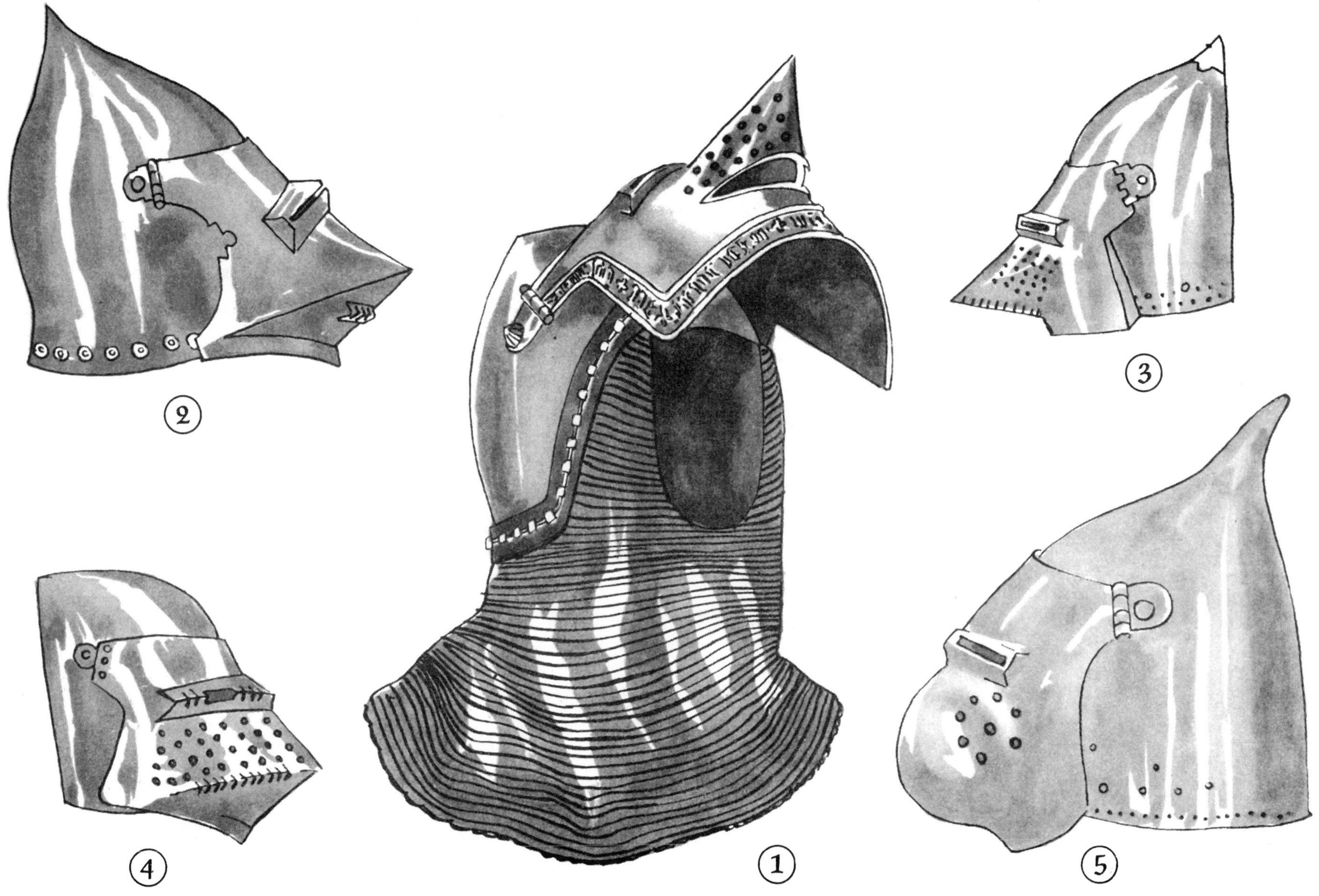

PLATE 4

(1) A basinet-type helmet, "pig-faced" with a bronze rim and biblical inscription (*The Armoury of the Castle of Churburg*, pl. XIV). (2) A 14th century helmet (Alteneck). (3) A visored basinet helmet of the late 14th century (*European Armour*, I, p. 249, pl. 294; also Boeheim, p. 35, pl. 20). (4) A basinet helmet from the 14th and early 15th century (*European Armour*, I, p. 249, pl. 294). (5) A helmet dating from between 1390–1430 (Alteneck 244).

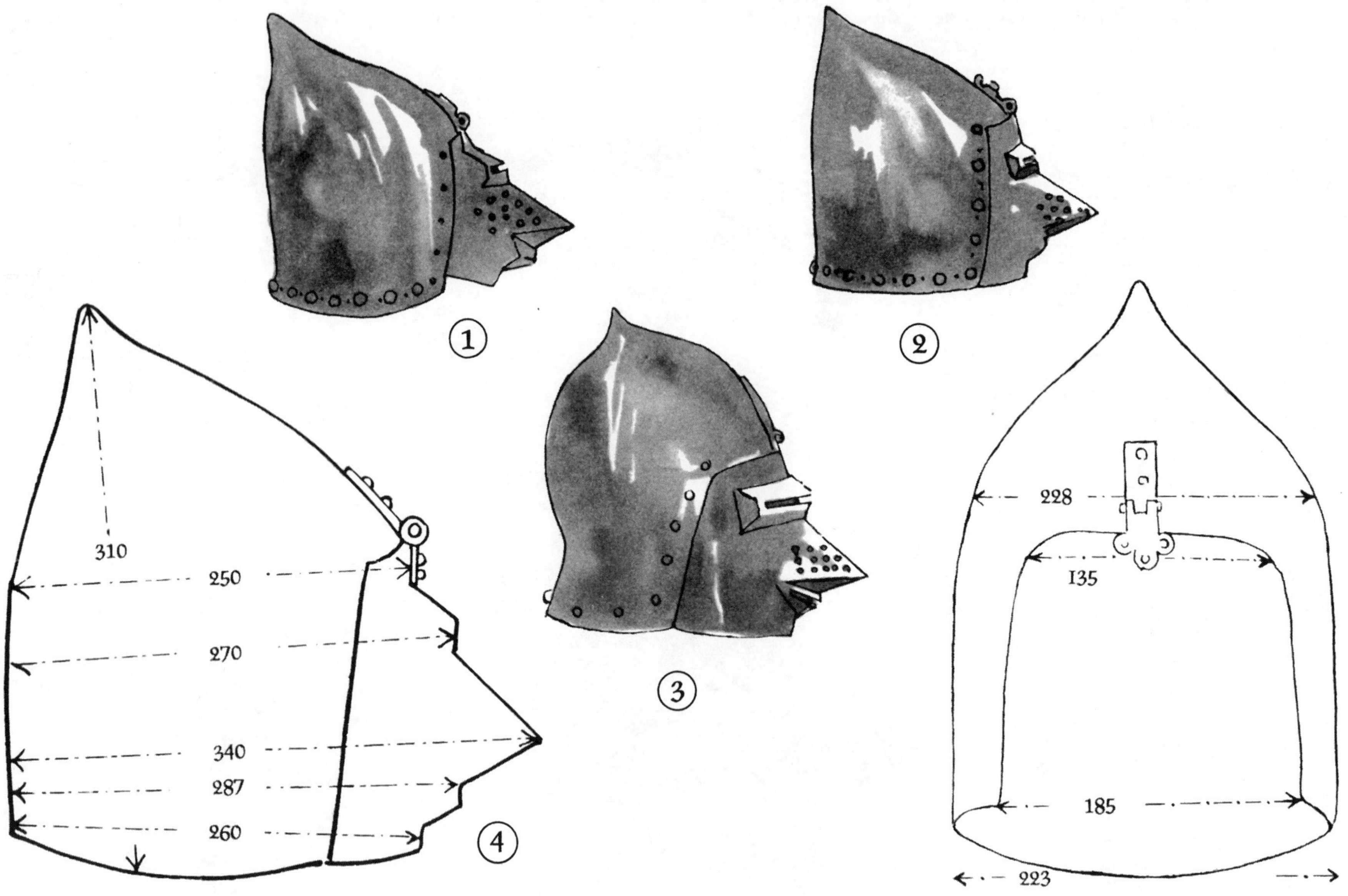

PLATE 5

(1) A basinet helmet, late 14th century (Boeheim, p. 35, pl. 19). (2) A basinet helmet, 14th century (*European Armour*, I, p. 238, pl. 282). (3) A 14th century basinet helmet (Stone, p. 103, pl. 132; also *Zeitschrift*, V, p. 37). (4) The measurements of the basinet helmet shown in *Zeitschrift*, VI, p. 45, pl. 5.

PLATE 6   PART III

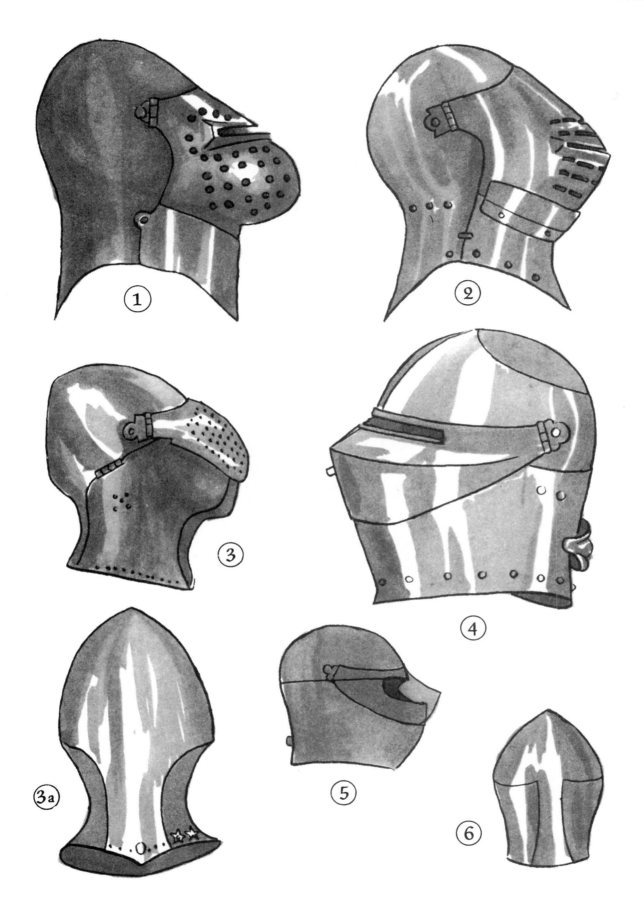

(1) Helmet about 1410 (*Zeitschrift für historische Waffenkunde*, 1936, p. 102, pl. 5; also Stone, p. 103, pl. 132). (2) A German helmet of about 1400 (Stone, p. 104, pl. 133). (3) A German basinet helmet of about 1460 (*European Armour*, I, p. 263, pl. 310, a, b; also *Zeitschrift*, VII, p. 19, pl. 7, 7a, and J. Launts, *Alte deutsche Waffen*, p. 7, dates it between 1430 and 1450). (3a) Back view of the same helmet. (4) An Italian basinet helmet of about 1440 (*European Armour*, II, p. 78, pl. 430). (5) Side view of the helmet (*ibid.*, II, p. 77, pl. 429a). (6) Back view of the same helmet (*ibid.*, II, p. 77, pl. 429b).

PLATE 7

Helmets of knights-at-arms dating from the late 14th and early 15th centuries, with fixed collar-piece. (1) See *European Armour*, I, p. 253, pl. 299; also *Zeitschrift*, V, p. 70. (2–3) Viollet le Duc, V, p. 164.

PLATE 8

PART III

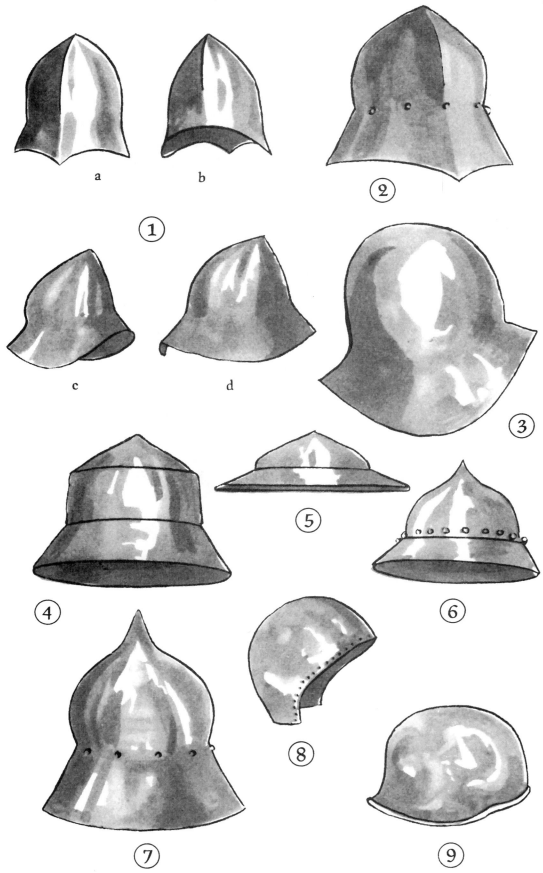

a   b   ②

①

c   d   ③

④   ⑤   ⑥

⑦   ⑧   ⑨

(1) A helmet dating from the early 15th century, preserved in the Kutná Hora Museum; a. front view, b. back view, c. and d. side views. (2) A helmet from turn of the 14th and 15th centuries, weighing 1.65 kilograms (*Zeitschrift*, VII, p. 270, pl. 4). (3) A salett of 1460 (*European Armour*, II, p. 28, pl. 370). (4) An iron hat dating from between 1450–90 (*European Armour*, II, p. 61, pl. 416; also Baron Cosson, *Le Cabinet des Armes*, pl. 7 (B7). (5) An English helmet of about 1340. (6) An English helmet of about 1250 (for (5) and (6) see Radnor, p. 45). (7) A pointed iron hat, possibly from first half of 15th century (*Zeitschrift*, VII, p. 269, pl. 1). (8) Iron skull cap dating from about 1390 (Estruch, *Museo armeria*, pl. XIII, no. 1263). (9) An English helmet of the 15th century (Radnor, p. 46).

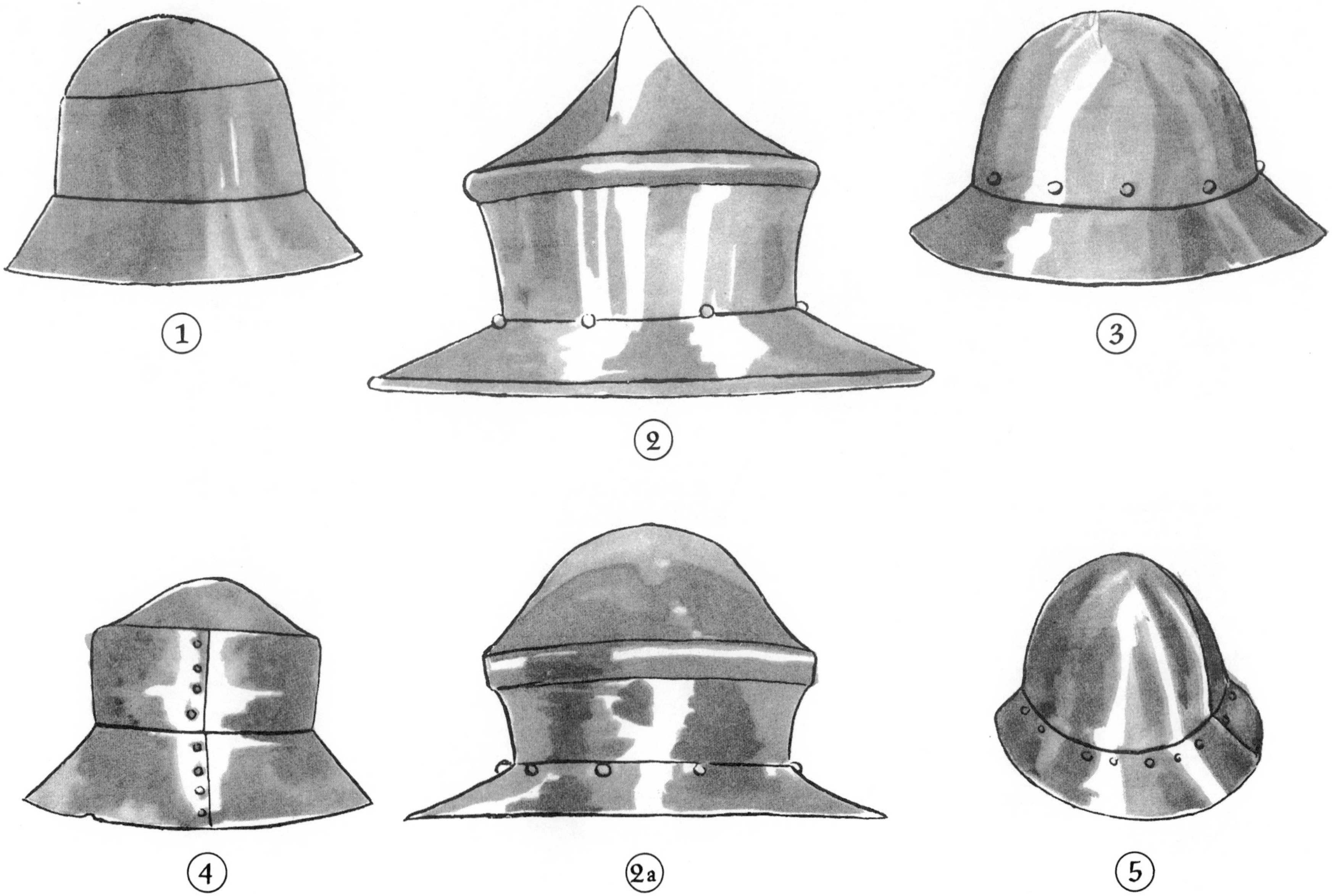

PLATE 9

PART III

Iron hats (1) A Swiss iron hat of the 15th century (Stone, p. 173, pl. 210). (2) An iron hat dating from between 1440–80 (*Zschille'sche Waffen-sammlung*, no. 40, pl. 6; also *European Armour*, II, p. 61, pl. 415). (2a) Side view. (3) Italian iron hat of the 15th century (Stone, p. 173, pl. 216). (4) An early 15th century iron hat: 25 cm. high, diameter of crown 33 cm., width of crown 11 cm., weight 3 kilograms (Szendrei, p. 250, pl. 799). (5) A 15th century iron hat (*Deutsches Leben*, pl. 546).

PLATE 10   PART III

The head of the armour bearer, from the paintings "The Stations of the Cross" in St. Martin's Church in Lorch am Rhein. Similar helmets are to be found in Bohemian Gothic panel paintings, such as the Crucifixion from Nové Sady and the Zátoň altar-piece.

PLATE 11   PART III

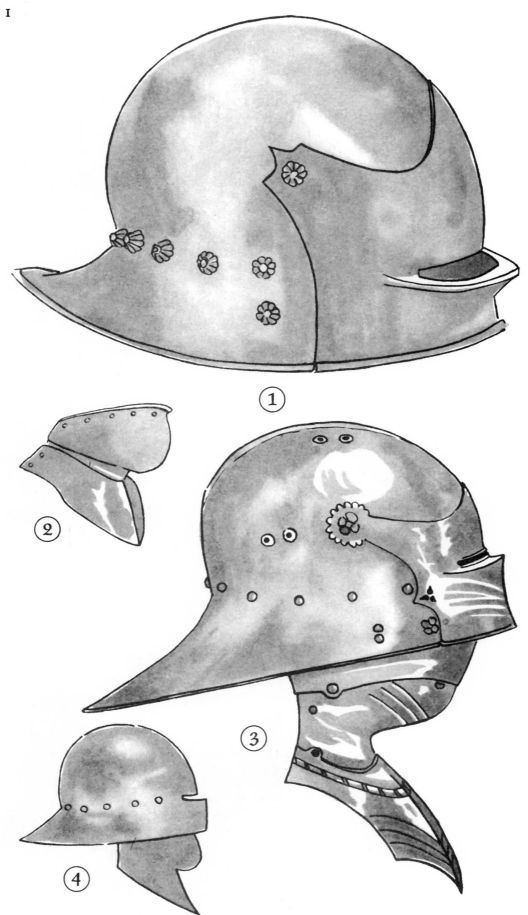

(1) A salett dating from about 1459, with a moveable visor with eye-slit (*The Armoury of the Castle of Churburg*, pl. XXIX, pl. 64.) (2) The bevor or chin-piece of the above-mentioned salett. (3) A German salett with bevor dating from about 1480 (*Die deutsche Soldatenkunde*, II, p. 104). (4) A salett with fixed eye-slit and bevor (*European Armour*, II, p. 27, pl. 368).

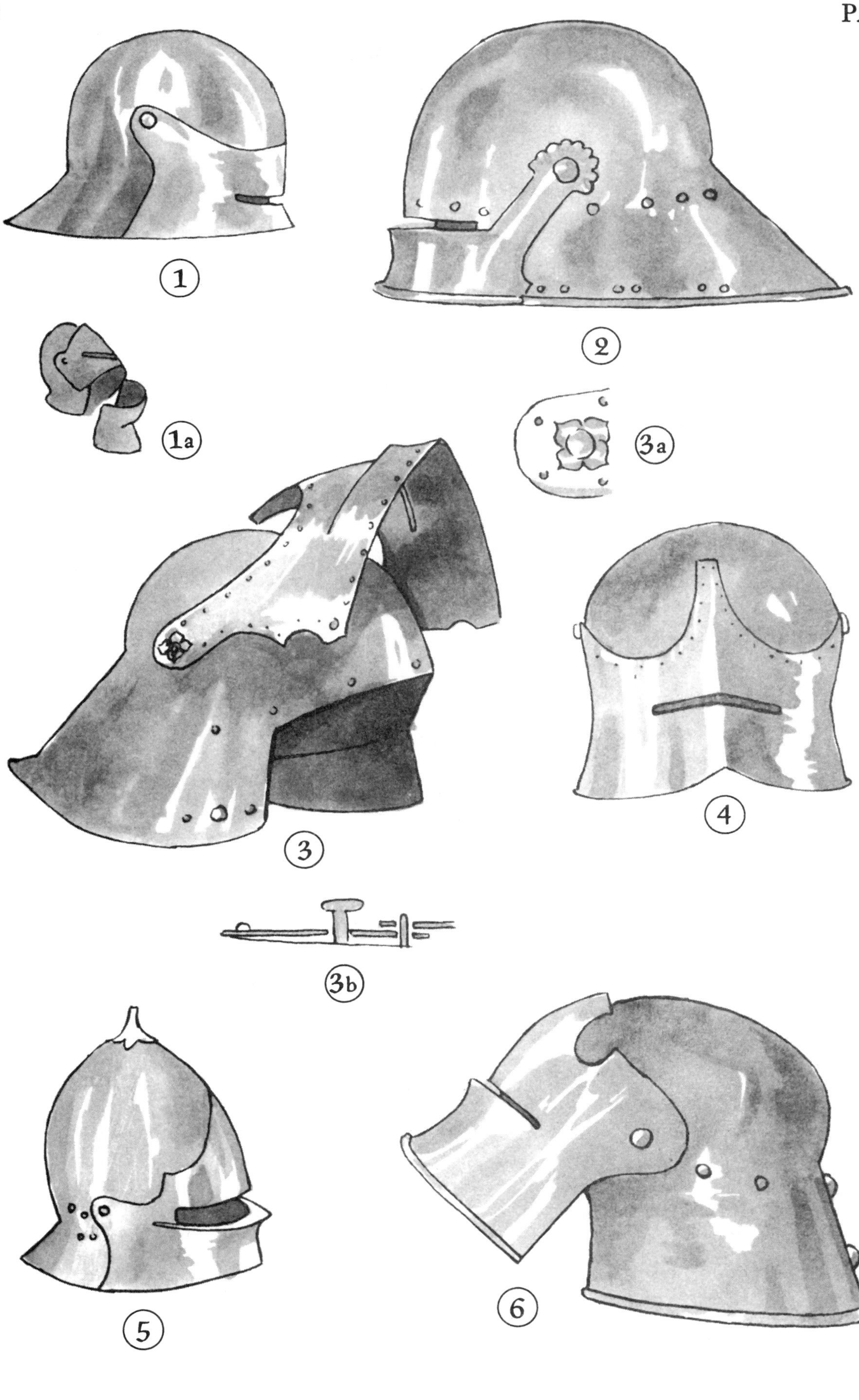

PLATE 12   PART III

(1) A French salett dating from about 1450 (*European Armour*, II, p. 24, pl. 361; also Stone, p. 537, pl. 867, fig. 5). (1a) The salett with bevor from the Trojan carpet in the Berne Museum about 1435 (*Zeitschrift*, 1936, p. 103, pl. 9). (2) A salett of about 1490 (*Churburg*, pl. XXXI). (3) A salett with the visor raised (Viollet le Duc). (3a) Detail of the rivet which holds the visor to the crown of the helmet. (3b) The spring which serves to hold the visor when lifted. (4) The same helmet seen from the front. (5) A French salett dating from about 1460 (*European Armour*, II, p. 26, pl. 365). (6) A salett which Szendrei (p. 252, pl. 801), possibly wrongly, dates as early 15th century. Height 27.5 cm., weight 3.95 kilograms.

PLATE 13

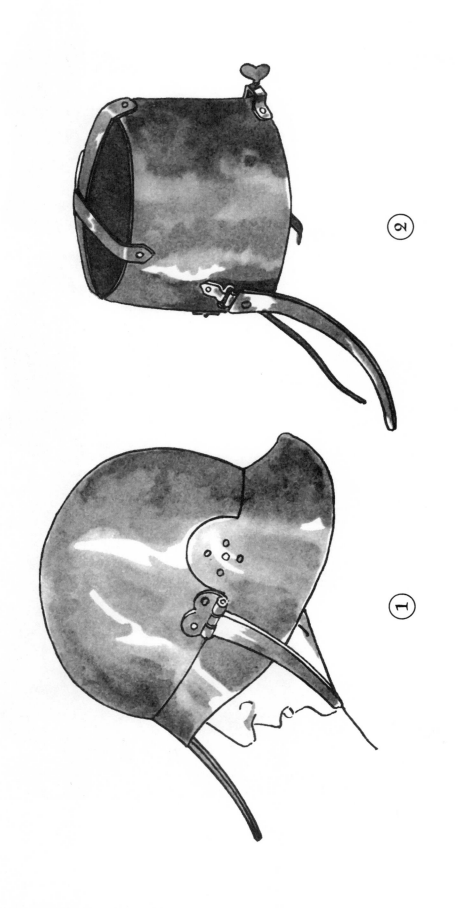

(1) A helmet with protective bands (copy of a study by Pisanello). (2) A helmet with protective bands, supposed to date from the 13th century but which may be 17th century. Height 13 cm., length of the bands 25 cm., weight 3.70 kilograms (Szendrei, p. 251, pl. 800). In the front there is obviously a fixture with a wing screw for a nose-piece, which reminds one of the method by which the loose nose-piece of the "Pappenheim" helmets was fastened in the 17th century.

PLATE 14   PART III

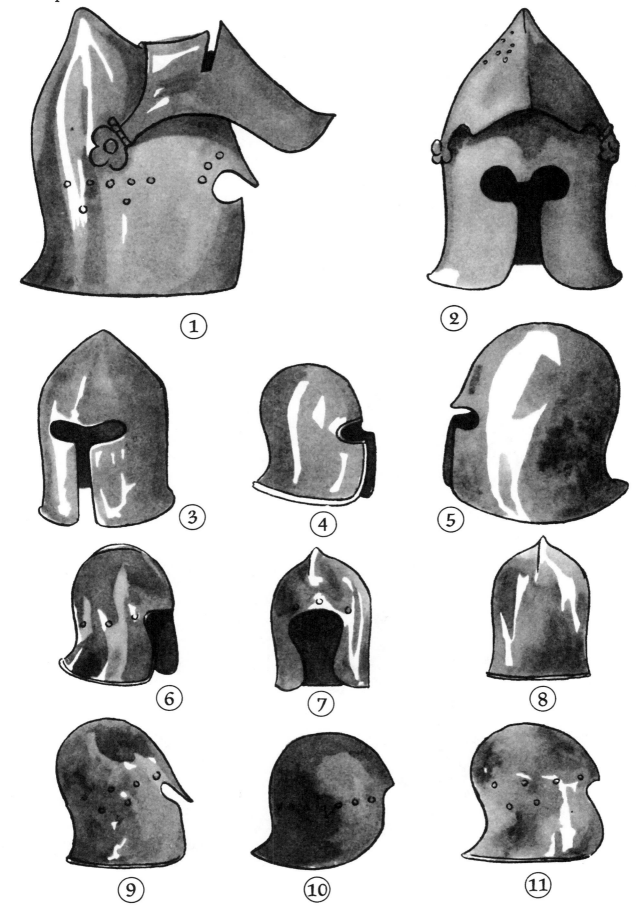

(1-2) Helmet dating from between 1350–1400 (Alteneck). Front and side view. (3, 5) North Italian helmets dating from about 1470 (*European Armour*, II, p. 9, pl. 342). (4, 6, 7, 8, 10), Italian 15th century helmets (*barbutes*). (Stone, p. 94, pl. 121). (9) A Spanish helmet dating from about 1450 (Stone, p. 94, pl. 121). (11) A Milanese helmet of about 1450 (Stone, p. 94, pl. 121).

PLATE 15　　　　　　　　　　　　　　　　　　　　　　　PART III

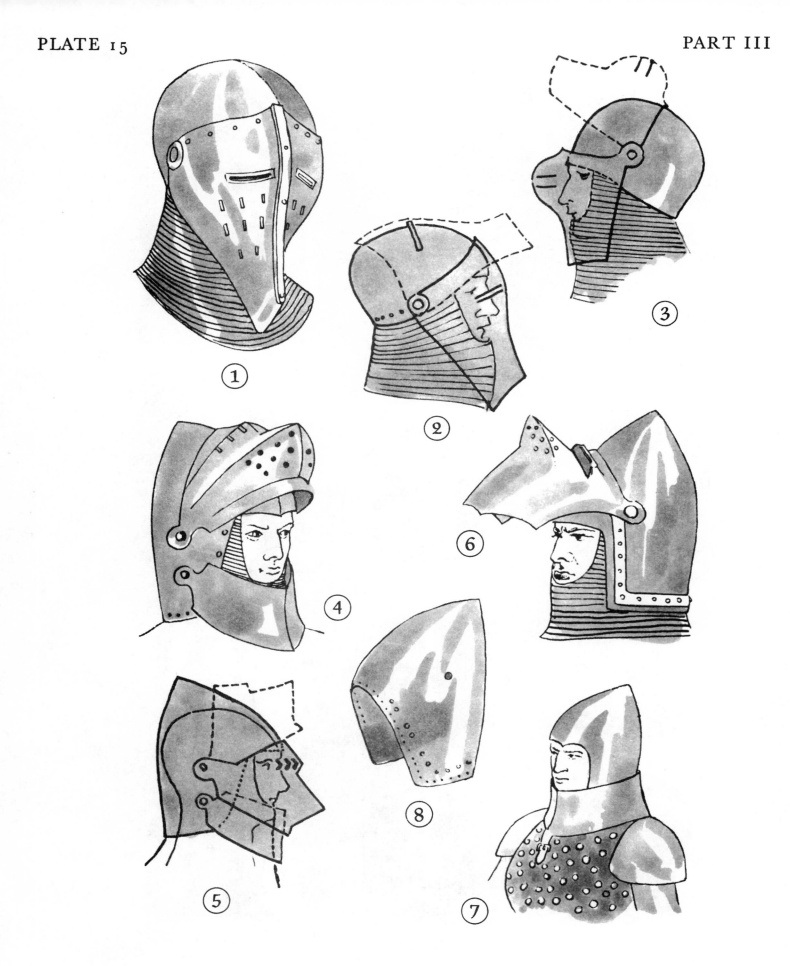

Helmets according to Viollet le Duc. (1–2) A helmet with moveable visor dating from about 1300 (V, p. 159). (3) A helmet dating from about 1310 (V, p. 158). (4–5) Helmets dating from 1350 (V, p. 160). (6) A Milanese basinet, dating from 1380 (V, p. 162). (7) A basinet with bevor fixed to the jacket, dating from about 1390 (V, p. 214). (8) A skull piece, of the 14th century (*European Armour*, I, p. 248, pl. 293).

PLATE 16   PART III

Helmets according to Viollet le Duc. (1–2) A knight's basinet dating from between 1400–10 (V, p. 167). (3–4) A combined helmet and iron hat dating from about 1350 (V, p. 208; also *European Armour*, II, p. 59, pl. 413). (5–6) A helmet dating from about 1375 (V, p. 214). (7) A knight wearing the helmet in (5) and (6), about 1375 (V, p. 256).

PLATE 17 PART III

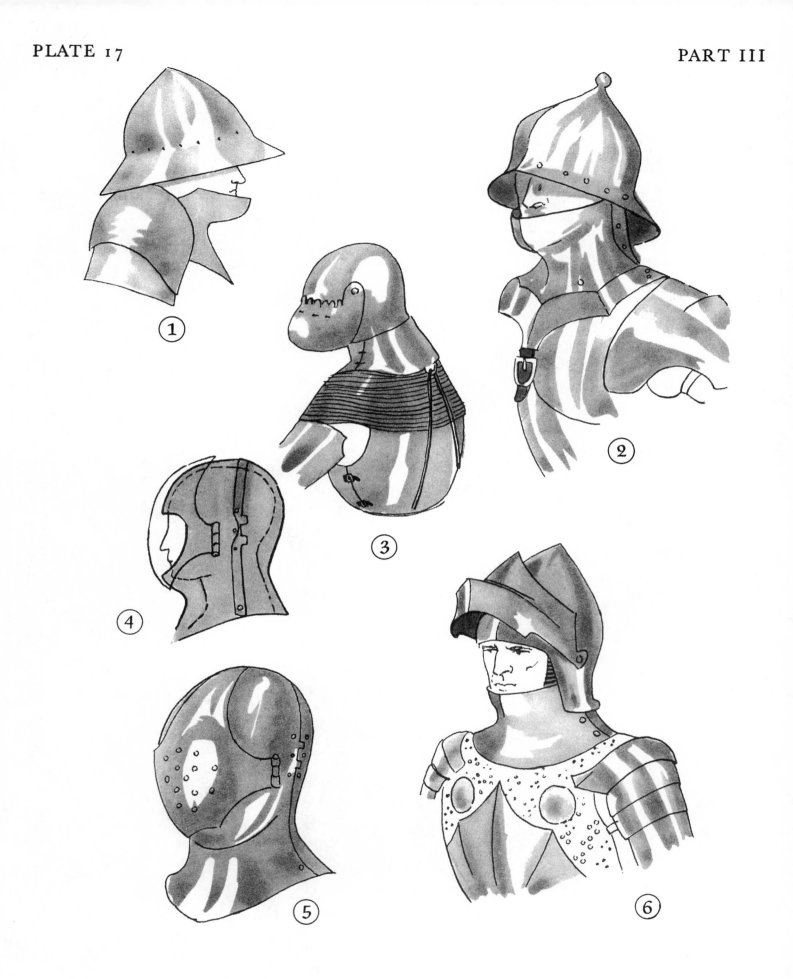

Helmets according to Viollet le Duc. (1) A helmet dating from about 1420 (V, p. 270). (2) A helmet dating from about 1440 (V, p. 280). (3) A helmet fastened by a thong over the camail and back-plate, dating from about 1400 (V, p. 283). (4, 5) A helmet dating from about 1430. The visor opens horizontally. (V, p. 313). (6) A salett with moveable visor and bevor, dating from about 1440 (V).

PLATE 18

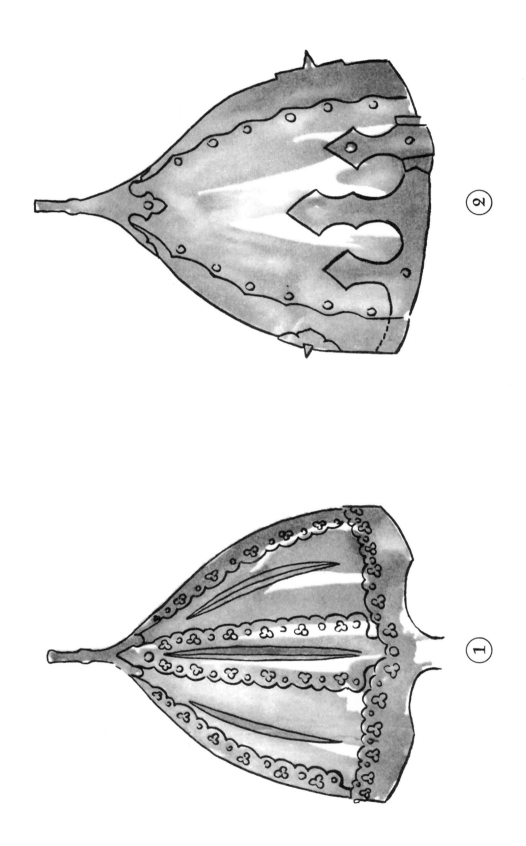

Eastern European Helmets. (1) A helmet discovered at Gniezdow. It dates from the second half of the 9th century (*Zeitschrift*, 1936, p. 30). (2) Early medieval helmets from eastern Europe. Discovered at Chernaya Mogyla near Cernigov (*ibid.*, pl. V).

PLATE 19   PART III

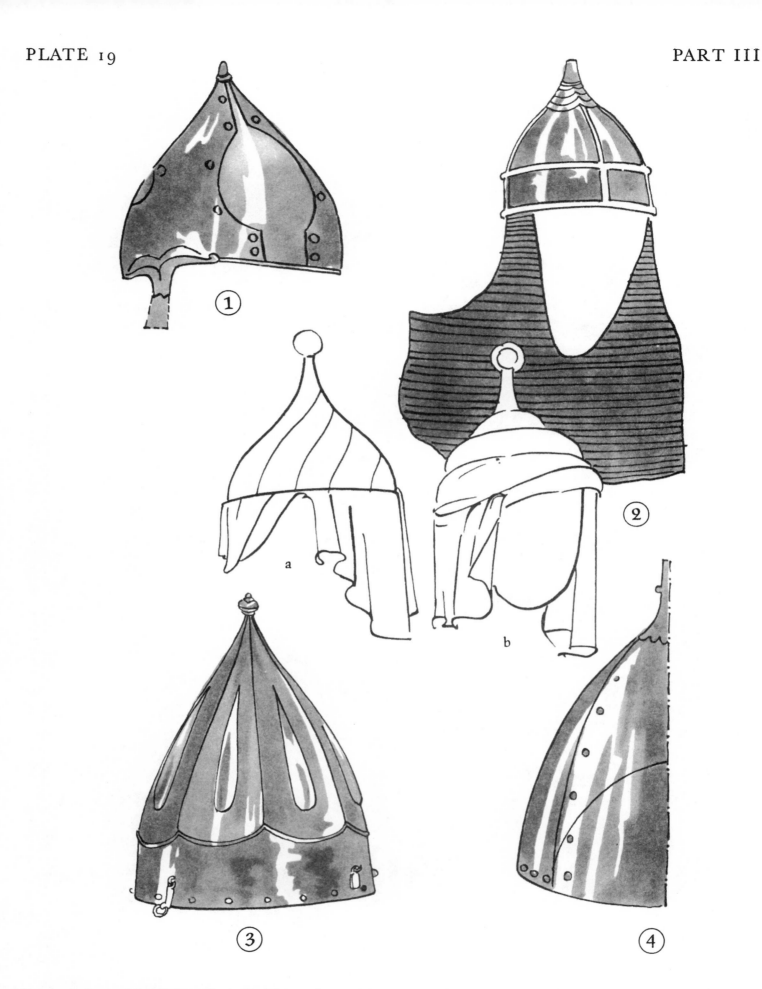

Eastern helmets. (1) A helmet from the 8th or 9th century, preserved in the Leningrad Museum (*Zeitschrift*, 1936, p. 36). (2) A southern Siberian helmet of the 16th or 17th century, preserved in the Moscow History Museum (*Zeitschrift*, 1936, pl. VI). (3) A Turkish helmet of the second half of the 15th century. Height 30 cm., width 21.5 cm., weight 1.80 kilograms (Szendrei, p. 267, pl. 827). (4) A helmet dating from the 9th century found in the Gulbish barrow near Chernigov (*Zeitschrift*, 1936, p. 30). a. A type of helmet appearing in Bohemian Gothic panel paintings about 1430, i. e. the Skalice Crucifixion (Matějček, pl. 241). b. This headdress from the same picture gives more the impression of a turban. It is possibly a similar helmet to that in Fig. a., with the addition of a veil.

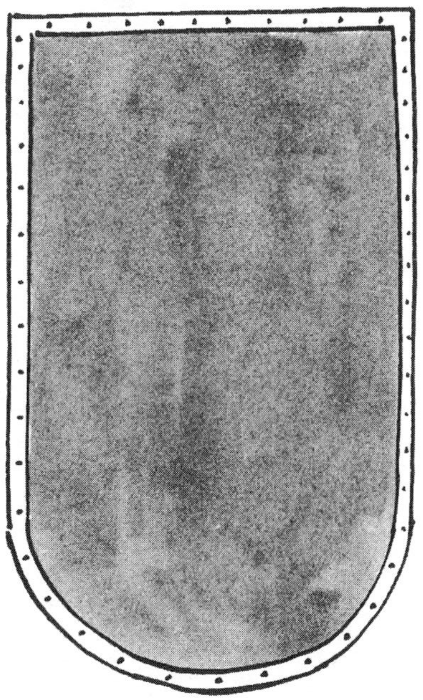

PLATE I

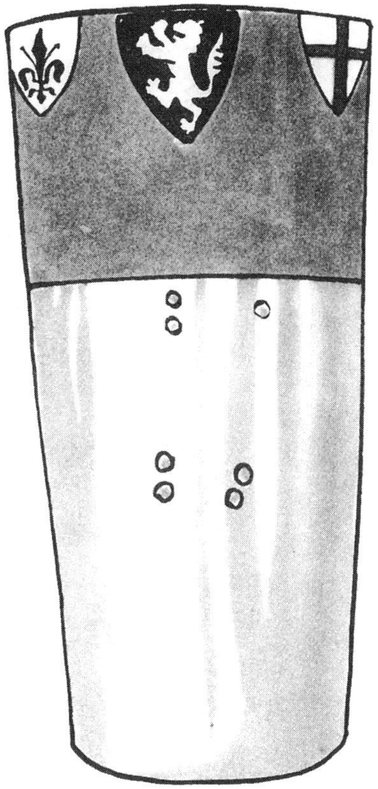

PART IV

(1) Shield of King Edward III, 1327–77 (*European Armour*, II, p. 224, pl. 586). (2) An Italian shield of the mid-15th century (*ibid*., II, p. 236, pl. 604). (3) An early 15th century shield (*ibid*., II, p. 225, pl. 588).

PLATE 2   PART IV

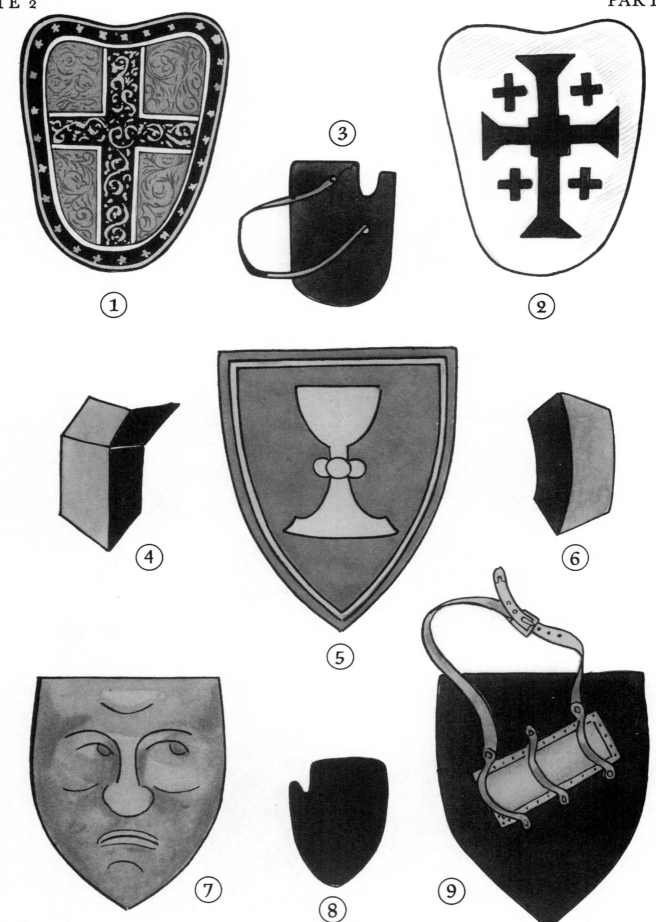

(1) A knight's shield, 1355–67 as carried by St. Maurice in the painting of the same name by Master Theodoricus (Matějček, pl. 68). (2) A knight's shield of the same date, as carried by the Holy Knight in the painting of the same name by Master Theodoricus (Matějček, pl. 69). (3) The back of a shield, in an illumination in the King Wenceslas Bible. (4, 6) Shields in illuminations in the King Wenceslas Bible. (5) A shield in an illumination in the Krumlov MS (fol. 40). (7) A shield in a miniature in the Krumlov MS (fol. 36). (8) A shield in an illumination in the King Wenceslas Bible. (9) The back of a shield showing the strap fastenings (*Zeitschrift*, II, p. 96).

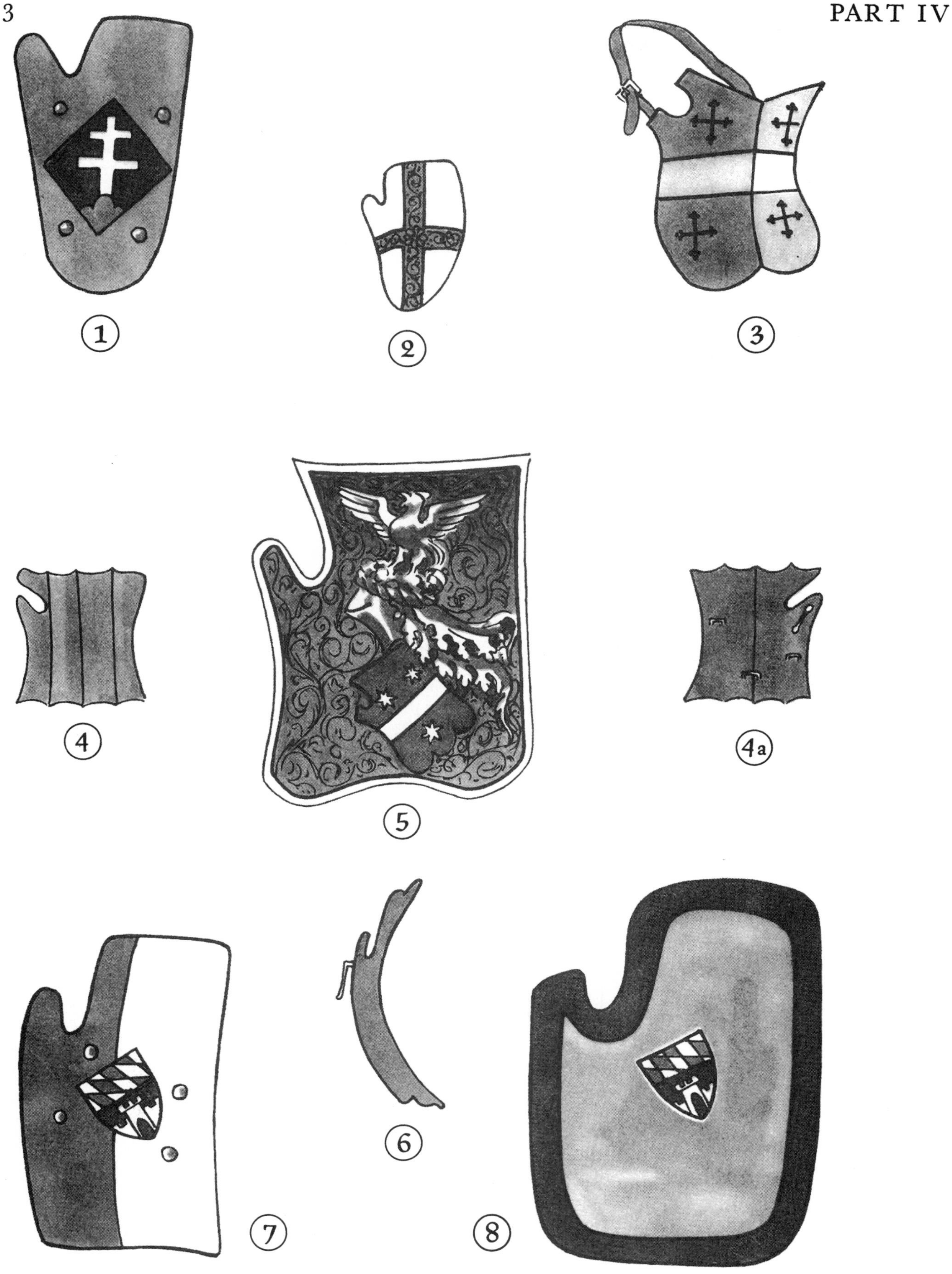

PLATE 3

PART IV

① ② ③

④ ⑤ ④a

⑥ ⑦ ⑧

(1) A 14th century shield (*Ungarisches Soldatentum*, pp. 56, 57). (2) A 14th century shield (*European Armour*, II, p. 70, pl. 424a). (3) A shield dating from between 1410-60 (Alteneck). (4–4a) A 15th century shield, front and back (Demmin, p. 564, pl. 33). (5) A Florentine shield from the middle of the 15th century, made of wood and covered with parchment: 63.5 cm. high and 50.8 cm. wide (*European Armour*, II, p. 228, pl. 591). (6) Side view of an equestrian shield (Demmin, p. 564, pl. 33). (7) A wooden shield covered with skin, carrying the heraldic bearings of the town of Deggendorf, first half of the 15th century (Boeheim, p. 182, pl. 194). See also (8). (8) An equestrian shield of the early 15th century. Height 73 cm., width 55 cm., weight 4.60 kilograms. The bouche for the lance is 20 cm. deep. The shield is covered with a skin. A dark green, almost black field, a broad red border. In the centre are the armorial bearings of the Bavarian town of Deggendorf. The upper part has blue diamonds on a white field, the lower is a red field with a white tower with battlements, fortification wall and open gate (*Waffen der Wartburg*, p. 249, pl. 51, text p. 80).

PLATE 4   PART IV

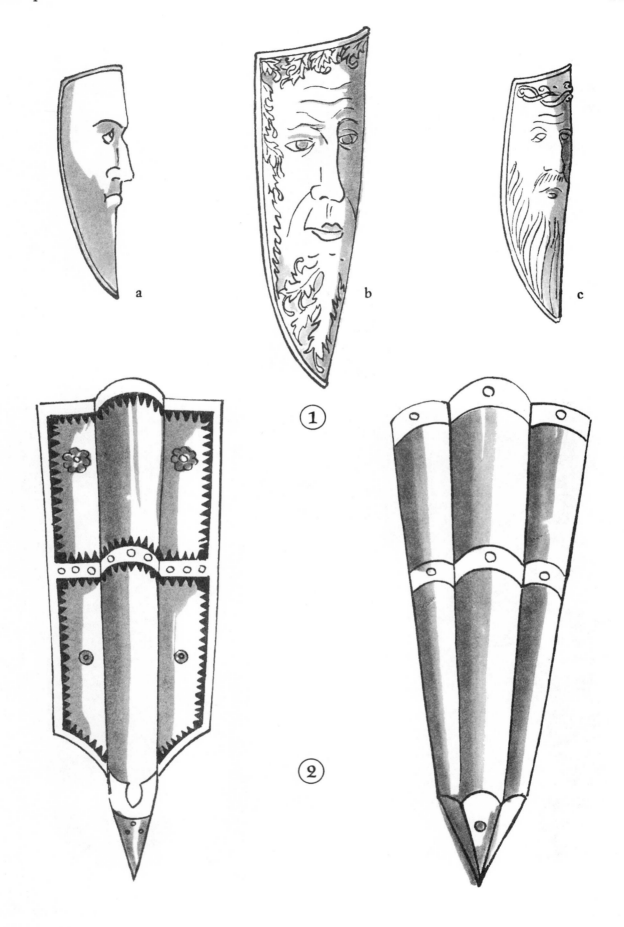

(1) "Face" shields, according to Bohemian Gothic panel paintings. a. From the St. Barbara Crucifixion, about 1380 (Matějček, pl. 114). b. The Crucifixion in the Zátoň altar-piece, dating from after 1430 (Matějček, pl. 222). c. The Crucifixion in the Reininghaus altar-piece, dating from after 1420 (Matějček, pl. 208). (2) Late 15th century pavises, from the Kutná Hora Bible (Zíbrt and Winter, II, p. 249, pl. 143).

PLATE 5

(1) A wooden Hungarian shield with painted skin cover, from the second half of the 15th century (Boeheim, p. 183, pl. 195). (2) The back of a wing-shaped Hungarian shield (Szendrei, p. 202, pl. 586; Boeheim also dates such a wing-shaped equestrian shield from the 13th century and gives its measurements as 127 cm. by 64 cm.; p. 143, pl. 560). (3) A 16th century wing-shaped shield (Szendrei, p. 132, pl. 334) – Szendrei, p. 176, pl. 494, gives the measurements of such Hungarian shields as being height 72 cm., width 37 cm., weight 3·30 kilograms. (4) A Saracen shield from the 15th century, covered with a red skin with gilt decoration (Boeheim). (5) A painted wooden shield of the early 15th century (*European Armour*, II, p. 229, pl. 593).

PLATE 6

PART IV

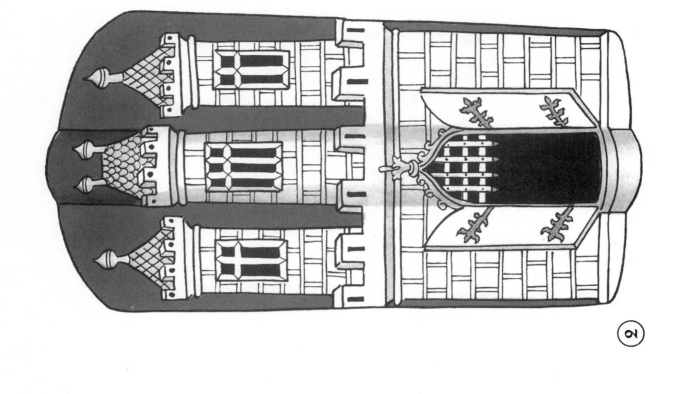

(1) A Czech pavise of the second half of the 15th century, with the favourite Hussite motif of David fighting the heavily-armed giant Goliath (property of the National Museum in Prague). (2) A Prague pavise of the middle of the 15th century (property of the Prague Municipal Museum).

PLATE 7

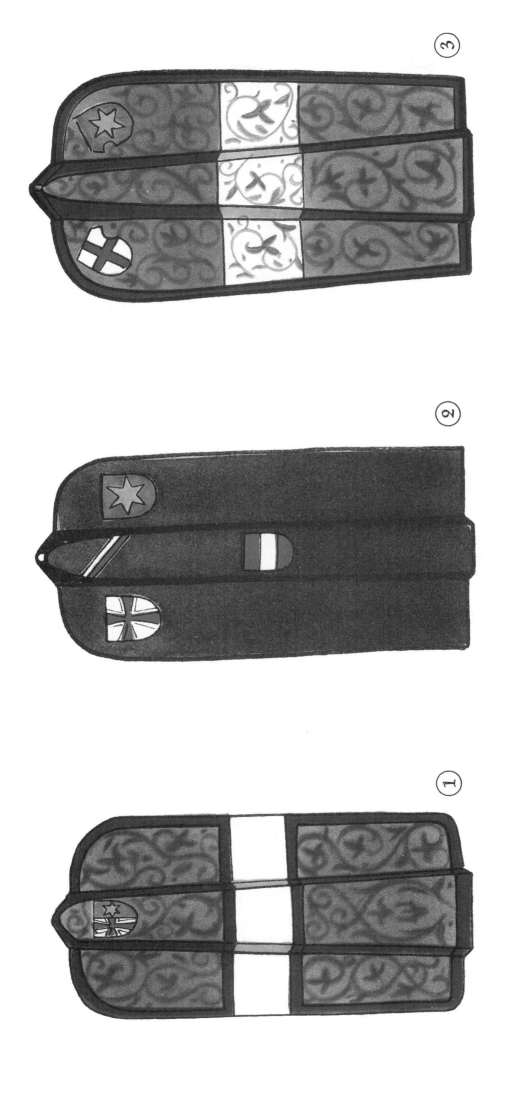

Austrian pavises of the 15th century. (1) Height 112 cm., width 57 cm. (2) Height 117 cm., width 56 cm. (central section is 15 cm. wide). (3) Height 117 cm., width at the base 60 cm. (central section 22 cm. wide). (*Zeitschrift für historische Waffenkunde*, 1929, pp. 159–64).

PLATE 8

PART IV

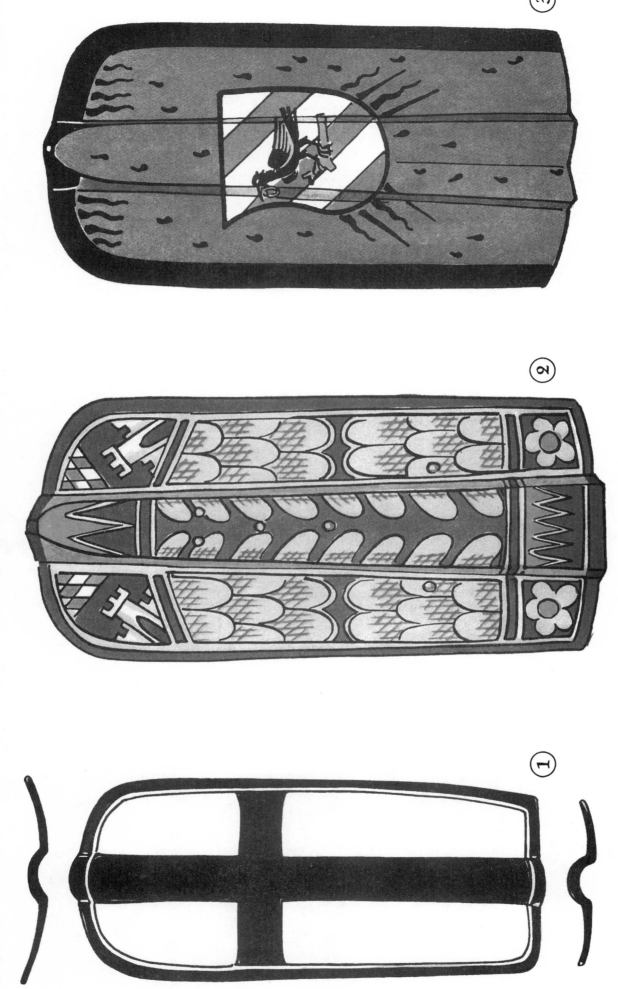

(1) The pavise of an Order of German knights; height about 105 cm., width at top 56 cm., at bottom 46.5 cm. (*Zeitschrift*, II, p. 95). (2) A pavise of the town of Deggendorf; height 127 cm., width at the top 63.5 cm., weight 14.5 kilograms (*Zschille'sche Waffensammlung*, pl. 21, no. 98). (3) A pavise with the bearings of Matthias Corvinus, possibly painted on later; height 115 cm., width at top 62 cm., with a border 5 cm. wide (Szendrei, p. 207, pl. 603).

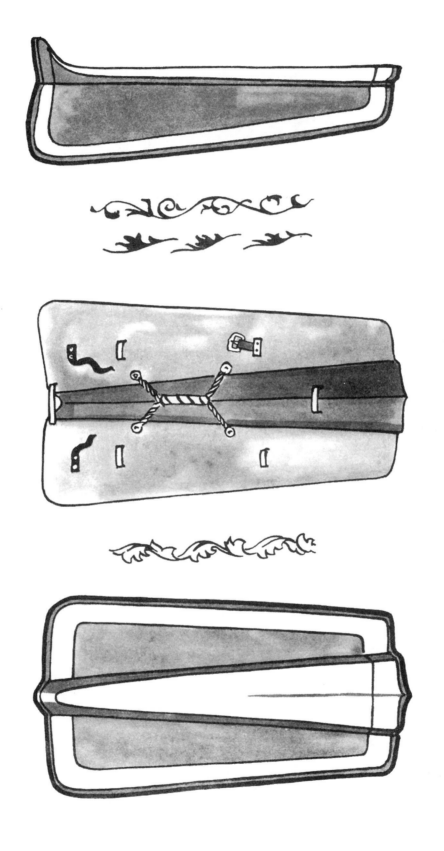

PLATE 9

A pavise from O. Frankenberger, *Naše velká armáda*, p. 30, pl. 11, of usual size. Between the pavises are the motifs used to decorate the shields. It is 130 cm. high, 64 cm. wide (77 cm. at the top). The central section is 21 cm. wide at the bottom and 17.5 cm. at the top; it projects 7.5 cm. An example of a painted pavise.

PLATE 10

PART IV

The monogram of the ruling king "W" Vladislav II, the Jagellon king of Bohemia from 1471–1516.

The chalice, symbol of the religious and political adherence of the town.

Typical symbols of the town, miners working a windlass, miners holding a shield with crossed implements.

Border, usually with religious inscription.

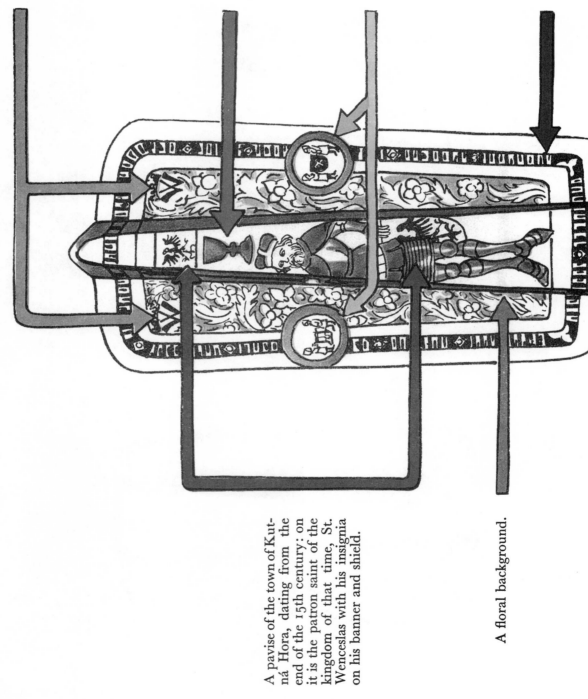

A pavise of the town of Kutná Hora, dating from the end of the 15th century: on it is the patron saint of the kingdom of that time, St. Wenceslas with his insignia on his banner and shield.

A floral background.

PLATE 11   PART IV

(1) A pavise or *taras* with supporting poles and observation slit, dating from 1405 (Bellifortis MS, fol. 128). (2) A pavise or *taras* with a slot for a weapon: both pavises are equipped with spikes at the lower edge and "crutches" at the back (*ibid.*). (3) The upper part of the supporting pole (from a Viennese MS dating from between 1437 and 1450). (4) The handle of the pavise from (2). (5) A pavise dating from the end of the 15th century (Boeheim, p. 179, pl. 190). (6) A pavise of the town of Ravensbrück (*Památky archeologické a místopisné*, 1902, XX, Bk. II, p. 175). (6a) The back of the same pavise. (7) Cross-section of the peep-hole of the same pavise.

PLATE 12 PART IV

The bearings of a Grand-master of an Order of German Knights, dating from the first quarter of the 14th century (*Zeitschrift für historische Waffenkunde*, II, p. 98). Various types of heraldic crosses from *Heraldry* by Král z Dobré Vody, V, pp. 165–7. (1) The ordinary cross of the monastery of St. George in Prague. (2) The potent or crutch-head cross. (3) The crosslet cross (as early as 1278). (4) The anchor or moline cross. (5) The liliate or pattée cross. (6) The Maltese cross. At the bottom centre is a botonée or clover-leaf cross.

PLATE 1   PART V

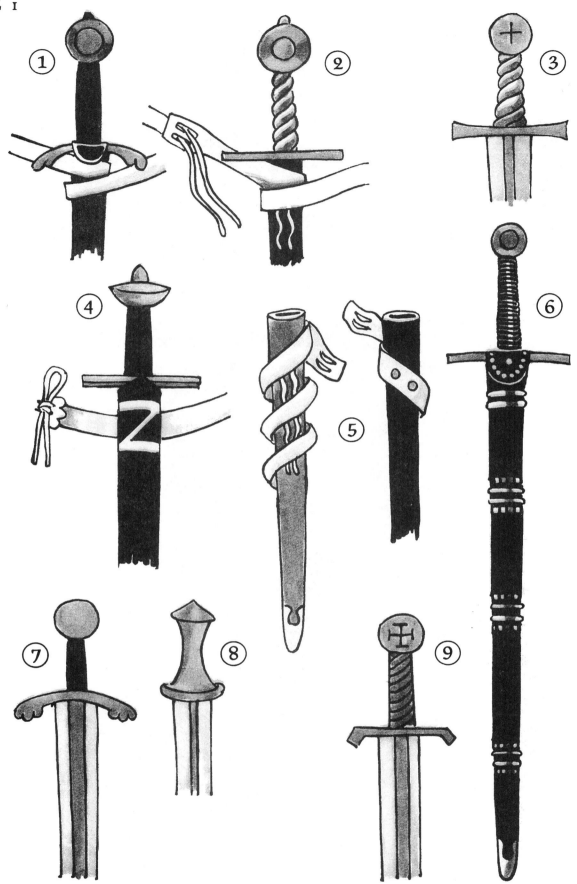

(1–2) A sword and its attachment to the belt, from the Velislav Bible (first half of the 14th century). (3) A sword, from the Velislav Bible. (4) A sword and its attachment to the belt, from the Velislav Bible. (5) Two scabbards from the Velislav Bible. (6) A sword, from the Krumlov MS (early 15th century). (7) A sword from the Velislav Bible. (8) A dagger, *ibid.* (9) A sword, *ibid.*

PLATE 2 PART V

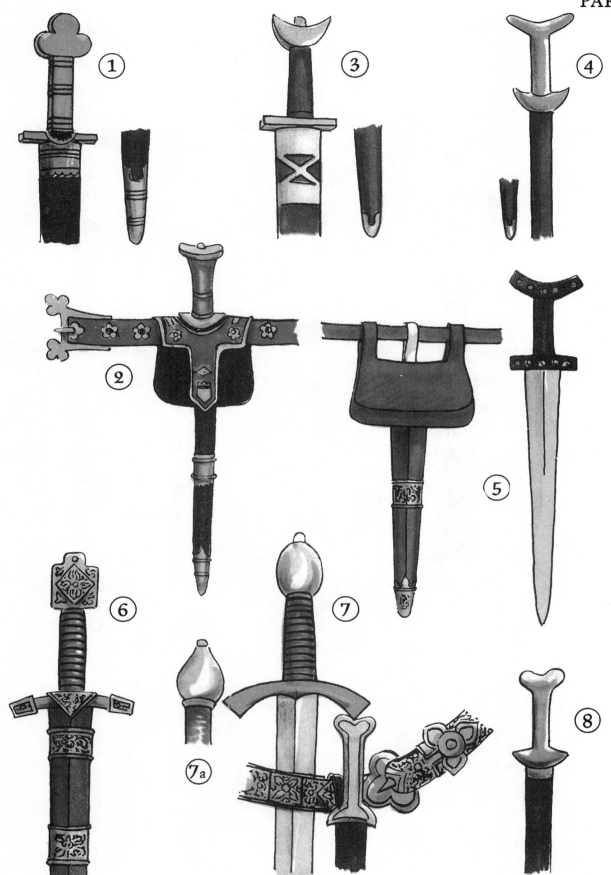

(1) From the Crucifixion by the Master of Vyšší Brod, about 1350. This sword and dagger (2) are worn by the captain (Matějček, pl. 14). (2) A dagger, length 50 cm., about 1350. See (1). (3) From the Resurrection by the Master of Vyšší Brod, 1350. The sword and dagger (4), length 50 cm., are worn by the guard at the Holy Tomb (*ibid.*, pl. 17). (5) From the Kaufmann Crucifixion, dating from after 1350. Dagger and sheath. The actual length of the weapon was about 50 cm (*ibid.*, pl. 33). (6) St. Catherine's sword, by Master Theodoricus, 1357–67 (*ibid.*, pl. 67). (7) The sword, dagger and belt of St. Maurice, according to Master Theodoricus, dating from 1357–67 (*ibid.*, pl. 68). (7a) The pommel of David's sword, according to Donatello. (8) The dagger of the young Wenceslas, from the Jan of Očko votive painting, after 1370; the length of the dagger in reality would have been about 50 cm. (*ibid.*, pl. 75).

PLATE 3

PART V

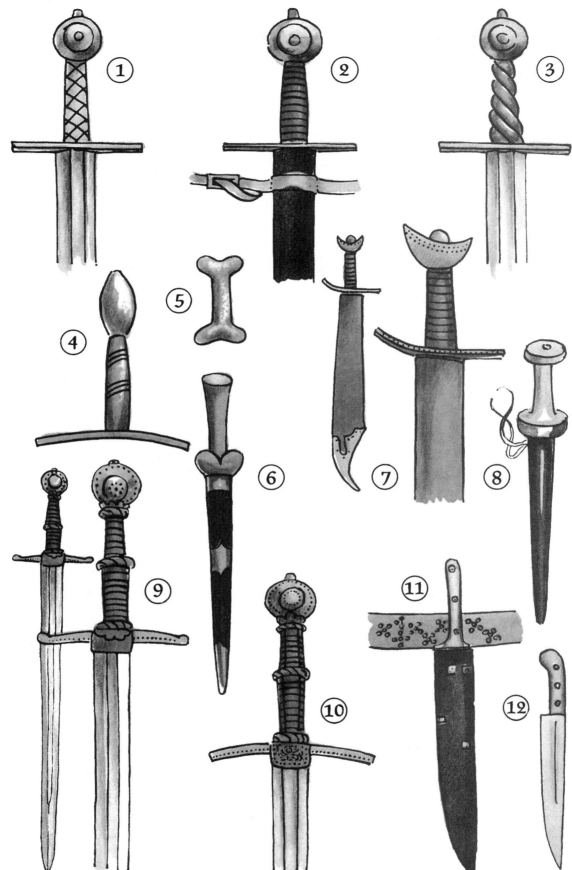

(1) The sword of St. Wenceslas, from the Jan of Středa's *Liber Viaticus* of about 1360. (2) A sword from the *Liber Viaticus* about 1360, fol. 268. (3) A soldier's sword, from before 1380, from the Crucifixion in the Emmaus monastery (Matějček, pl. 81). (4) The hilt of a sword, about 1385, from the Mulhouse altar-piece (*ibid.*, pl. 87). (5) A dagger hilt often to be found in Bohemian Gothic paintings; a similar one is to be seen in the Emmaus Monastery Crucifixion (*ibid.*, pl. 81). (6) A dagger dating prior to 1380, from the Emmaus Monastery Crucifixion (*ibid.*, pl. 81). (7) A soldier's falchion, dating from about 1380, from the Resurrection by the Master of the Třeboň altar-piece (*ibid.*, pl. 96). (8) A soldier's dagger, dating from about 1380 (*ibid.*, pl. 101). (9) A sword dating from about 1385, from the Three Saints by the Master of the Třeboň altar-piece (*ibid.*, pl. 93). (10) A captain's sword, dating from about 1400, from the St. Barbara Crucifixion (*ibid.*, pl. 114). (11) Soldier's knife, with part of the belt, dating before 1400, source as in (10). (12) A knife depicted in the Jena Codex.

PLATE 4   PART V

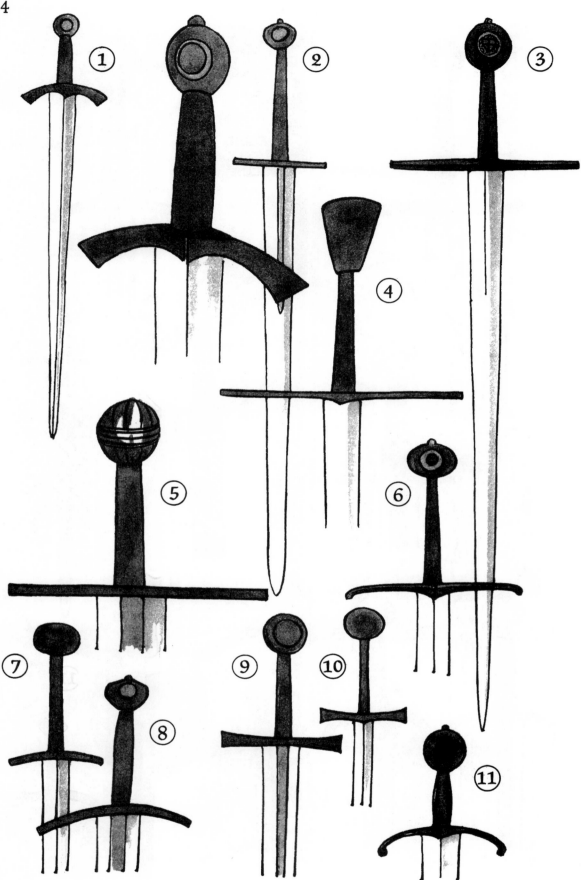

(1) An early 15th century sword (Dreger, *Waffensammlung*, pl. 23, fig. 50, p. 86). (2) A 14th to 15th century sword (*Zeitschrift für historische Waffenkunde*, VIII, p. 250, pl. 2a). (3) A sword from the first quarter of the 15th century (*European Armour*, II, p. 262, pl. 639). (4) A mid-14th century sword (*European Armour*, I, p. 132, pl. 164). (5) An English sword with a spherical pommel, from the first half of the 14th century (*European Armour*, I, p. 134, pl. 167). (6) A sword dating from the middle of the 14th century (*European Armour*, I, p. 140, pl. 174). (7) A 14th–15th century sword about 124 cm. long (*Zeitschrift*, VIII, p. 252, fig. 4b). (8) A sword about 115 cm long, dating from 1308 (*Zeitschrift*, VIII, p. 360). (9) A 13th to 14th century sword (*Zeitschrift*, VII, p. 214, pl. 1c). (10) A 14th–15th century sword in the Steyer Museum in Graz (*Zeitschrift*, VIII, p. 252, pl. 4a). (11) A late 14th century German sword (Stone, p. 592, pl. 761; similarly *European Armour*, II, p. 264, pl. 641, middle of the 15th century).

PLATE 5 PART V

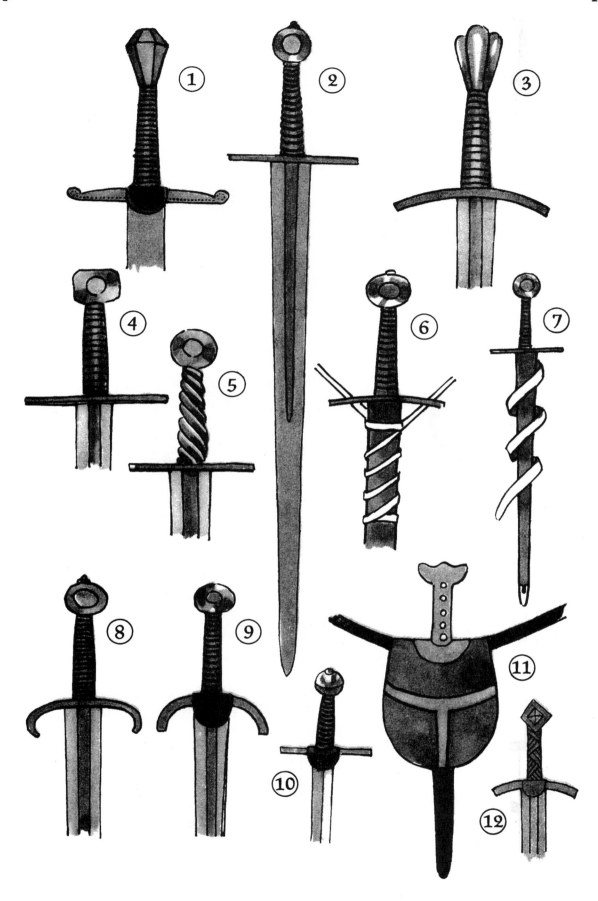

(1) The sword of St. Wenceslas, before 1400. (Dubeček panel, Matějček, pl. 138; similar in *European Armour*, II, p. 323, pl. 701). (2–5) Swords from the King Wenceslas Bible. (6) A method of attaching the scabbard, from the King Wenceslas Bible. (7) The girding of a sword, from the King Wenceslas Bible. (8–9) Swords from the King Wenceslas Bible. (10) A dagger dating from about 1420 (the Reininghaus altar-piece, Mary Magdalene and St. Lucy, Matějček, pl. 211). (11) A dagger and pouch from the King Wenceslas Bible. (12) The hilt of a sword, in a painting of St. Felix of Adauctus; middle of the 15th century.

PLATE 6   PART V

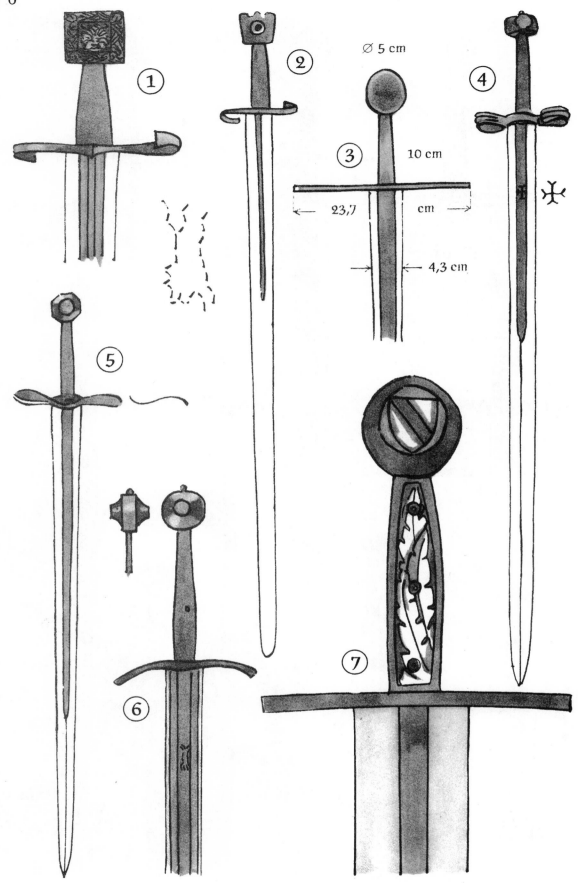

(1) A late 15th-century Spanish sword (Stone, p. 592, pl. 761, fig. 5). (2) A sword from the middle of the 15th century. The cross-guard in the shape of a horizontal letter S (*Zeitschrift für historische Waffenkunde*, I, p. 83, pl. 7). The sword bears the running wolf mark, see detail. (3) A 13th to 14th century sword (*ibid.*, VII, p. 214, pl. 1d). (4) A late 15th century sword, 111 cm. long (Zschille, pl. 65, p. 258; similar in *European Armour*, II, p. 287, pl. 688, second half of the 15th century, and *Zeitschrift*, pl. X, p. 152). (5) A 15th century sword. Blade 95 cm. long, 5 cm. wide, hilt 12 cm. long, haft 12 cm. long, pommel 5 cm. (Szendrei, p. 189, pl. 555). (6) A 15th century sword, with drooping quillons, and a running wolf marked on the blade (*Zeitschrift*, I, p. 83, pl. 8). (7) The sword of Margrave Rudolph VI of Baden. 1353–72 (*ibid.*, I, p. 262).

PLATE 7   PART V

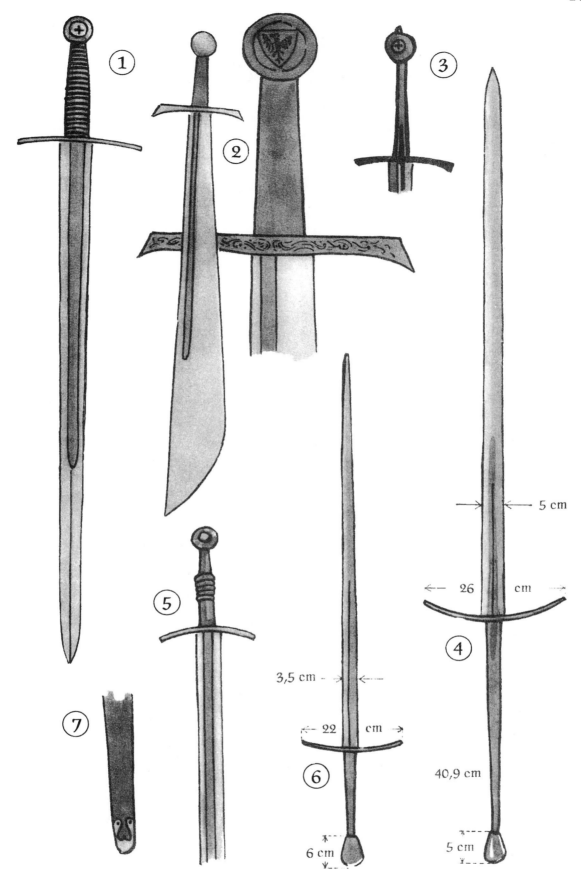

(1) A 14th century sword (*Zeitschrift*, III, p. 261, pl. 24). (2) An early 14th century falchion (*European Armour*, I, pp. 128, 129, pl. 157 and 158). (3) A 14th–15th century sword (*ibid.*, VIII, p. 253, pl. 5a). (4) A 15th century "two-handed" sword, 151 cm long (Copenhagen National Museum, *ibid*, VIII, p. 251, pl. 6a). (5) A sword of the second half of the 15th century; 108.5 cm. long, cross-guard 23.5 cm. long (K. Gimbel, *Waffensammlung*, text p. 21, no. 358). (6) A sword, about 1386. 103 cm. long, blade 83 cm. long, 3.5 cm. wide, cross-guard 22 cm. long, pommel 6 cm. high. (7) A chape: the metal plate often found on the lower tip of the scabbard. (*Zeitschrift*, II, p. 203).

PLATE 8　　　　　　　　　　　　　　　　　　　　　　　　　　PART V

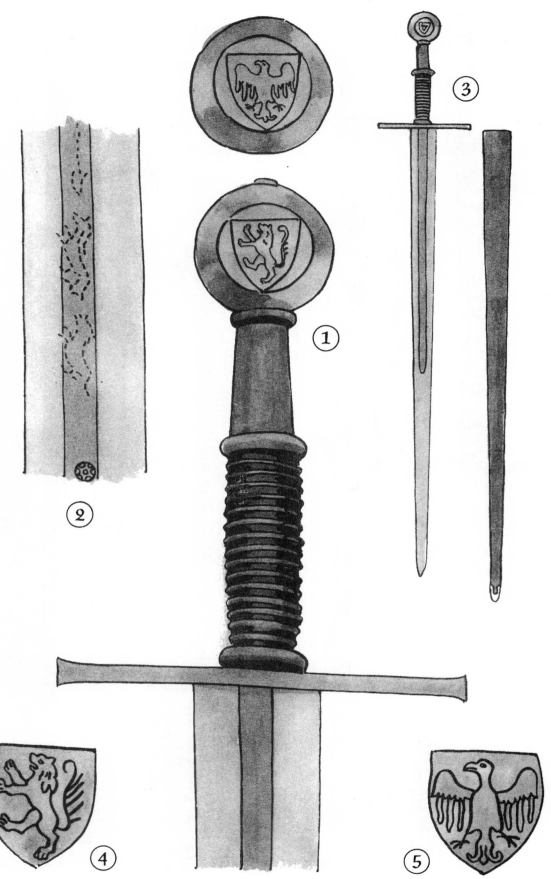

(1) The sword of the Emperor Albrecht II, 1438–9 (Jan Lauts, *Alte deutsche Waffen*, pl. 6). (2) The swordsmith's mark on the groove of the Emperor Albrecht's sword (Szendrei dates the sword from the end of the 14th century: pp. 190, 191, pl. 560). (3) A sword and its scabbard. Blade 98.5 cm. long, 5.9 cm. wide, haft 17 cm. long, pommel 6.3 cm. (*Zeitschrift* n. d., p. 25, pl. 1). (4) A lion on an escutcheon on the pommel of a sword, inlaid brass (Szendrei, p. 191, pl. 560). (5) An eagle on an escutcheon on the pommel of a sword (*ibid.*, p. 25, pl. 2 and 3).

PLATE 9   PART V

(1) A Bohemian sword dating from about 1430 (Matějček). (2) The pommel of a sword, inscribed with a cross (*Zeitschrift*, n.d., p. 25). (3) A sword in its scabbard as carried by an executioner, 1430–1440 from the St. James altar-piece, "The Capture of St. James" (Matějček, pl. 253). (4) A sword dating from 1430, from the Skalice Crucifixion (*ibid.*, pl. 239). (5–6) Swords from the Prague Municipal Museum, drawn in proportion to one another (14th–15th centuries). Sword, (5), cat. no. 11473, has the following measurements: length 117.5 cm., blade 90 cm. long, 7 cm. wide, pommel 5.5 cm., cross-guard 21 cm. long. Sword, (6) is 90.5 cm. long, blade 73 cm. long, 4.2 cm. wide, pommel 5.5 cm., cross-guard 16.5 cm. long. (7) A 15th century sword from Levoča. (*Zeitschrift*, I, p. 83, pl. 12). (8) A soldier's sabre, dating from about 1430, from the Skalice Crucifixion (Matějček, pl. 239). (9) A dagger and pouch, dating from between 1430–40, from the St. James altar-piece, "St. James attends the Sick" (*ibid.*, pl. 254). (10) Part of falchion, from the Badra fortress (Sedláček, XII, p. 21). Blade 46.4 cm. long, 5 cm. wide.

PLATE 10   PART V

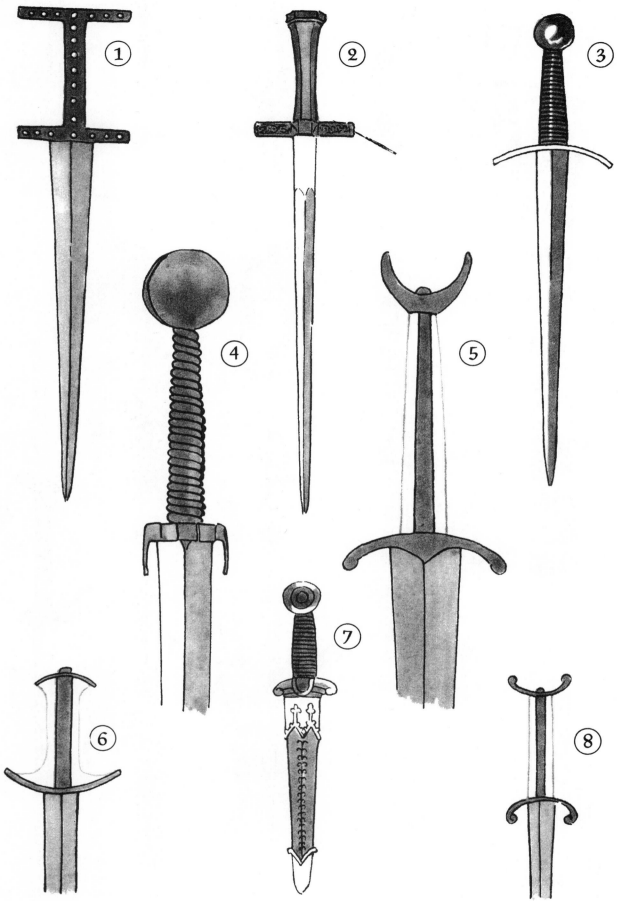

(1) A basilard dagger, early 15th century (*European Armour*, III, p. 10, pl. 748). (2) A dagger dating from about 1400 (*ibid.*, III, p. 5, pl. 733). (3) A late 14th century dagger (*ibid.*, III, p. 4, pl. 729). (4) A dagger dating from about 1390 (*ibid.*, III, p. 5, pl. 731). (5) An early 15th century Italian dagger (*ibid.*, III, p. 6, pl. 736). (6) A dagger dating from about 1386 (*Zeitschrift*, VI, p. 207; original in a museum in Zurich). (7) The dagger from the effigy of John Cray, dating from 1392 (*European Armour*, III, p. 4, pl. 730). (8) A dagger from the middle of the 14th century (*European Armour*, III, p. 6, pl. 735).

PLATE 11   PART V

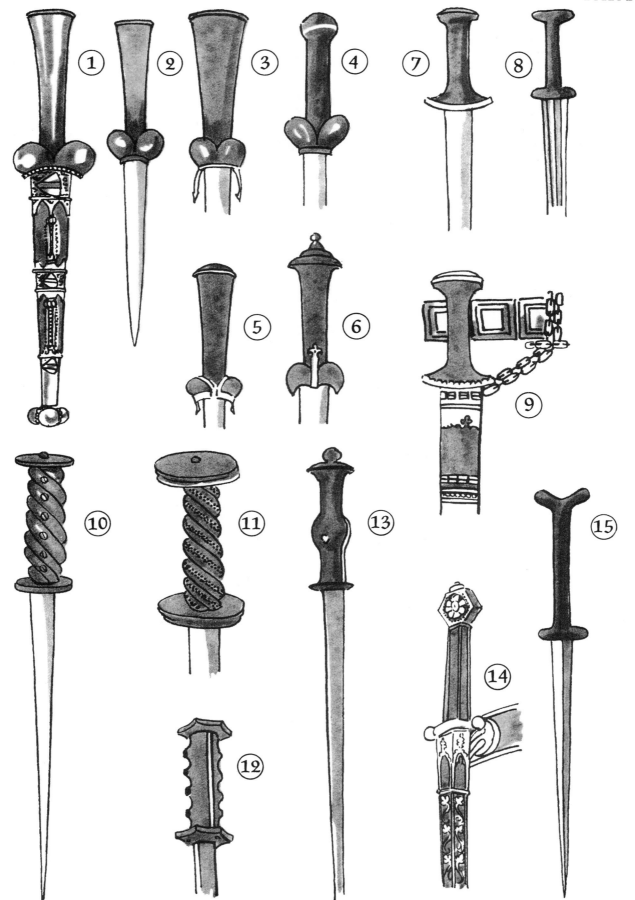

Daggers. (1) A Danish 14th century dagger (*Zeitschrift für historische Waffenkunde*, 1929/1931, p. 269, pl. 2). (2) A 14th century Bohemian dagger in the Prague Municipal Museum. (3) A dagger dating from between 1430–50 (*European Armour*, III, p. 33, pl. 796). (4) A dagger dating from between 1400–20 (*European Armour*, III, p. 32, pl. 795). (5) An English dagger dating from between 1450–60 (*ibid.*, III, p. 35, pl. 798). (6) An English dagger 1440–50 (*ibid.*, III, p. 36, pl. 803). (7) A late 14th century German dagger (*ibid.*, III, p. 10, pl. 747). (8) Early 15th century German dagger (*ibid*, III, p. 10, pl. 750). (9) A method of fastening the scabbard to the belt, dating from 1390 (*ibid.*, III, p. 9, pl. 743). (10) A 15th century French dagger (*Zschille'sche Waffensammlung*, pl. 149, no. 421). (11) An early 15th century dagger (*European Armour*, III, p. 17, pl. 765). (12) An English dagger dated 1430 (*ibid.*, III, p. 19, pl. 770). (13) An English dagger about 1440 (*ibid.*, III, p. 21, pl. 774). (14) An early 14th century sword, showing attachment to the belt (*ibid.*, III, p. 3, pl. 725). (15) A slender dagger, dating from about 1420 (*ibid.*, III, p. 11, pl. 752).

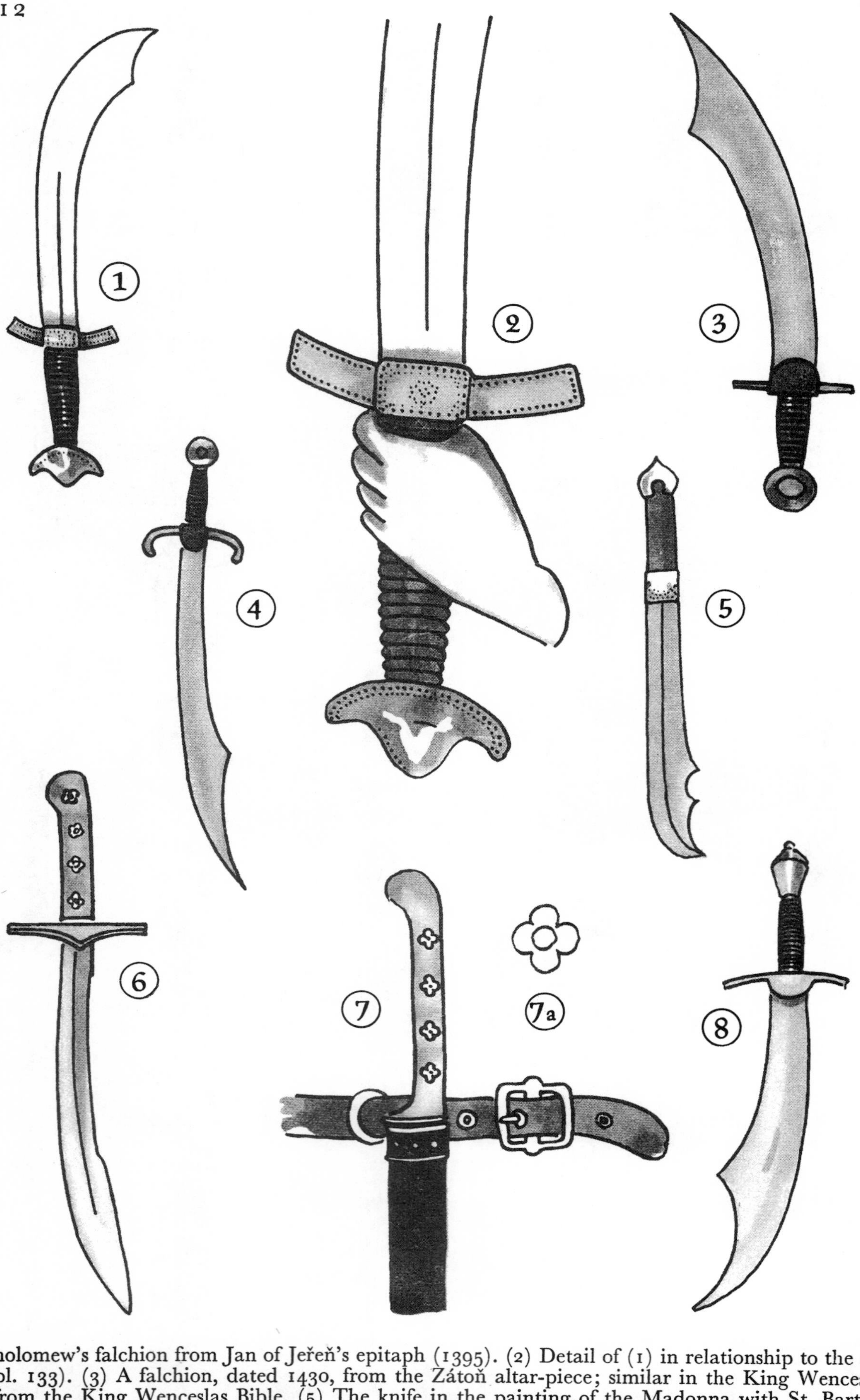

PLATE 12   PART V

(1) St. Bartholomew's falchion from Jan of Jeřeň's epitaph (1395). (2) Detail of (1) in relationship to the size of a hand (Matějček, pl. 133). (3) A falchion, dated 1430, from the Zátoň altar-piece; similar in the King Wenceslas Bible. (4) A falchion from the King Wenceslas Bible. (5) The knife in the painting of the Madonna with St. Bartholomew and St. Margaret, dating from about 1400 (Matějček, pl. 130). (6) A soldier's sabre, prior to 1420, from the Rajhrad altar-piece painting of the Carrying of the Cross (Matějček, pl. 181). The sabre hangs from the soldier's wrist by a narrow strap. In reality the hilt of the sabre would be about 22 cm. long, the blade 56 cm. (7) A falchion dating from about 1430, from the Hýrov votive altar-piece, "The Madonna with the Donors" (Matějček, pl. 219). (7a) An ornamental rivet on the previous falchion. (8) A falchion dating prior to 1420, from the Rajhrad altar-piece painting of the Resurrection. There is a similar weapon in the Zátoň altar-piece, dating from after 1430, in the painting "The Execution of St. John the Baptist" (ibid., pl. 227).

PLATE 13

PART V

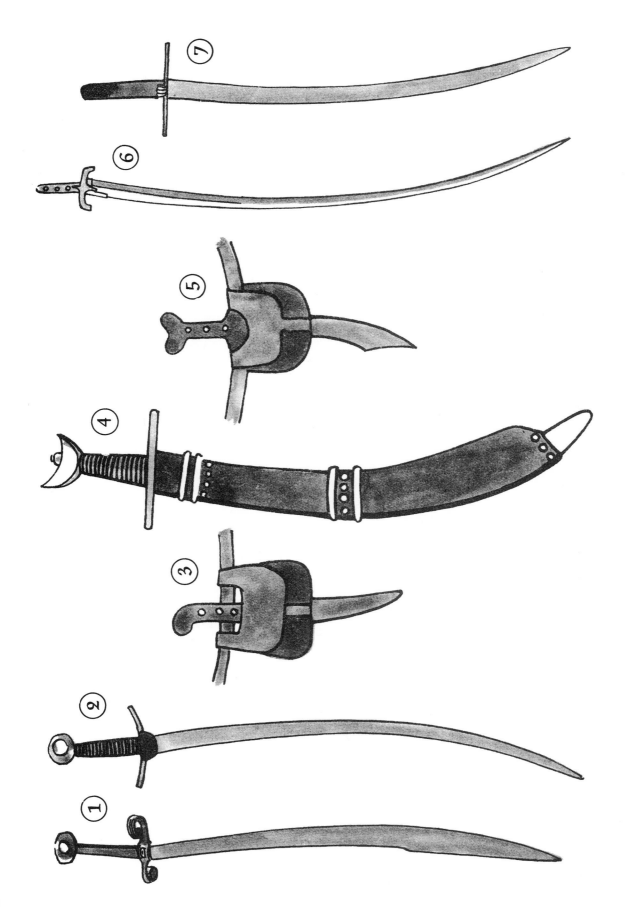

(1) A sabre from the middle of the 15th century (*Zeitschrift für historische Waffenkunde*, 1935, pl. X, following p. 152, no. 8). (2) A sabre from the King Wenceslas Bible. (3) A knife and pouch from the King Wenceslas Bible. (4) A falchion from the King Wenceslas Bible. (5) A knife and pouch from the King Wenceslas Bible. (6) A Tartar sabre (Turkish) of the early 13th century. Length 109 cm., width 3.3 cm. (*Zeitschrift*, 1934, p. 43). (7) A late 15th century sabre, similar to that of George Castriota (Scanderberg, 1403–67). Length of blade 91 cm., width 3.5 cm., haft 17.3 cm., cross-guard 21.5 cm. There is an upturned hook on the outer side of the cross-guard (Szendrei, pp. 177–90, pl. 557).

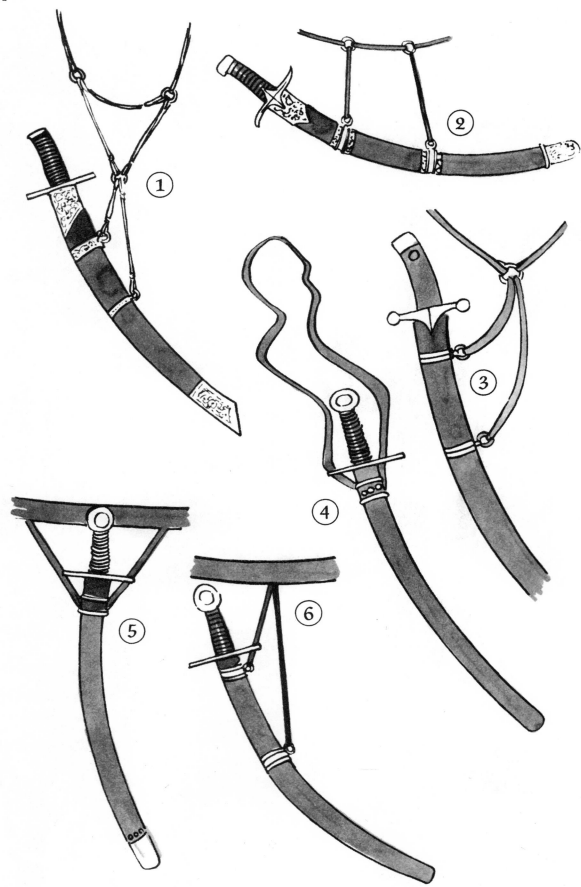

(1) Straps for hanging the sabre over the right shoulder (from the painting "The Beheading of St. Barbara", by Hans Schüchlin, died 1505, in the Prague National Gallery). (2) Method of hanging a sabre from a belt (Arthur Wesse, *Skulptur und Malerei in Frankreich im 14. und 15. Jahrhundert*, p. 51, pl. 64). (3) Method of hanging a sabre over the right shoulder, according to a drawing by Jost Amman (Schoenbeck, p. 174, pl. 278; also *Zeitschrift*, II, p. 363, pl. 6). (4) A sabre and its hanging strap, from the King Wenceslas Bible. (5–6) Methods of hanging a sabre from a belt from the King Wenceslas Bible.

PLATE 15   PART V

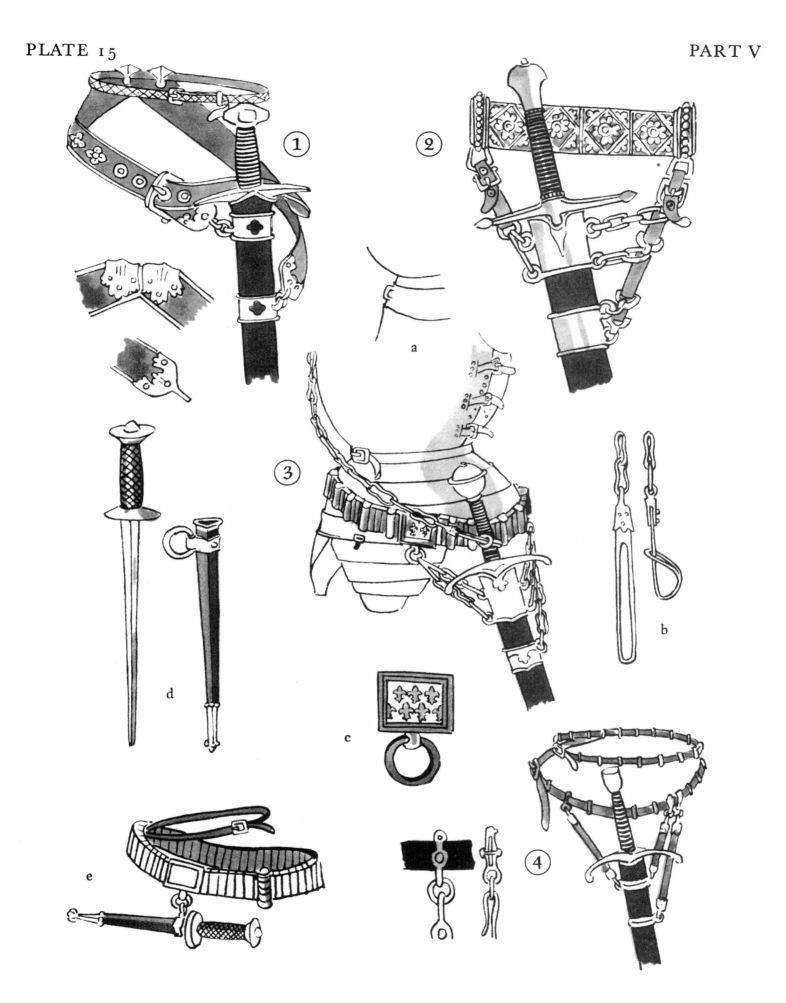

Knightly girdles and methods of attaching the sword, from the 14th and 15th centuries, according to Viollet le Duc. (1) Dating from 1323, with details of the belt fastenings. (2) Dating from between 1380–1400. (3) From about the year 1400, with details: a. the metal ring fixed to the armour at the hip for threading the strap or throng; b. a link in the chain by which the sword is suspended; c. one of the metal plates of the belt, with a ring for suspending a dagger; d. the dagger and its sheath; e. the dagger as suspended from the belt. (4) The attachment of a sword dating from between 1409–10, with details of the straps used.

PLATE 16   PART V

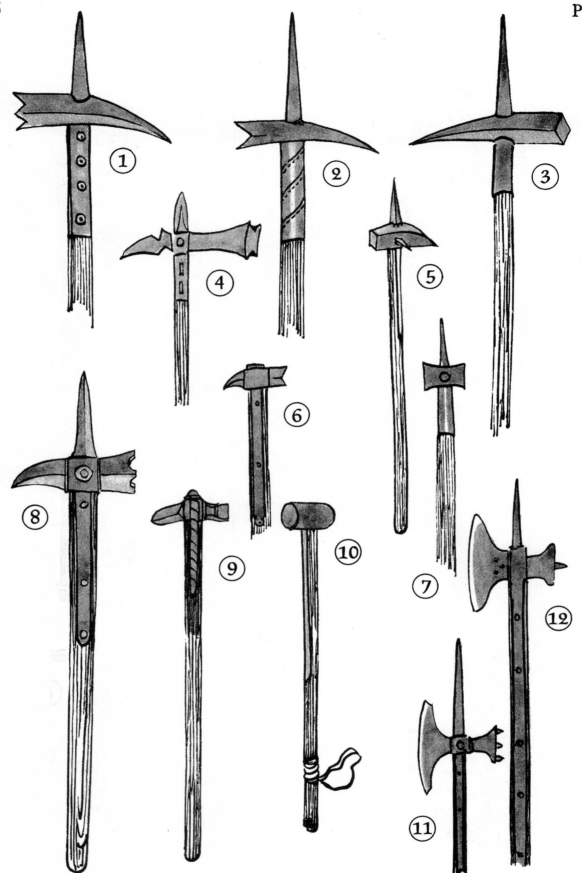

War-hammers. (1) A war-hammer from the painting by the Master of the Třeboň altar-piece, "Christ on the Mount of Olives", dating from 1389 (Matějček, pl. 88). (2) A war-hammer from the Třeboň church of St. Barbara painting of the Crucifixion (*ibid.*, pl. 114), now in the Prague National Gallery. (3) From the Skalice Crucifixion, now in the Prague National Gallery (*ibid.*, pl. 239). (4) A Lucerne war-hammer of the late 14th century (Boeheim, p. 364, pl. 430). (5) A French war-hammer dating from 1350 (Boeheim, p. 364, pl. 429). (6–7) 14th century war-hammers (*Die Geschichte der Französischen Armee*, p. 76). (8) A war-hammer dating from the first half of the 15th century (*European Armour*, III, p. 88, pl. 873). (9) A war-hammer (a parrot's beak), probably of the 14th century (K. Gimbel, no. 605, p. 40). Zschille places this hammer in the middle of the 16th century: p. 899, pl. 194. (10) A French lead mallet, with an iron grip on the haft, about 150 cm. long (Boeheim, p. 364, pl. 428). Dated 1495. (11) A mid-15th century pole-axe (Zschille, p. 186, pl. 808). A similar pole-axe is depicted in the Bamberg altar-piece, dating from 1429. (12) A pole-axe of the middle of the 15th century (Szendrei, p. 504, pl. 178).

PLATE 17   PART V

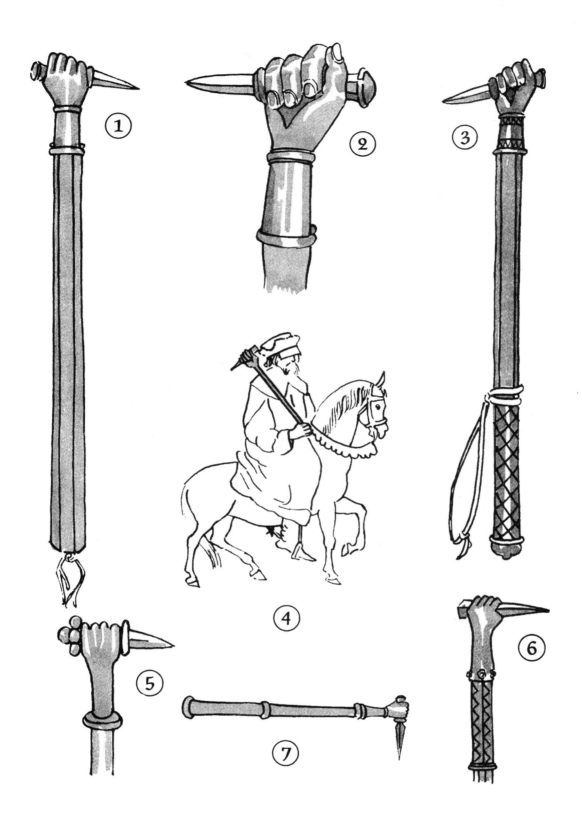

(1) A bronze dagger-mace of the 14th century; total length of mace haft 52 cm., length of dagger 11.5 cm. (*Zeitschrift für historische Waffenkunde*, V, p. 79). (2) Enlargement of a "dagger in the fist" mace (*ibid.*, 1940/1942, p. 25, pl. 1, dates such a mace from the second half of the 15th century). (3) A dagger-mace (*ibid.*, II, 1926/1928, p. 288, pl. 1 and 2). (4) Jan Žižka with a dagger-mace as depicted in the Konáč's translation of the *Czech Chronicles* by Eneas Silvius, 1510 (*Žižkův sborník*, pl. VII). (5) A reproduction of a pen-drawing of a mace in "Hus being led to the stake (*Zeitschrift*, VII, p. 322, pl. 1 and 2). (6) A dagger-mace (*ibid.*, V, p. 81, pl. 3). (7) A 14th century dagger-mace (K. Gimbel, *Waffensammlung*, pl. XV, no. 581).

PLATE 18   PART V

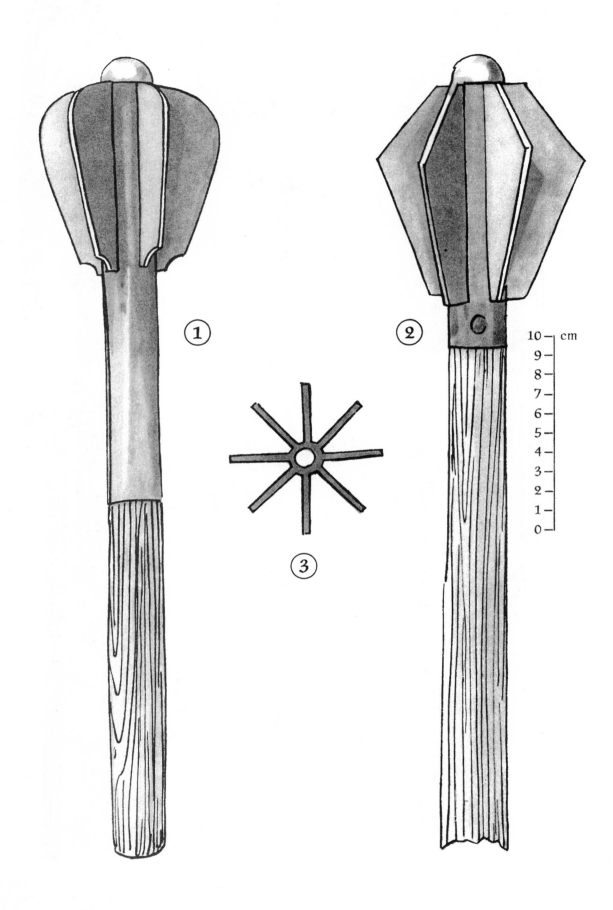

(1) A mace discovered at Tábor, about half its actual size. (Prague National Museum). (2) The head of a six-bladed mace of the 14th century, about 16 cm. long. The base of the blade is about 12 cm. long. (*European Armour*, p. 90, pl. 875). (3) A cross-section of an eight-bladed mace head.

PLATE 19   PART V

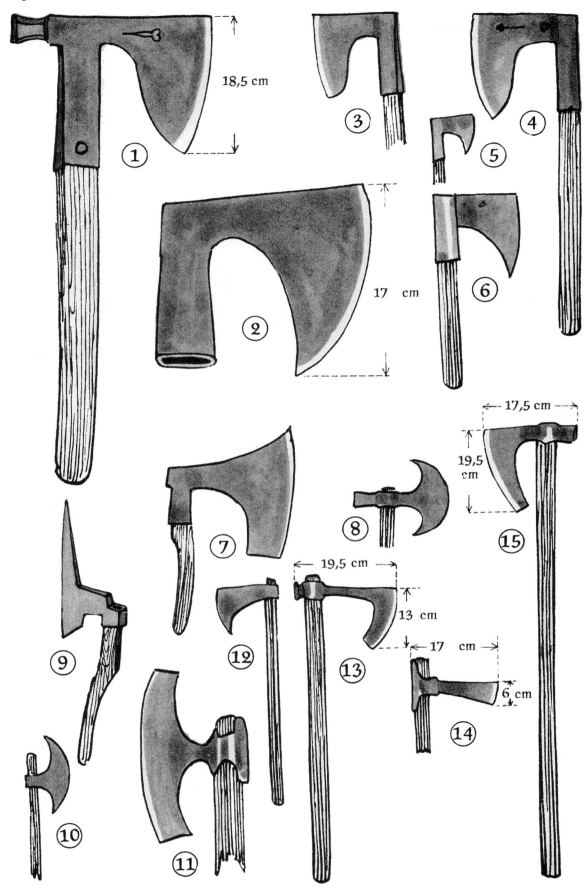

(1) A war-axe from the Tábor museum. Length 24.5 cm., length of blade 18.5 cm., length of socket 19 cm. (2) A war-axe discovered among the remains of the Badra fortress. Length of blade 17 cm. (Sedláček, *Hrady a zámky*, XII, p. 21). (3) A war-axe dating from 1420, from the Crucifixion in the Rajhrad altar-piece (Matějček. pl. 184). (4) A war-axe dating from about 1440 (from a painting in the St. Magdalene church in Třeboň). (5) A war-axe from the first half of the 14th century (Velislav Bible). (6) A war-axe from the first half of the 14th century (from the *Legends of the Bohemian Patron Saints*). (7) A mounted soldier's war-axe of the 15th century (K. Gimbel, no. 678, p. 41). Similar war-axes are recorded for foot soldiers of the 14th and 15th centuries, but with longer hafts (Zschille, no. 562, pl. 164). (8) A late 15th century war-axe (Szendrei, p. 128, no. 331). Length 15 cm. (9) A mounted soldier's war-axe of the 15th century, on a short haft (Boeheim, p. 820, pl. 17). (10) A war-axe depicted in the Velislav Bible. (11) A 14th century German war-axe (Stone, p. 80, pl. 100). (12) An early 15th century war-axe. Length 19.5 cm., length of blade 13 cm. (Szendrei, p. 154, no. 393). (14) An early 15th century war-axe (?), length 17 cm., length of blade 6 cm. (Szendrei, p. 144, no. 393). (15) A 14th century war-axe, length 17.5 cm., length of blade 19.5 cm. (see diagram). (Szendrei, p. 133, no. 334).

PLATE 20   PART V

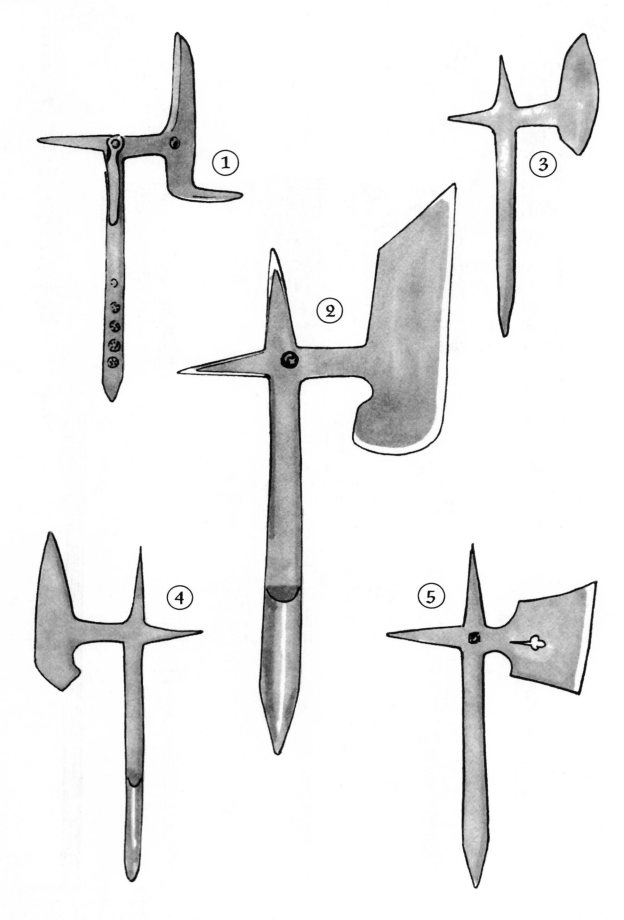

Throwing axe or hurlbats of the 14th and 15th centuries. (1) A 14th century throwing axe. (2–5) Early 15th century throwing axes (*Zeitschrift für historische Waffenkunde*, II, pp. 241, 356).

PLATE 21   PART V

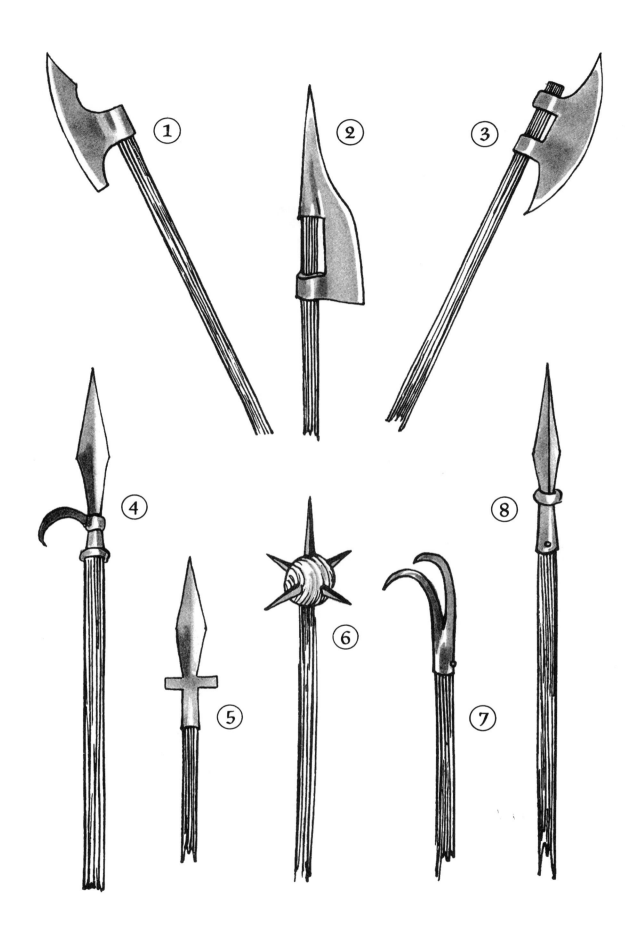

15th century weapons as depicted in the King Wenceslas Bible. (Photographic reproductions in the State Documentary Centre, Prague). (1) A war-axe. (2) A voulge. (3) A primitive halberd. (4) A lance and hook or boar pike. (5) The "eared" javelin. (6) A spiked mace. (7) A "talon" pike or double-pronged fork. (8) A spear.

PLATE 22   PART V

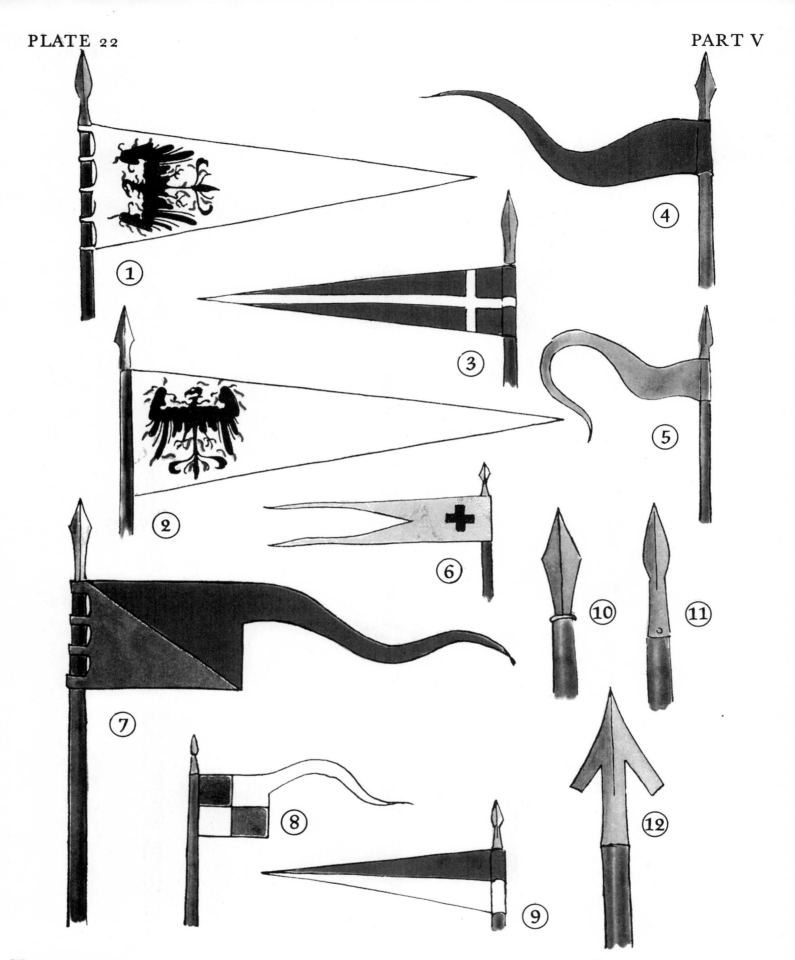

(1) St. Wenceslas's pennon in the Jan Očko of Vlašim votive painting, dating about 1370 (Matějček, pl. 75). (2) St. Wenceslas's pennon in the Mulhouse altar-piece, dating from 1385 (*ibid.*, pl. 87). (3) The pennon from the border of the Vyšší Brod painting of the Madonna, dating from after 1420 (*ibid.*, pl. 204). (4–5) Lances with pennons, from the Krumlov MS. (6) The Holy Knight's pennon, from the painting by Master Theodoricus, dating from between 1357–67 (Matějček, pl. 69). (7) A banner from the Skalice painting of the Crucifixion, dating about 1430 (*ibid.*, pl. 239). (8) The shape of a banner dating between 1430–40. From the Doudleby picture of the Madonna; reverse side; "The Adoration of the Child" (*ibid.*, pl. 242). (9) A pennon dating from 1430, from the Vyšší Brod painting of "The Carrying of the Cross" (*ibid.*, pl. 235). (10) A lance-head as commonly depicted in Bohemian Gothic painting. (11) A lance-head as frequently found among preserved relics. Less common in paintings. (12) A javelin of unusual shape, about 1420. From the Nové Sady picture of the Crucifixion in the Rajhrad altar-piece (Matějček, pl. 184).

PLATE 23   PART V

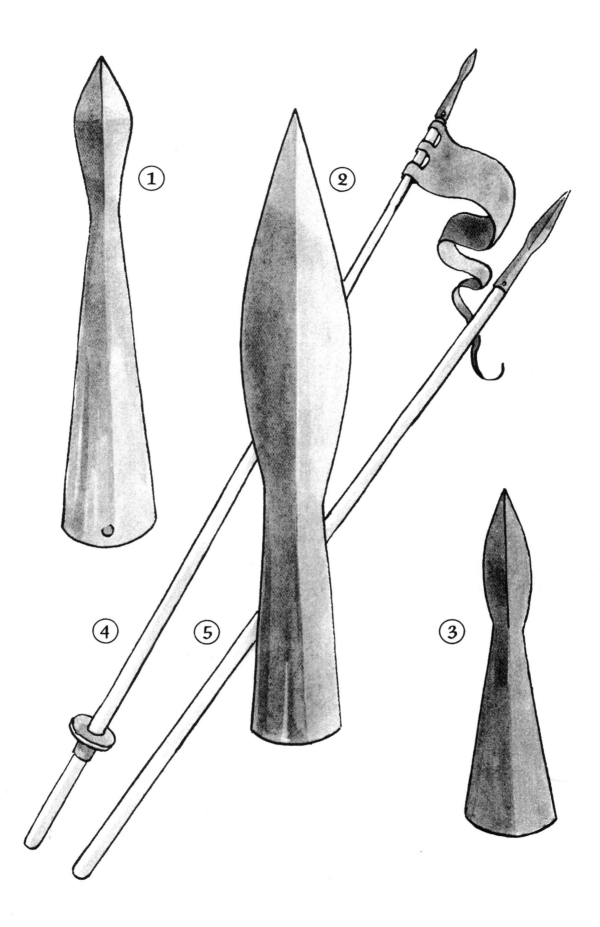

(1) The head of a 15th century lance, preserved in the Prague Municipal Museum. Total length of the head 26 cm., length of headless socket 8 cm. (2) The head of a lance in the Military History Museum in Prague. Length 34.5 cm., greatest width 5 cm. The length of the blade without socket is 22 cm, the diameter of the socket is 4 cm. (3) The head of a 15th century lance. Prague Municipal Museum. Length 18 cm. (4) A common form of lance, fitted with a support ring, frequently to be found in medieval Czech manuscript illuminations. (5) A foot soldier's spear, which is frequently to be found in Bohemian Gothic paintings.

PLATE 24   PART V

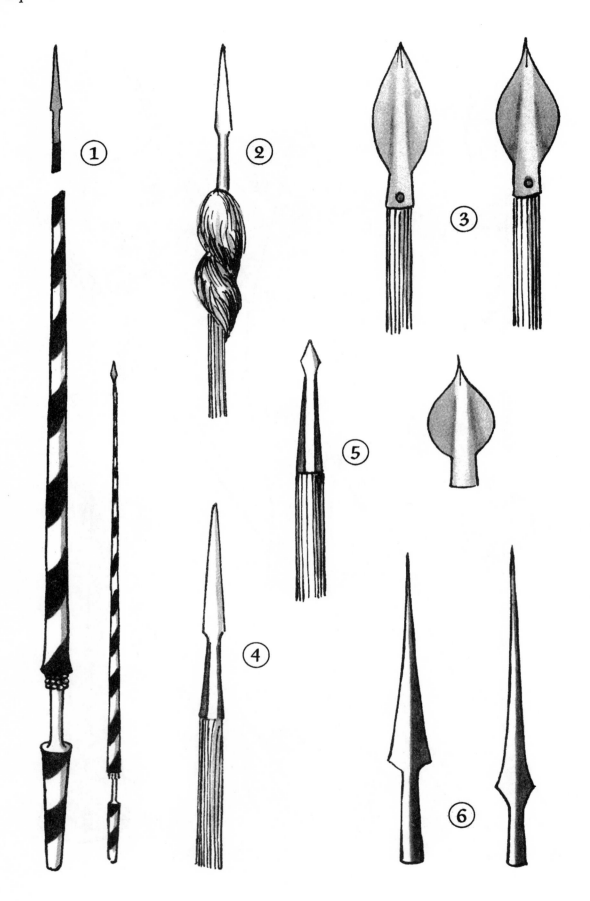

(1) A 15th century lance with a narrow grip for the hand, at the upper end of which there are rows of tiny steel balls (Boeheim, p. 326, pl. 386). (2) The head of a lance ornamented with a fox tail, dating from about 1480 (*ibid*, p. 326, pl. 385). (3) The heads of 15th century Spanish lances (Stone, p. 408, pl. 512). (4) The head of a lance from the second half of the 15th century (Boeheim, p. 314, pl. 366). (5) The head of a French lance of the 15th century (Stone, p. 408, pl. 512). (6) Heads of 14th century lances (*European Armour*, I, p. 141, pl. 176 a, b).

PLATE 25

PART V

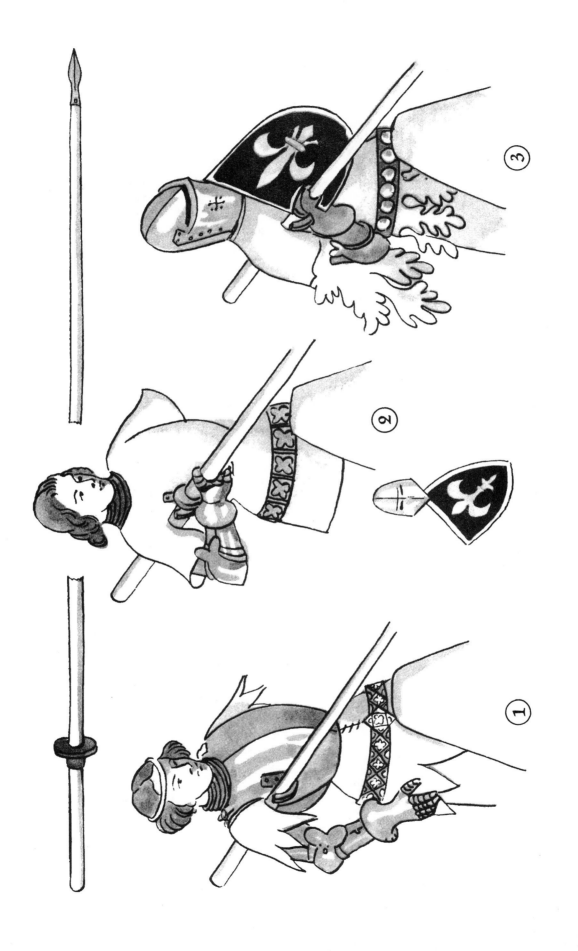

The rest used for supporting the lance. (1) The hook was fixed to the breastplate on the right side of the breast. It helped to balance the lance in action. (2) At the lower end of the lance shaft there was a metal ring, which probably rested against the hook during a thrust at an opponent, giving additional force to the thrust and distributing the shock of the blow over the entire breastplate. (3) The method of holding the lance and shield for attack. (This angle of holding the shield is reflected in the heraldic bearing, see detail.)

PLATE 26   PART V

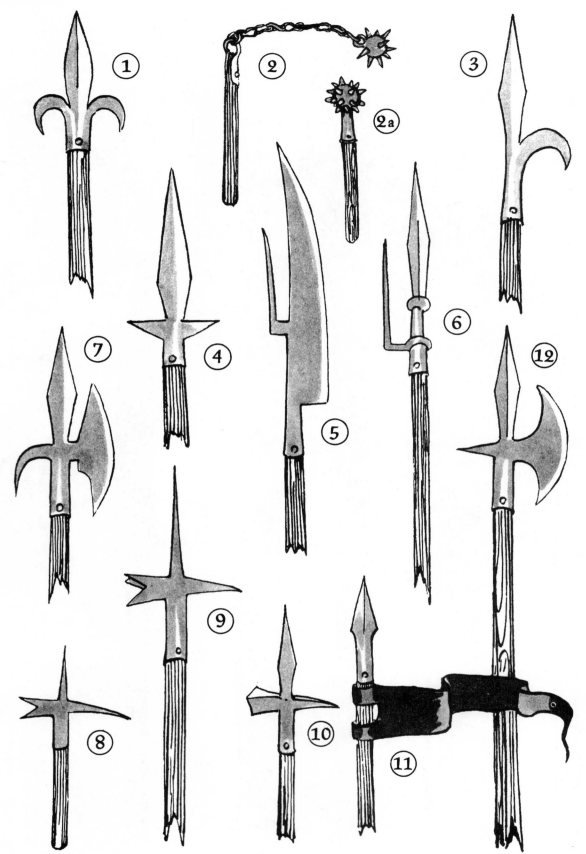

Various types of weapons used in Bohemia during the late 14th and early 15th centuries. From illuminations in the King Wenceslas Bible. (Photographic reproductions in the State Documentary Centre, Prague). (1) A spear with two hooks. (2) The so-called "holy-water sprinkler". (2a) A spiked mace. (3) A boar pike with one hook. (4) A partizan or Bohemian "ear-spoon". (5) A glaive. (6) A lance with ring below the blade, and below that a long guisarme-type spike. (7) A pole-axe-type halberd. Judging by the frequency with which this type of weapon appears in Bohemian paintings of the 14th and 15th centuries, it must have been very common among Bohemian soldiers. (8–10) War-axes. (11) A lance and pennon. (12) A halberd.

PLATE 27   PART V

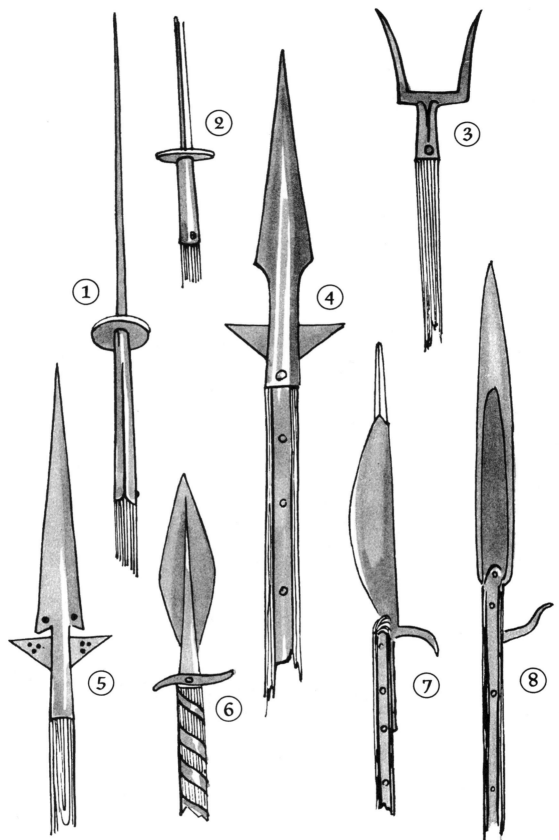

(1, 2) The awl-pike is a thrust weapon with a long pike or head, at the lower end of which there is a disk, set in a short stave. Taking Bohemian sources we find it appearing in the early 15th century in the Krumlov MS (the painting "Eleazar defeating the Elephant" and in the Göttingen Codex in a miniature of Žižka at the head of the army). Szendrei (p. 238) gives its measurements as follows: the head with its socket 1.34 metres, the head alone being 1.18 metres, the diameter of the disk 9 cm., length of the staff 90 cm. to 1 metre. Boeheim mentions an awl-pike dating from 1470, with a pike 83 cm. long. (Boeheim, p. 5, pl. 363). (3) A Hussite two-pronged fork, from the picture of Žižka leading the army in the Göttingen Codex. (4) A Bohemian "two-eared" lance or partizan (Military Museum, Prague). This type probably dated from the second half of the 15th century. The pike head is 47 cm. long. (5) A 15th century Bohemian ear-spoon (Stone, p. 122, pl. 159). Demmin mentions a similar weapon from the 15th century, with a blade 36 cm. long (p. 830, pl. I). (6) A boar-spear from the painting of Žižka at the head of the army in the Jena Codex. (7) A gisarme from the second half of the 15th century (*Zschille'sche Waffensammlung*, no. 812, pl. 187). (8) A 15th century voulge.

PLATE 28   PART V

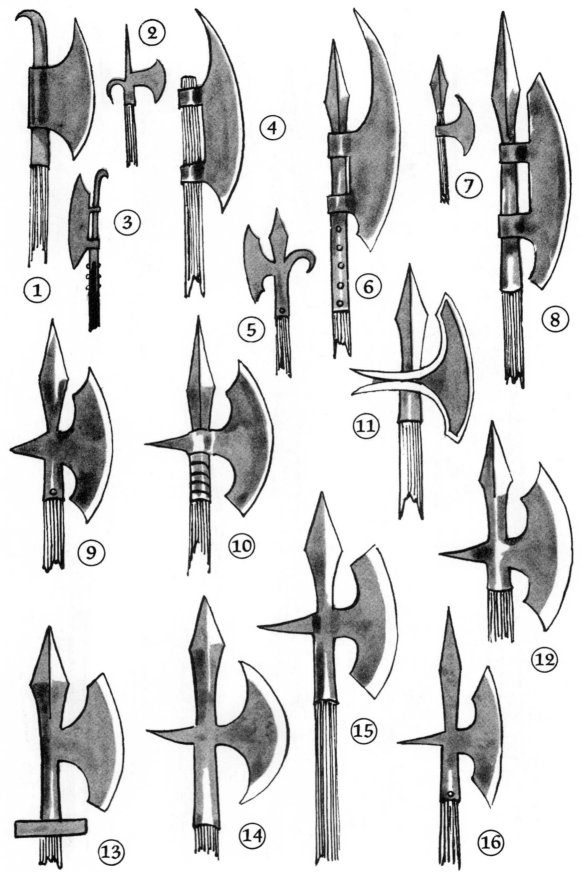

(1) An axe with a hook, on a long stave, from a painting by the Master of Vyšší Brod, dating from about 1350 (Prague National Gallery). (2) A pole-axe from *Legends of the Bohemian Patron Saints* (pl. 17), 1340. (3) A Scottish pole-axe (Demmin, p. 819, pl. 13). (4) A pole-axe from the Jan of Středa's *Liber Viaticus* (1350–60). (5) A halberd from the Velislav Bible. (6) A pole-axe type of halberd dating from 1380, from the painting of the Resurrection in the altar-piece by the Master of Třeboň. (7) A halberd from the Velislav Bible. (8–9) Halberds from the St. Barbara Crucifixion, dating from about 1380 (Prague National Gallery, from the workshop of the Master of Třeboň). (10) A halberd from the Rajhrad altar-piece of the Resurrection, prior to 1420 (Matějček, pl. 190). (11) A halberd from the Rajhrad altar-piece of the Carrying of the Cross, prior to 1420 (*ibid.*, pl. 181). (12) From the Rajhrad altar-piece of the Crucifixion (*ibid.*, pl. 184). (13) From the painting of the Crucifixion, dating from after 1430, found in the church of St. Simon and St. Judas in Skalice, near Soběslav (now in the Prague National Gallery). (*Ibid.*, pl. 239). (14) From a panel in the Prague National Gallery, dated 1430. (15) From the Rajhrad altar-piece painting of the Crucifixion, found in Nové Sady, dating from before 1420 (*ibid.*, pl. 184). (16) A halberd from the end of the 15th century, according to the Jena Codex.

PLATE 29

PART V

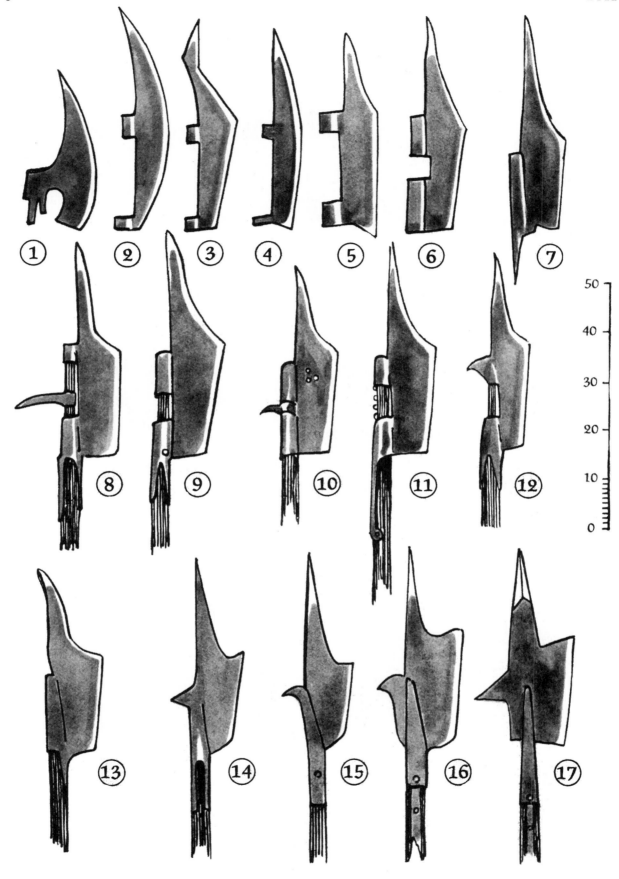

According to *Zeitschrift für historische Waffenkunde*, V, pp. 275 and 276, the voulge-type halberd developed in the following manner: (1–4) to about 1315, (5–9) to the end of the 14th century, (10–14) to about 1421, (15–17) to about 1468.

PLATE 30   PART V

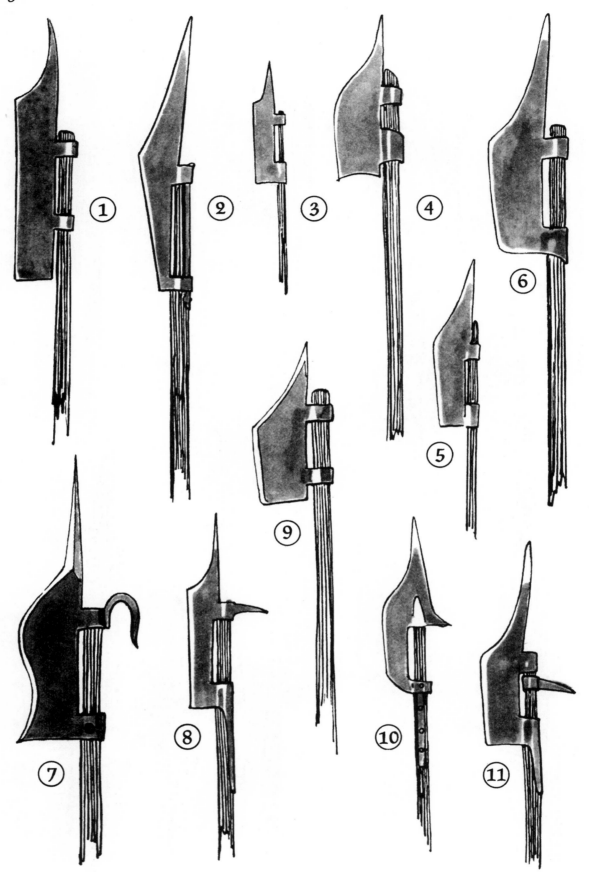

(1) A 14th century voulge-type halberd (*Zschille'sche Waffensammlung*, pl. 166, no. 583). (2) A 14th century voulge (Szendrei, p. 240, no. 756). Blade about 48 cm. long. (3) A voulge from the middle of the 14th century (*Zschille'sche Waffensammlung*, pl. 173, no. 649). (4) A voulge from the painting of Christ before Pilate by Hans Multscher (1427–67). (5) A voulge from Morgarten (Jähns, p. 50). (6) A 14th century Swiss voulge (*Armi ed Armaioli*, p. 16; also *Die Geschichte der französischen Armee*, p. 16). (7) A Scottish Jedburg-axe in use from the 15th century onwards (Stone, p. 321, pl. 405). (8) A Swiss voulge (*Zschille'sche Waffensammlung*, pl. 166, no. 581). (9) A voulge from the Crucifixion painting from the Emmaus Monastery, dated 1375, now in the Prague National Gallery. (10) A voulge of about the year 1400 (*Zschille'sche Waffensammlung*, pl. 166, no. 580). (11) A Swiss voulge of the 14th century (Stone, p. 654, pl. 835).

PLATE 31   PART V

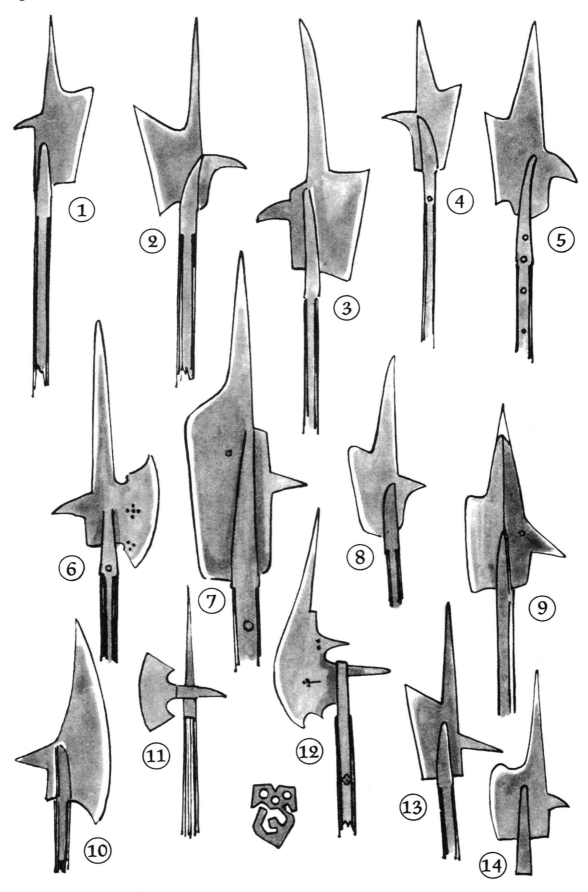

(1) A halberd dating from 1400 (Zschille, pl. 166, no. 579). (2) A Gothic halberd of the 15th century (*ibid.*, pl. 166, no. 578). (3) A halberd from the middle of the 15th century (*ibid.*, pl. 168, no. 603). (4) An early 15th-century halberd (*ibid.*, pl. 167, no. 588). (5) A mid 15th-century halberd (*ibid.*, pl. 168, no. 605). (6) A mid 15th-century halberd (*ibid.*, pl. 168, no. 602). (7) A Sempach halberd, early 15th century (*European Armour*, II, p. 120, pl. 925). (8) A 15th century halberd (Zschille, pl. 167, no. 594). (9) A 14th-century German halberd. Length without stave 34 cm., length of hatchet blade 18 cm. (Szendrei, p. 240, no. 749; also Zschille, pl. 167, no. 595). (10) A halberd from the middle of the 15th century (Zschille, pl. 168, no. 599). (11) A pole-axe-type halberd from the middle of the 15th century (*ibid.*, pl. 167, no. 592). (12) A Swiss halberd of the late 15th century, with its maker's mark (Szendrei, p. 238, pl. 762). Length of the blade is 43 cm. (Zschille, pl. 186, no. 799). (13) A 15th century halberd (*ibid.*, pl. 167, no. 596). (14) A halberd (*ibid.*, pl. 167, no. 592).

PLATE 32   PART V

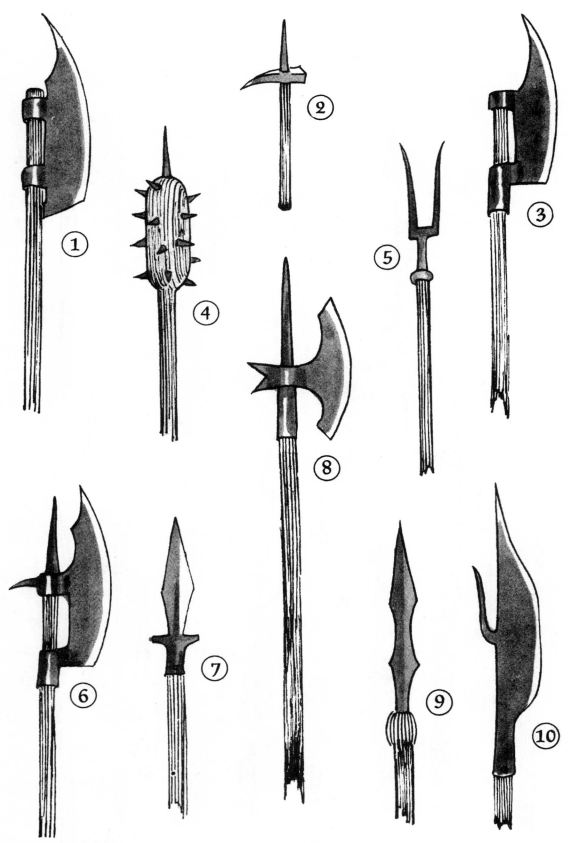

(1) A voulge dating from about 1384 (Burger-Schmidt-Beth, *Die deutsche Malerei der Renaissance*, p. 234, pl. 282). (2) A war-axe from the middle of the 15th century by a Bavarian Master (*Die alt-deutsche Malerei*, p. 109, pl. 73). (3) A voulge dating from the middle of the 15th century by a Bavarian Master (*ibid.*, p. 109, pl. 73). (4) A spiked cudgel or holy-water sprinkler dating from 1429, from a painting by the Frankish Master of the Bamberg altar-piece (*ibid.*, p. 30, pl. 18). (5) A two-pronged military fork dating from 1447, from a painting by the Frankish Master of the Crucifixion of Christ (*ibid.*, p .119, pl. 79). (6) A voulge dating from the middle of the 15th century by the Bavarian Master (*ibid.*, p. 109, pl. 73). (7) A javelin or boar-pike dating from 1429, from a picture by the Master of the Bamberg altar-piece (*ibid.*, p. 30, pl. 18; also Hans Multscher, 1427–67, *ibid.*, p. 105, pl. 71). (8) A pole-axe dating from 1429, from the Bamberg altar-piece (*ibid.*, p. 30, pl. 18). (9) A pike from the middle of the 15th century, according to the Bavarian Master (*ibid.*, p. 109, pl. 73; also in the *Liber Viaticus*, 1350–60). (10) A fauchard dating from about 1429, from a picture by the Frankish Master of the Bamberg altar-piece (*Die alt-deutsche Malerei*, p. 30, pl. 18). Also from the Crucifixion by the Bavarian Master, middle of the 15th century (*ibid.*, p. 109, pl. 73).

PLATE 33 PART V

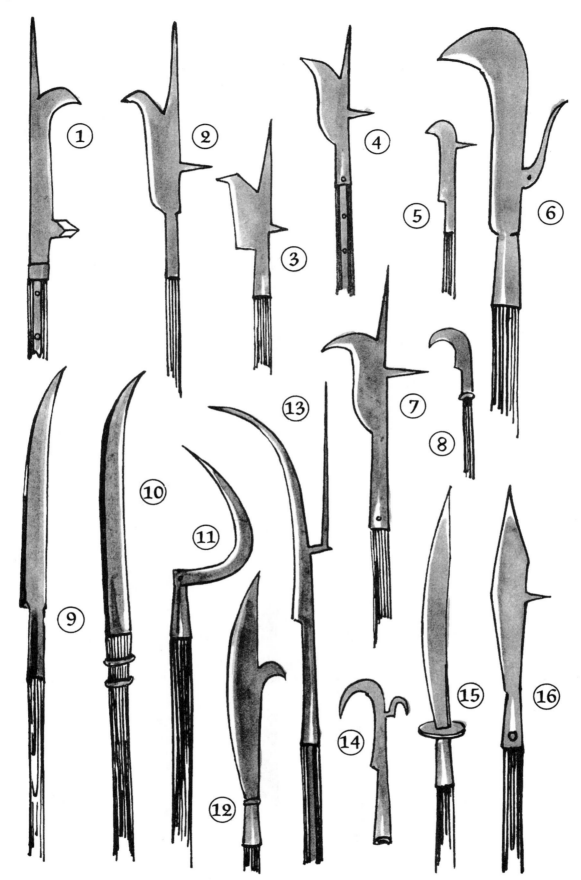

(1) A late 15th century Swiss bill (Demmin, p. 804, pl. 4). (2) An Italian bill from the middle of the 15th century (Boeheim, p. 330, pl. 391). (3) A 15th-century bill (Stone, p. 116, pl. 149). (4) A bill dating from about the year 1500 (Zschille, pl. 186, no. 801). (5) A bill (Stone, p. 116, pl. 149). (6) A bill from northern Italy, 15th century (Stone, p. 255, pl. 314). (7) A bill in the Military History Museum, Prague; length of blade 46 cm., length of spike 10–12 cm. (8) A Bohemian battle-scythe of the 14th century, Velislav Bible (Demmin, p. 798, no. 2). (9) A glaive of the 14th century; Paris. (Demmin, p. 798, no. 3). (10) A Swiss glaive of the 14th and 15th centuries (Solothurn), with a blade 130–40 cm. long. (Demmin, p. 798, no. 4; Jähns, p. 54). (11) A peasant sickle, 15th century (Zschille, pl. 173, no. 647). (12) A Burgundian bill of the middle of the 15th century (Jähns, p. 54). (13) An English guisarme of the 14th century (Boeheim, p. 355, pl. 44; also Stone, p. 255, pl. 315, and dated as 1450. Demmin places in the 12th century). (14) A Swiss guisarme from the 13th century (Demmin, p. 804, no. 2). (15) A French glaive dated between 1440 and 1450 (Demmin, p. 798, no. 3). (16) A 14th century bill (*Die Geschichte der französischen Armee*, p. 76).

PLATE 34   PART V

(1) A bill dating from 1425 (Radnor, *It All Happened Before*, p. 47; similar in *European Armour*, III, p. 113, pl. 913. The author here gives it as an early 16th century weapon). (2) A 15th century guisarme (K. Gimbel, *Waffensammlung*, no. 731, text p. 44). (3) A guisarme in *Musei armeria*, considered to date from the 14th century (pl. XIII, no. 592). (4) A late 15th-century Italian guisarme (Boeheim, p. 340, pl. 393). (5) A guisarme preserved in the Prague Military History Museum. The blade is 66 cm. long, the hook is 25 cm. long, the spike 8 cm. (6) A 15th century guisarme (*European Armour*, III, p. 112, pl. 908). (7) An English guisarme of the late 15th century (Demmin, p. 804, no. 5). (8) A Swiss guisarme from the middle of the 15th century (Jähns, p. 54, pl. 14). (9) A 15th century Italian guisarme with a blade 71.8 cm. long (Szendrei, p. 217, pl. 693). The German term for this weapon is *Rosschinder* or horse killer. According to *European Armour*, III, p. 111, pl. 907 such a weapon was known as early as the 13th century. The master-painter from the Middle Rhine who painted "The Crucifixion of Christ" in 1440 also depicts a similar weapon. Pinturicchio painted this weapon into a fresco in Sienna in 1507–9 (Ullstein, *Weltgeschichte, Mittelalter*, p. 427).

PLATE 35   PART V

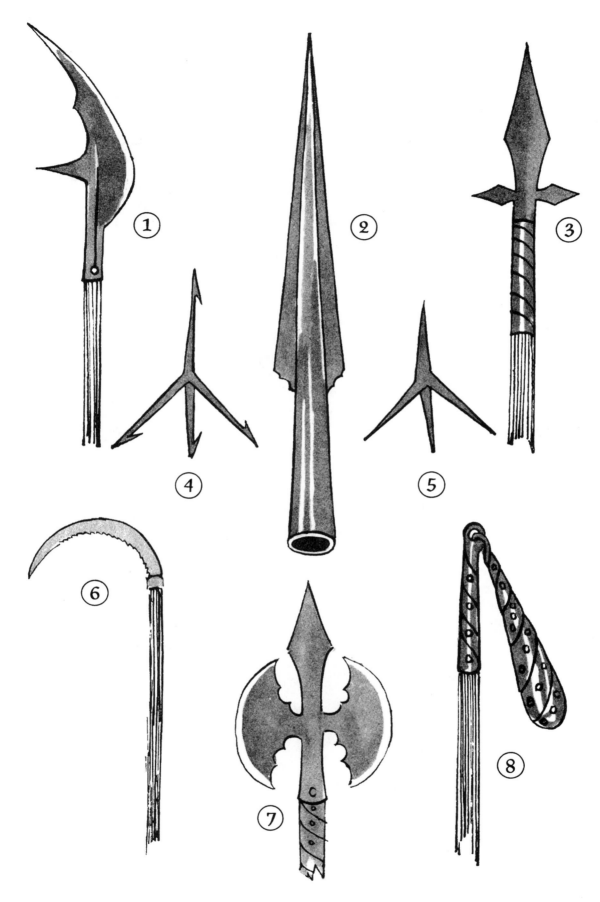

Weapons as depicted in the Bellifortis MS, dating from 1402–5. (1) A primitive halberd. (2) The head of a lance, 35 cm. long. (3) A spear. (4, 5) Calthrops planted in the ground to lame the horses of the attacking cavalry. They were between 6 and 8 cm. high. (6) A scythe. (7) A halberd with two sharp blades. (8) A military flail, completely covered in metal.

PLATE 36   PART V

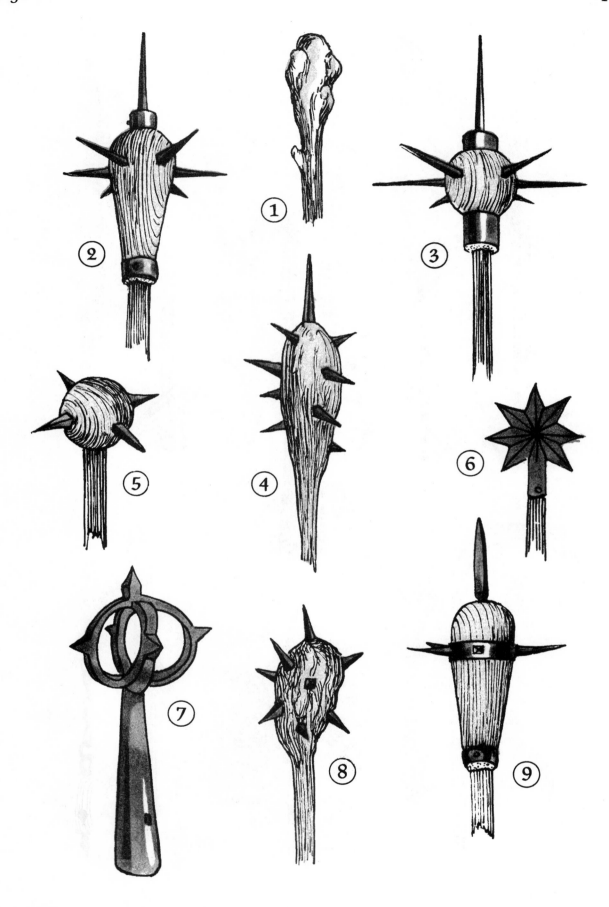

(1) A cudgel from the St. Barbara painting of the Crucifixion, dating from about 1380. Now in the Prague National Gallery. (2) A spiked cudgel or a "morning star" (Zíbrt and Winter, p. 281, pl. 164). (3) A German holy-water sprinkler of the early 16th century (Stone, p. 297, pl. 2). (4–5) A reconstruction of holy-water sprinklers from a Viennese manuscript dated 1437: the painting of "The Battle with the Hussites". (6) A mace, from the Kaufmann painting of the Crucifixion, dated about 1350 (Matějček, pl. 33). (7) An iron mace of the 15th century. The head is 9.5 cm. in diameter, the neck 12.5 cm. (Szendrei, p. 145, no. 305). (8) The holy-water sprinkler from the painting "Žižka at the Head of the Army" in the Göttingen manuscript. (9) A German holy-water sprinkler of the 15th century (Boeheim, p. 360, pl. 423).

PLATE 37 PART V

(1) A military flail: a wooden ball stuck with metal spikes, suspended on a chain. There are several examples of this type of weapon in the Prague National Museum. (K. Gimbel, *Waffensammlung*, pl. XV, no. 592, text p. 39). (1a) A metal ball with spikes (property of the Prague National Museum). (2) A sword pommel on a chain used as a flail. The pommel is 5.5 × 4.2 cm. the stave 68.5 cm. long, the links of the chain 6.5 × 2.5 cm. the chain itself 31 cm. long. (Military History Museum, Prague). (3) A late 15th-century metal flail (Zíbrt and Winter, II, p. 280). (4) An early medieval flail (Demmin, p. 794, fig. 1). (5) A chain-flail (Demmin, p. 794, fig. 4). (6) A spiked metal ball on a twisted iron chain, from the Military History Museum, Prague. (7) A wooden ball stuck with 13 forged nails, a chain hanging from a stave 57 cm. long. (Demmin, p. 794, fig. 3). He terms it a *Žižka star*. (7a) The shape of the nails.

PLATE 38
PART V

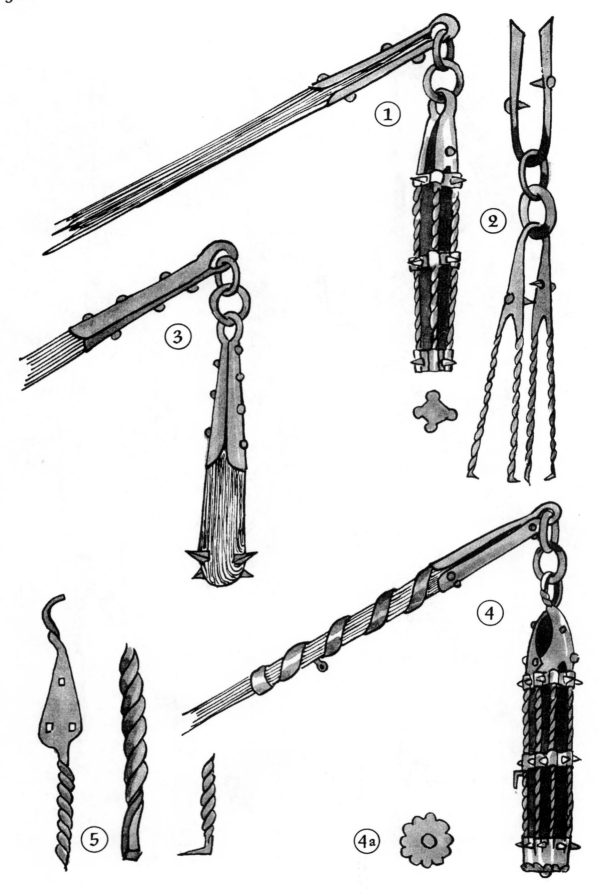

(1) A 15th-century flail. Swingle 41 cm. long, 4 cm. at base; it is constructed of 4 twisted metal throngs, 3 bands, and studded with 12 nails (Prague Municipal Museum). (2) Detail: to show its metal construction. (3) A flail according to the picture in the Viennese manuscript, "The Fight with the Hussites", dating from 1437–50. (4) A 15th-century flail, in the Prague National Museum. Cat. no. 36. The swingle is 41 cm. long, it has 8 forged twisted metal throngs, 4 metal bands (see 5, detail), and is studded with 24 nails. There is a metal plate shaped like a rosette hammered on to the bottom. Detail: the metal rosette.

PLATE 39   PART V

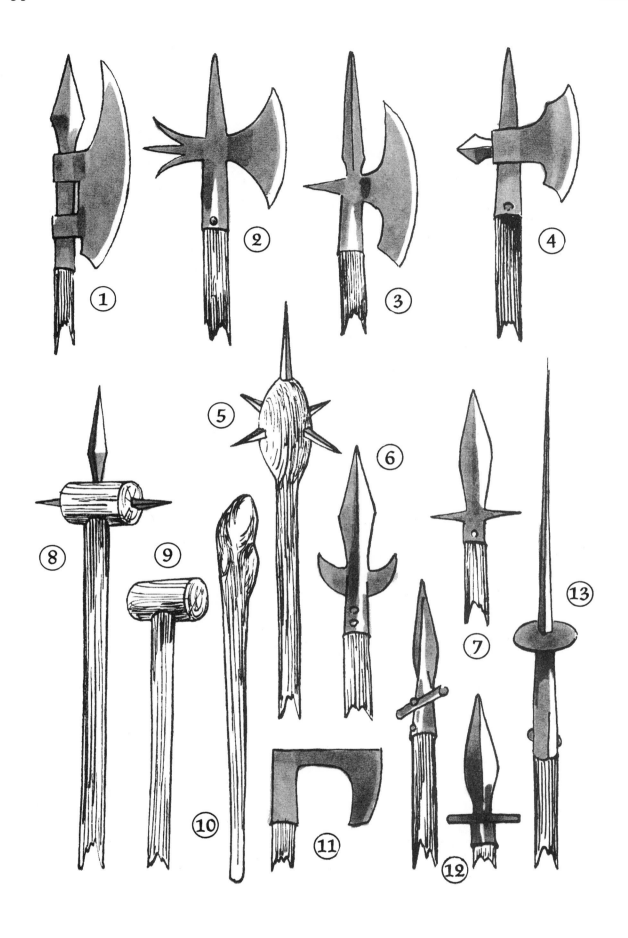

The typical weapons of an infantry unit about the year 1410, from *Mittelalterliches Hausbuch*. (1–4) Pole-axe-type halberds. (5, 8, 9, 10) Maces and cudgels. (6, 7, 12) Spears and boar spears. (11) An axe. (13) An awl-pike.

PLATE 1   PART VI

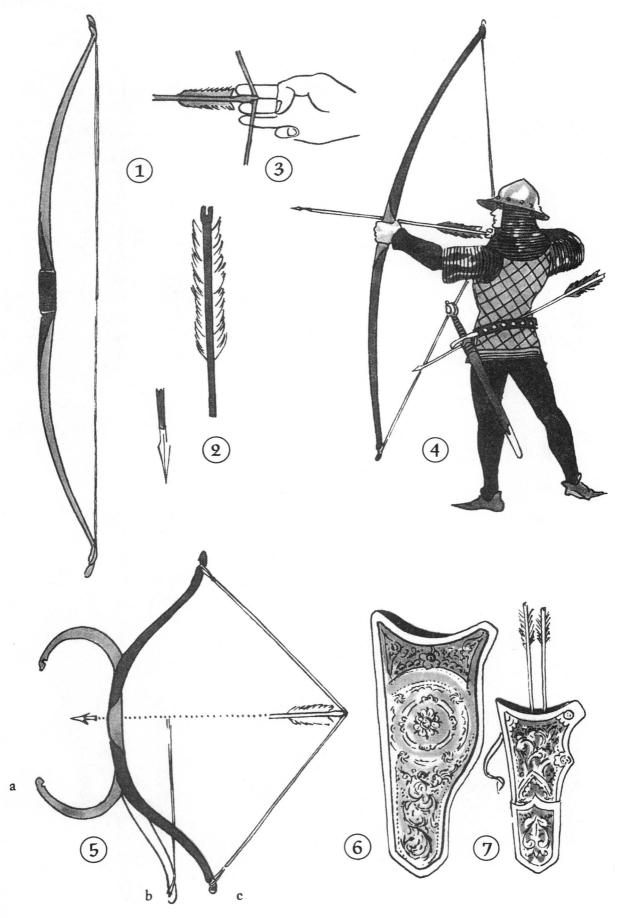

(1) A bow. (2) The head and feathered end of the shaft of an arrow, showing the notch for the bowstring (Boeheim, p. 399, pl. 476). (3) The method of holding the arrow and drawing the bowstring (Stone, p. 135, pl. 173). (4) How the bow was held when shooting (Boeheim, p. 394, pl. 971). (5) An Eastern bow, mostly used by cavalry soldiers. a. The bow unstrung. b. The bow with its string. c. The bow drawn for shooting (Boeheim, p. 390, pl. 475). (6) A Turkish sheath for a bow. (7) A Turkish quiver. Both sheath and quiver date from the middle of the 16th century (Boeheim, p. 400, pl. 478).

PLATE 2

PART VI

(1) The stance of the archer with a crossbow when shooting. The archer did not balance the crossbow on his shoulder, but merely placed the butt of the stock against his cheek (*Zeitschrift für historische Waffenkunde*, II, p. 262). Methods of spanning the arbelest: (2) the windlass (Hauner, *Vývoj pozemního válečnictví*, supplement p. 28, pl. 31). (3) The rack and pinion jack (*Die alt-deutsche Malerei*, p. 247, pl. 166). (4) Spanning by means of a cord and pulley attached to the belt, from a picture depicting the siege of a town in the Velislav Bible.

PLATE 3 PART VI

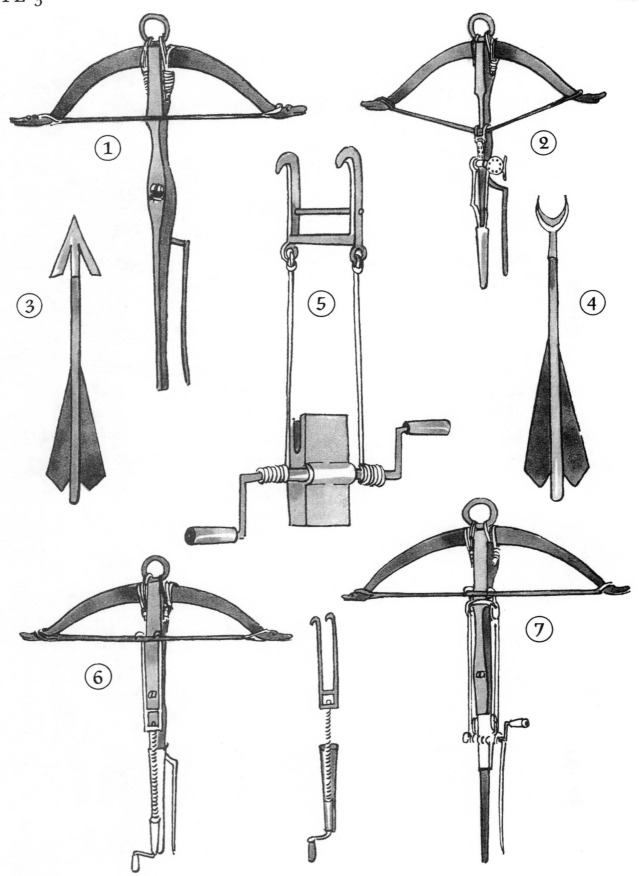

(1) An arbalest or crossbow. The ends of the bow are carved. (2) A crossbow with a ratchet which is fixed to the lower part of the stock by means of a socket. When the wheel was turned it also turned a cylinder which wound up a belt with claws hooked round the cord, which was thus drawn backwards. (3–4) Bolts; similar ones are to be found in the Velislav Bible. (5) A bow-charging windlass, without pulleys. The cords holding the hooks are wound direct on to the winding handle. (6) A crossbow with screw tackle. By turning the handle at the bottom, the connecting rod screwed up the grasp hooks and drew back the bowstring. Detail: the screw tackle. (7) A crossbow fitted with a tackle block, consisting by now of a windlass and pulleys (Bellifortis MS, 1402–5).

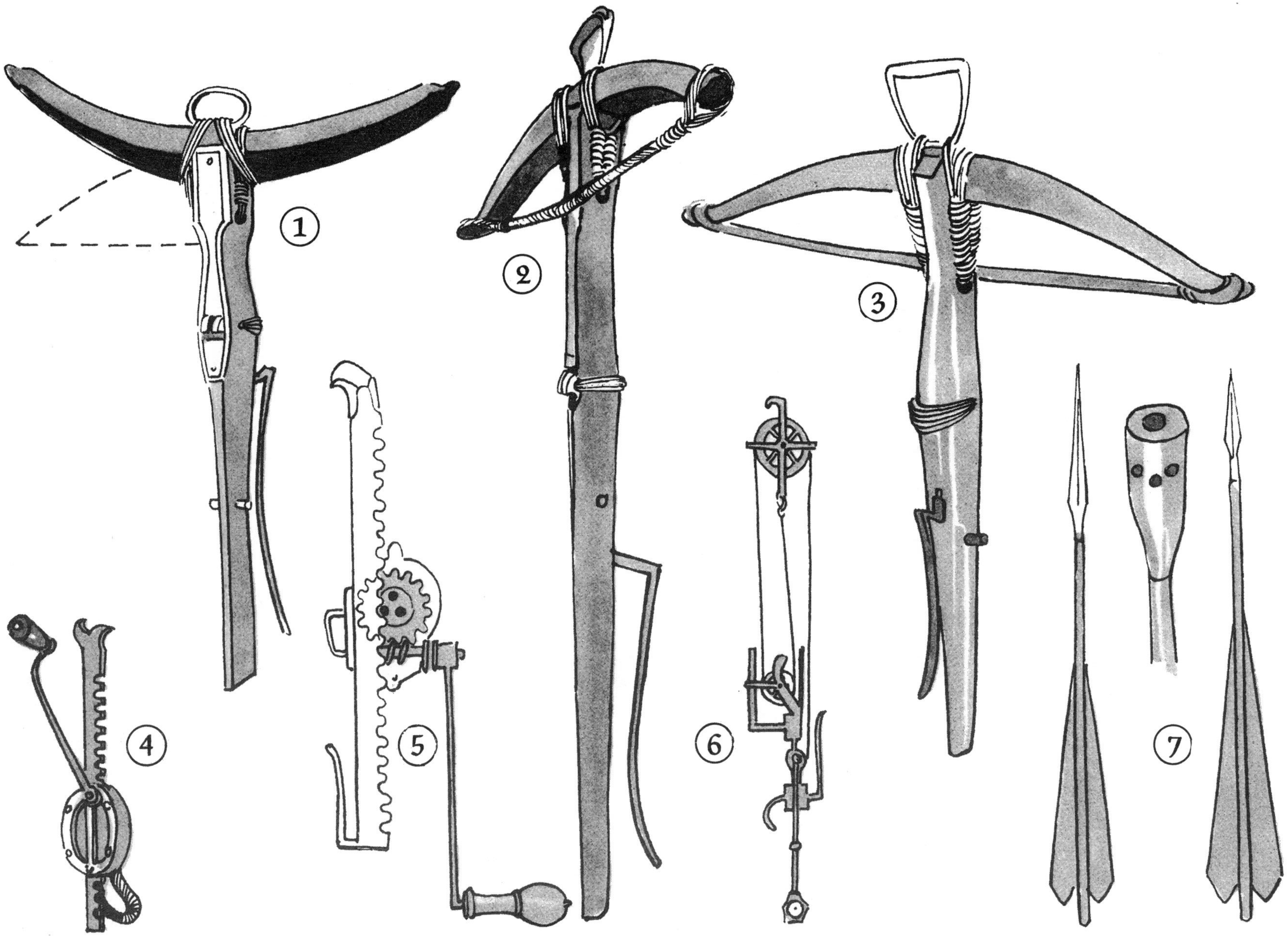

PLATE 4

(1) A heavy crossbow dating from about 1450. The stock is 110 cm. long, and is fitted with a winder-pin, for the German type tackle block. It is a crossbow, 1 metre long, made of horn, marked with the name Andreas Baumkircher, who was shot in 1471 (Boeheim, p. 470, pl. 484). (2) A 15th century arbalest (*Zeitschrift*, 1932/1934, p. 100). (3) The underside of the arbalest. (4) The type of rack and pinion with which the archer tensed the crossbow (Demmin, p. 904). (5) A cross-section of a rack and pinion dating from 1563 (Boeheim, p. 412, pl. 491). The rod turned by the handle has a thread which sets the cog-wheel in motion. Around the centre of the cog-wheel are three pins which in turn move the serrated rod which draws back the bowstring. (6) The principle of the windlass à tour, which by means of pulleys is more able to overcome the resistance of the bow. The turn of the handle winds the cord around a cylinder, setting the pulleys in action. (7) Bolts dating from 1405, according to drawings in the Bellifortis MS. In between them is the head of a whistling bolt.

PLATE 5   PART VI

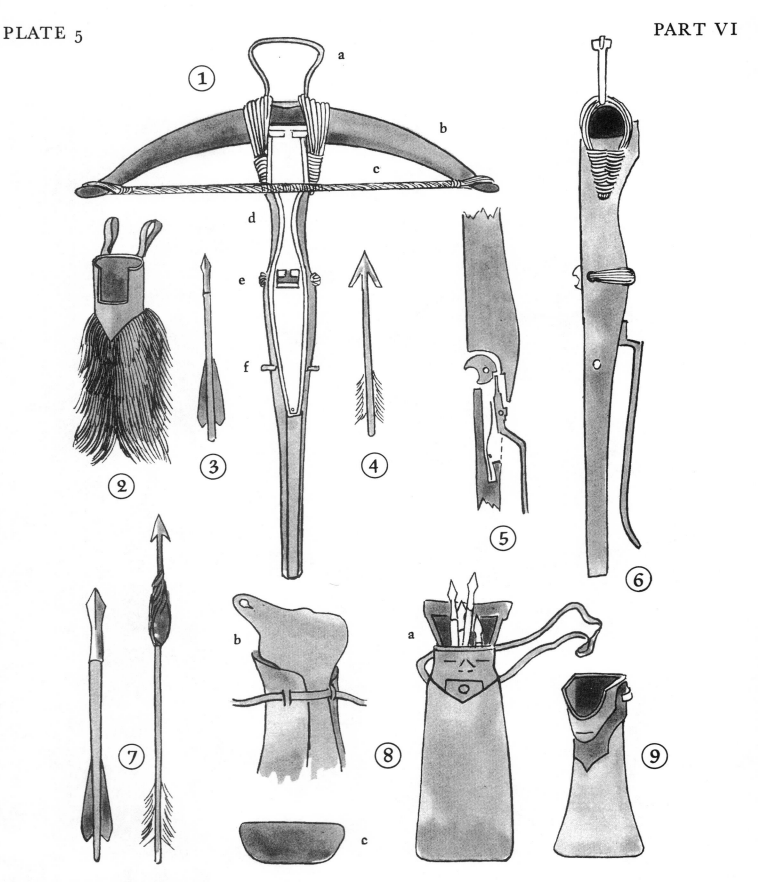

(1) An arbalest or crossbow of the 15th century (drawn from an original in the Prague Military History Museum; cat. no. 4000). a. The stirrup, used for tensing the bow. 10 × 10 cm. b. The bow, made of horn, wrapped in sinew, with a span of 72 cm. It is lashed to the stock with a cord. c. The bowstring is plaited string; it tenses the bow and propels the arrow towards its target. d. The stock or tiller of the crossbow. 81.5 cm. long, 5 cm. wide at its broadest point. e. The winder-pin is a bone cylinder with an aperture through its centre, around which it can turn; also a slit in which to catch the string. It is 3.2 cm. wide and placed 56.5 cm. from the butt end of the stock. f. The pegs for holding down the tackle block are 39 cm. from the butt end of the stock. (2) A quiver, the case for arrows, which were packed in heads uppermost (see Viennese MS, "The Battle with the Hussites"). (3) An arrow with a heavy head, and a "vane" of leather, skin or parchment. (4) The bolt with the barbed head was more common in the 14th century; it usually had a vane of goose feathers (Master of the Třeboň altar-piece, "Three Saints", dating from 1380, Matějček, pl. 109). (5) A cross-section of the mechanism of a crossbow (Boeheim, p. 404, pl. 483). When renovating a crossbow in the Prague Military History Museum, V. Holec discovered that originally the crossbow did not have a spring, but the tension was provided entirely by the hooking back of the bowstring into the winder-pin, when it was charged. (6) Side view of a crossbow

PLATE 6   PART VI

Crossbowmen of the first half of the 14th century (Velislav Bible). (1) 14th-century bolt-head, 10 cm. long. (2) 14th-century bolt-head, 12.5 cm. long (Szendrei, p. 138, no. 364).

showing the way the bow is fastened to the stock, also the winder-pin. Thickness of the stock at the top 7 cm, at the bottom 4 cm. Length of iron catch 38.5 cm. (7) A penetrating bolt and a fire bolt. The latter has some inflammable material wound round the shaft near the head (Boeheim, p. 426, pl. 504 and 505). (8) The usual shape of the quiver, according to Viollet le Duc (also Boeheim, p. 429, pl. 508); a. front view, b. backview, c. shape of the base of the quiver. Height 42 cm, width 15.5 cm. (9) A 15th century quiver (Boeheim, p. 429, pl. 509).

PLATE 7   PART VI

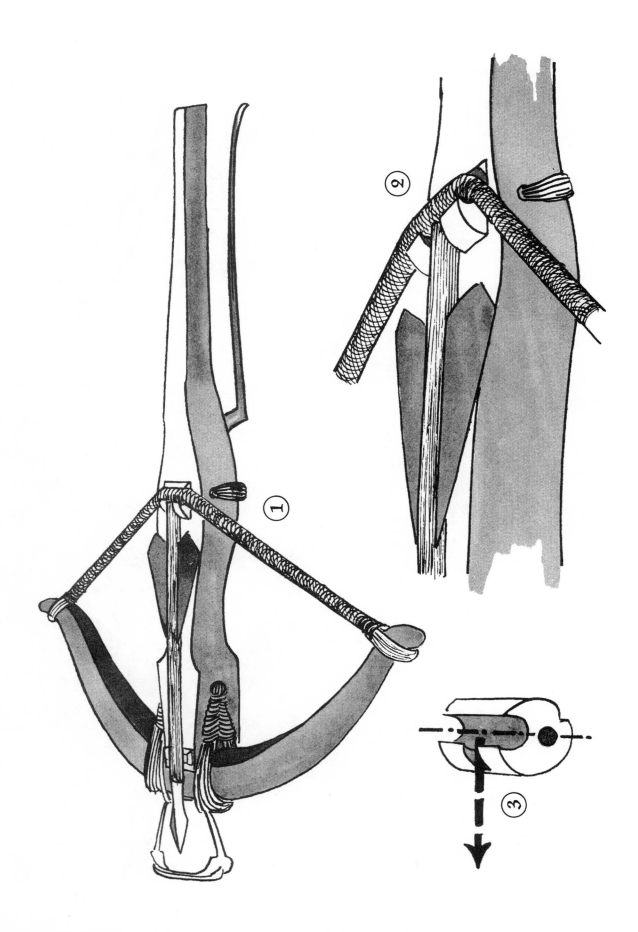

How the bolt is set in the crossbow. (1) Complete view of a crossbow "charged". The tensed string is held by the notch of the winder-pin, which is in turn held by a short arm of the catch inside the stock. The feather end of the bolt is pressed into the notch so that it touches the bowstring. By pressing the catch, the winder-pin was freed, turned in the direction of the bowstring, which it had held tensed; it was thus released, at the same time propelling the arrow towards its target. (2) Detail of the way the arrow is set against the string and notch. (3) The winder-pin.

PLATE 8

PART VI

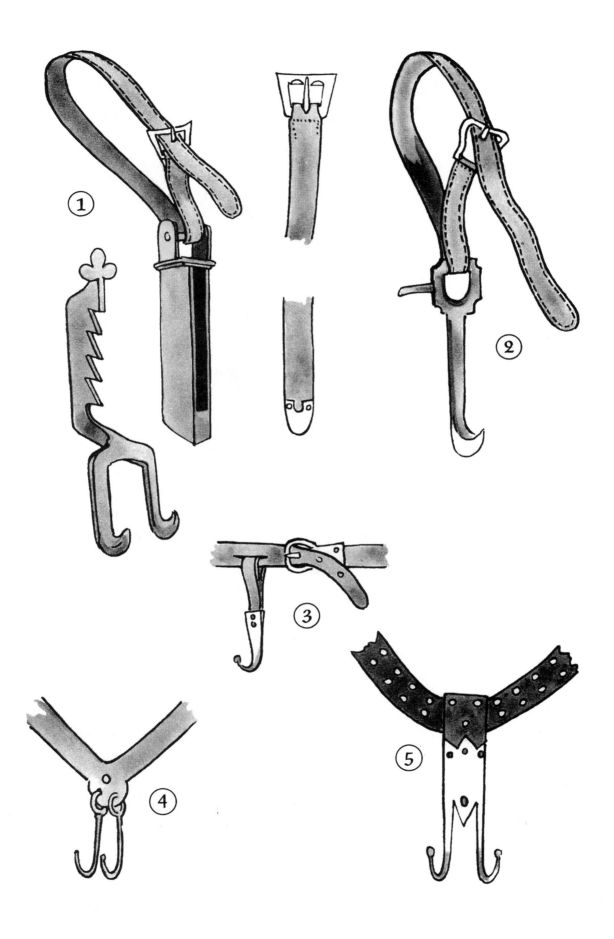

Belt-hooks for tensing the crossbow. (1–2) Belt-hooks dating from 1405 (Bellifortis MS). In between the two hooks there is a diagram of the belt. (3) A belt-hook or "claw", from the first half of the 14th century (Velislav Bible). (4–5) Belt-claws dating from the 13th to 15th century (Demmin, p. 902; Boeheim, p. 410, pl. 487).

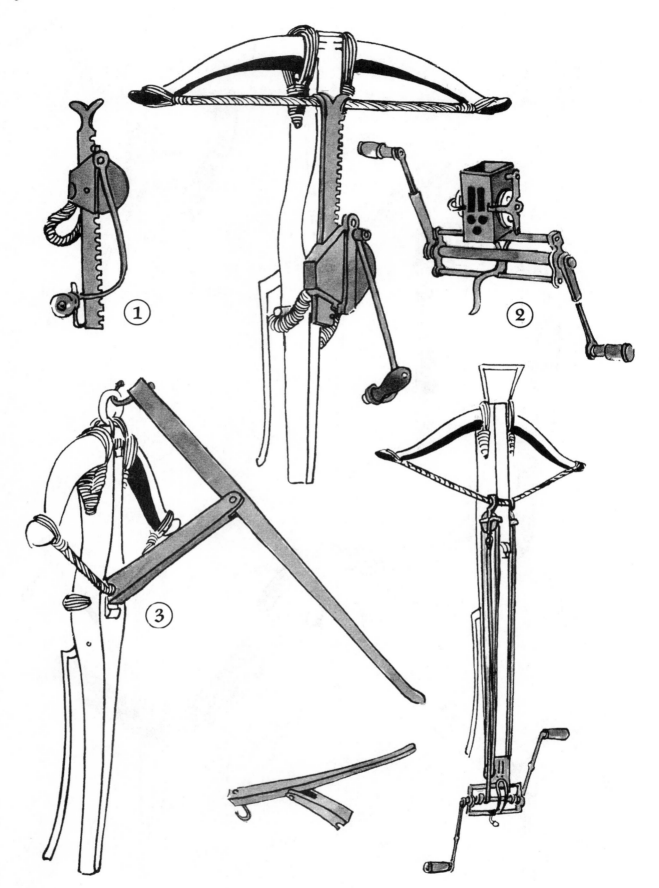

The tensing of the crossbow and the machines used for charging it. (1) A German ratchet windlass and the way it was fixed to the stock. These windlasses probably date from the second half of the 15th century and later. But nevertheless there are some pictures, dating from about 1400, where the crossbow is already charged in this manner. (Demmin, p. 904 and *Soldatenkunde*, p. 132). (2) A windlass à tour and the winding handle, in detail, including the pulley wheels (Boeheim, p. 411, pl. 488). The turning of the handle winds up the cords on either side of the stock and draws back the bowstring as far as the notch. (3) A "goat's foot" lever. At the end of a long bar there is a hook which slips into the ring at the front of the bow. A short arm, hanging freely from the long bar is notched to fit over the bowstring. When the archer pulls down the upper bar, the lower one pulls the bowstring back to the winder-pin, until it falls into the groove (Jähns, p. 57, pl. 8).

PLATE 10   PART VI

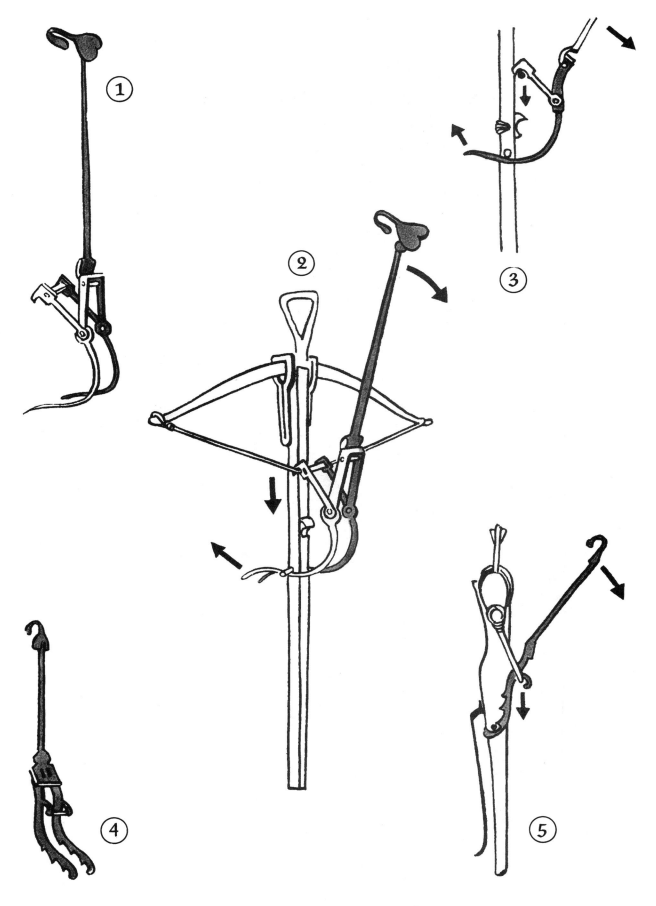

(1) A French "goat's foot" lever of the late 15th century, according to Viollet le Duc (Boeheim, p. 416, pl. 494). (2) How it was fitted to the crossbow. The lever with the claws was hooked over the bowstring. The curved lever hooked round the notch in the stock; by drawing back the long, straight upper lever the curved ones slipped round the notch and the bowstring was drawn back to the winder-pin. Detail showing how it functioned. (4) A "goat's foot" lever, according to Jähns, p. 57, pl. 7. (5) How it worked.

PLATE II

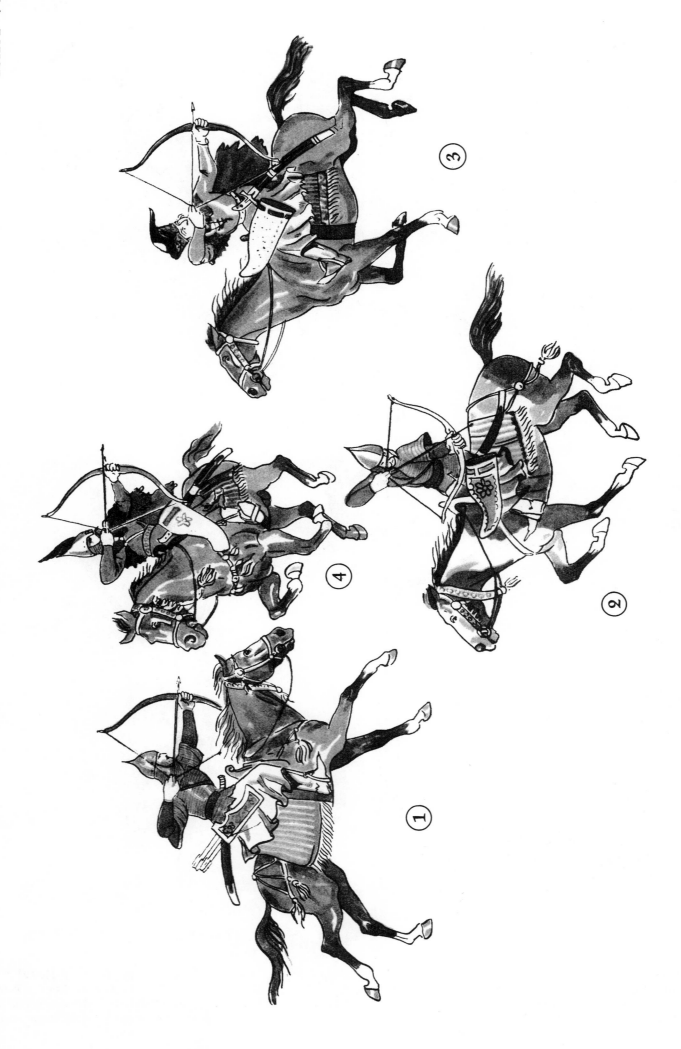

Archers on horseback. Drawn freely from Carl Diem, *Reiterspiele*, pp. 58–63. (1) Straight ahead. (2) Downwards. (3) Backwards. (4) To the side.

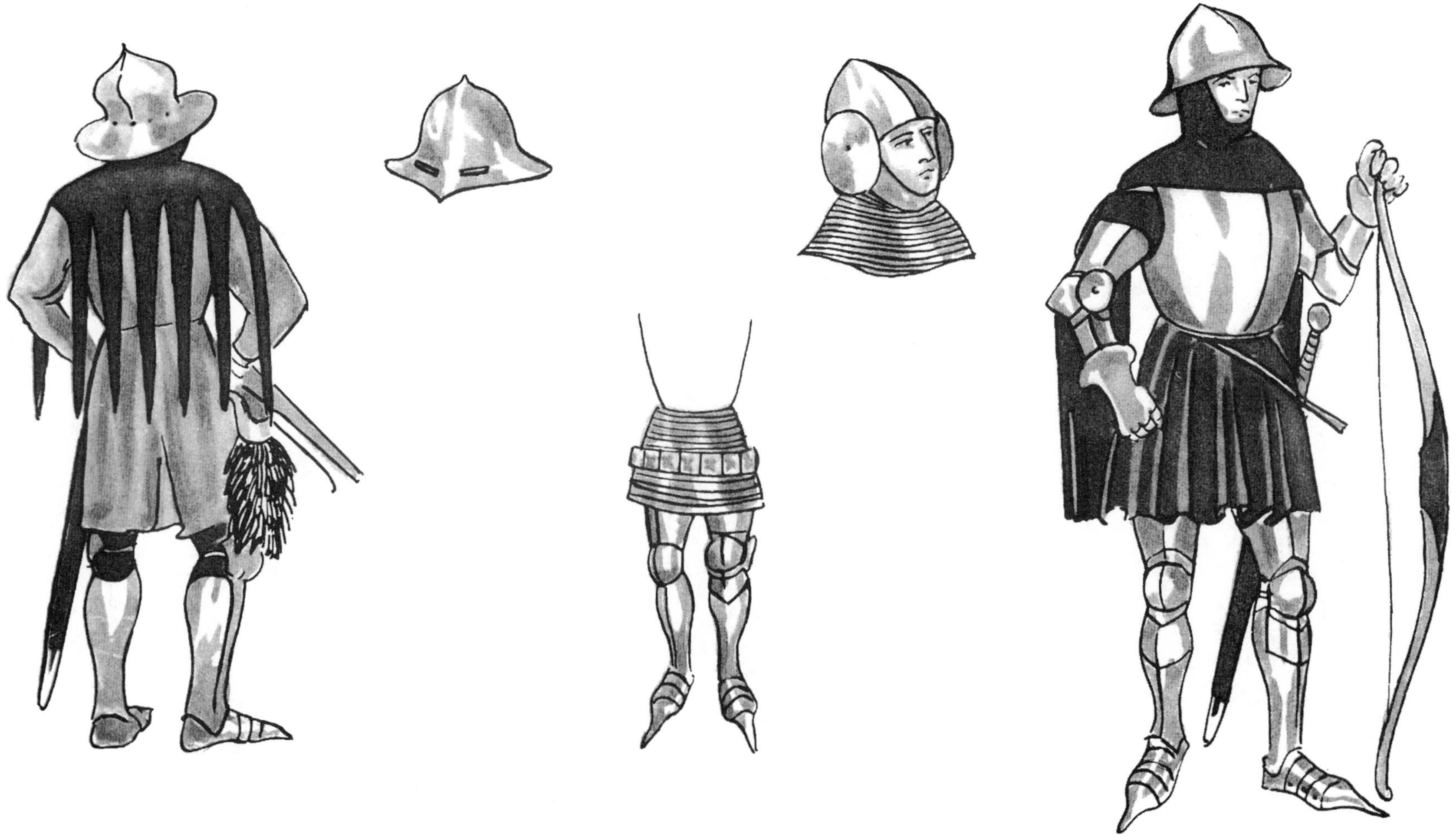

PLATE 12

Archers, from the picture ,,The Battle with the Hussites'', in the Vienna MS (1437—50).

PLATE 13

(1–2) German archers with crossbows dating from the years 1430–50 (Essenwein, pl. B. 5; *Zeitschrift*, I, p. 249; 1420–1440). (3) An archer with an arbalest, from the picture "The Battle with the Hussites" in the Viennese manuscript (1437–50).

(1) A running fight between a mounted crossbowman and a lancer. (Thalhofer's *Fechtbuch*, 1467, p. 267). The crossbowman being chased, holds the reins with his left hand, with his right he balances the crossbow, backwards, along his arm, ready to loose his bolt as soon as his pursuer comes sufficiently close. (2) A fight between an archer and a lancer (Thalhofers *Fechtbuch* 1467, p. 269). The crossbowman holds his arbalest in the normal way.

PLATE 15

A fight between a crossbowman and a lancer (Thalhofer's *Fechtbuch*, 1467, p. 268). The archer wards off the lance with his crossbow and at the same time looses his bolt into his opponent's breast.

PLATE 16   PART VI

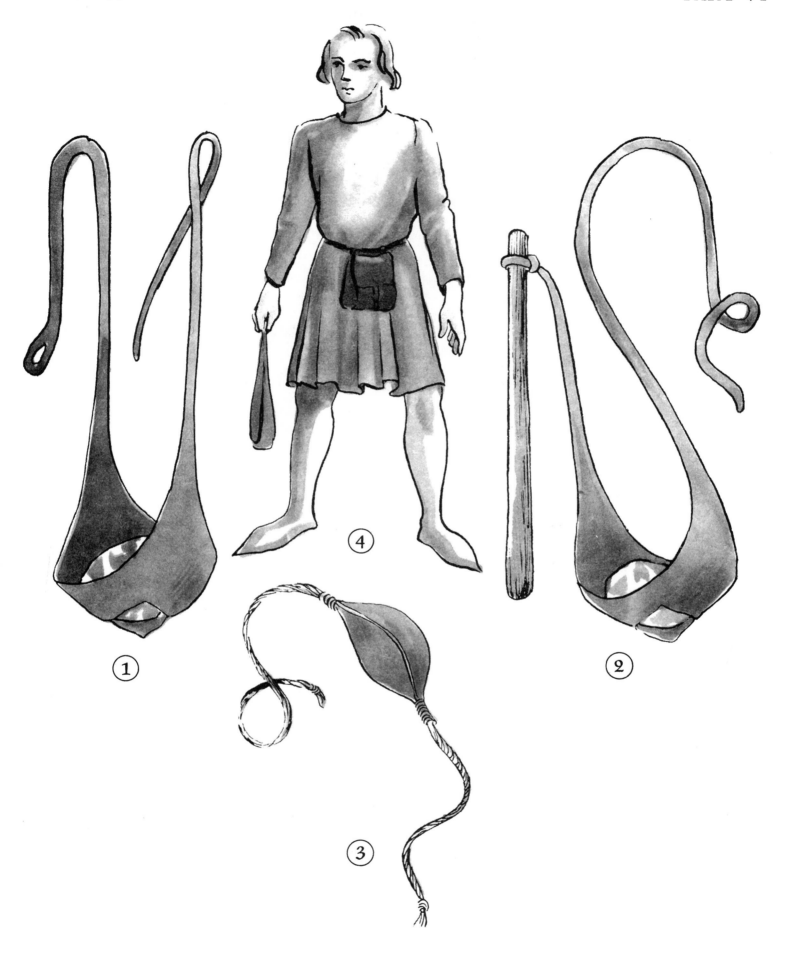

(1) A hand-sling, from an illustration in the Bellifortis MS, 1405. (2) A similar sling, for hurling stones, but attached to a handle. (3) A sling, according to Boeheim, p. 386, pl. 462. (4) The figure of David with his sling, from a picture in Jan of Středa's *Liber Viaticus* MS, dating from about 1360.

PLATE 17

PART VI

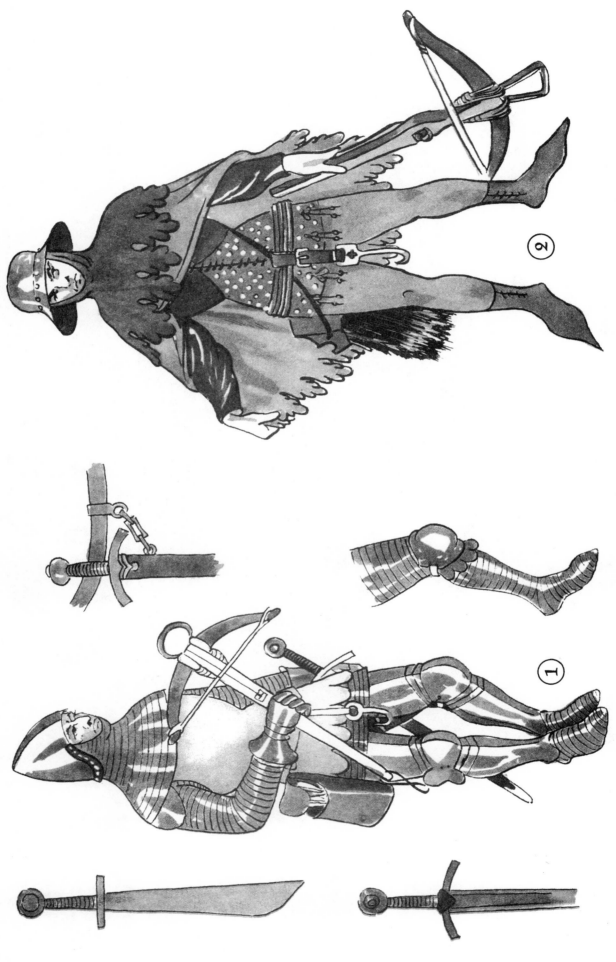

(1) A crossbowman with his arbalest, dating from after 1349 and probably even as late as the early 15th century (from "The Guard at the Holy Sepulchre", Hagenau). The falchion and hanging sword are from the Holy Grave in Strasbourg (*Zeitschrift für historische Waffenkunde*). (2) A crossbowman with a crossbow, dating from about 1430 (*Deutsches Leben*, p. 585).

PLATE 18   PART VI

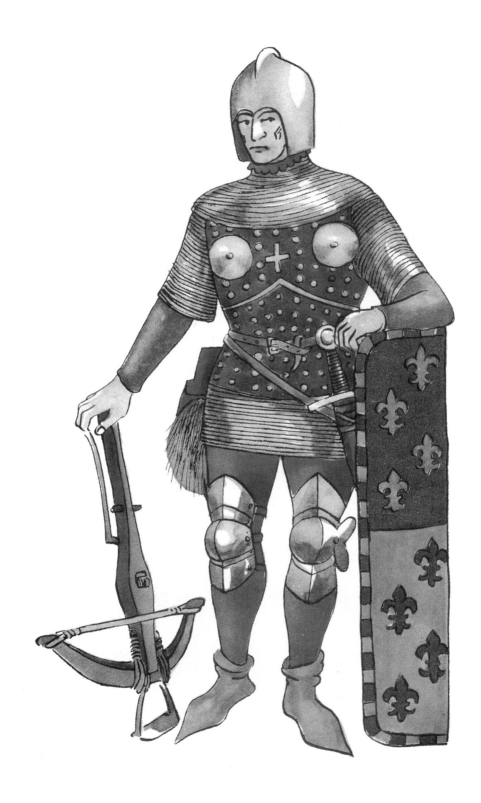

A French crossbowman, dating from 1430 (Tilke, pl. 41).

PLATE 19

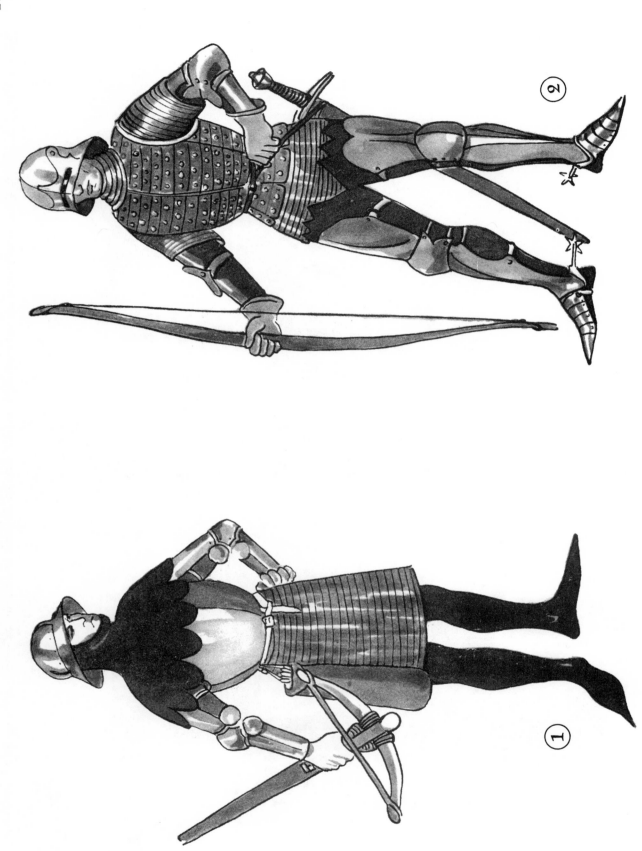

(1) A crossbowman with his arbalest, dating from the 15th century (*Zeitschrift*, VI, p. 384). (2) A mounted archer of Charles VII's army, dating from about 1450 (Viollet le Duc; also Jähns, *Atlas*, p. 57, pl. 16).

PLATE 20

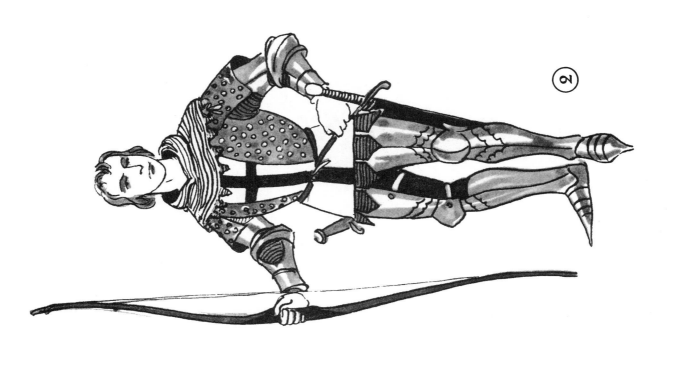

(1) A 14th century English archer, from an illustration showing archery practice (*Die Geschichte der französischen Armee*, p. 75). (2) Guillaume May, the captain of Louis XI's 120 archers. 1423–1461–1483; *ibid.*, p. 106).

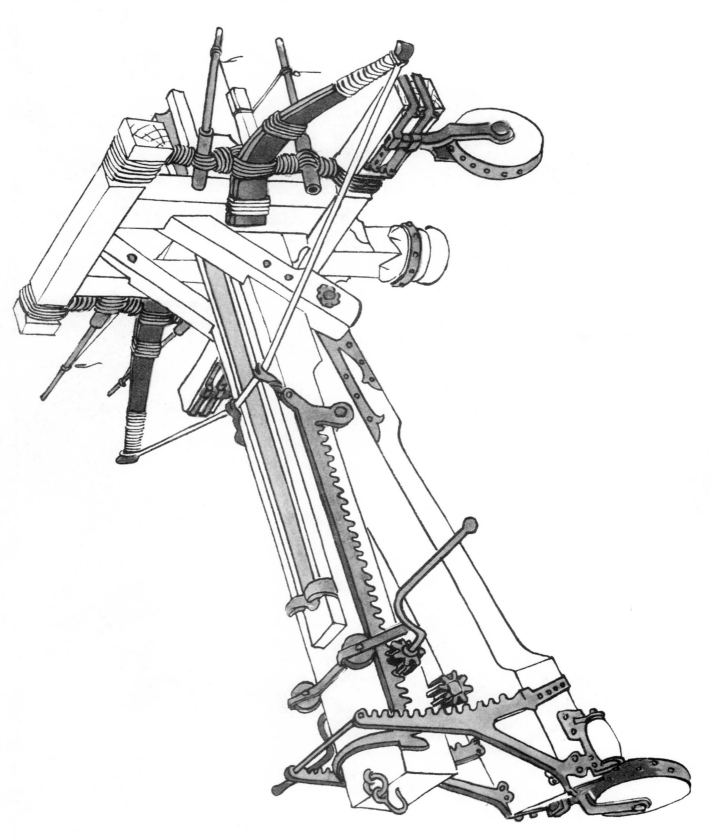

A catapult (Viollet le Duc, V, p. 242).

PLATE 21

PLATE 22

PART VI

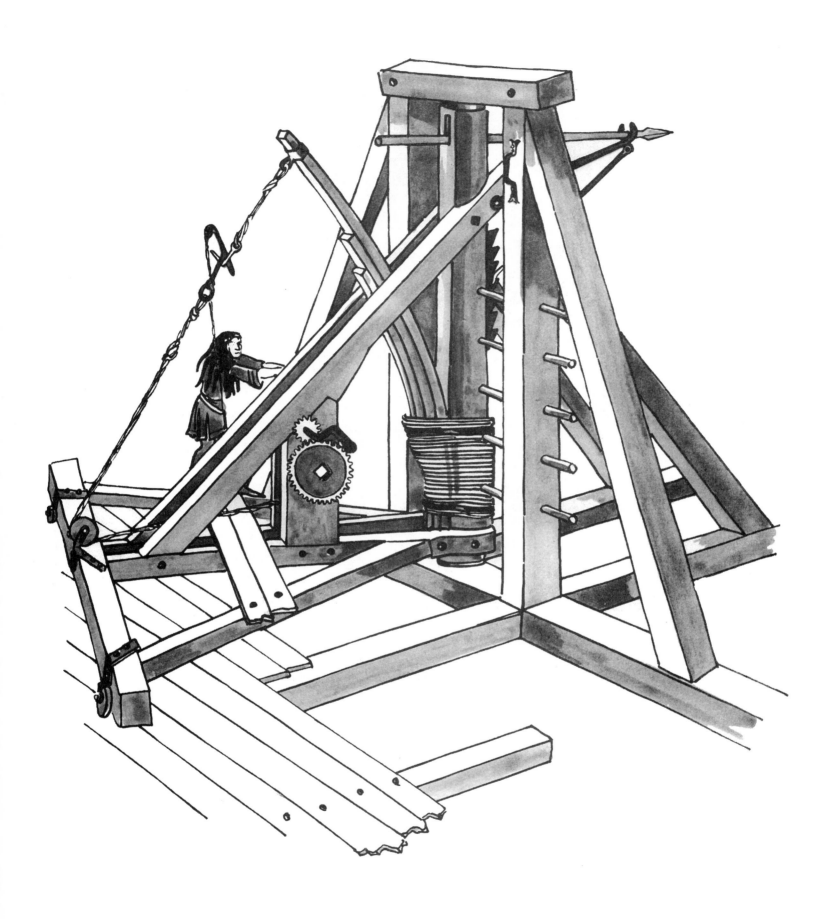

A catapult which shot darts (Viollet le Duc, V, p. 244).

PLATE 23

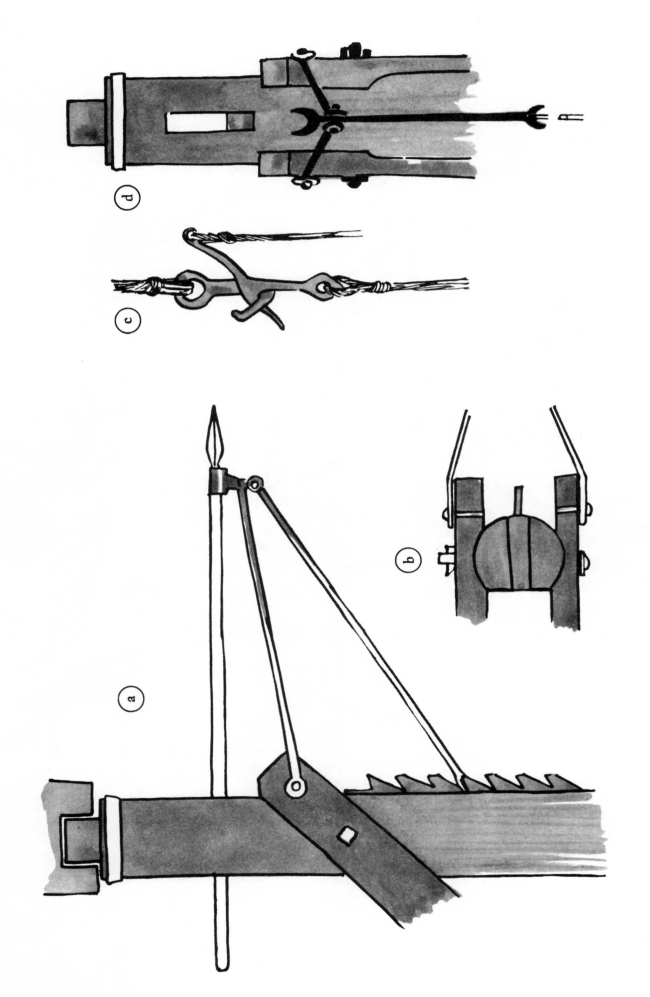

Details of the previous machines (Viollet le Duc, p. 244). a. Side view of the main supporting pillar showing how the arrow was aimed. b. The same seen from above. c. The catch. d. Front view of the main pillar, including the fixture for aiming the arrow.

PLATE 24

PART VI

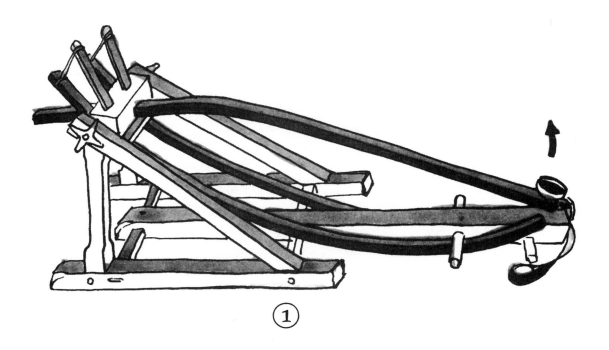

①

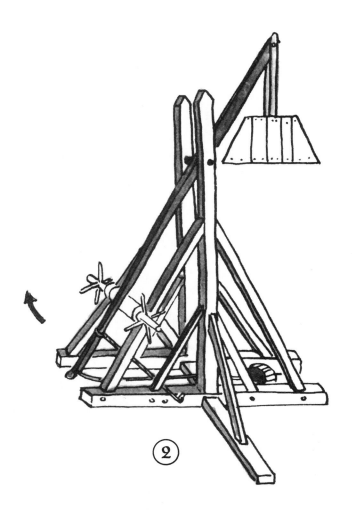

②

Catapults for hurling light missiles. (1) Gilber Anger, *Illustrierte Geschichte der K. u. K. Armee.* (2) A catapult of about 1404 (Jähns, pl. 73).

PLATE 25

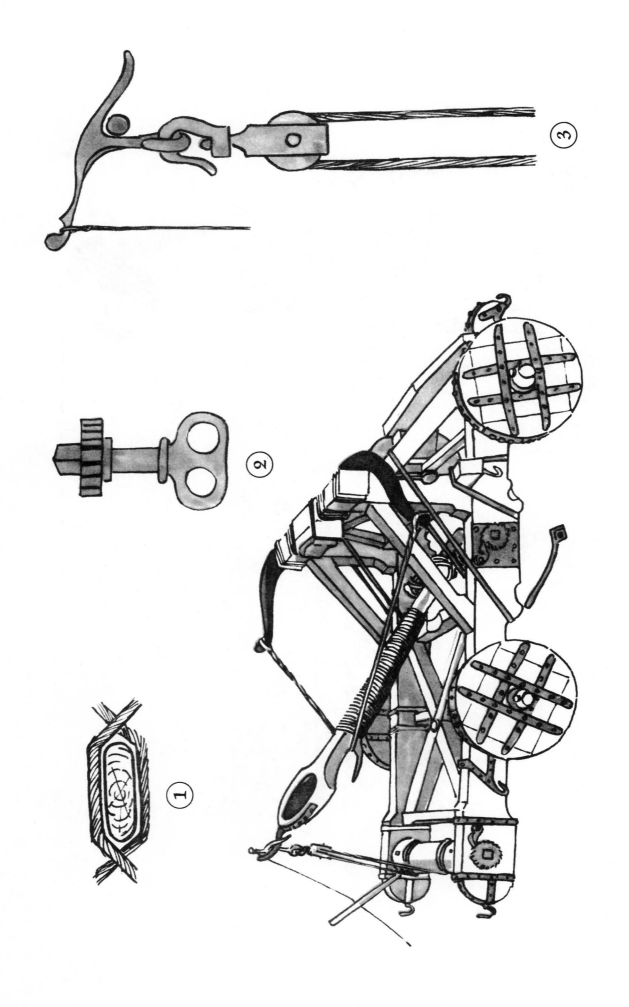

A low mobile catapult (Viollet le Duc, V, p. 222). (1) Detail of the rope holding down the catapult lever at its lower end. (2) The cog-wheel, by means of which it is possible to wind up the rope holding the catapult lever. (3) The charger and at the same time the release-catch.

PLATE 26

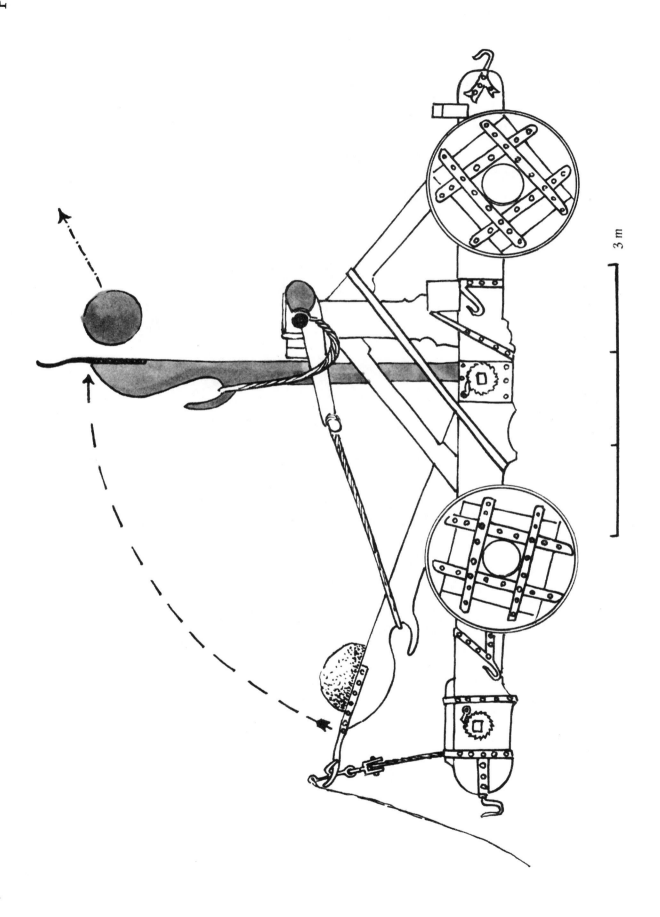

A side view of the previous catapult (Viollet le Duc, V, p. 223).

3 m

PLATE 27

PART VI

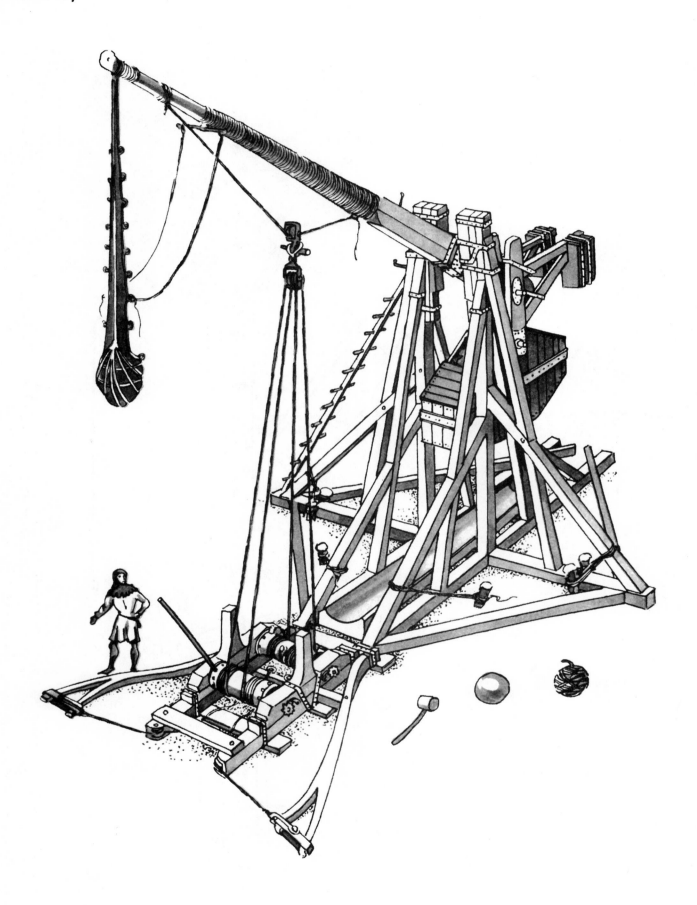

The great catapult or trebuchet, as depicted by Viollet le Duc, V, p. 227.

PLATE 28

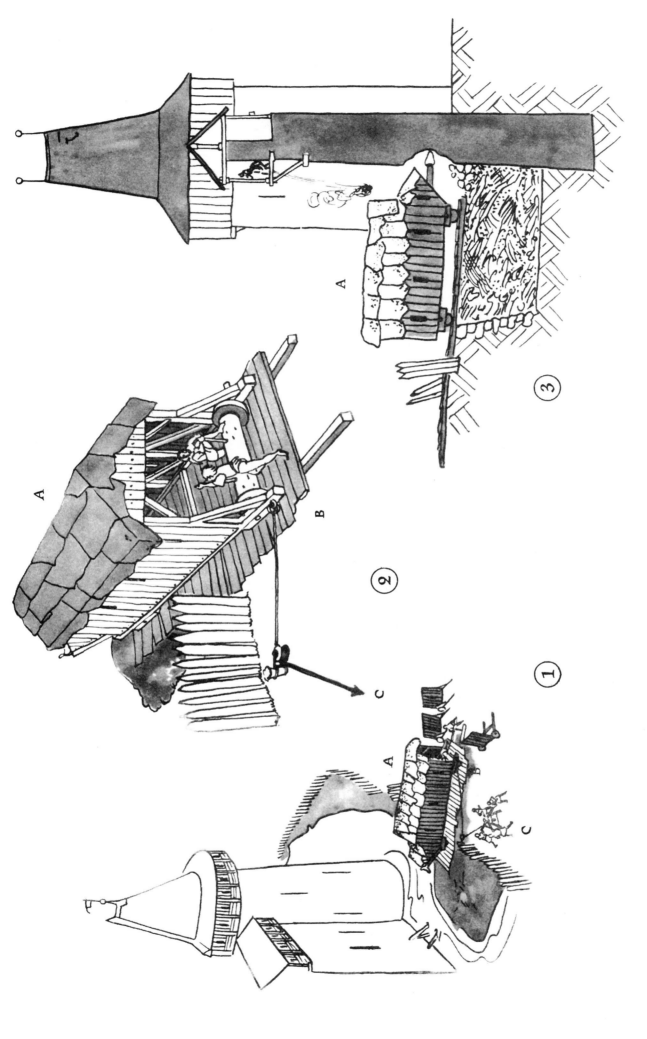

(1) The mobile wooden construction which protected the battering ram (A) was pushed on a wooden platform (B) by means of a capstan (C). To fill up the moat all kinds of material were thrown from the front of the construction. (Viollet le Duc, I, no. I, p. 363). (2) When the capstan could lever the machine no farther, it was pushed the rest of the way by those inside it and under cover. (3) The battering-ram, which had been concealed inside it, in action. (Imaginary reconstruction.)

PLATE 29   PART VI

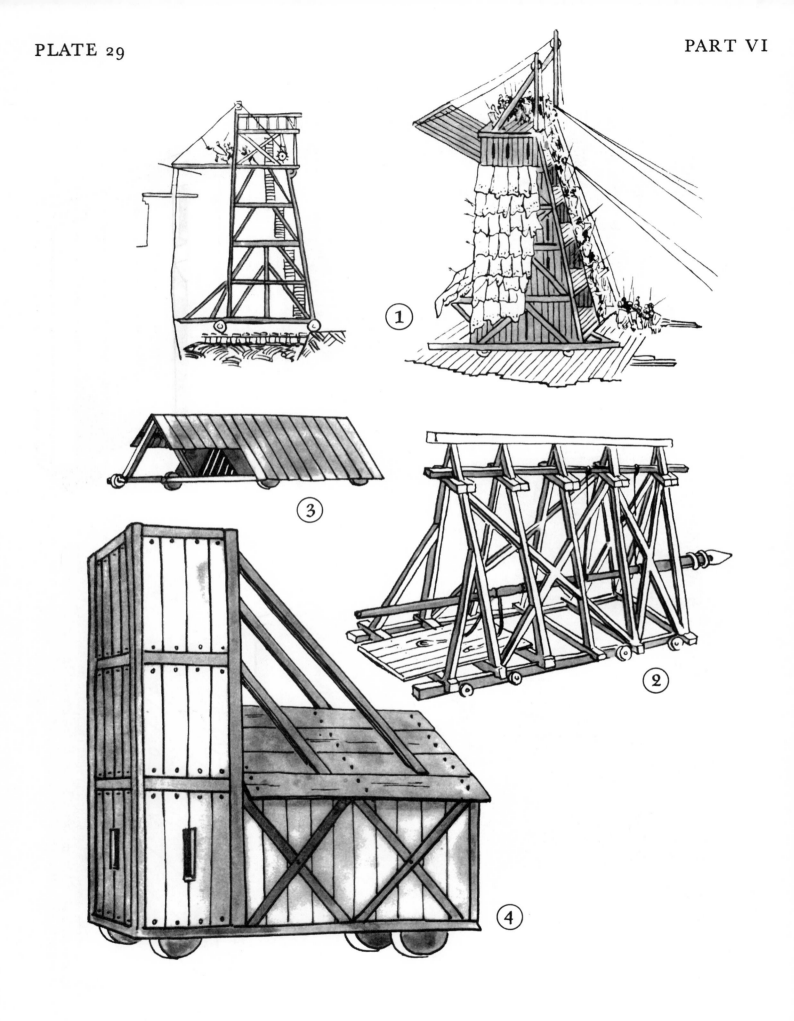

(1) A breaching tower or belfrey. (Viollet le Duc, I, no. 1, p. 363). a. picture of a belfrey in action. b. in cross section.
(2) A battering-ram without its roof. (3) The moveable roof of boards, 15th century (Jähns, p. 68, pl. 5). (4) A breaching
tower or belfry covered with boards, early 15th century (Bellifortis MS).

PLATE 30 PART VI

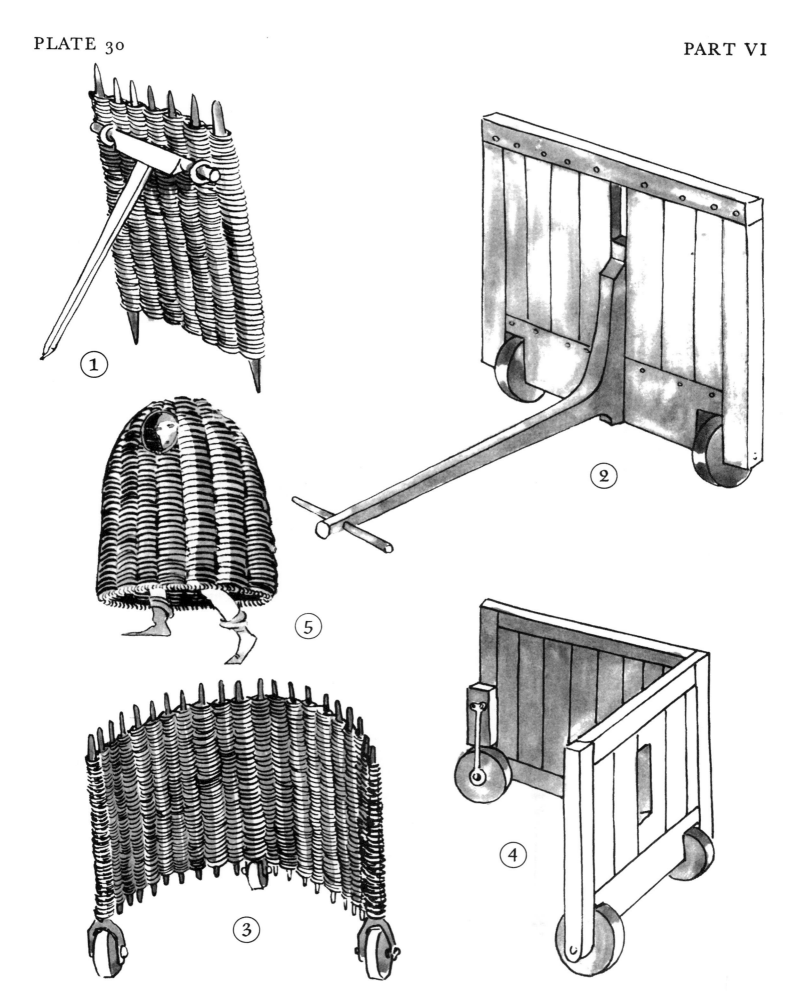

(1) A fixed shield of woven osiers. (2, 4) A mobile wooden shield on wheels (Viollet le Duc, p. 269). (3) A mobile convex wattle shield (*ibid.*, p. 268). (5) An "approach" basket made of wattle (Bellifortis MS).

PLATE 1   PART VII

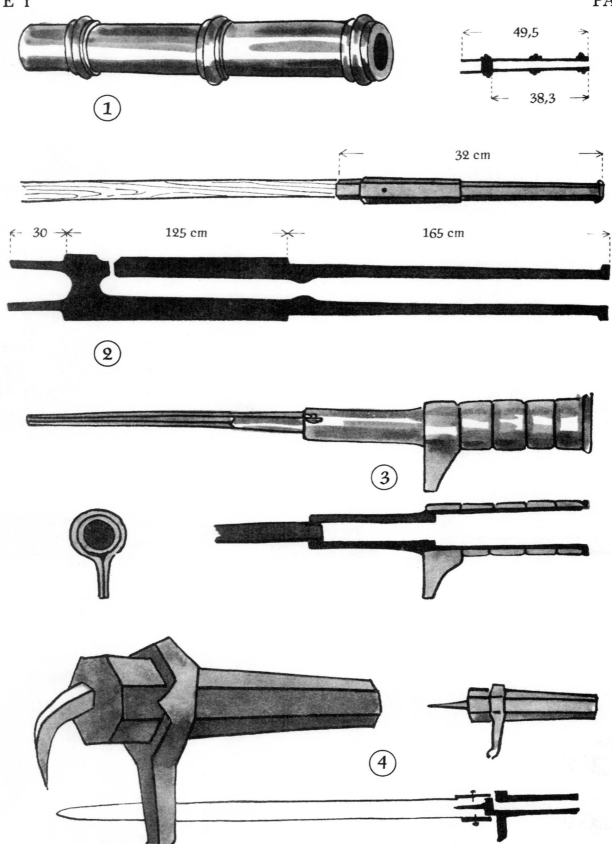

(1) A bronze hand gun dating from about 1350, 49.5 cm. long, 44 mm. calibre, and weighing 8.5 kilograms. The vent is 14.5 cm. from the mouth. The barrel is 38.3 cm. long, the socket 9.8 cm. (Rathgen, *Das Geschütz im Mittelalter*, pl. 9). (2) The Tannenberg hand gun, made of bronze and dating from before 1399. 14.5 mm. bore, weighing 1.2 kilograms. Length of barrel 32 cm. (a. Rathgen, pl. 9; b. *Deutsches Leben*, p. 404; c. *Zeitschrift für historische Waffenkunde*, III. pl. 3.) (3) A wrought iron hand gun for firing stone shot. The gun chamber is forged from one piece of iron 26 cm. long, with a bore of 6 cm. The back of the chamber is closed by an iron stock. The vent is on the right-hand side at the back and is fitted with a little pan. The barrel is forged on a welded iron plate and strengthened by five iron rings each about 10 cm. wide, the last of which is drawn out into a 12 cm. long ring. The barrel is 50 cm. long, with a calibre of 12 cm. Weight of the stone shot 1.9 kg, powder priming 0.414 kg. The gun dates from the first decade of the 15th century (*Zeitschrift für historische Waffenkunde*, II, pp. 317, 8, pl. 73). (4) An iron hand gun from Braunfels, with a hook for fastening it to its support (1/5th actual size). (Rathgen, pl. 9.)

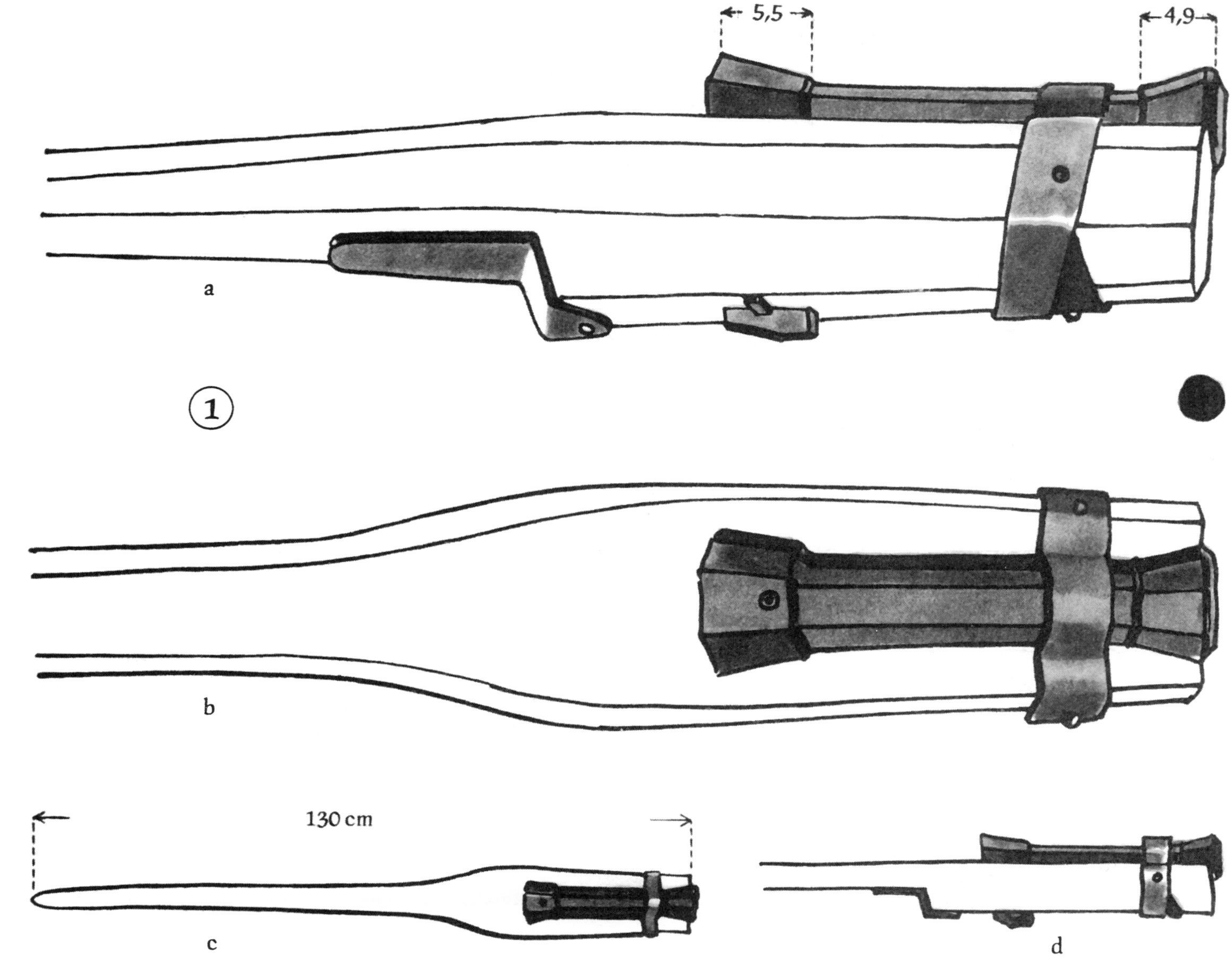

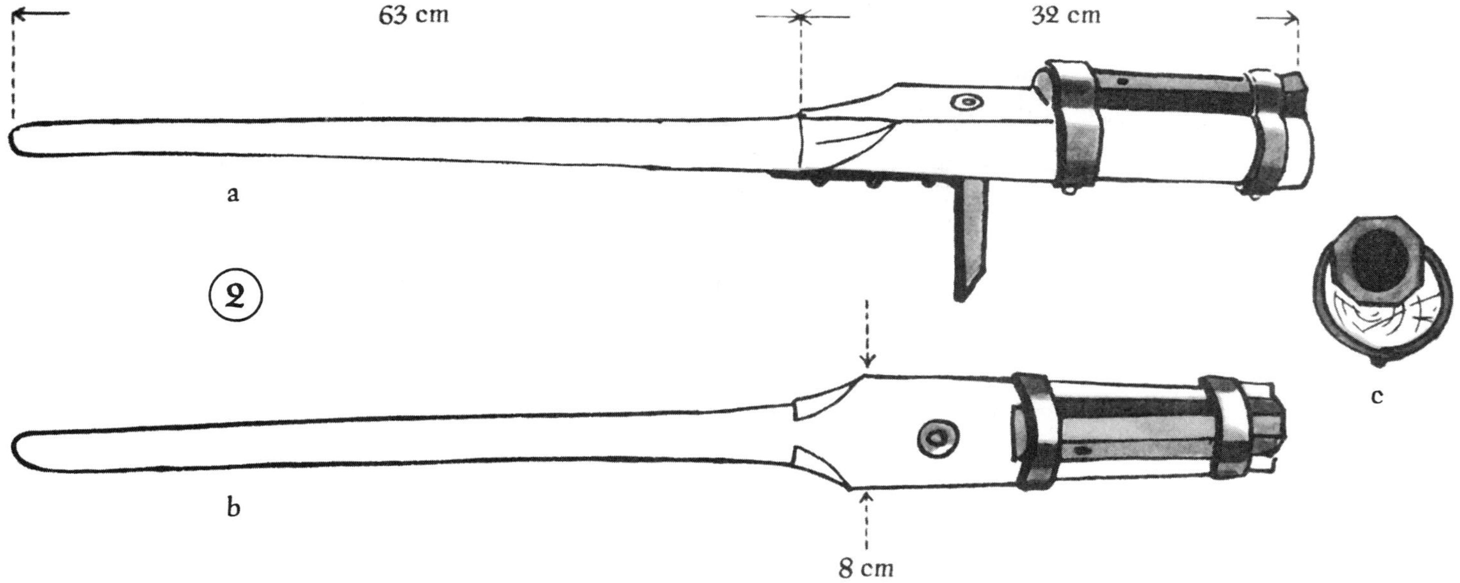

PLATE 2

PART VII

(1) A 14th-15th-century hand-gun (J. Koula, *Vývoj českých pušek*, pl. 1). The original is in the Plzeň Museum. Calibre 25 mm. length of barrel 29 cm. The width of reinforcement at the rear end of the barrel is 55 mm, that at the muzzle end 49 mm. The vent is 3.5 cm. from the end of the barrel. a. seen from the side. On the underside of the stock one can see the metal-plated ridge for supporting the weapon when firing and for absorbing the recoil. b. from above. c. the overall length of the weapon, together with stock, 130 cm. d. side view of the hand-gun. (2) A hand gun from the Berne History Museum. A copy in the Prague Military History Museum. 14th century. Length of weapon with stock 95 cm, length of barrel 18 cm. The vent is 13 cm from the muzzle; 31 mm calibre. a. side view. b. seen from above (width of stock 8 cm). c. front view. (*Zeitschrift für historische Waffenkunde*, I, p. 182.)

PLATE 3   PART VII

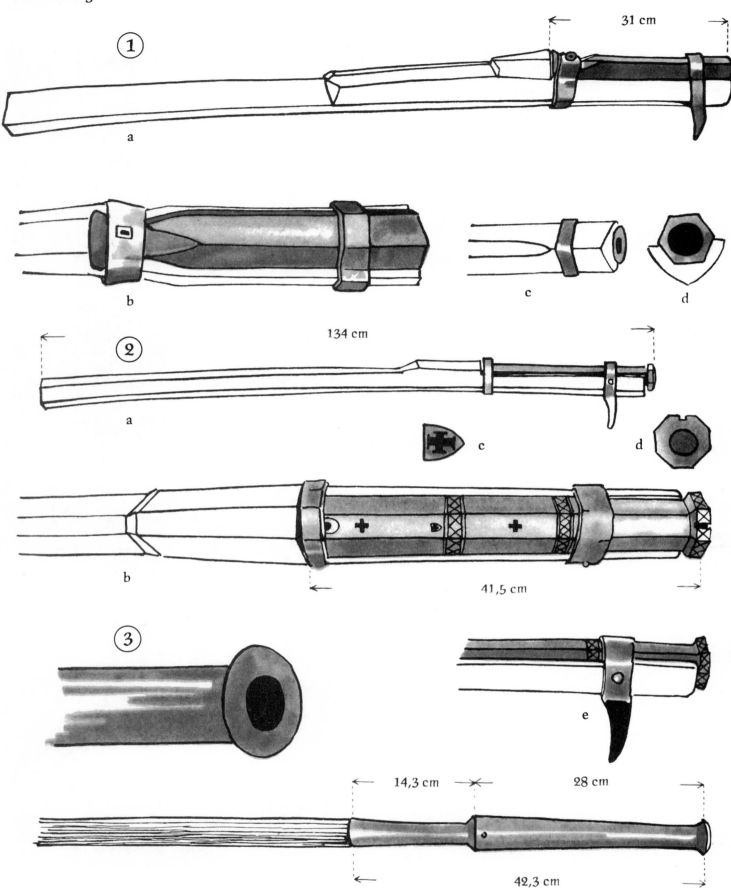

(1) A Plzeň arquebus, 105 cm long (J. Koula; *Zeitschrift*, II, p. 164, pl. 63). a. side view. b. seen from above. c. seen from below. d. the muzzle. (2) A Plzeň arquebus (J. Koula; *Zeitschrift*, II, p. 165, pl. 64). a. view of the complete weapon, 134 cm. long. b. seen from above, showing the details of the markings and ornamentation of the barrel. c. the marking: a cross in an escutcheon. d. the muzzle of the barrel with a slot obviously used as a sight. e. detail of the hook. (3) A Tábor musket (now in the Tábor Municipal Museum; an exact copy is to be seen in the Prague Military History Museum). Total length 42.3 cm. length of barrel 28 cm. calibre 18 mm.

PLATE 4

PART VII

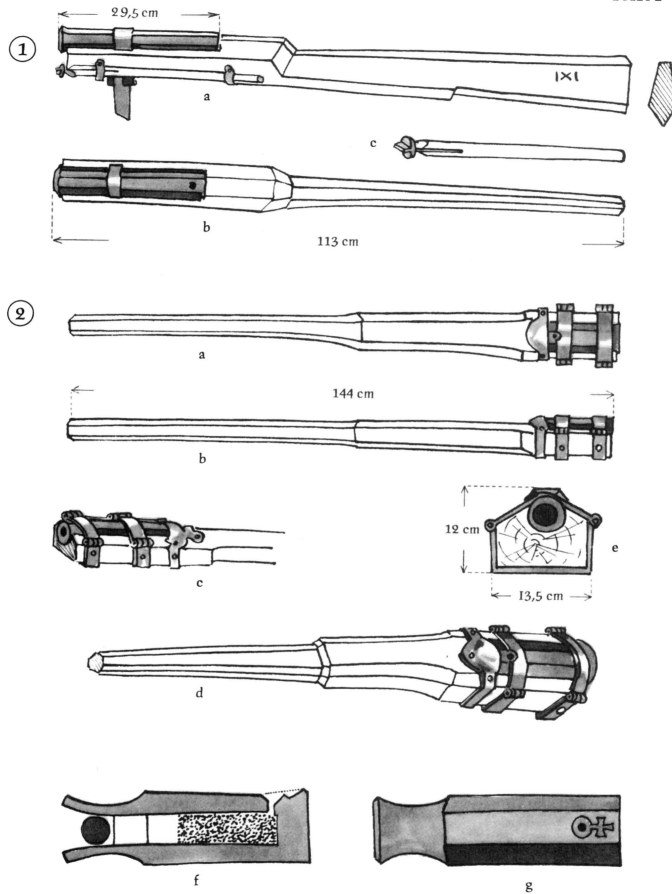

(1) A 15th century hand gun, the property of the Prague National Museum (J. Koula). a. side view; the ramrod is fastened on the left side. b. view from above. c. the ramrod. (2) A 14th century Nuremberg hand gun (*Zeitschrift für historische Waffenkunde*, I, p. 182, pl. 6). Total length 144 cm. barrel 19 cm. a. seen from above. b. side view. c. diagonal view (*ibid.*, I, p. 129), 1/10th actual size. d. an iron hand gun, see (2) (*Deutsches Leben*, p. 404, pl. 591 and 592). e. section of the same hand cannon from the front. f. cross-section of its barrel (*Zeitschrift*, I, p. 183), calibre of shot 25 mm. diameter of the muzzle of the barrel 42 mm. g. view of the barrel from above, with the vent in a circle with a cross (*ibid.*, II, p. 101, pl. 5).

PLATE 5

(1) A gunner firing a hand cannon, dating from 1405 (Bellifortis MS, 1402–5). (2) A gunner priming a hand cannon, dating from 1410 (Essen-wein, *Quellen zur Geschichte der Feuerwaffen*, pl. B-1). (3) Two gunners, the one on the right is taking aim, and the other is priming the cannon (Vienna MS, dating between 1437–50, from the painting "The Battle with the Hussites").

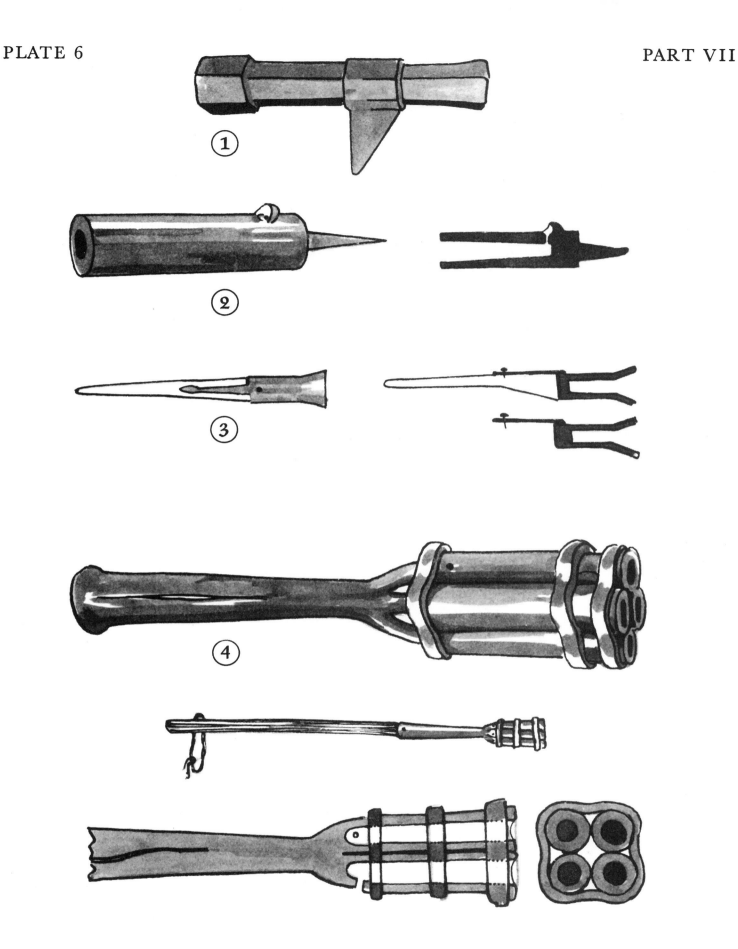

(1) An iron hand cannon dating from about 1420, Zurich Regional Museum. Weighs 7 kg. 1/5th actual size, i. e. about 38–39 cm. long (Rathgen, pl. 9). (2) The barrel of a hand cannon from Linz, with spike for securing it firmly. On the upper side is a small rising fan, protecting the back of the vent. (*Zeitschrift für historische Waffenkunde*, I, p. 129 and II, p. 412.) Dating from the end of the 14th century. 19 cm. long, a round barrel, 8.3 cm. long spike, 15.3 cm. long bore. The diameter of the gun is 52.5–60.4 mm. (3) An Italian gun; calibre 4 cm. Diameter of the muzzle 6.4 cm. View from above and two cross-sections (*ibid.*, I, p. 83). (4) A four-barrel hand gun dating from the end of the 14th or early 15th century; about 24 cm. long. After firing it was used as a cudgel (*ibid.*, IV, p. 57; V, p. 98).

PLATE 7

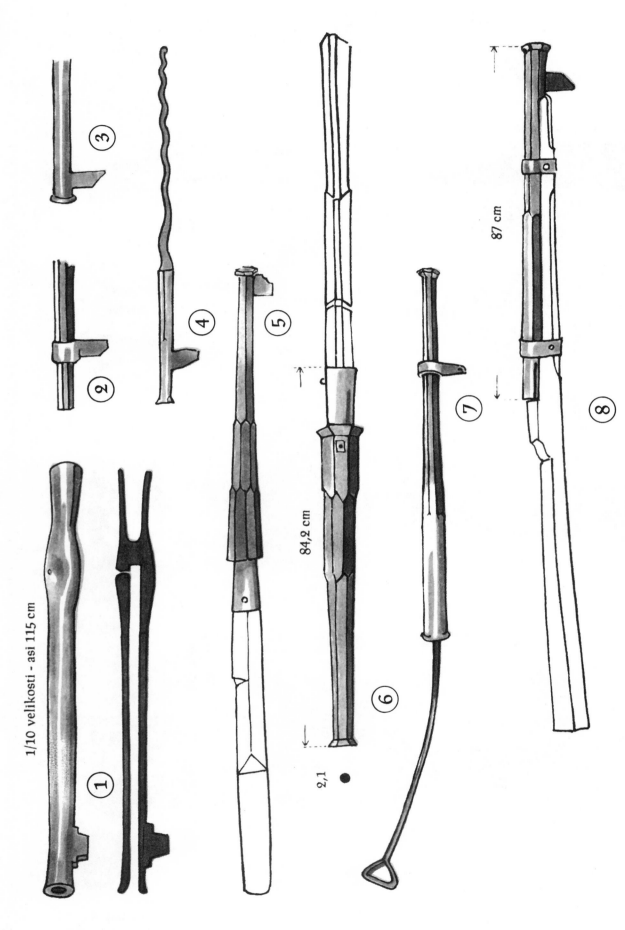

1/10 velikosti - asi 115 cm

84,2 cm

2,1

87 cm

(1) A hand gun dating from about 1440; about 115 cm. long (*Zeitschrift für historische Waffenkunde*, I, p. 131, pl. 6). 1/10th actual size. (2) How the hook was fastened to the barrel on a socket. (3) Weld. (4) A Nuremberg arquebus (*Deutsches Leben*, p. 404; *Zeitschrift*, II, p. 166, pl. 65). The rear part of the barrel is pentagonal, 37.5 cm. long; the complete weapon is 1 metre long, with a calibre of 21 mm. Weighs 4.65 kg. (5) An arquebus from the Plzeň Museum (J. Koula). Barrel 84.2 cm. (6) An arquebus from the Plzeň Museum (J. Koula). (7) An iron arquebus from Berlin (*Zeitschrift*, II, p. 387, pl. 71). There is a similar one in Luxembourg (*Zeitschrift*, II, p. 387, pl. 71). It is one of the oldest of the great arquebuses. Weighs almost 20 kg., the barrel is 43.3 cm. long, calibre 5 cm. calibre ratio 1:8.5. From the first decade of the 15th century. (8) A Plzeň arquebus with a barrel 87 cm. long.

PLATE 8

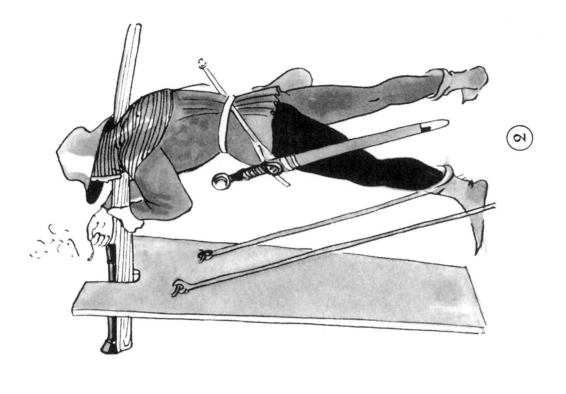

(1) A gunner priming a hand gun. (Viollet le Duc; Jähns; Radnor). (2) A gunner primes an arquebus protected by a *taras* with "crutches and slot".

PLATE 9

(1–2) German gunners with an arquebus (Essenwein, pl. BI; *Zeitschrift*, I, pp. 249–50). (3) A gunner with an arquebus dating from the years 1437–50 (Vienna MS, from the painting "The Battle with the Hussites").

PLATE 10

German gunners dating from the years 1420–40 (Essenwein, pl. BI; *Zeitschrift*, I, p. 249, pl. 22). The last gunner is wearing a cap woven from rope or a helmet made of metal plates.

PLATE 11   PART VII

(1) A wrought iron gun dating from the 14th century; 37 cm. long, 55 mm. calibre (Szendrei, p. 206, pl. 598). (2) An Italian gun (*Zeitschrift für historische Waffenkunde*, 1923/1925, p. 119, pl. 7). (3) A cross-section of a Turin bombard, 50 cm. long, width of the barrel 150–180 mm. the chamber 50–68 mm. Weight of the stone shot 5.182 kg. (*ibid.*, I, p. 222, pl. 12). (4) The stone ball fired from the great Frankfurt gun from the Castle of Tannenberg, dating from 1399. Calibre 47 cm. weight 110 kg. (Rathgen, pl. 8, fig. 28.) (5) A bombard made in two parts, the barrel and the chamber. Total length 144 cm., weight 15 kg. (*Zeitschrift*, 1923/1925, p. 117). (6) The shot from the same bombard, calibre approx. 48 cm. (*ibid*). (7) A 14th–15th century bombard (Toman, *Husitské válečnictví*, p. 152, pl. 1a). (8) A Thuringen cast gun, dating from about 1400. 150 mm calibre (1/5th actual size). (Rathgen, pl. 8, fig. 25.) (9) A Landskronen cast gun, dating from about 1400. 215 mm. calibre, weight 115 kg., 1/15th actual size (Rathgen, pl. 8, fig. 25; *Zeitschrift*, VIII, p. 13, pl. 8).

PLATE 12   PART VII

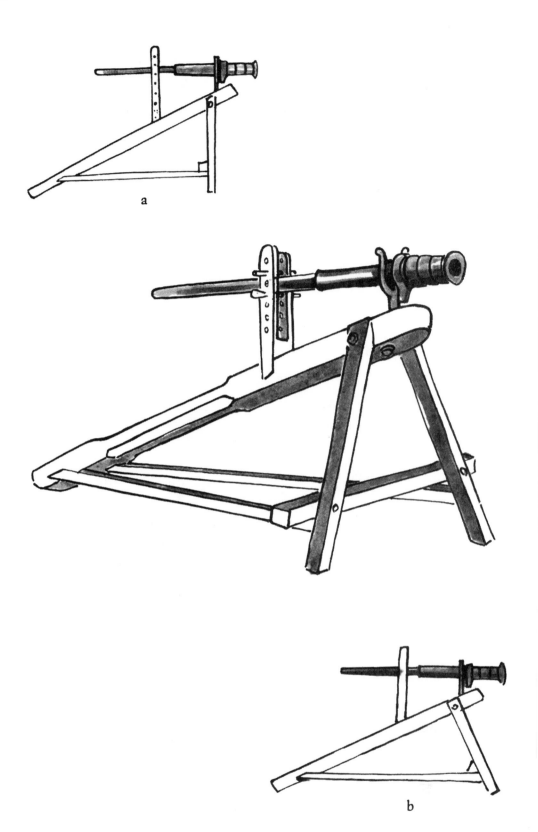

A gun support dating from between 1420–30 (*Zeitschrift*, I, p. 248, pl. 21). a. the legs of the stand were either placed perpendicular to the ground or, as in b., were at an angle to the central bar.

PLATE 13   PART VII

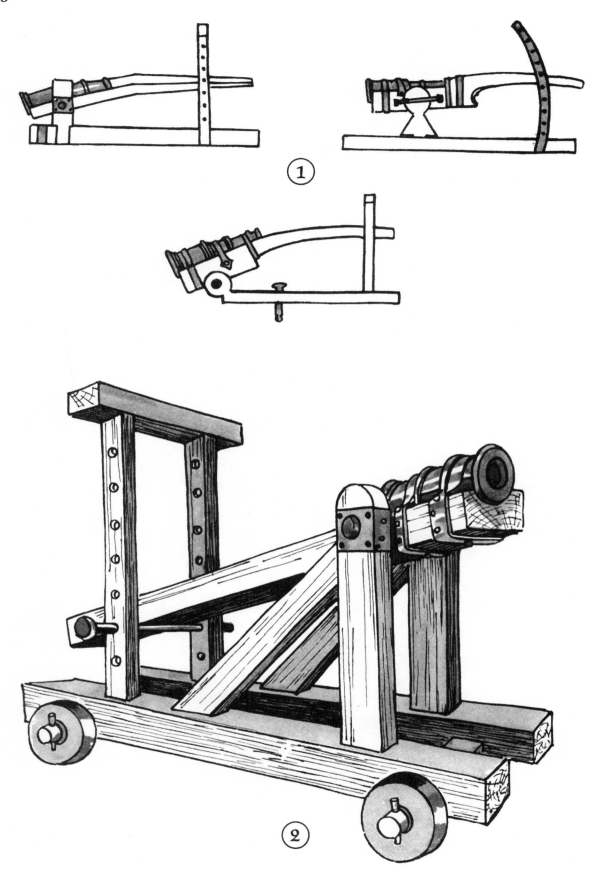

(1) Guns on wooden supports with aiming devices, dating from about 1400 (W. Herman, *Das Feuerwerker Buch von 1420*, p. 139, pl. 42–3). (2) A gun on a wheeled carriage, dating from between 1390–1400 (a reconstruction according to Essenwein, *Quellen zur Geschichte der Feuerwaffen*, A VII).

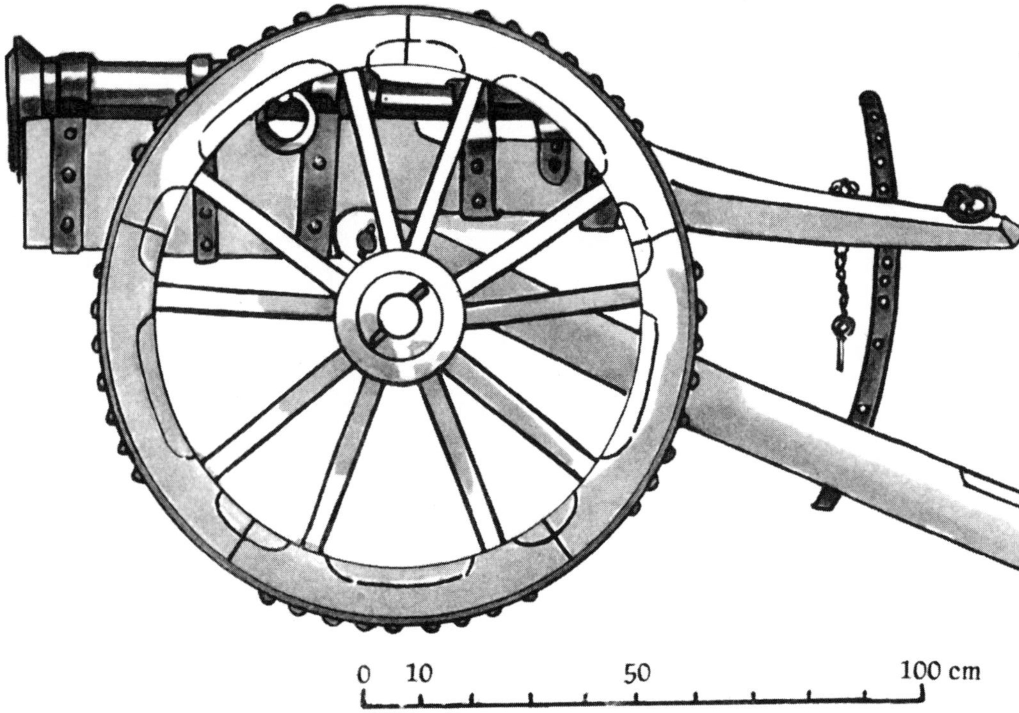

PLATE 14

0   10   50   100 cm

(1) A howitzer from the Vienna arsenal, usually dated from about 1450, firing cannon balls, 160 mm. calibre, length of barrel and chamber 98 cm., i. e. approximately 6 times the calibre. The iron barrel is welded from iron rods held together by transverse rings. It rests on a wooden block. The wooden gun-carriage has an iron sight. (Toman, *Husitské válečnictví*, pl. II). (2) A similar gun on a wooden wheeled carriage with iron sight, dating from 1390 (Rathgen, *Das Geschütz im Mittelalter*, pl. 3).

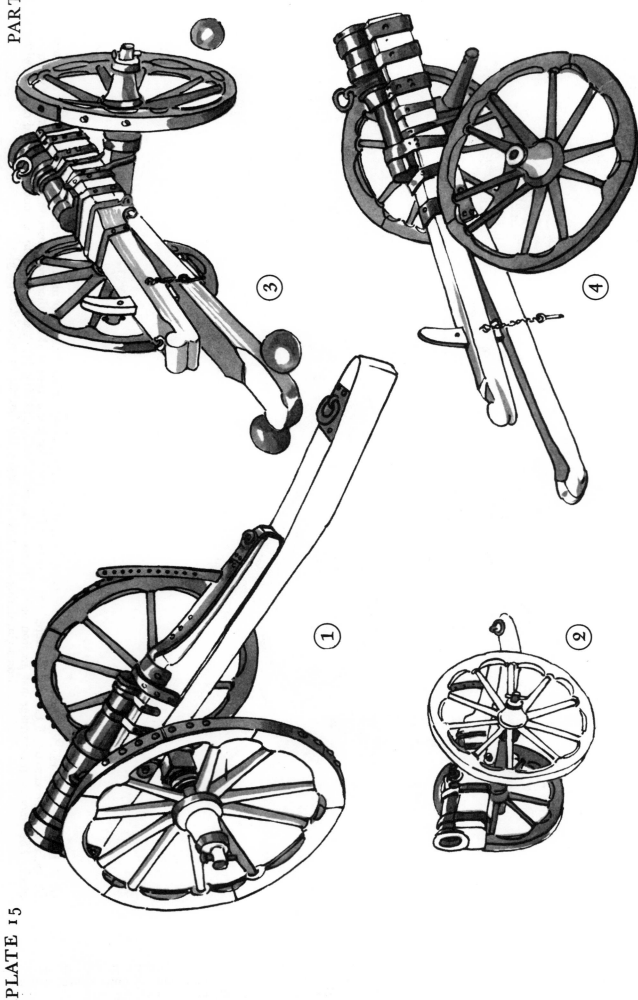

PLATE 15

(1) A view of a howitzer preserved in the Vienna arsenal (*Zeitschrift für historische Waffenkunde*, 1937/1939, p. 153). (2) The same howitzer from V. J. Hauner, *Vývoj pozemního válečnictví*, supplement, p. 35, pl. 42. (3) A Burgundian howitzer dating from between 1450–76, in the Berlin Museum. The howitzer fired cannon balls of 8 cm. calibre; length of barrel and chamber 80.5 cm. (*Geschichte des I. Kurhessischen Feldartillerie-Regiments, Nr 11, und seiner Stammtruppen*, Dr. Wilhelm Has). (4) The same howitzer from a different position (Ullstein, *Weltgeschichte: Dr. J. von Pflug-Harttung, Neuzeit*, I, plate following pl. 560, fig. 10).

PLATE 16   PART VII

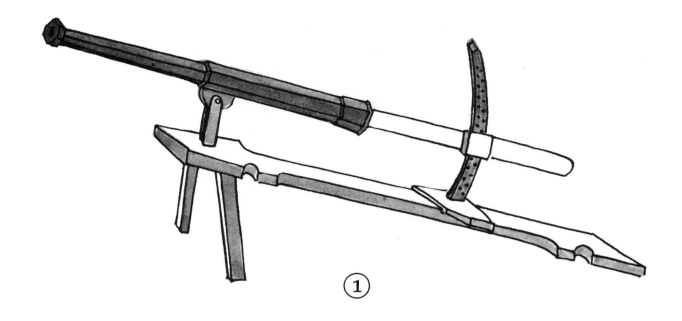

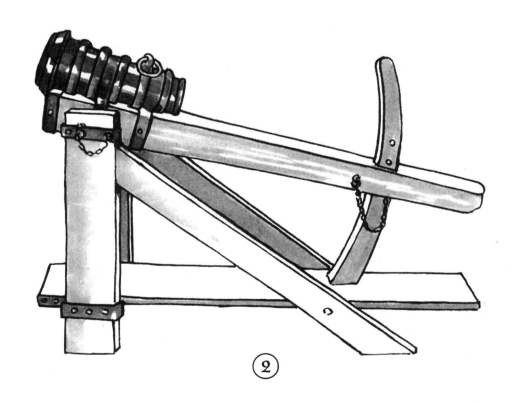

(1) *tarasnice* or palissade gun, on a wooden plank with a wooden trestle and sighting device (Toman, p. 161, pl. 4). (2) A mortar, dating from between 1450 and 1470, from the Berlin Armoury. Barrel 84 cm. long, 15 cm. calibre, weight of shot 3 kg (Ullstein, *Weltgeschichte*, Pflugt-Harttung, *Neuzeit*, I, plate following p. 560, fig. 18).

PLATE 17   PART VII

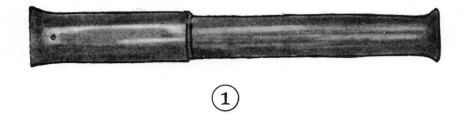

①

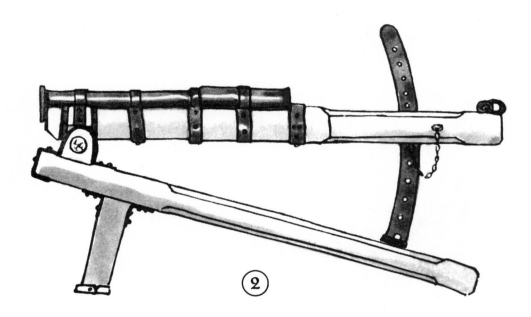

②

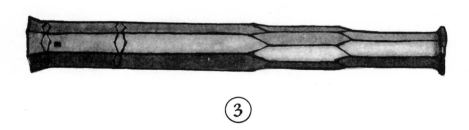

③

(1) A wrought-iron gun of the early 15th century (Plzeň Municipal Museum, cat. no. H. T. 2). Cylindrical barrel 1080 mm. long, outer diameter 106 mm. with a strengthening bracket at the butt end, 46 mm. calibre. (2) A diagram of the carriage required for the gun in (1). (3) A wrought-iron gun of the first half of the 15th century (Znojmo Municipal Museum, cat. no. Zb 512). The octagonal barrel is 1084 mm. long, strengthened twice, 40 mm. calibre. The gunsmith's mark is a wreath of flowers. Diameter of the barrel at the muzzle is 92 mm.

PLATE 18

A palissade gun from the Spanish Military Museum. The 160 cm. barrel is fastened to the wooden support by ropes (Estruch, *Museo ameria*, pl. XXVI).

PLATE 19   PART VII

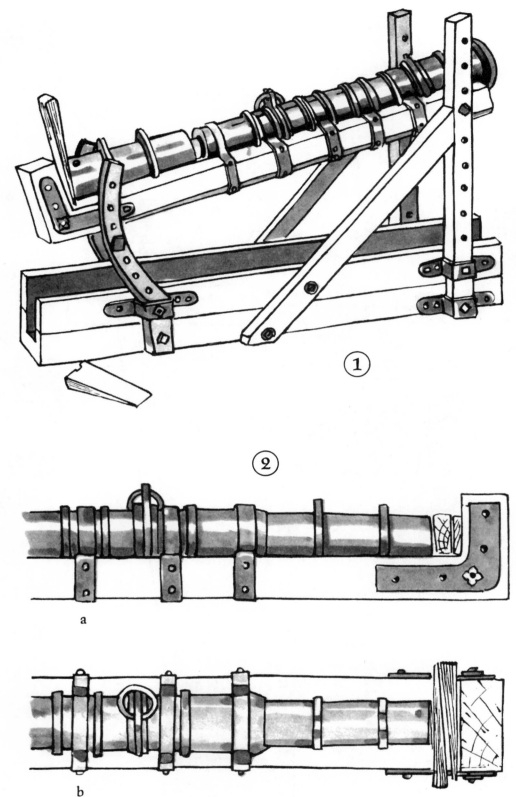

(1) A wrought iron breechblock gun, on a wooden support; 105 mm. calibre. The barrel is 160–180 cm. long including the chamber. Dating from about 1420. (Rathgen, pl. 10). (2) Detail of the attachment of the chamber. a. side view. b. view from above (*Zeitschrift für historische Waffenkunde*, II, p. 4, pl. 1).

PLATE 20

PART VII

b

a

② ①

c

(1) A breechblock gun on a wooden gun-carriage, with securing wedge on a chain and the block in position. By the sight, there are two pegs on chains for holding the gun steady. This picture is reconstructed from a copper engraving by Israel van Meckenen, "Judith killing Holofernes" (1470–80). (2) A breechblock gun drawn precisely according to the above mentioned source (also Essenwein, *Quellen zur Geschichte der Feuerwaffen*, pl. A LXVI). The wedge and breechblock are lying beside the gun, also a leather pouch for powder. a. Side view of a breechblock gun, with its block removed. b. The front part of the barrel lying on its rest, seen from above. c. The back part of the wooden carriage, with one of the pegs for setting the sights.

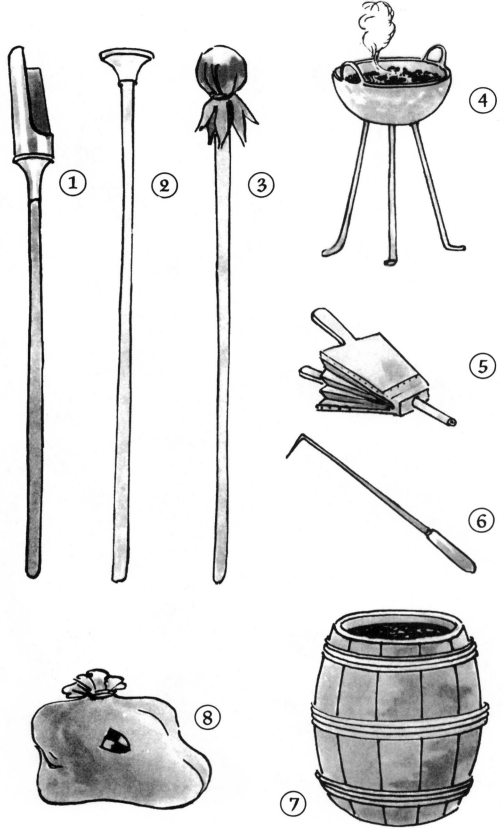

The gunner's equipment. (1) A powder measure (Boeheim, p. 489, pl. 567). (2) A ramrod. (Viollet le Duc, V, p. 256). (3) A cleaning rod. (4) A trivet brazier with glowing coals for lighting the match. (5) Bellows, from a picture in the Jena Codex. (6) The match, shaped like a furnace rake. (7) A powder barrel. (8) A leather pouch as depicted in the copper engraving by Israel van Mechenen, "Judith killing Holofernes" (*Kulturgeschichte des Deutschen Volkes*, I, pp. 272, 273).

PLATE 22

PART VII

During the siege of Vyšehrad castle in 1420, the soldiers of the Prague faction placed a gun in a chapel about 300 metres from the walls of the castle. They knocked a hole in the wall for firing through (Toman, p. 312). This illustration is based on one in the *Zeitschrift für historische Waffenkunde*.

PLATE 23   PART VII

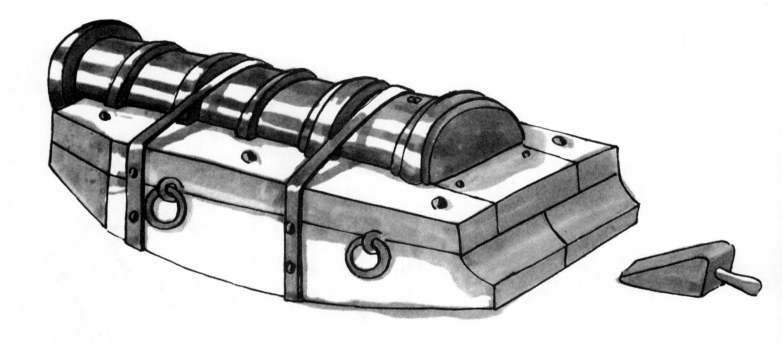

A cannon in its support; barrel is about 160 cm. long (Viollet le Duc, p. 254).

PLATE 24   PART VII

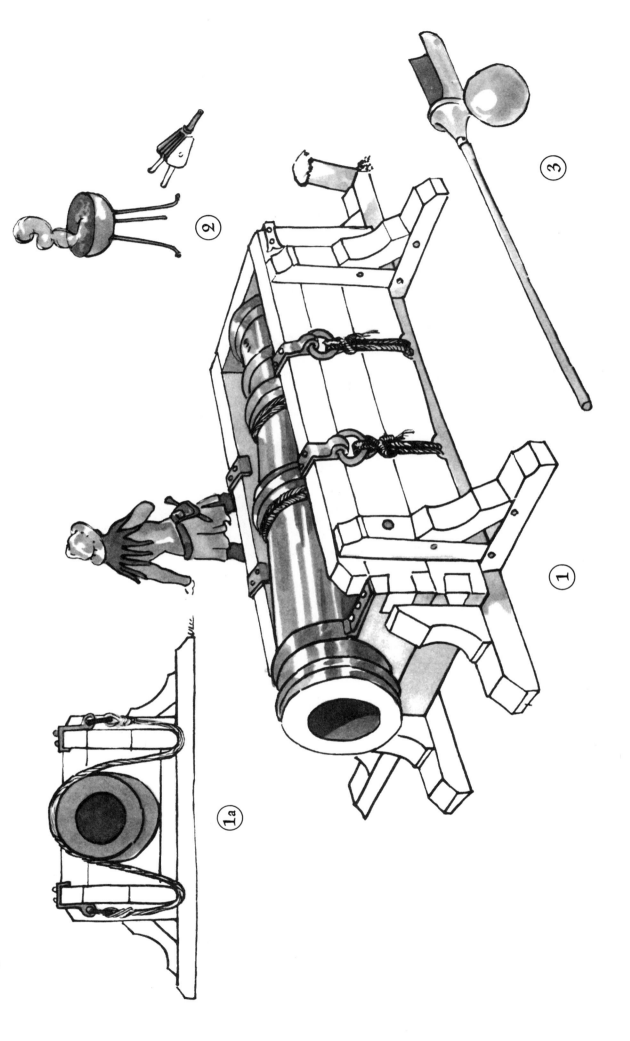

(1) A crude cannon in its wooden support, secured by ropes and pegs. (1a) The method of securing the gun barrel with a rope (from the front). (2) A brazier for lighting the match, usually in the shape of a hearth rake. (3) A powder measure and cannon ball (Viollet le Duc, V, p. 255).

PLATE 25

The firing position of a bombard and its discharge (reconstructed).

PLATE 26   PART VII

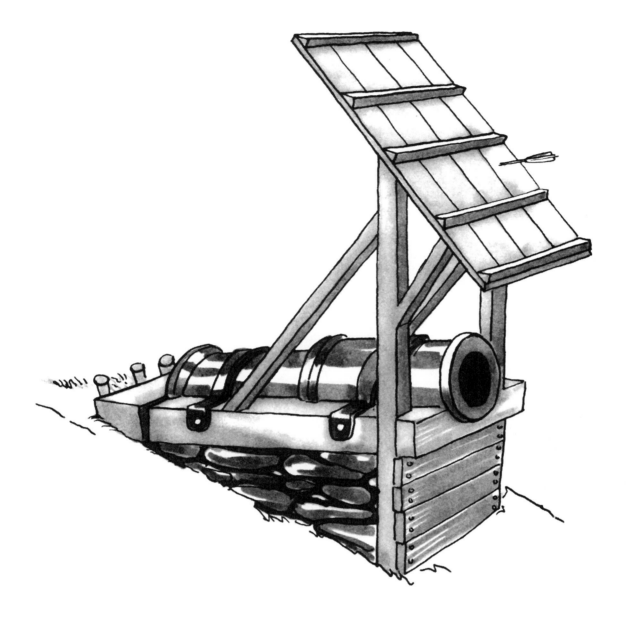

A gun placed for firing on a slope. The gun is placed in a support which is held in place at the front by planks, covered by a defensive "roof". The gun support is wedged with stones. From an old French tapestry, dating from the 15th century, in Rheims Cathedral.

PLATE 27   PART VII

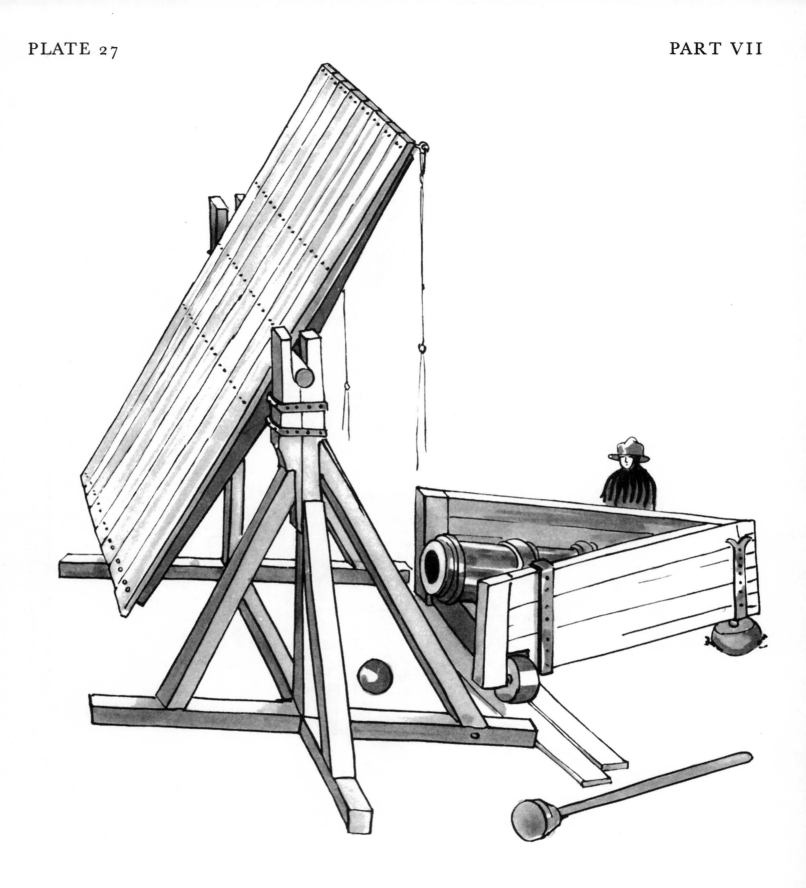

A crude piece, with the possibility of lateral adjustment of the line of fire; also its ramrod and the lowered defensive shield (Viollet le Duc, V, p. 256).

PLATE 28

PART VII

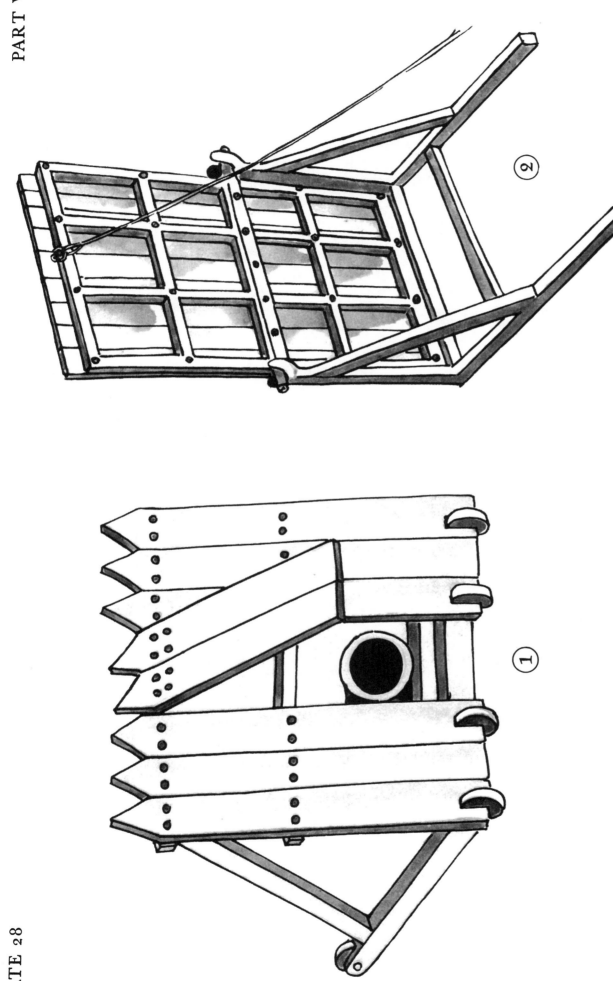

Artillery shields or *taras*, of the 15th century. (1) A gun and its shield dating from the first half of the 15th century (Jähns, p. 59, pl. 12). (2) A 15th century gun shield or *taras* (*Zeitschrift für historische Waffenkunde*, n. d.).

PLATE 29

PART VII

The firing position of a great gun, with trench and defensive shield. From a miniature in the MS *Grandes Chroniques de France*, 15th century (*Histoire de la marine française*, p. 20).

PLATE 1   PART VIII

(1) A banner dating from about 1380, from the painting of the Resurrection by the Master of the Třeboň altar-piece (Matějček, pl. 96). (1a.) Detail of the cross of the above-mentioned banner. (2) A banner dating from about 1420, from the painting of the Resurrection by the Master of the Rajhrad altar-piece (*ibid.*, pl. 190). (3) A banner from the *Liber Viaticus*. (4) A pennon, dating from 1420, from the frame of the Vyšší Brod painting of the Madonna (Matějček, pl. 205). (5) A pennon from the Krumlov MS, early 15th century.

PLATE 2

PART VIII

(1) Hussite cavalry banner, from the picture "The Fight of the Hussites with the Crusaders" in the Jena Codex MS. (2) A Hussite infantry banner, from the picture "Jan Žižka at the Head of the Army" in the same Codex. (3) A pennon inscribed with a goose, from the picture of the Hussites fighting the Crusaders in the Viennese MS dating from between 1437–50. (4–5) Signalling banners, which were carried on the leading waggons on the outside columns, one colour on one side, and another on the other.

(1, 2, 4) Banners and pennons inscribed with crosses, from the Ghent altar-piece, dating from the first half of the 15th century (Van Eyck). (3) A pennon with a cross, from the Jena Codex ("The Hussites fighting the Crusaders"). (5) A banner from a painting of the siege of Rhodes (*Die Geschichte der französischen Armee*, p. 57). (6) A pennon (*Zeitschrift für historische Waffenkunde*, II, p. 203, pl. 2a). (7) A banner, from a painting in the *Flanders Book of Tournaments*, dated 1433 (similar in *Vie militaire et religieuse au moyen âge*, p. 442).

PLATE 4

A military pennon and shield bearing the symbol of the Czech lion.

PLATE 5

PART VIII

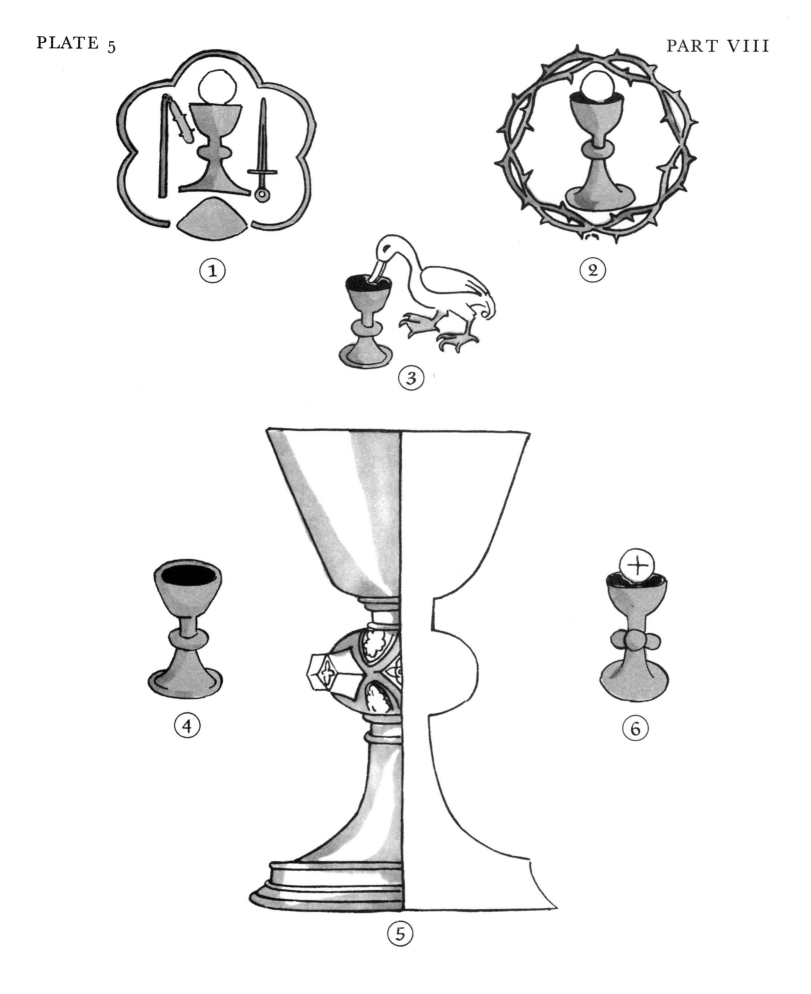

Hussite symbols and marks of identification. (1) The symbol of the Tábor community, from a seal. (2) The Tábor community field symbol, from a seal. (3) A goose drinking from a chalice (from the Viennese MS, 1437–50). (4) The chalice on a tent's escutcheon, from the same source. (5) The shape of the actual Gothic chalice, from which the Hussite symbol was derived. (6) A chalice on a pennon, from the picture of Jan Žižka leading his army in the Göttingen Codex.

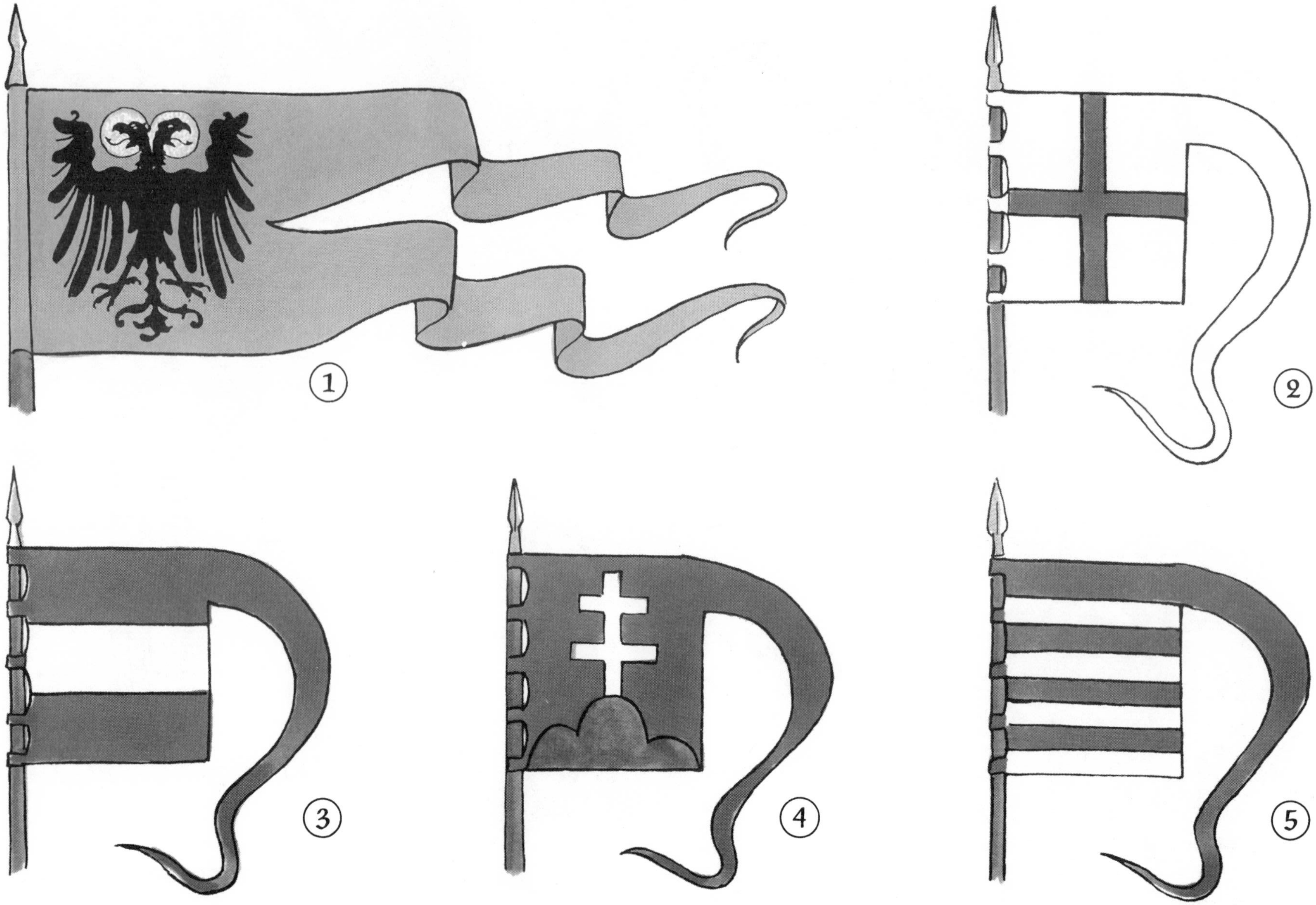

PLATE 6

PART VIII

(1) An imperial banner of the 15th century (*Mittelalterliches Hausbuch*, a waggon phalanx). (2) A banner with a cross, dating from between 1437–50. (Viennese MS, "The Battle with the Hussites"). (3) An Austrian banner from the same source. (4–5) A 14th century Hungarian banner (*Ungarisches Soldatentum*). The banner in (4) bears the Slovak symbol.

PLATE 7   PART VIII

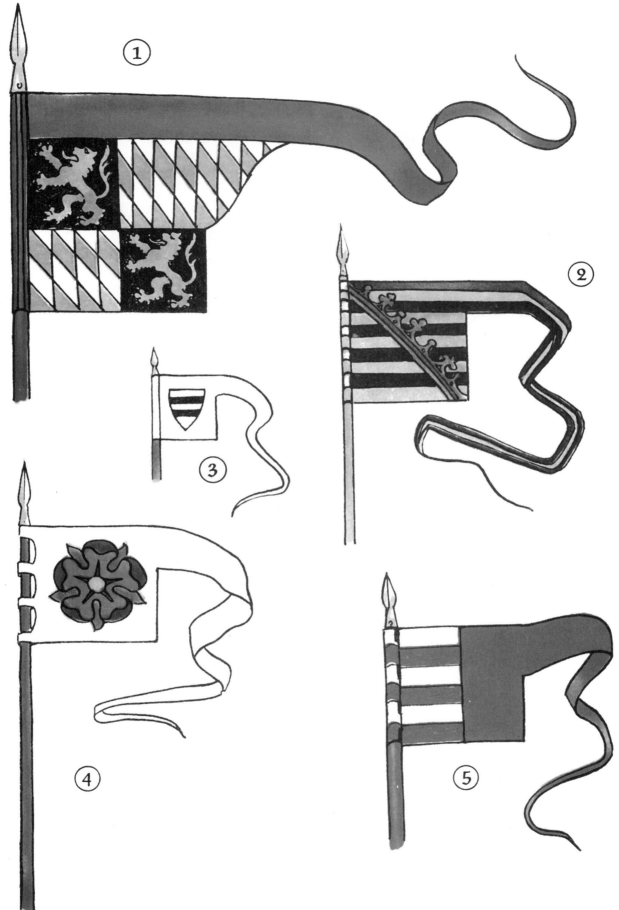

Various positions for the insignia and heraldic bearings on a banner. (1) A banner with the Bavarian symbol. (2) A banner from Saxony. (3) A banner with an escutcheon. (4) The Rožmberk banner. (5) The banner belonging to Švihovský of Ryzemberk.

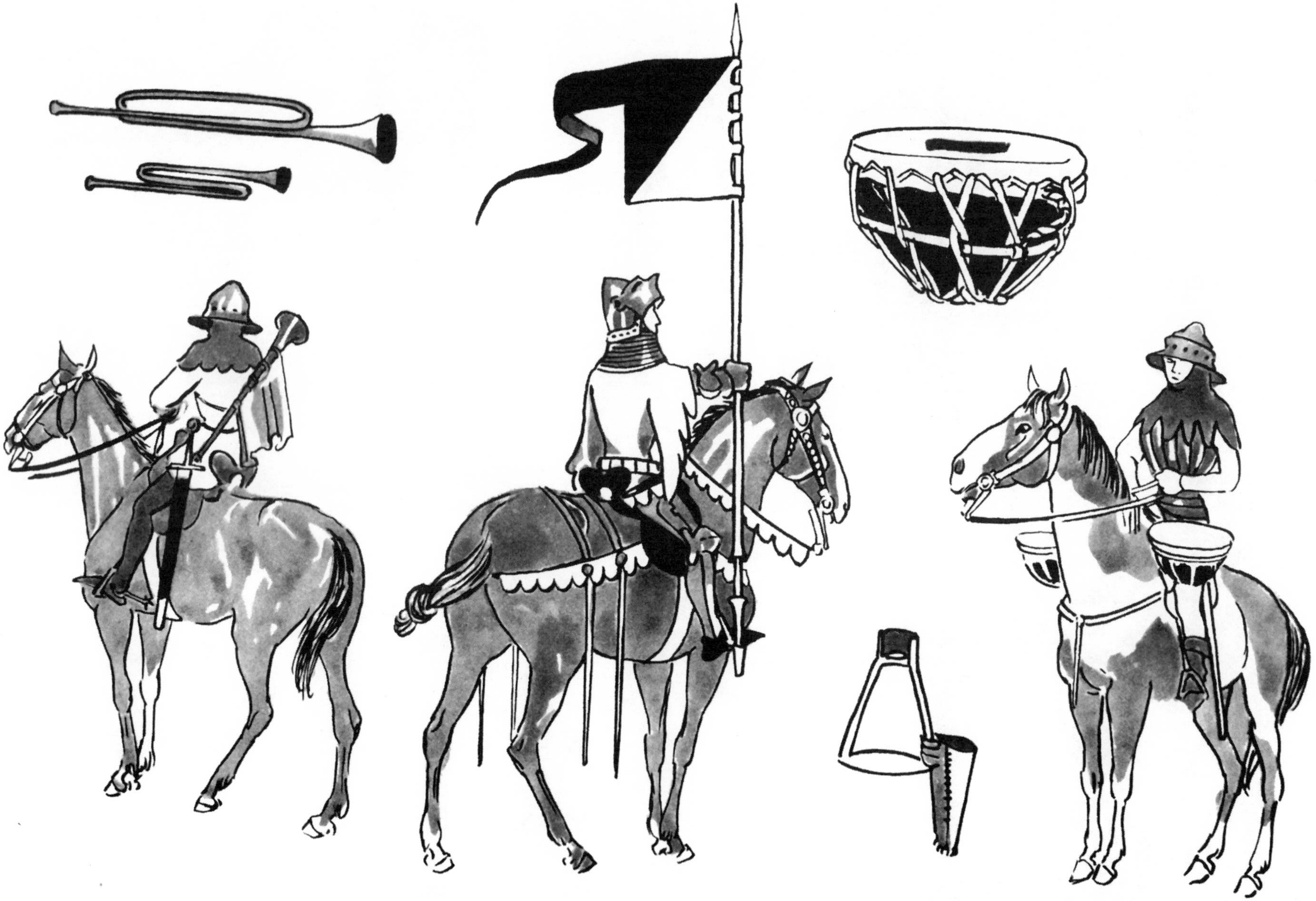

(1) A mounted trumpeter; the trumpet and the way it was carried (*Mittelalterliches Hausbuch*). (2) How the lance and banner was carried by a mounted soldier. It is probable that a leather case was fixed to the stirrup, which held the lower end of the lance stave. (3) Mounted drummer. For the drums, see Zibrt and Winter, Vol. II, p. 627, pl. 353.

PLATE 8

PLATE 9   PART VIII

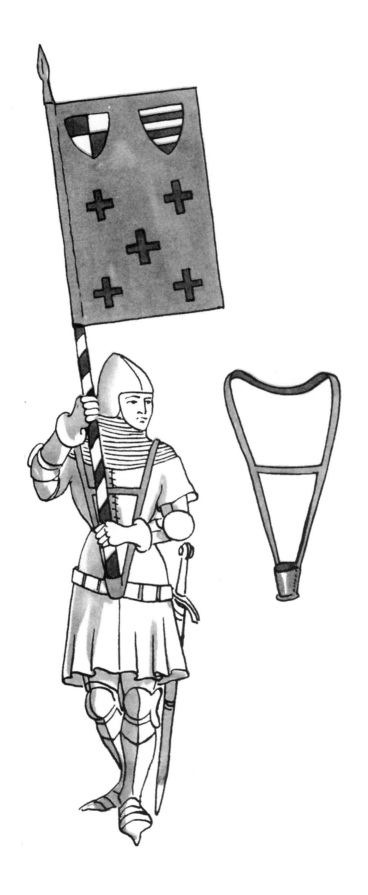

The standard bearer of an infantry unit (Lacroix, *L'Armée française*, p. 225, pl. 142).

PLATE 10

An Italian trumpeter, dating from 1450, and another 15th century trumpeter (Tilke).

PLATE 1   PART IX

The correct mediaeval riding seat. Donatello's statue of Condottiere Gattamelato (Gustav Weise, *Das Meisterwerk Do-natellos*, pl. 16).

PLATE 2

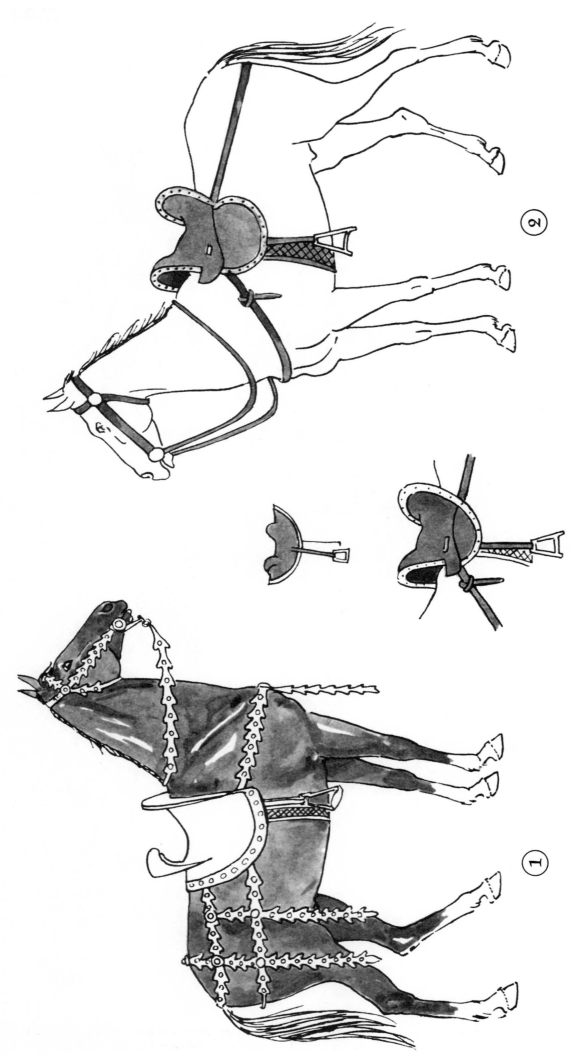

(1) A horse's saddle and bridle from an illumination in the King Wenceslas Bible. (2) A saddle dating from the first half of the 14th century (Velislav Bible, fol. 50).

PLATE 3   PART IX

The trappings of a knight's horse, dating from about 1373 (the statue of St. George at Prague Castle). In actual fact the loose ends of the straps would probably have ended in tassels, as indicated in the detail.

PLATE 4

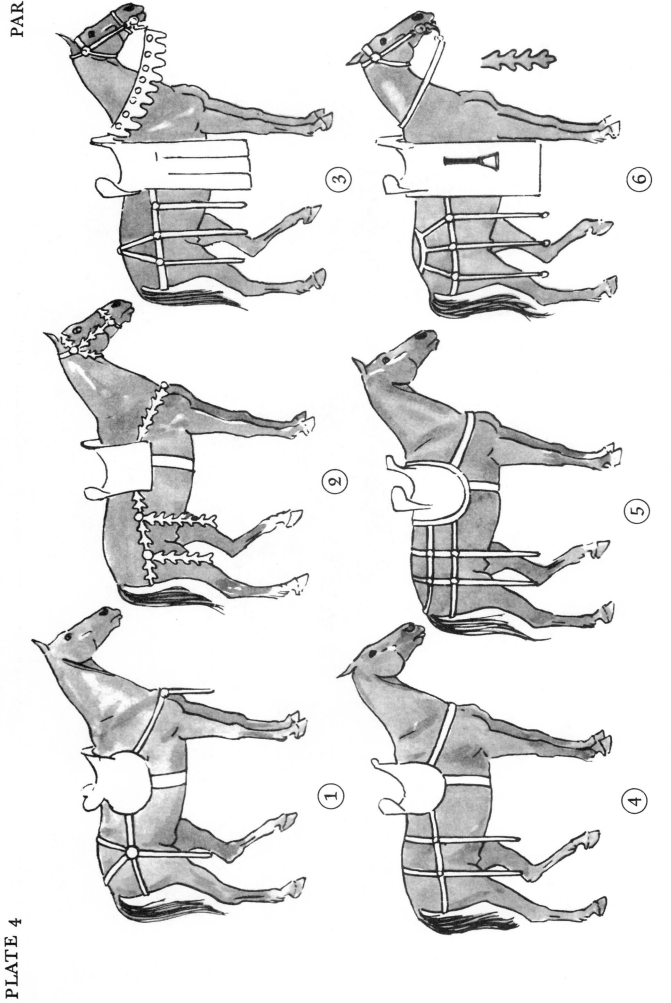

Illustrations of various types of saddles and bridles from illuminations in the King Wenceslas Bible.

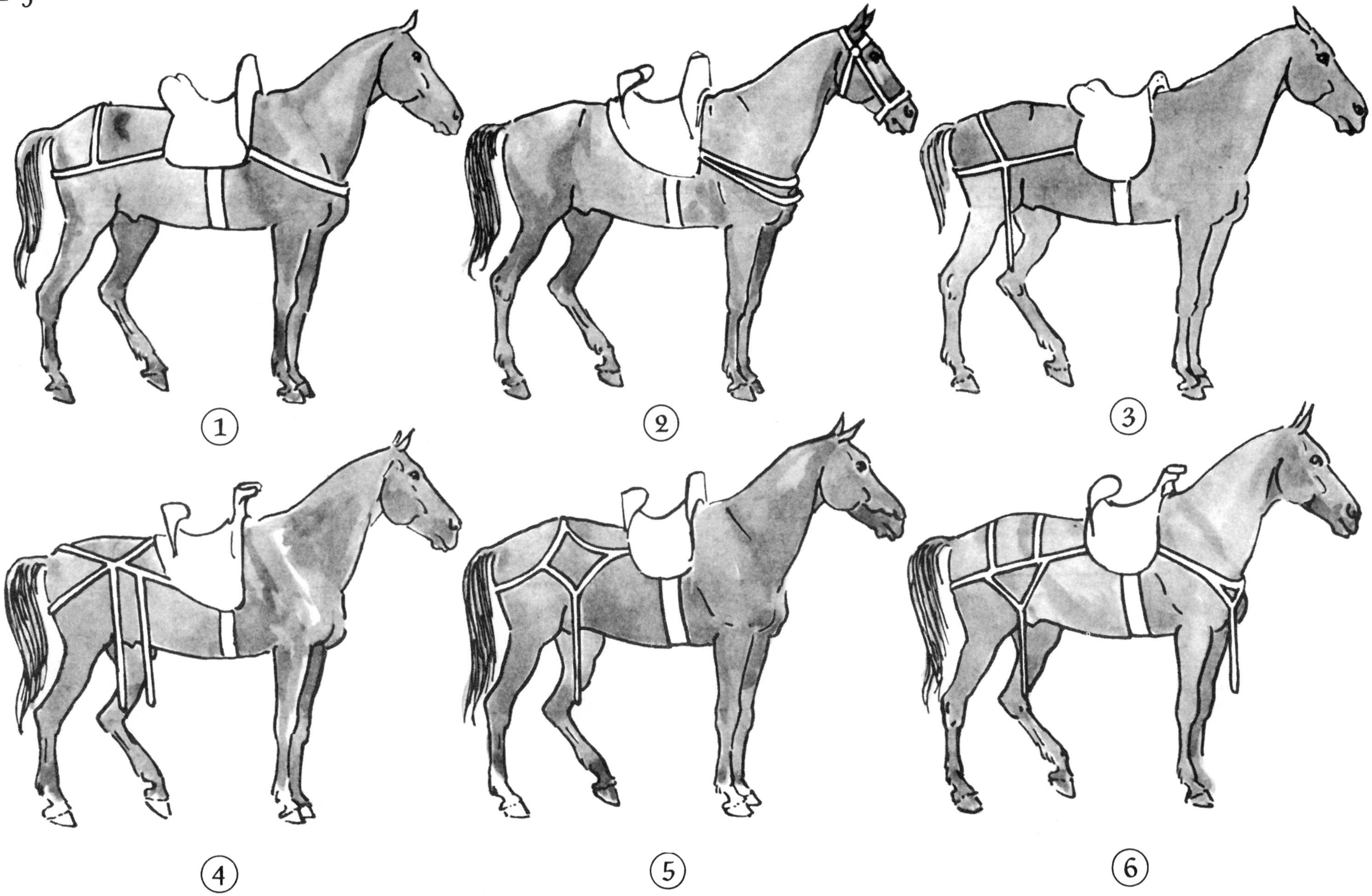

PLATE 5

Various saddles and horse trappings from illuminations in the King Wenceslas Bible.

PLATE 6
PART IX

Saddles and caparisons from illuminations in the King Wenceslas Bible.

PLATE 7   PART IX

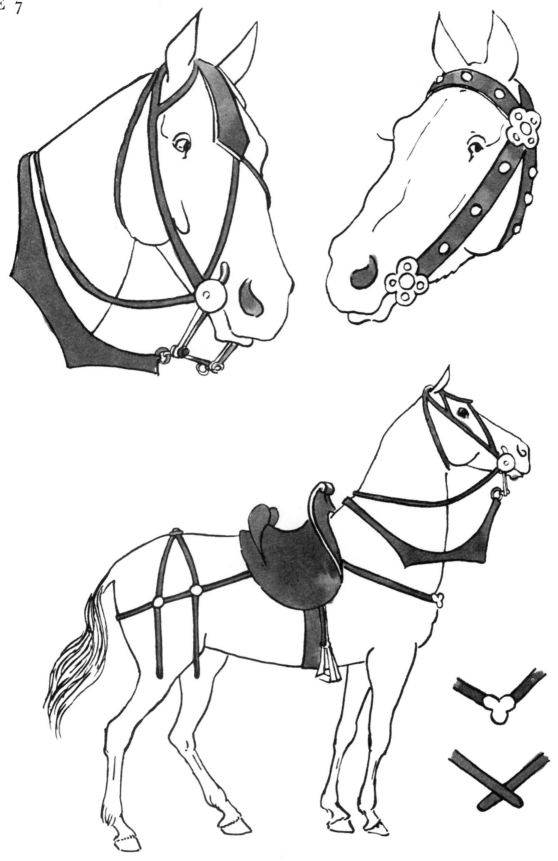

Saddle, bridles and parts of the breast-collar from a picture in the Jena Codex.

PLATE 8   PART IX

The saddle and bridle, from the altar-piece of St. George's church (Prague National Gallery). (1) The saddle. (2) The ends of the straps finished off with metal tags. (3) Rosettes on the bridle. (4) The stirrup. (5) The rosette on the breast-band. (6) The bridle.

PLATE 9   PART IX

(1) A horse's harness dating from 1380 (*Zeitschrift für historische Waffenkunde*, 1932/1934, p. 167). (2) A saddle fitted with breeching, from a painting by Jan van Eyck. (3) A saddle and bridle from the tomb of Simon de Laval, in the church at Basècles (died 1407).

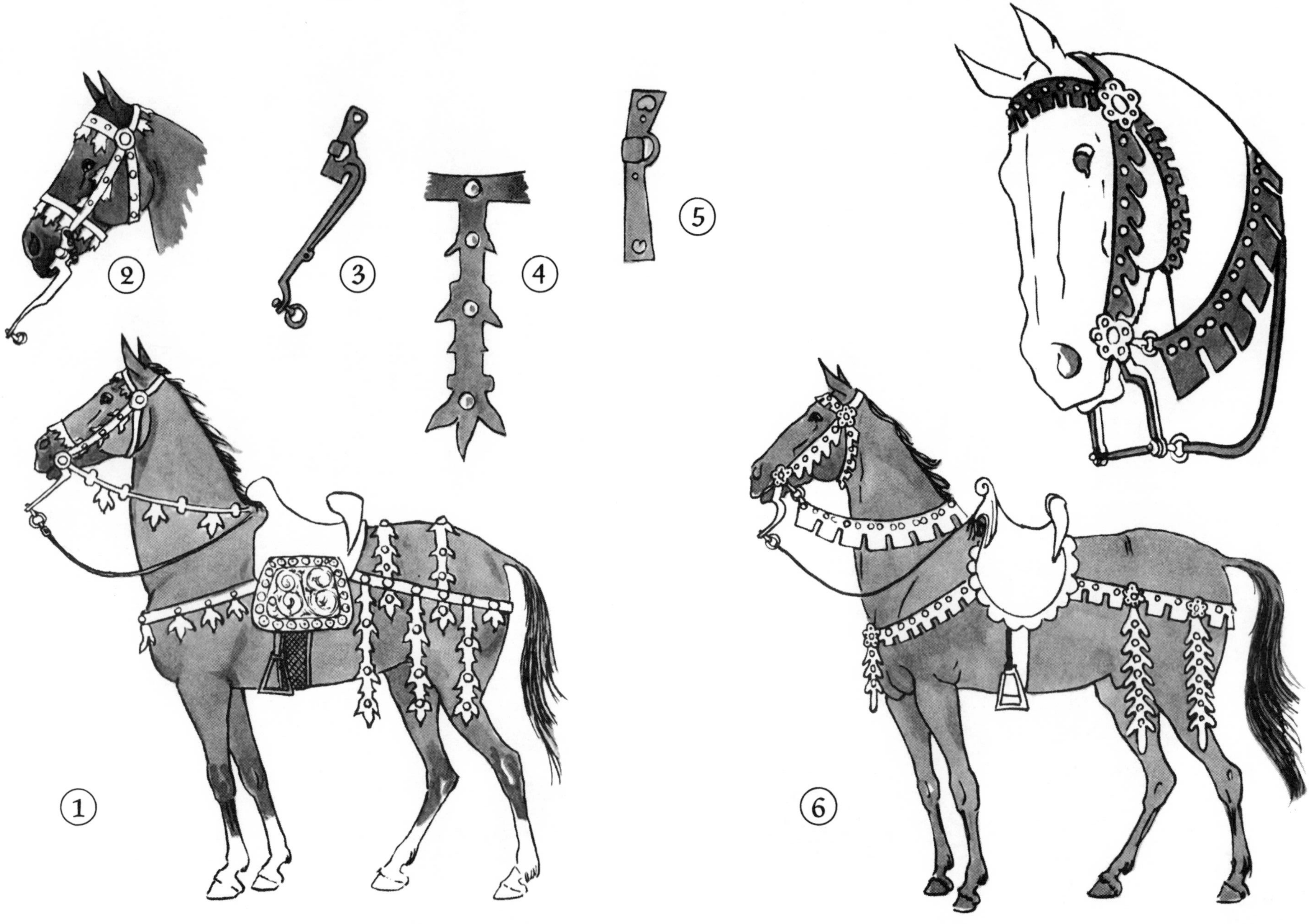

PLATE 10

(1) The saddle and bridle of a knight's horse (Viollet le Duc, VI, p. 59). (2) A bridle with a curb bit (*Chic à cheval*, p. 84). (3) The left-hand bar of a curb bit. (4) The left-hand bar of a 14th century curb bit (*ibid*, p. 82). (6) A hunting saddle with breast-collar and breeching, bridle and reins (*Meister der Reitkunst*, p. 24).

PLATE 11

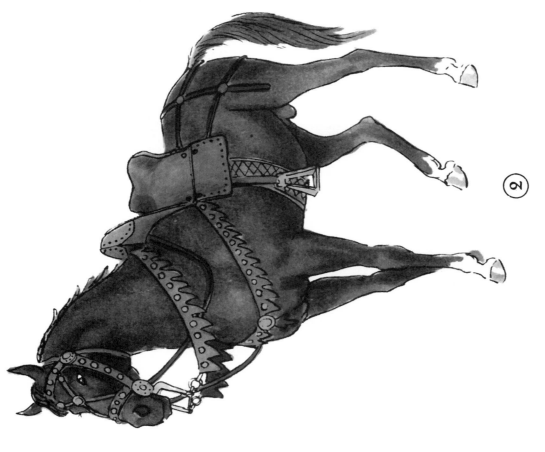

(1) Saddle and bridle from a painting of the Crucifixion by Giovanni de Alamaguio (died 1450) now in the Prague National Gallery. (2) The horse's saddle and bridle, from the painting "The Adoration of the Magi" by Geertgen tot Sint Jans (1460–95). Prague National Gallery.

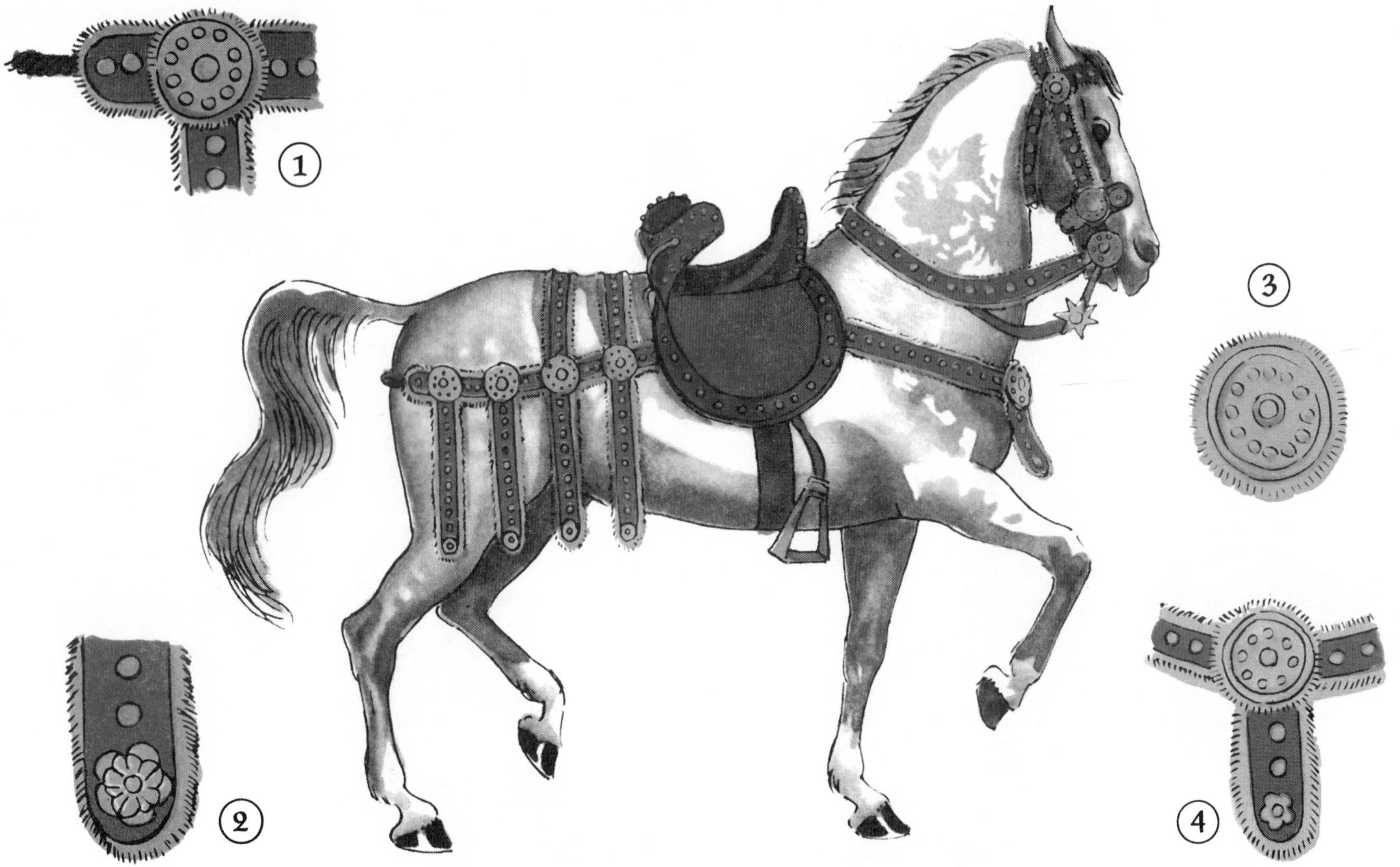

PLATE 12

PART IX

A reconstruction of the saddle and bridling from the portrait of St. Hubert by Antonio Pisanello (Dagenhart, *Pisanello*). (1) Part of the breeching. (2) The lower end of one of the breech straps, ornamented with a rosette. (3) The rosette on the breast-band. (4) Part of the breast-band with its rosette.

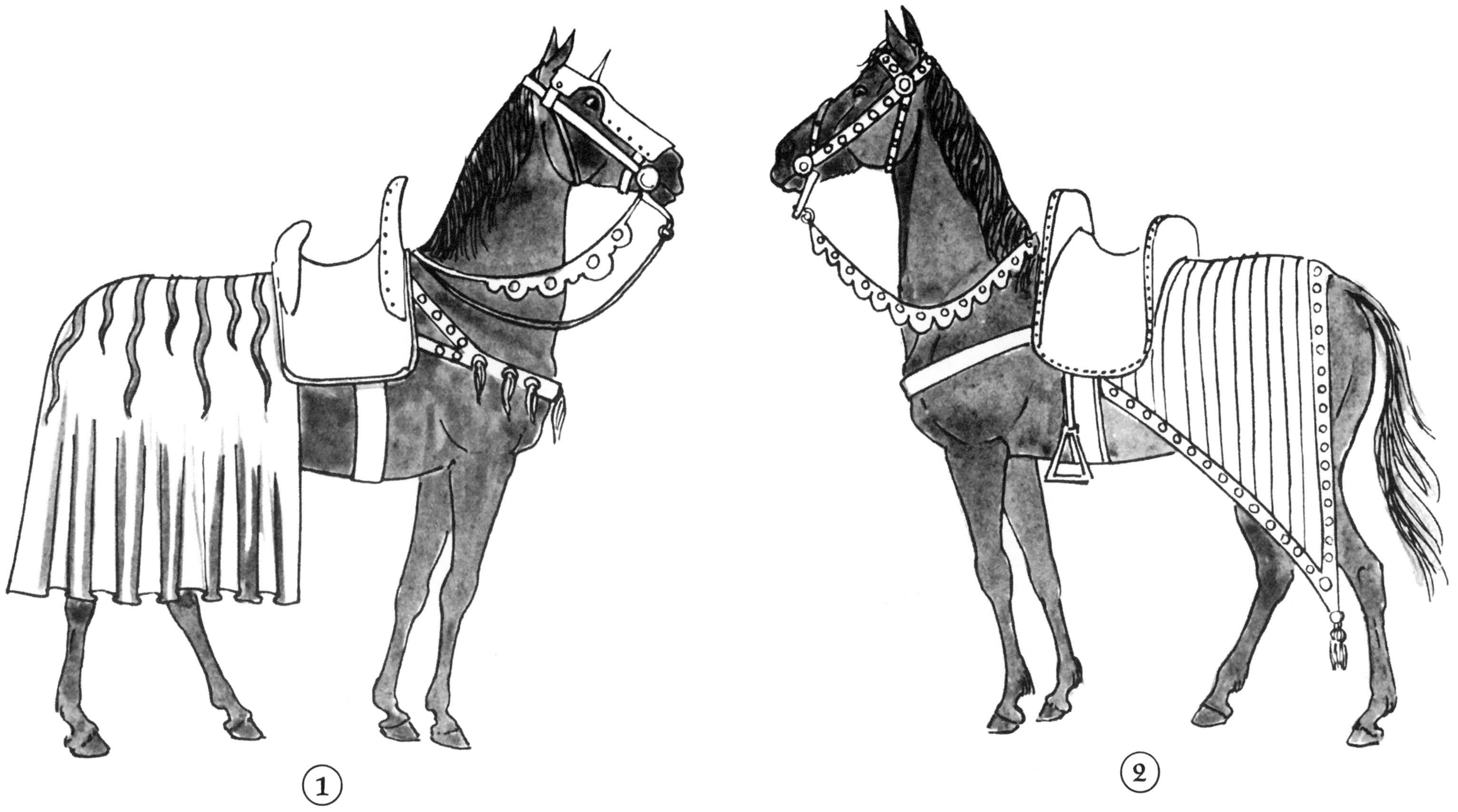

PLATE 13

(1) Saddle and bridle and caparison dating from 1440 (Hauner, *Vývoj pozemního válečnictví*, supplement, p. 27, pl. 30). (2) Saddle and caparison dating from the second half of the 15th century (from the painting "The Adoration of the Magi" by Geertgen tot Sint Jans. Prague National Gallery).

PLATE 14   PART IX

(1) A shield, banner and caparison bearing the insignia of Wolfram von Eschenbach (Hans Neumann, *Die Minnesinger in Bildern der Manessischen Handschrift*. (2) The shield and caparison of Uldrich von Lichtenstein (*ibid.*). (3) A caparison from a painting "Esquestrian Warfare" by Walther von Klingen (*ibid.*).

PLATE 15

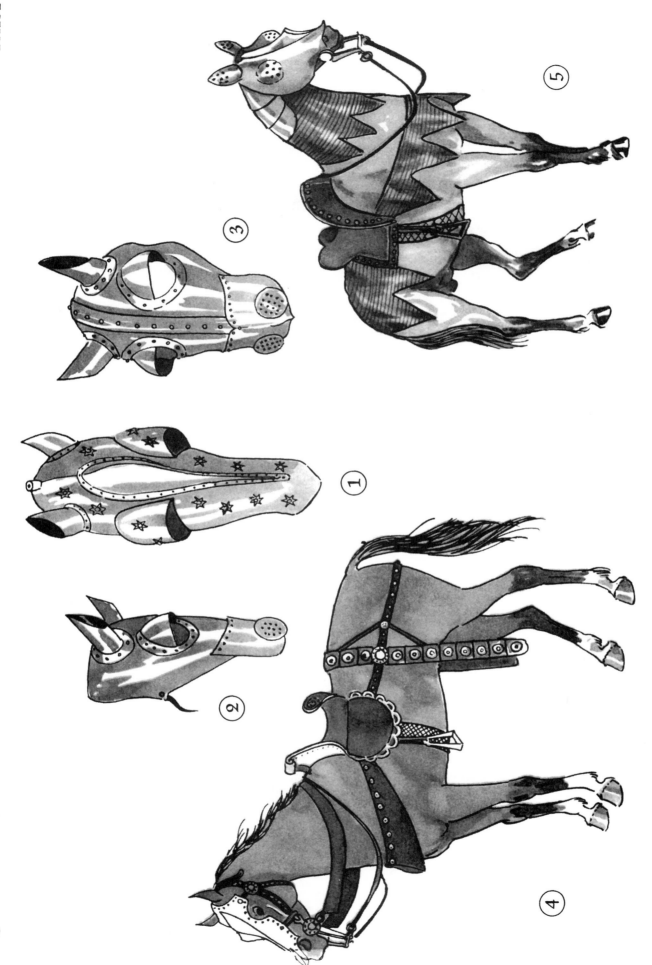

(1) Protection for the horse's head, known as a chamfron, with arched blinkers; ornamented with small stars. 14th–15th century (*European Armour*, III, p. 153, pl. 960). (2–3) 14th century chamfrons (Viollet le Duc, III, p. 264). (4) A knight's horse, according to a reproduction of the painting "The Battle of Poitiers" (Ullstein, *Weltgeschichte, Mittelalter*, p. 359). (5) The saddle and horse armour or bardings of a knight's horse, dating from about 1420 (*European Armour*, III, pl. 154, pl. 961).

PLATE 16

(1) A horse on a martingale. In order to prevent the horse from throwing back its head, the rein runs through rings on the breast-collar and the rider thus draws in the horse's head towards its chest. From the Duke of Berry's guard (Arthur Weise, *Skulptur und Malerei in Frankreich im XV. und XVI. Jahrhundert*, p. 51, pl. 64). (2) A bundle or saddle bag at the back of the saddle dating from the 15th century. Freely drawn from a painting by H. Memling, "The Seven Joys of Mary" (*Deutsches Leben*, pl. 636).

PLATE 17

PART IX

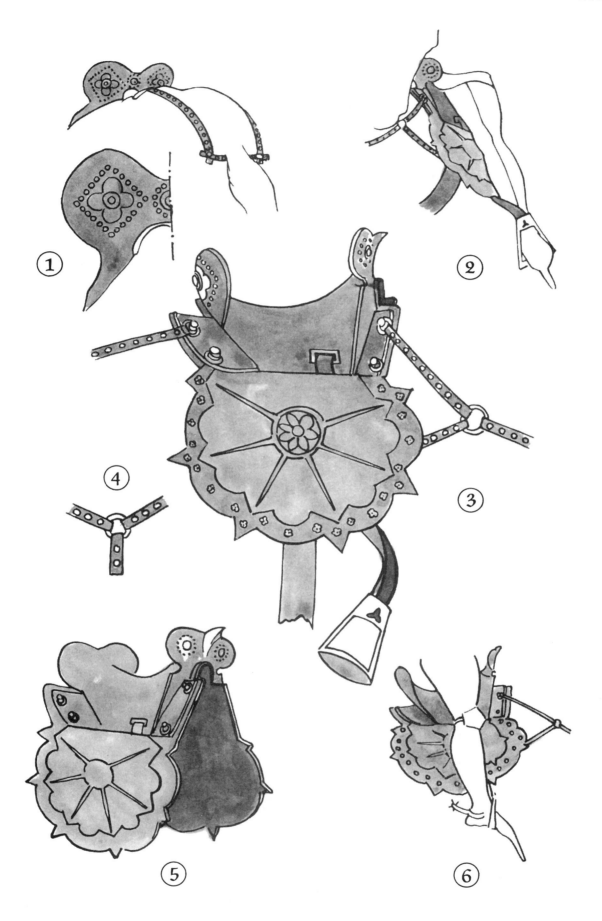

Details of the saddle of the St. George statue at Prague Castle, dating from 1373. (1) The hind bow of the saddle or cantle and crupper. (2) Part of the pommel and breast-band. (3) View of the saddle from the right side. (4) The middle section of the breast-band. (5–6) Side views of the saddle.

PLATE 18   PART IX

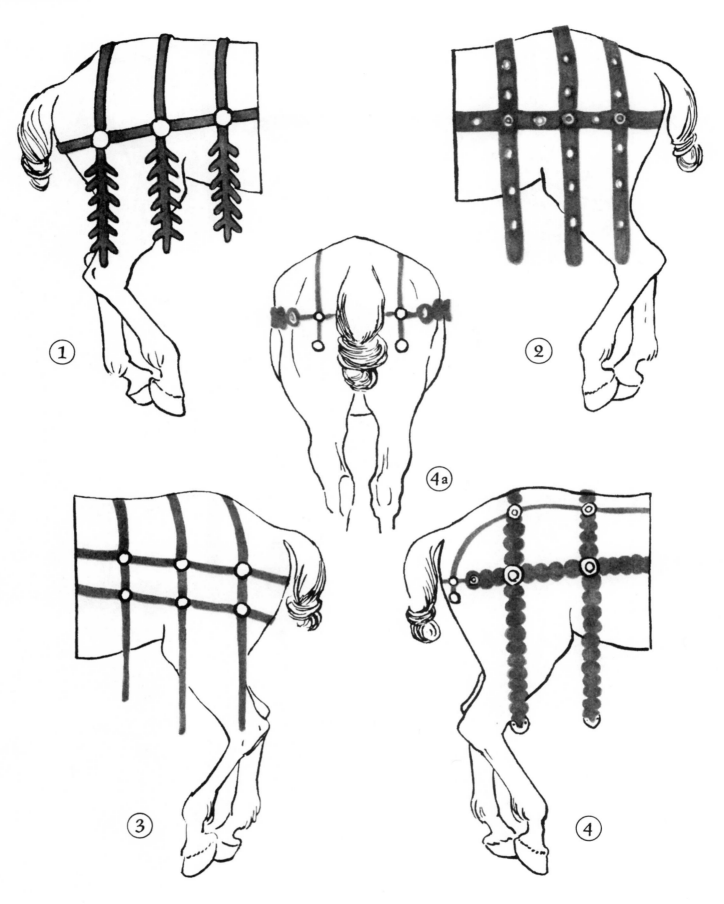

Cruppers and breeching. (1–3) Thalhofer's *Fechtbuch*, 1443, pl. 18, 36. (4–4a) Details from a painting of Calvary by Johann Pleydenwurff, dated about 1465 (Dehio, *Geschichte der deutschen Kunst*, II, p. 380, pl. 453).

PLATE 19

PART IX

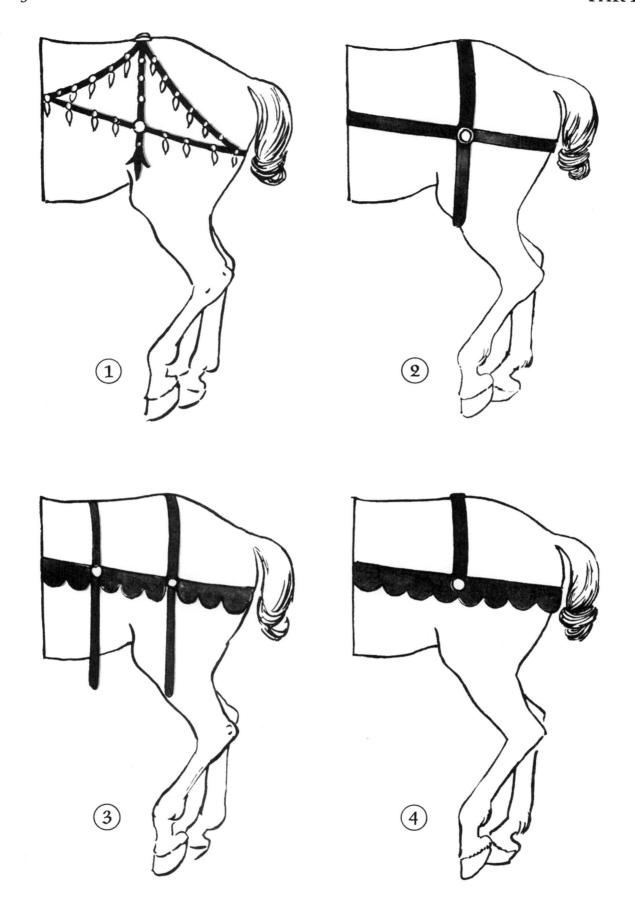

Cruppers and breeching. (1) From an illustration in *Ungarisches Soldatentum*, pp. 56, 57. (2–4) From a picture of the Emperor and Pope's Procession in the Richenthal Chronicle.

PLATE 20

PART IX

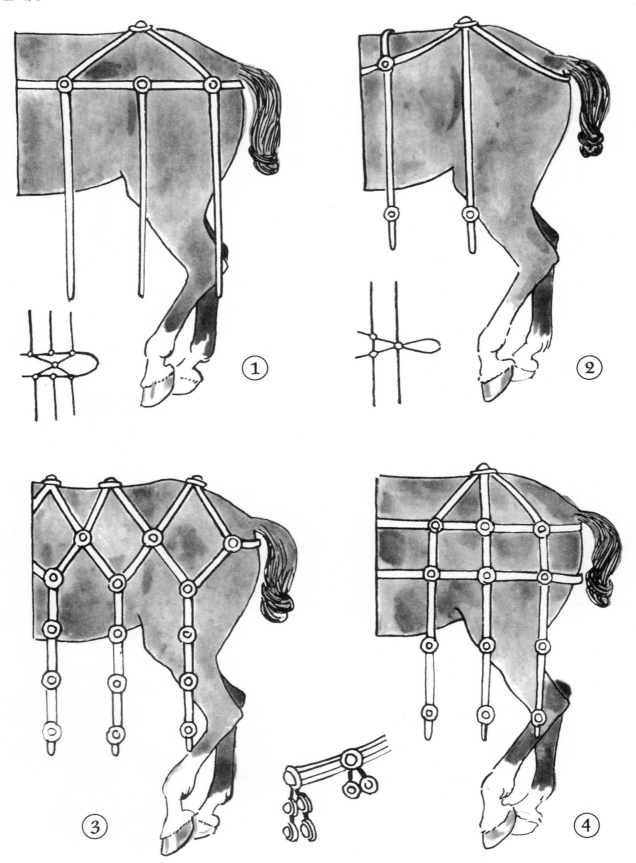

(1) A crupper of about 1420 (*Die deutsche Malerei der Renaissance*, p. 419, pl. 513). (2) A crupper of about 1410 (*ibid.*, p. 412, pl. 501). (3-4) Cruppers and breeching dating from 1410 (*ibid.*, p. 383, pl. 464).

PLATE 21 PART IX

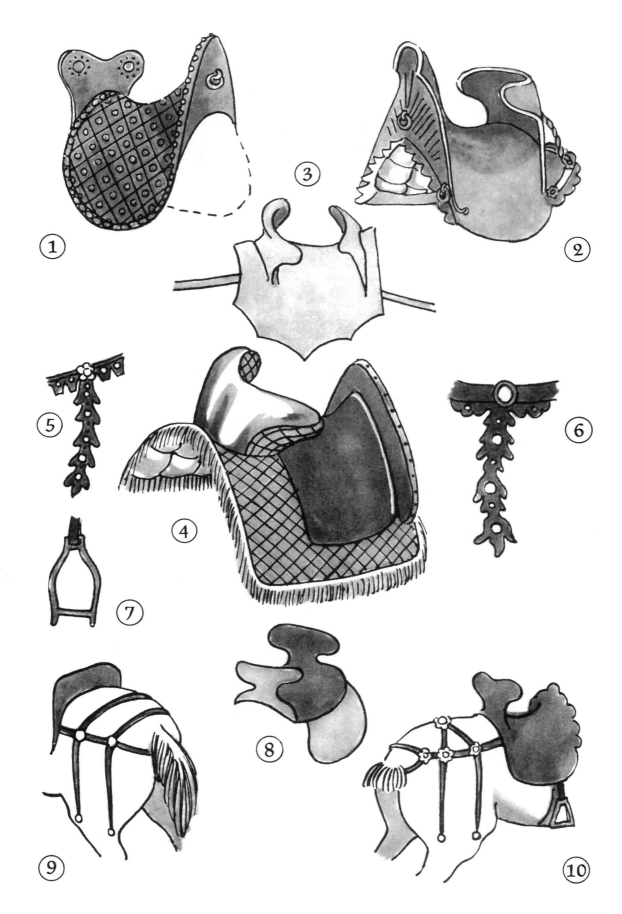

(1) A 15th-century saddle (Viollet le Duc, VI, p. 61). (2) A mid-15th-century saddle (*Chic à cheval*, p. 80). (3) A saddle (Viollet le Duc, III, p. 436). (4) Late-15th-century saddle (Viollet le Duc, III, p. 447). (5–6) Pendents from the breast-collar (Viollet le Duc, III, p. 437). (7) A stirrup (Viollet le Duc, III, p. 437). (8) A saddle (Viollet le Duc, VI, p. 60). (9–10) Cruppers and breeching (Viollet le Duc, III, pp. 439, 437).

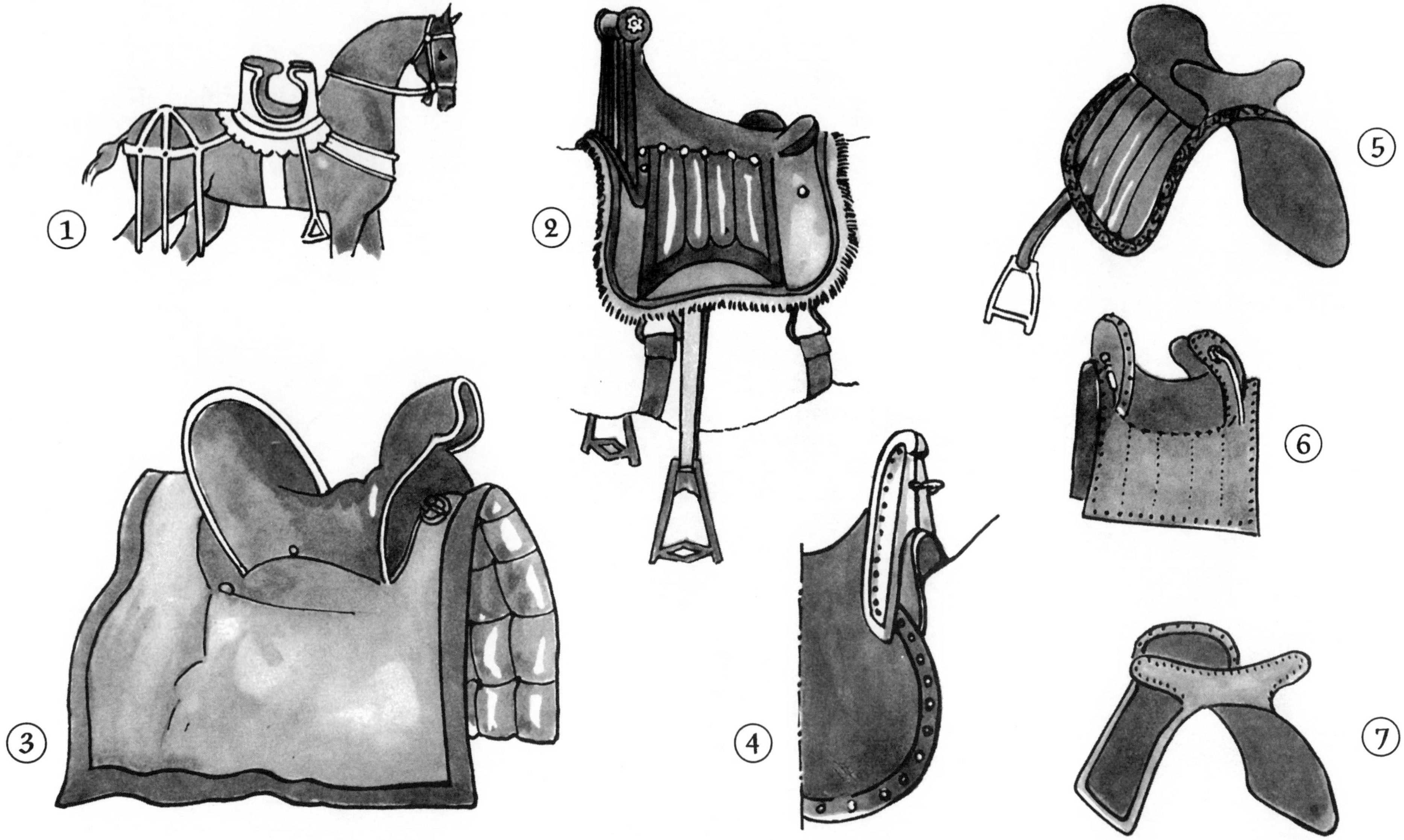

PLATE 22

(1) A saddle of about 1378 (Boeheim, p. 201, pl. 218). (2) A rider's pack-saddle (Degenhart, *Pisanello*, pl. 69). (3) An early 16th century Hungarian saddle (Boeheim, p. 221, pl. 232). (4) The pommel of a knight's saddle from the Ghent altar-piece (Jan van Eyck). (5) A saddle of 1425, according to a painting by Gentile da Fabriano (Degenhart). (6) A saddle of about 1435. From "The Adoration of the Magi" by Stefano da Verona (Degenhart). (7) The saddle from the painting "St. George goes out to fight the Dragon" by Pisanello (1380–1455). There is a similar one on a medalion by Domenico Malatesta, dating from about 1460 (*European Armour*, II, p. 427).

PLATE 23   PART IX

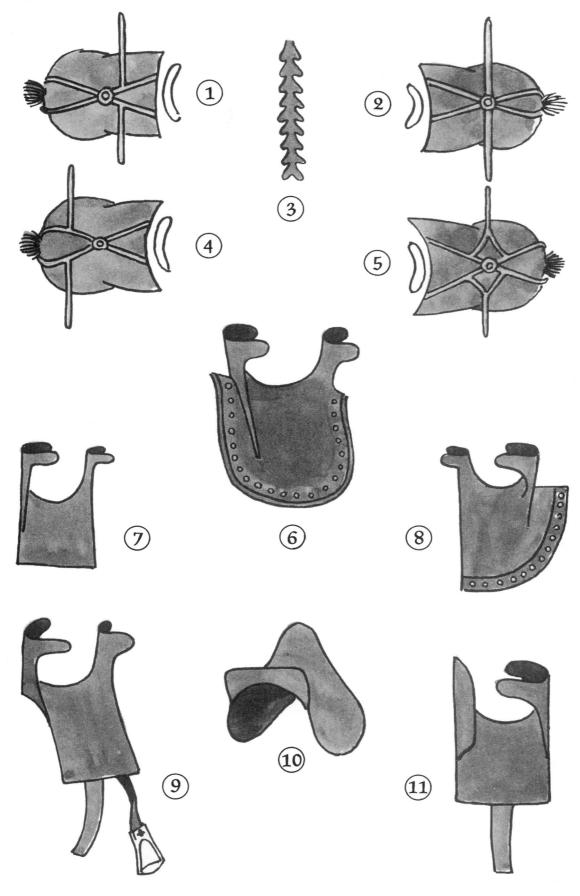

(1, 2, 4, 5) Cruppers from the King Wenceslas Bible. (3) Dagged straps, from the same source. (6–11) Saddles from illuminations in the King Wenceslas Bible.

PLATE 24

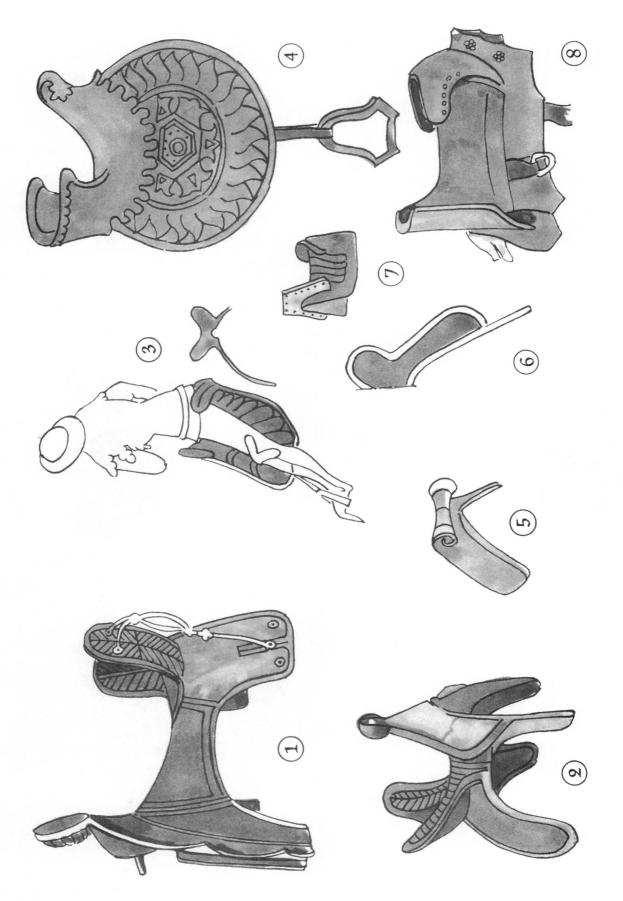

(1) A saddle of the early 15th century (Boeheim, p. 202, pl. 220). (2) A 15th century jousting saddle (Demmin, p. 644, pl. 15). (3) A rider's seat according to a study by Stefano da Verona. (4) A French hunting saddle of the 14th century (Boeheim, p. 203, pl. 221). (5) A simplified diagram of the pommel of the equestrian statue of Condottiere Gattamelato (Donatello. See Schoenbeck, *Das Pferd*, p. 9). (6) The left half of the burrplate or pommel of the equestrian statue of Colleoni (Verrocchio. See Schoenbeck, p. 8). (7) A German saddle of the second half of the 15th century (Demmin, p. 642, pl. 9). (8) The Aragon saddle of King James I., 1206–76 (Boeheim, p. 200, pl. 217).

PLATE 25

PART IX

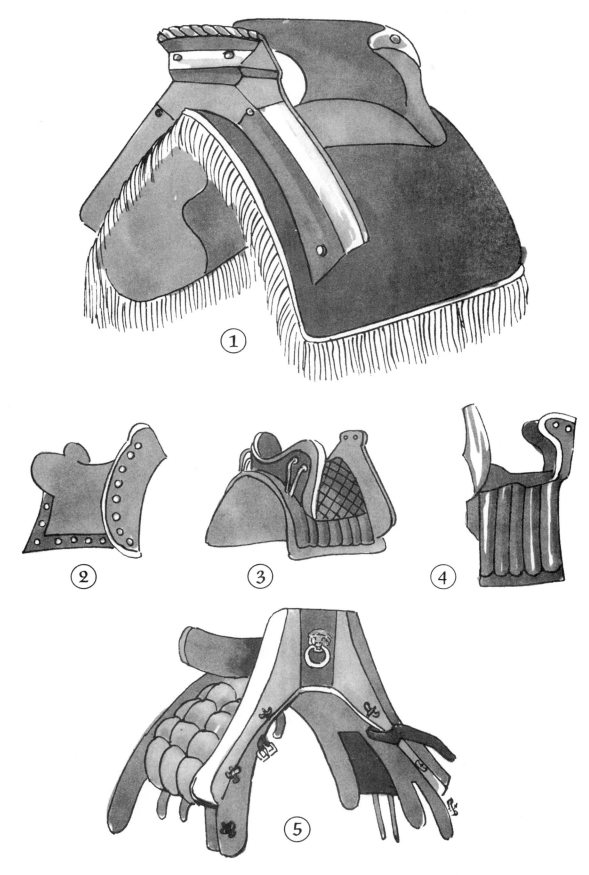

(1) A 15th-century saddle richly covered (Estruch, pl. XXIII, p. 532). (2) A knight's saddle, according to a miniature in 1420 (*European Armour*, p. 154, pl. 961). (3) A jousting saddle of about 1500 (Schoenbeck, *Das Pferd und seine Darstellung in der bildenden Kunst*, pl. 11d). (4) A jousting saddle dating from between 1470–90 (Schoenbeck, pl. 11C). (5) A saddle of the middle of the 15th century, designed for the heavy equestrian armour of Maximilian I (Boeheim, p. 201, pl. 219).

PLATE 26   PART IX

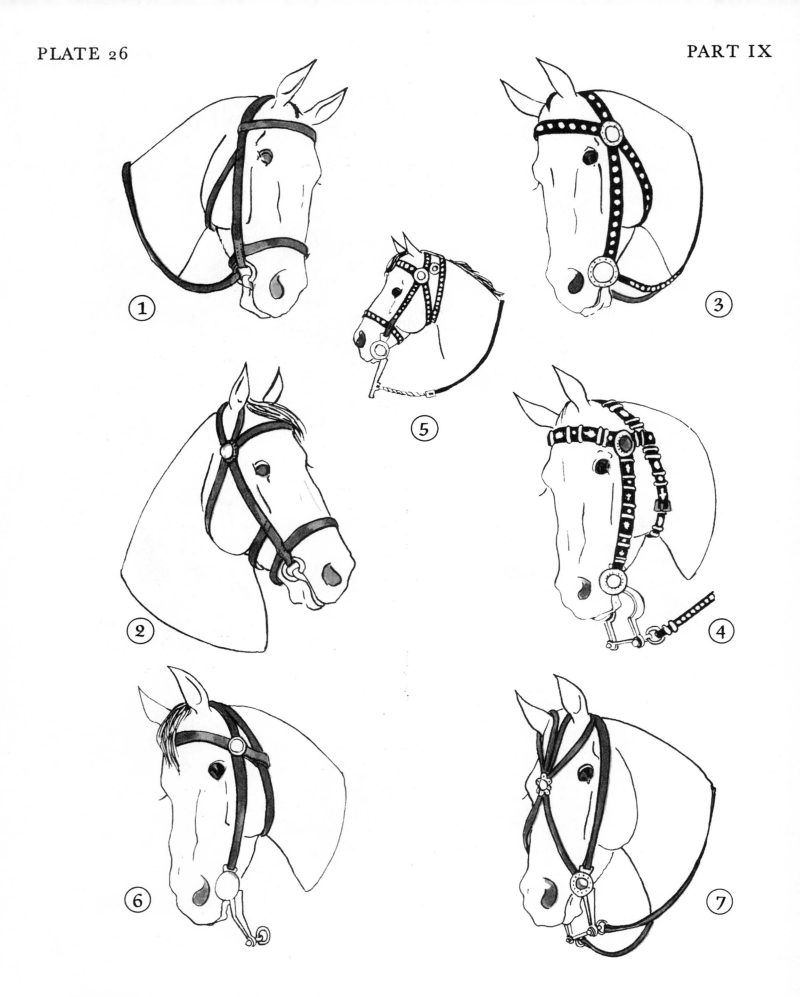

(1–2) Bridles from illuminations in the King Wenceslas Bible. (3) The normal type of bridle found in Czech illuminated manuscripts. (4) An ornamental bridle from the painting "Ten Thousand Martyrs" by Vittorio Carpaccio, dating from the beginning of the 16th century (*European Armour*, III, p. 183, pl. 992). (5) A bit and bridle from the middle of the 13th century (Viollet le Duc; also Hauner, *Vývoj pozemního válečnictví*, supplement p. 25, pl. 28). (6) A bit and bridle from the 15th–16th century (Schoenbeck, p. 48, pl. 54 and pl. 55: also p. 165, pl. 256). (7) A bridle, from the painting "The Adoration of the Magi" by Geertgen tot Sint Jans, 1460–95 (Prague National Gallery).

PLATE 27   PART IX

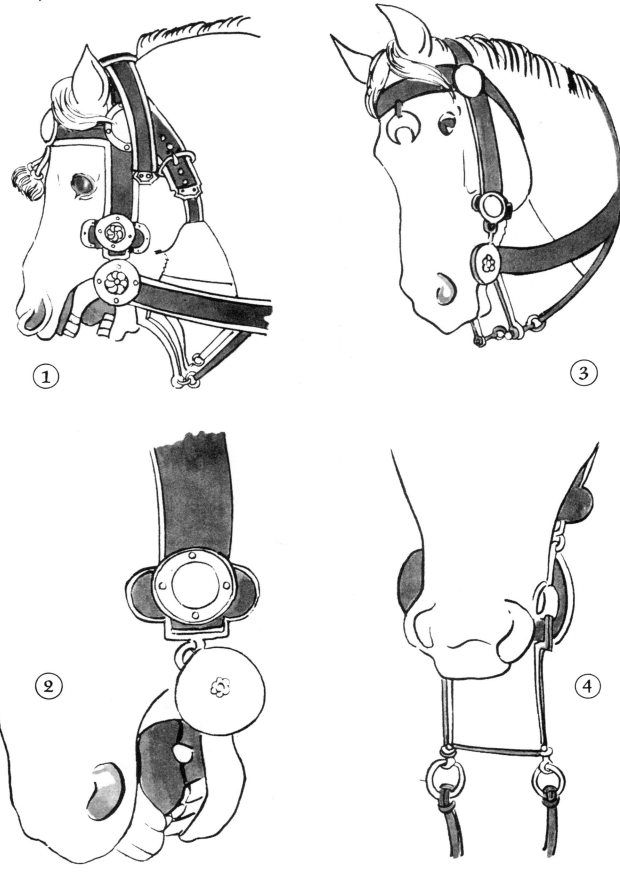

Studies of bits and bridles by Pisanello (Degenhart). (1) A picture of the complete bridle (*ibid.*, p. 75). (2) Lower part of the cheek-strap with snaffle bit and metal plate. (3) A bridle (*ibid.*). (4) Front view of bit.

PLATE 28   PART IX

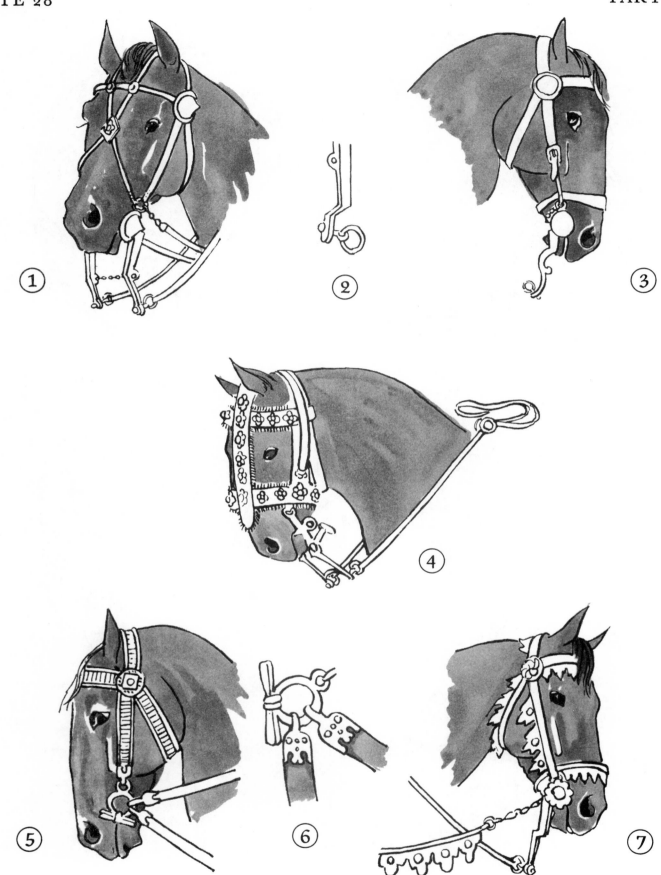

(1) A bridle (Viollet le Duc, III, p. 444). (2) Detail of the lower end of the cheek-bar. (3) A bridle (*ibid.*, III, p. 436).
(4) A pack-horse bridle (Degenhart, pl. 69). (5) A bridle with double rein, dating from the statue of Barnaba Visconti
(*Chic à cheval*, p. 72). (6) Detail. (7) A bridle (Viollet le Duc, III, p. 437).

PLATE 29   PART IX

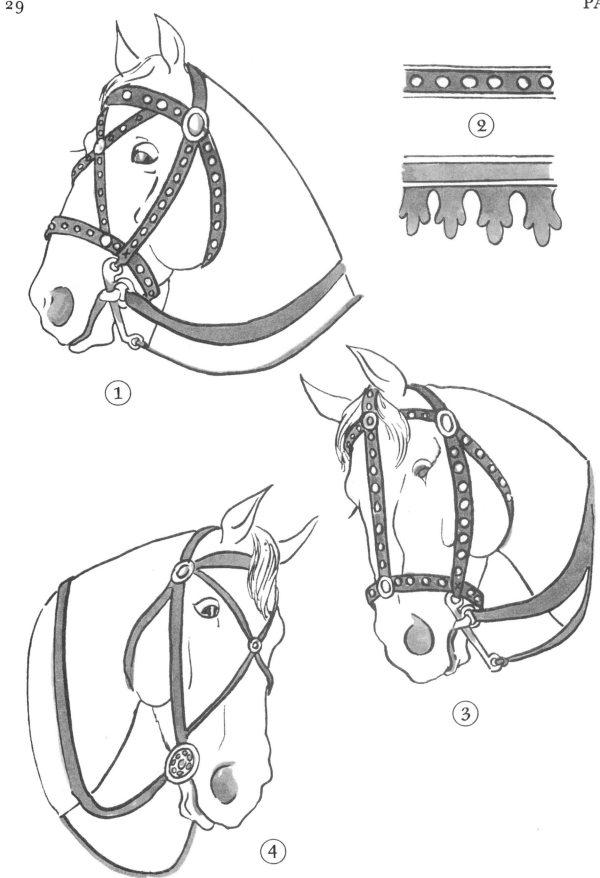

(1) A bridle of about 1385 (Kosina, *Illustrované dějiny světové*, II, p. 477). (2) Part of the breast-band (*ibid.*). (3) A bridle dating from about 1385 (*ibid.*; also Schoenbeck, p. 170, pl. 267; 15th–16th centuries). (4) The bridle on Jan Žižka's horse in the Jena Codex picture of "Žižka at the Head of his Army".

PLATE 30   PART IX

(1) The bit and bridle of the knight's horse in the Ghent altar-piece by Jan van Eyck. (2) A bridle of about 1423, from the painting "The Adoration of the Magi" by Gentile da Fabriano. (3) A type of bridle freely copied from the painting by B. Gazoli, "The Procession of the Magi". (4) A type of bridle of about 1497, freely copied from the epitaph of J. Řepický; in the Prague National Gallery.

PLATE 31   PART IX

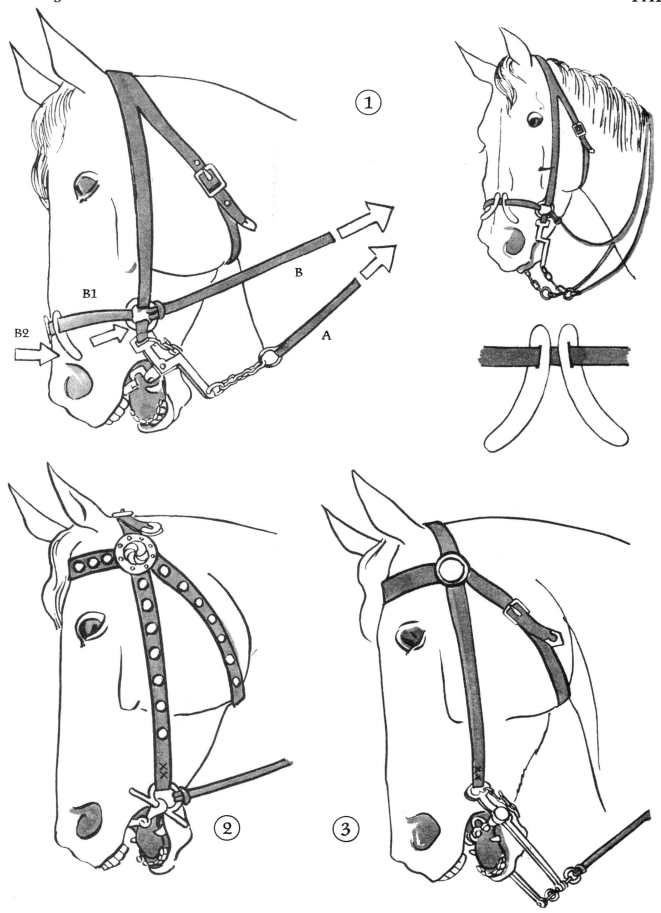

(1) A bridle with "breathers". The curb bit is normal, but the slender rein is linked with a nose-piece, on which there are two half-moon-shaped "breathers". By pulling on the upper rein they press on the nostrils, which prevents the horse from breathing properly, which curbs its speed when galloping or charging (Degenhart). A. curb rein, B. upper rein, C. nose-piece, D. detail: "breather". (2) A snaffle bit and narrow rein. (3) A bridle and curb bit.

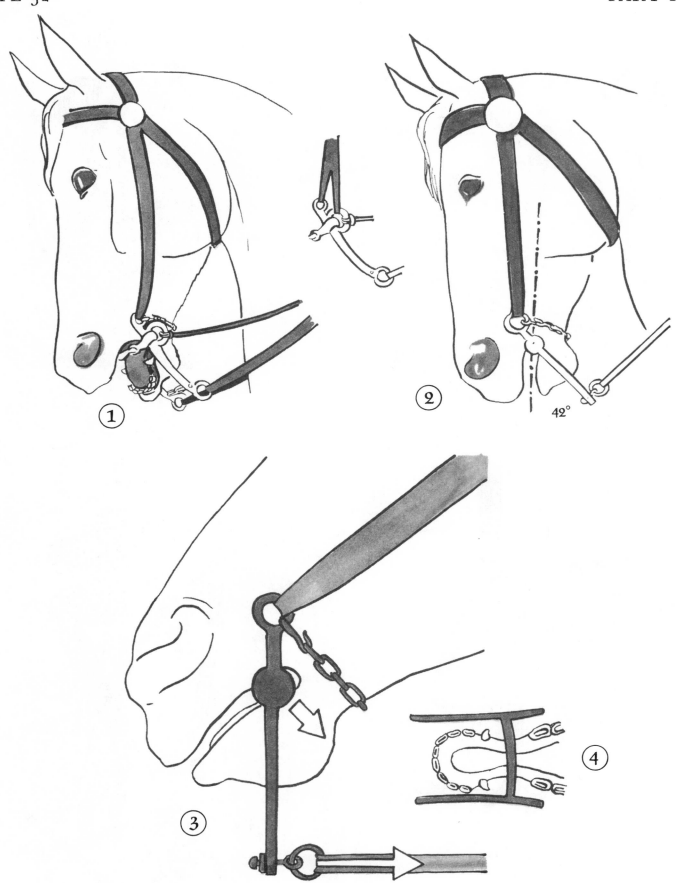

PLATE 32

PART IX

(1) A combination of the curb and snaffle bit, known as the Pelham bit. In the centre is a detail of the left cheek bar of the curb with a divided cheek-strap. (2) The correct angle for the curb bit in relation to the horse's mouth is 42°. (3) A curb bit is composed of a single-branched bit and a chain under the horse's lower jaw. The strain is taken by the horse's gums, where the bar of the bit presses, and the pressure is intensified by the lever action of the long cheek bar which is drawn back by the curb chain. (4) The position of the curb bit on the horse's gums.

PLATE 33

PART IX

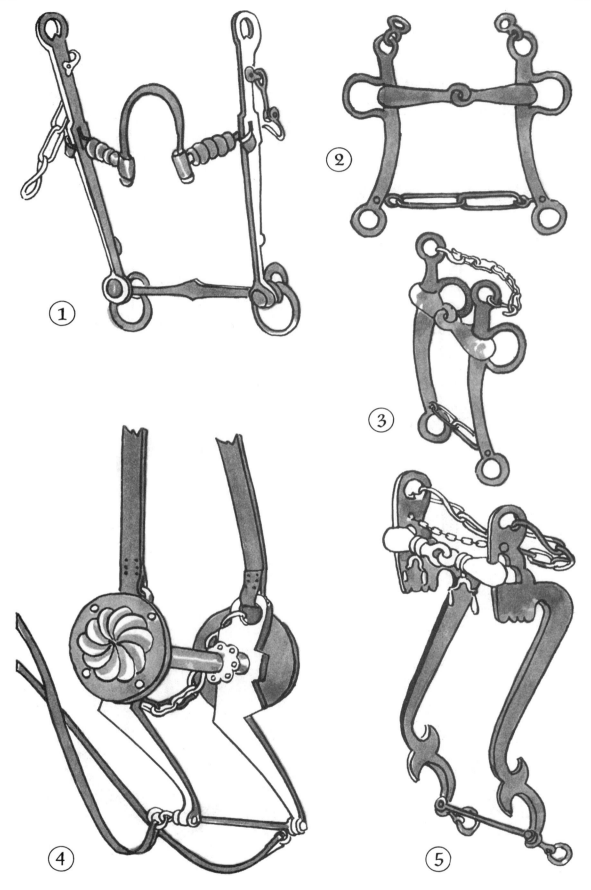

(1) A 14th-century bit. The cheek bars are slightly curved at the end where they are ended with a ring, 1.7 cm. in width. The bar is 17 cm. long, each link of the chain 3 cm. the hook 5 cm. (Szendrei, p. 131). (2) A bit from Tannenberg, dating from 1399 (Demmin, p. 662, pl. 15). (3) The same bit with a curb chain (seen from the left-hand side). (4) A 15th-century jousting bit, with curb chain, cheek-strap and curb rein (Boeheim, p. 551, pl. 639). (5) A late 15th-century curb bit and chain (Boeheim, p. 194, pl. 208).

PLATE 34   PART IX

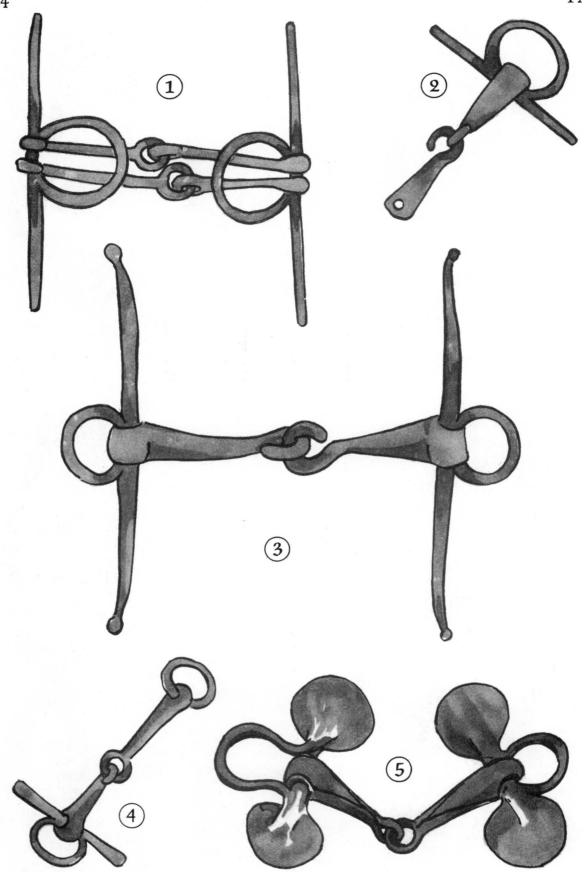

(1) A 14th-century bit, the rings are 5 cm. in diameter (Szendrei, p. 133, pl. 336). (2) A snaffle bit from Tannenberg, dating from about 1399 (Demmin, p. 662, pl. 14). (3) A snaffle bit (Szendrei, p. 63, pl. 107). (4) A bit from Tannenberg, of about 1399 (Demmin, p. 662, pl. 13). (5) A late 14th century snaffle-type bit. Length of the bars 9 cm., diameter of the plates 5 cm., diameter of the rings for the reins 4 cm. (Szendrei, p. 147, pl. 411; *European Armour*, III, p. 162, pl. 966 dates this bit from the 13th century). A similar bit is in the collection at the Prague National Museum.

PLATE 35   PART IX

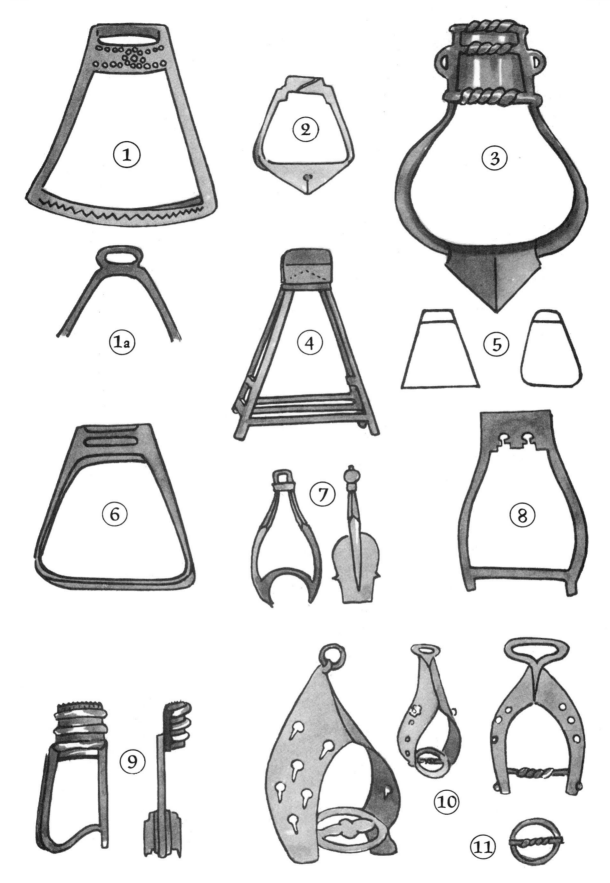

(1) A bronze 15th century stirrup. The stirrup bar is 15 cm. long, 4.5 cm. wide. The stirrup is 17 cm. high (Szendrei, p. 253, pl. 804). (1a) The upper part of a 14th century stirrup. The measurements are 16×16 cm. (Szendrei, p. 255, pl. 806). (2) A French 15th century stirrup (Stone, p. 585, pl. 754). (3) An old Hungarian pear-shaped stirrup of the 15th century. 15 cm. high, 12 cm. wide (Boeheim, pl. 213, pl. 235; Szendrei, p. 271, pl. 833). (4) A 14th-century Italian stirrup (Stone, p. 585, pl. 764). (5) The basic shape of the stirrup from the 9th to the 13th century (*European Armour*, I, p. 104, pl. 125). (6) A Bohemian stirrup, 13.4×13.4 cm., from the Badra fortress (Sedláček, *Hrady a zámky*, XII, p. 21). (7) A 13th century Aragon stirrup (Boeheim, p. 199, pl. 212). (8) A Swiss stirrup dating from about 1386 (*Zeitschrift*, VI, p. 202, pl. 16). (9) A mid-15th century iron stirrup (Boeheim, p. 207, pl. 226). (10) A 15th-century Italian stirrup (Stone, p. 585, pl. 754). (11) The shape of the stirrup bar.

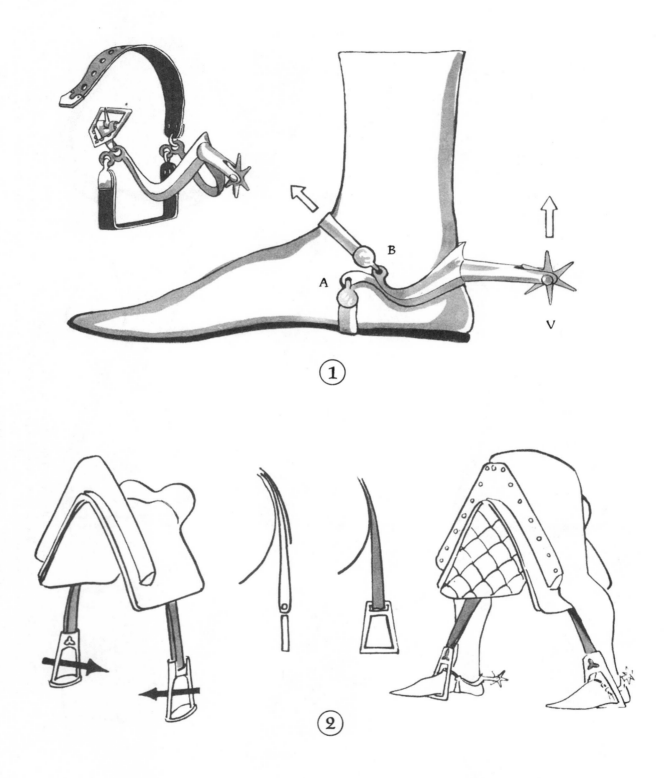

(1) How the spur was fastened on. The arch of the spur, carrying a long spike is made in the form of a two-armed lever. The lower strap fixes the spur at point A, the upper strap lifts it at point B and counterbalances the weight of "V", i. e. the long shank, and thus maintains its horizontal position. (2) The way the stirrups are hung from the saddle. The feet are placed in the stirrups from the outer side so that the stirrup straps lie flat against the leg. If the feet were put into the stirrup from the inner side the edges of the straps would cut into the leg.

PLATE 37

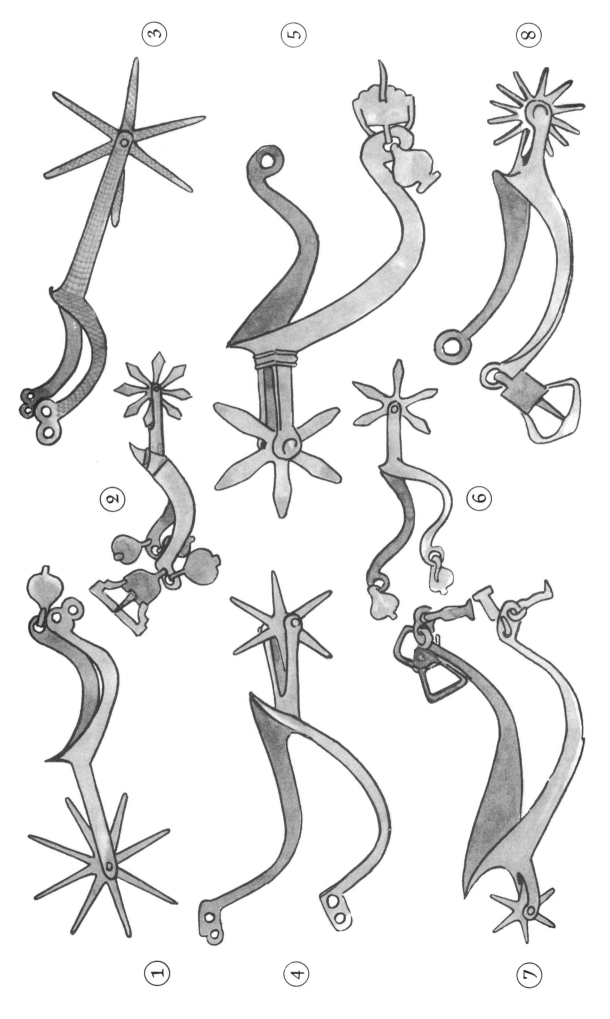

Rowel spurs. (1) An early 15th century bronze Florentine spur (*European Armour*, III, p. 165, pl. 970). (2) A 14th century spur (Rosenberg, pl. 62; Jähns, pl. 50, p. 12). (3) A bronze Italian spur dating from about 1380, carved which gives the impression of snake skin. Only the tips of the rowels are smooth (*European Armour*, III, p. 168, pl. 973a). (4) A 14th century spur. Width between the arch 8 cm, its height 6 cm. (Szendrei, p. 211, pl. 675). (5) A late 14th century spur (Szendrei, p. 185, pl. 535). (6) A 14th century spur. Length of neck 4 cm., width of arch 7.5 cm (Szendrei, p. 220, pl. 695). (7) A 15th century spur (Szendrei, p. 233, pl. 725). (8) A 15th century spur. The shank is 2.7 cm. wide, 4 cm. long, the rowel has 12 spokes and a diameter of 5 cm. (Szendrei, p. 232, pl. 725).

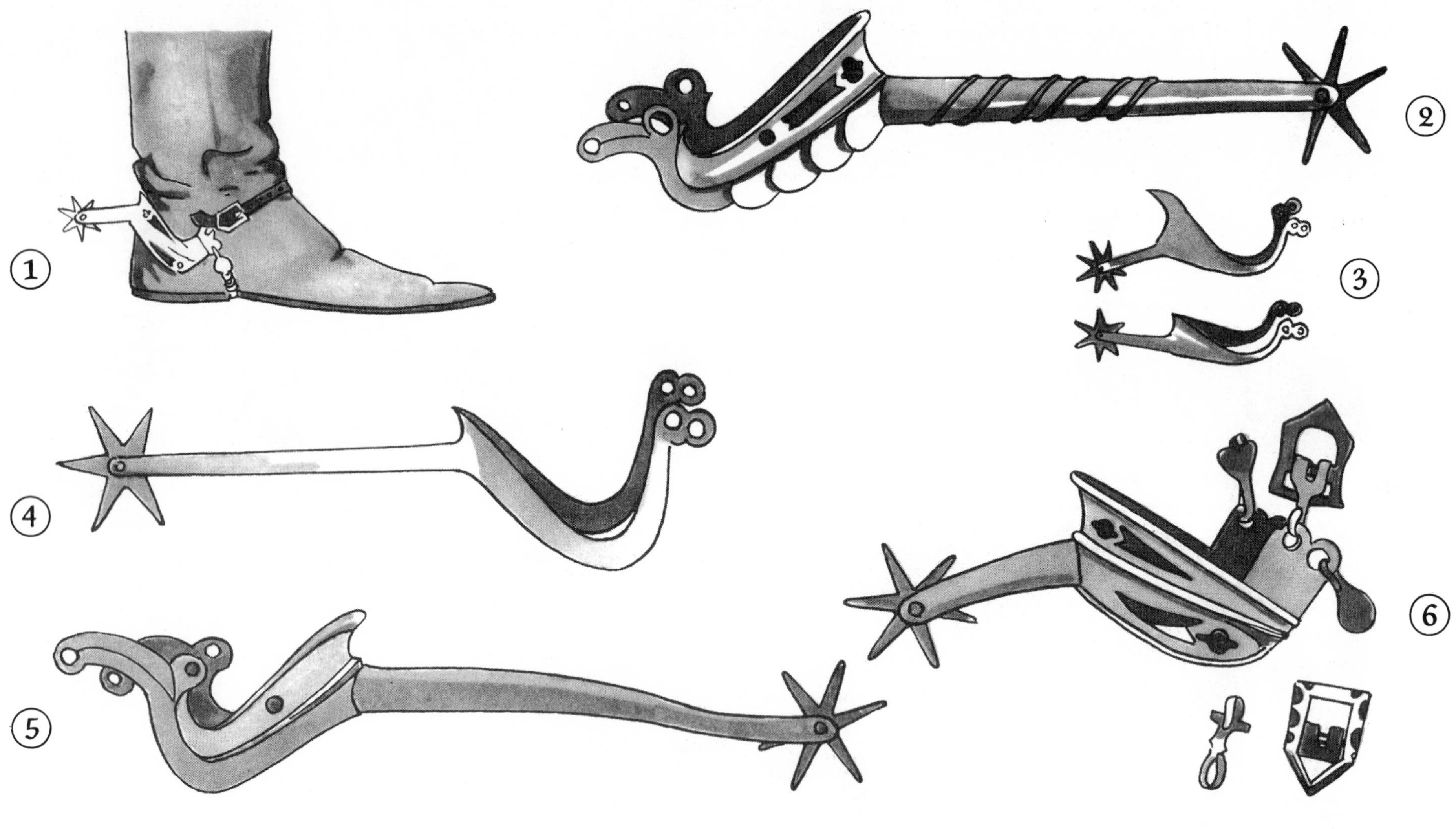

PLATE 38

(1) A Bohemian spur according to a drawing by Koula (Zíbrt and Winter, p. 150). (2) A spur in the Prague National Museum (*ibid.*, p. 155, pl. 265). (3) A spur found in the Badra fortress. The upper part is bronze, the lower iron; it is 12.8 cm. long, the neck 5 cm. (Sedláček, *Hrady a zámky*, XII, p. 21). (4) A bronze spur in the Prague City Museum. (5) A spur in the Prague National Museum (Zíbrt and Winter, p. 153, pl. 264). (6) A Bohemian spur with enlarged details (*ibid.*, p. 151, pl. 262).

PLATE 39

PART IX

(1) A 15th century German spur (Jan Lauts, *Alte deutsche Waffen*, pl. 9). (2) A 15th century jousting spur; the shank is 18.5 cm. long, the six-pointed rowel is 3.5 cm. in diameter, the width of the arch 7.1 cm., 3.5 cm. wide (Szendrei, p. 154). (3) A late 14th century spur, the shank is 9.5 cm. long, the arch 8 cm. wide (*ibid.*, p. 154). (4) A German spur dating from 1440 (*European Armour*, III, p. 168, pl. 974). (5) A late 15th century jousting spur. Shank 18.8 cm. long, diameter of rowel 8 cm., width of arch 8.5 cm., height 3 cm. (6) A 15th century spur with a flat arch, pierced in a number of places. The shank is 11 cm. long, the arch 9 cm. wide (Szendrei, p. 139, pl. 372).

PLATE I PART X

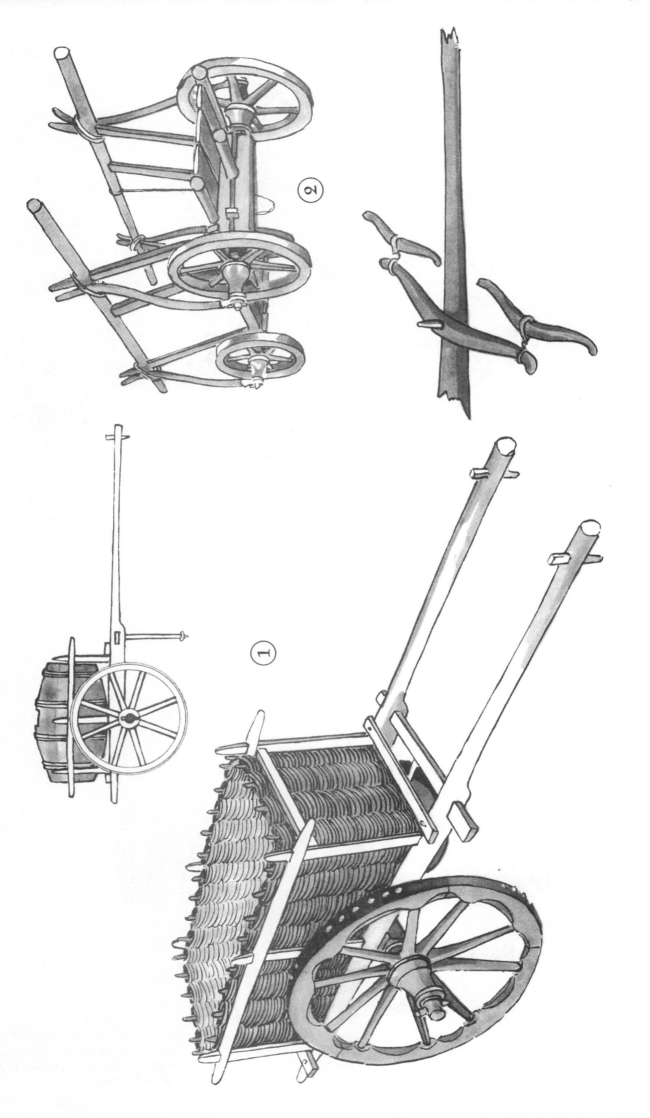

(1) Cart dating from 1405 (Bellifortis MS). (2) A farm waggon of the second half of the 15th century (Jena Codex). A simple cart with six-spoked wheels. The swingle-tree is pivotted on a bar projecting from the shaft of the cart.

PLATE 2 PART X

(1) A Bohemian covered merchant waggon with a chest at the front (Zíbrt and Winter, II, p. 271, pl. 159). (2) An illustration of part of a waggon phalanx, according to a Munich MS (H. Toman, *Husitské válečnictví*, p. 202). (3) An approximate reconstruction of the positioning of late 15th century military waggons. From a picture of a waggon phalanx encamped and on the march (*Mittelalterliches Hausbuch*). (4) A waggon from the time of Maximilian I (Dolleczek, p. 98, pl. 49). (5) A waggon dating from about 1542 (*Der Soldat in der deutschen Vergangenheit*, p. 60). (6) A 16th-century waggon, from Nuremburg (*Kulturgeschichte des deutschen Volkes*, plate behind p. 252).

PLATE 3

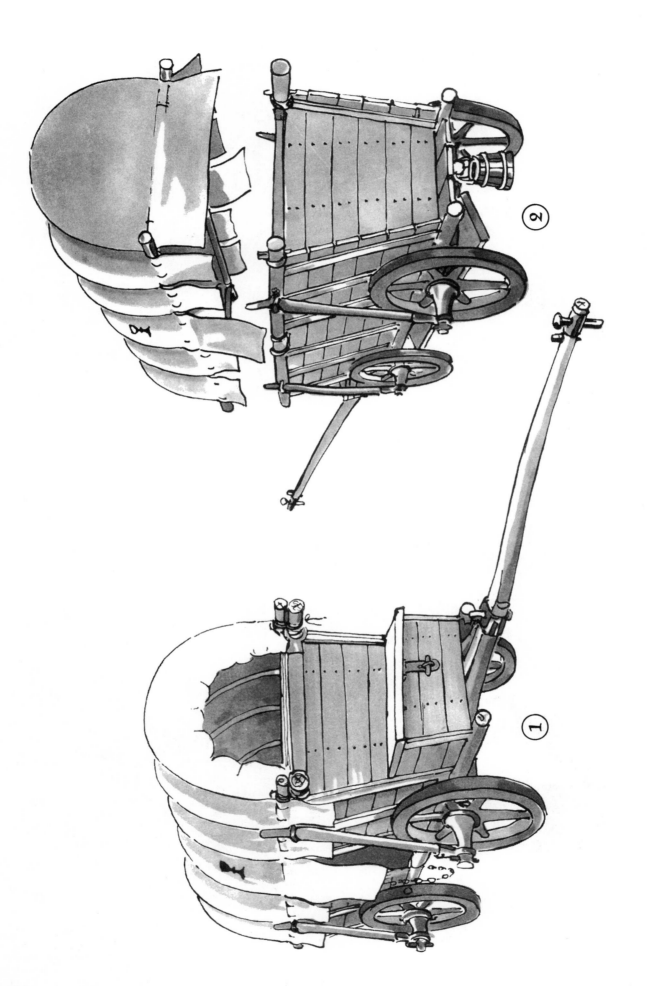

A transport waggon with a canvas top on its own frame. (1) Front view of the waggon, showing the tub of axle grease hanging underneath. The framed canvas roof is to be seen in the Viennese MS 1437–50, in an illumination showing a defence rampart composed of waggons. In that picture the canvas is protected on the outer side by pieces of wood hung over it. (2) Back view showing the chest for tools.

PLATE 4

①  ②

Picture of the outermost waggon, (1) as seen from the camp, (2) as seen from "the field". The waggon bearing the signalling banner is at the head of the row (Wagner, *Jak válčili husité*).

PLATE 5

PART X

①    ②

Other forms of protective boarding. (1) Boards in the form of a fence (Toman., *Husitské válečnictví*, p. 202). (2) A similar boarding, but with holes for shooting, is to be found in a picture of a waggon phalanx on the march (*Mittelalterliches Hausbuch*).

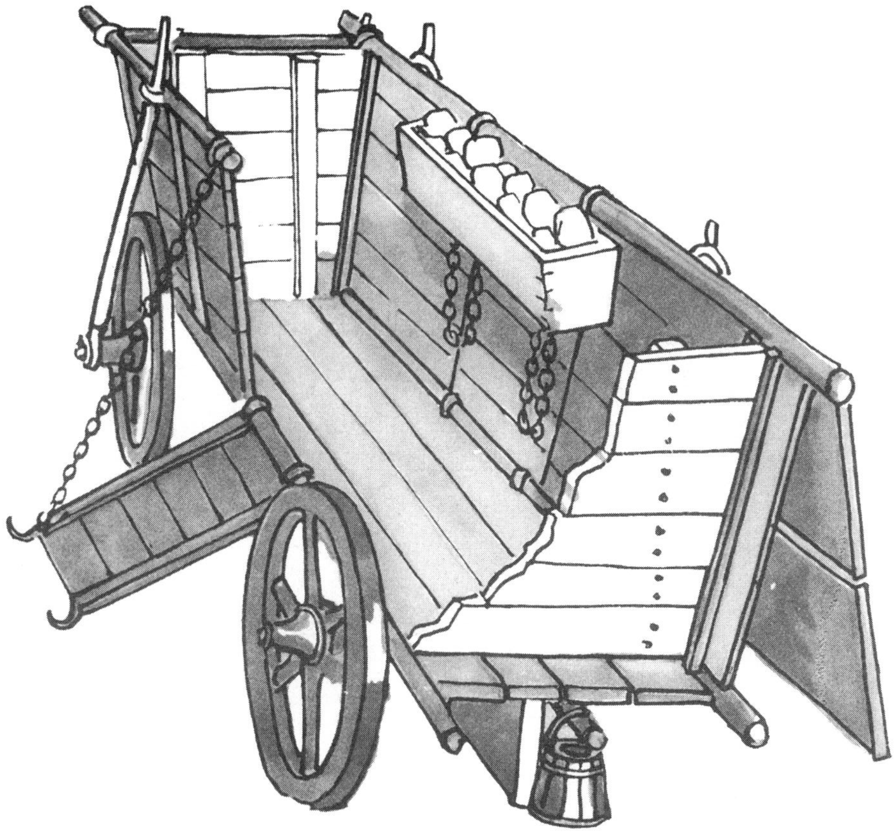

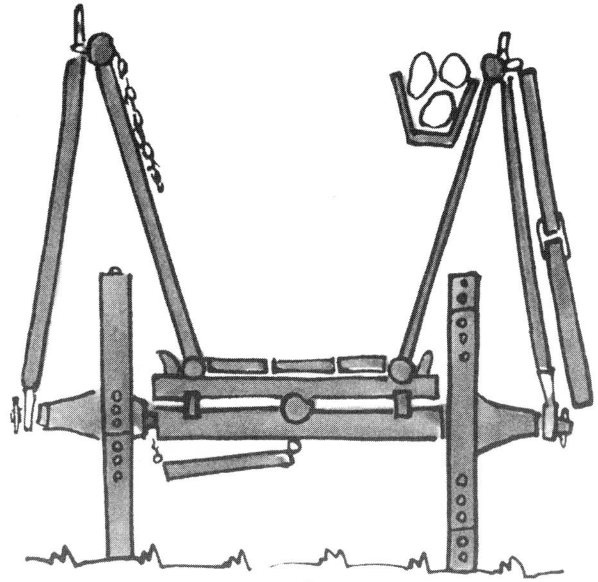

PLATE 6

(1) A diagram of a military or "battle" waggon. On the outer side, facing the enemy, are the protective boards, and below the waggon, the boards with holes for shooting. Attached to the upper beam is a trough for feeding the horses, now filled with stones. (2) When on the move the gang-plank between the wheels was raised. (3) A battle waggon in fighting position, with (in section) open gangway on the inner side, for communication. The plank could be let right down to the ground unless archers were shooting from beneath the waggon.

PLATE 7

PART X

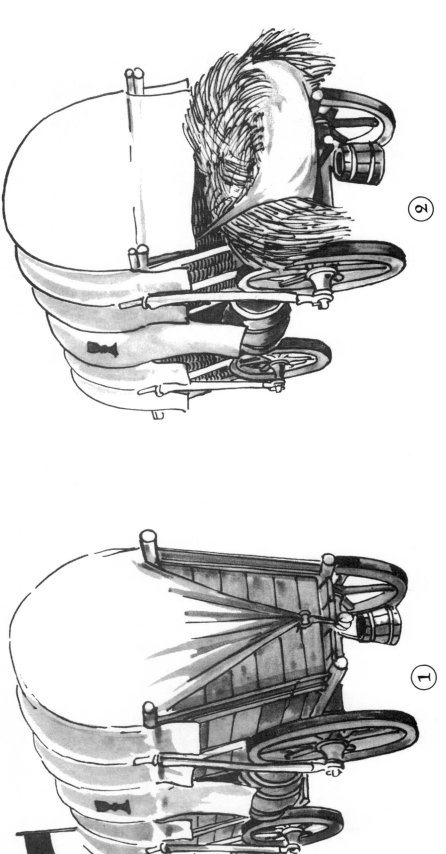

Supply waggons with canvas roofing. (1) The curved frame which carried the canvas was fixed direct to the waggon (Toman, p. 201, pl. 6). (2) A supply waggon of wattle, with canvas cover (Dolleczek, p. 92, pl. 49).

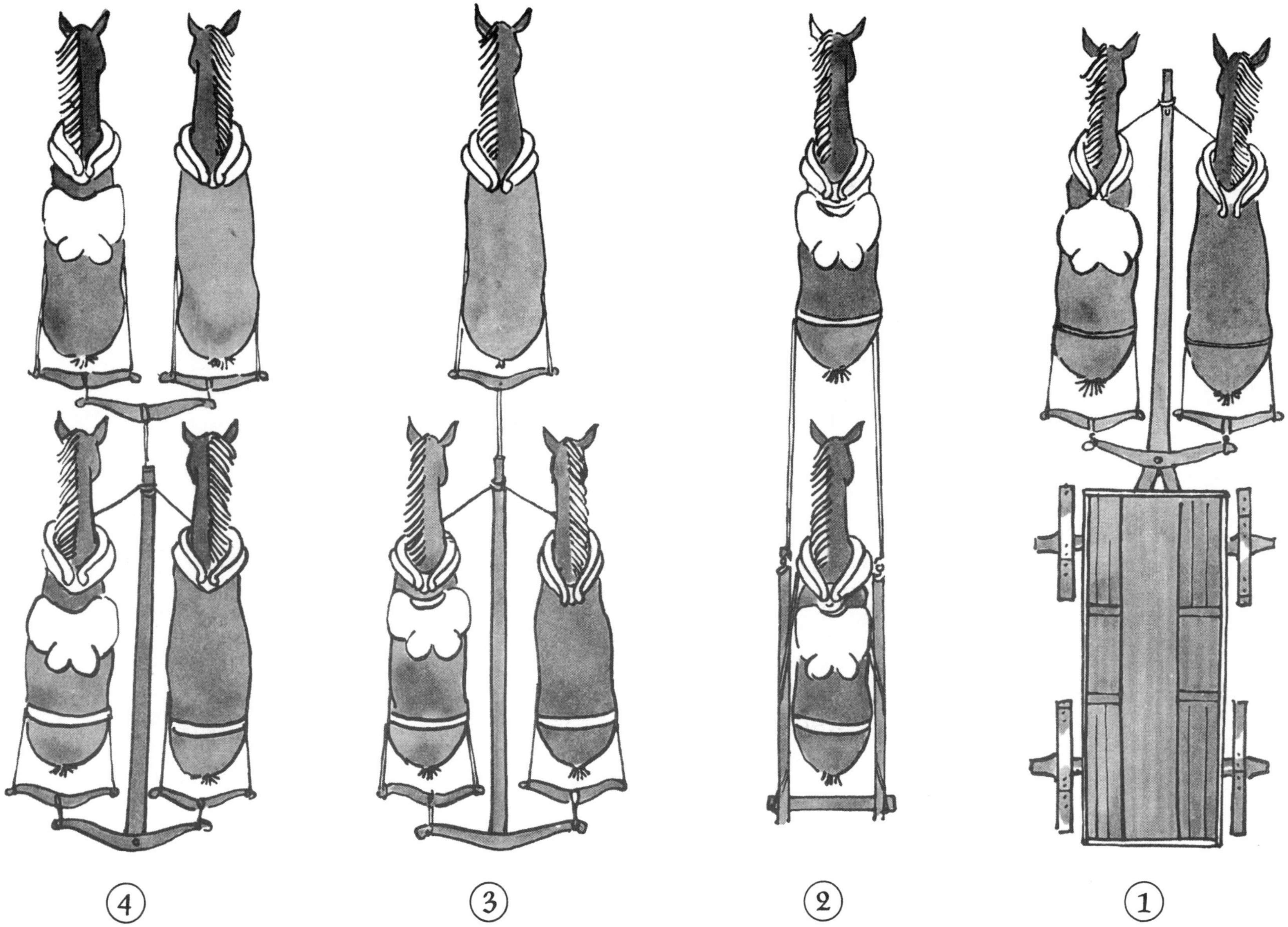

PLATE 8

PART X

① ② ③ ④

The normal medieval methods of harnessing animals in teams. (1) A simple team of two horses. (2) A tandem team. (3) A triple team. (4) A double team.

PLATE 9   PART X

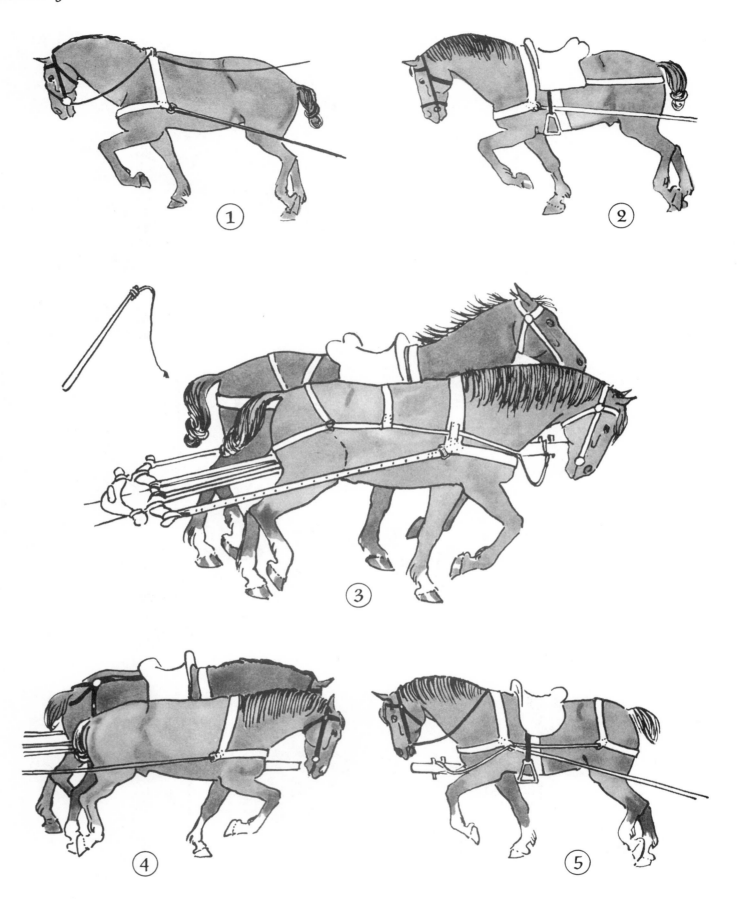

(1) A breast-collar draught harness from an illustration in the King Wenceslas Bible. (2) A breast-collar draught harness (with postillion's saddle) from a picture in the King Wenceslas Bible. (3) A team of horses from a picture in the King Wenceslas Bible. (4) A team of horses depicted in the King Wenceslas Bible. (5) Breast-collar draught harness (postillion's saddle) from an illumination in the King Wenceslas Bible.

PLATE 10   PART X

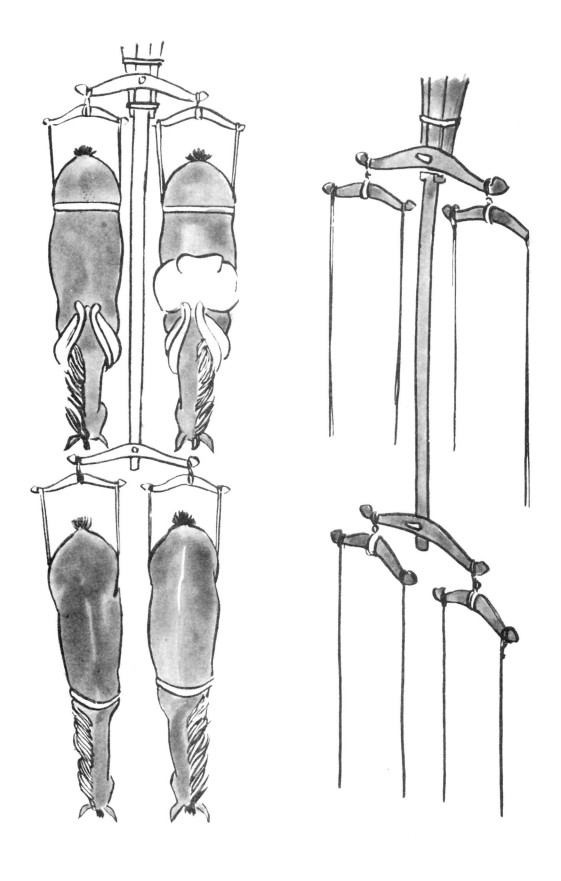

A double team in harness, according to the picture "A Waggon Phalanx on the March" (*Mittelalterliches Hausbuch*). In this picture the swingle-tree of the front pair is fitted direct, a pin being driven into the front part of the shaft.

PLATE 11 PART X

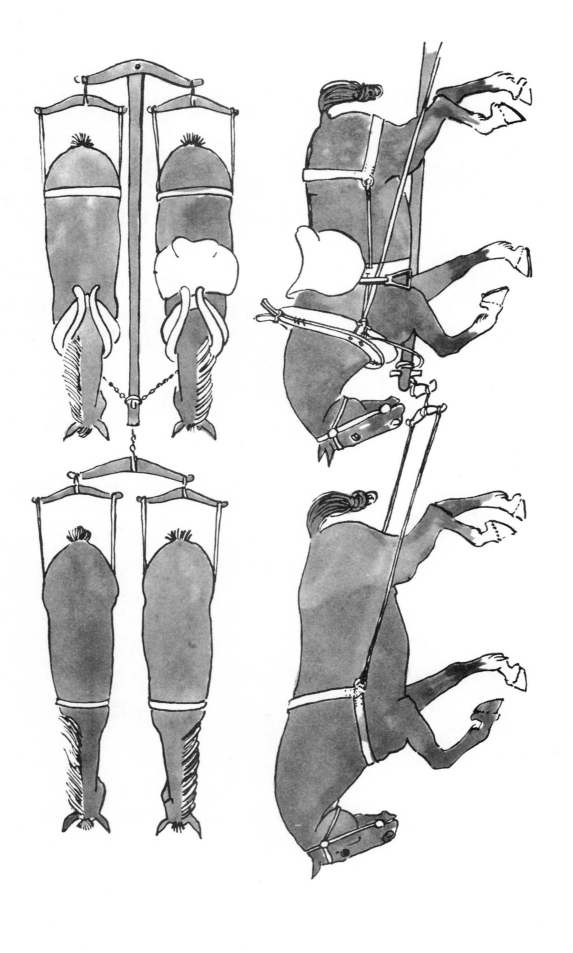

A double team, from the painting "A Waggon Phalanx on the March" (*Mittelalterliches Hausbuch*). The front pair have breast-collar draught harness, whereas the shaft pair have horse-collar harness and hame. There was only one driver for four draught horses.

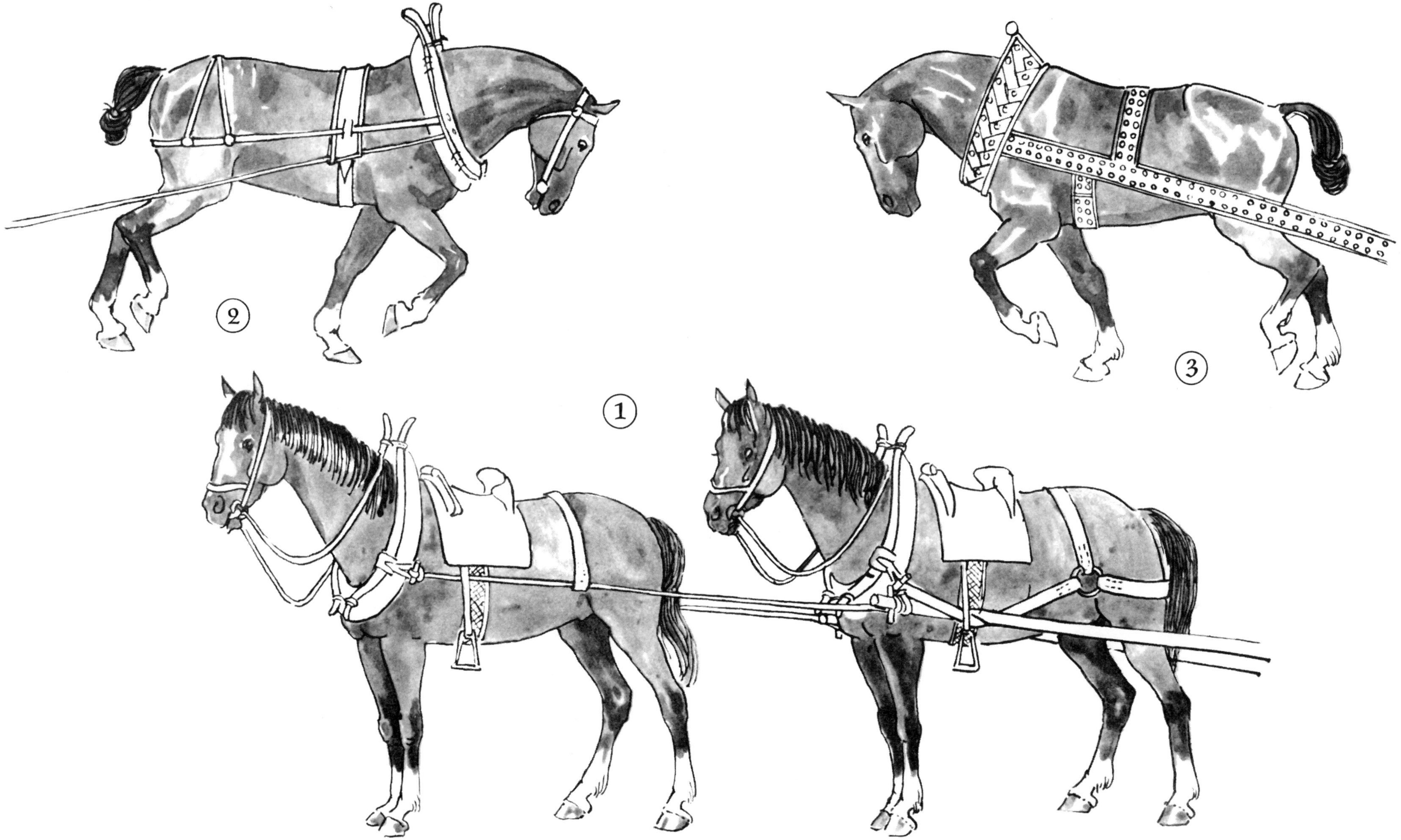

PLATE 12 PART X

(1) A tandem team of the 14th century (*Kulturgeschichte des deutschen Volkes*, I, p. 247). (2) Halter harness of the late 14th century (*Od dřevěného kola k automobilu*, p. 36). (3) Halter harness dating from 1390–1400 (Degenhart, p. 59).

PLATE 13

PART X

(1) Draught harness of the 15th century (*Od dřevěného kola k automobilu*, p. 28). (2) Draught harness dating from the first half of the 16th century, from the painting by Peter Breughel, "Hay-making", in the Prague National Gallery. (3) Draught harness dating from 1536 (*ibid.*, p.27).

PLATE 14

PART X

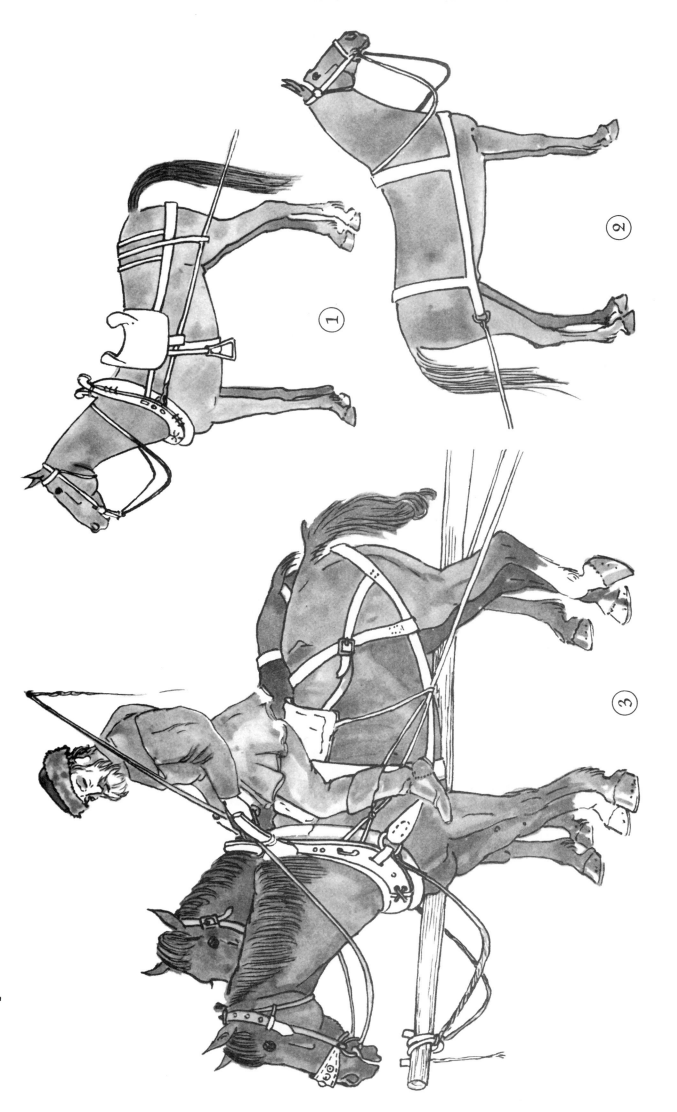

(1) Draught harness with a saddle, dating from the 14th century (*Od dřevěného kola k automobilu*, p. 24). (2) Breast-collar draught harness (Zíbrt and Winter, II, p. 271, pl. 159). (3) Agricultural harness, from a painting by Peter Breughel, 1515–69.

PLATE 15

PART X

Breast-collar draught harness from the Jena Codex. (1) A saddle horse. (2) A horse guided by hand.

PLATE 16

PART X

(1) A packhorse with packsaddle (Henne am Rhein; *Kulturgeschichte des deutschen Volkes*, I, p. 201). (2) Cat-o'-nine-tails. (3) A packsaddle, of about 1500 (Dolleczek, p. 117, pl. 55). (4) A donkey or mule loaded with barrels (King Wenceslas Bible illustration.) (5) Detail of the girth of the packsaddle, see (3). (6) A packhorse loaded with baskets, from the illumination in the King Wenceslas Bible.

PLATE 1   PART XI

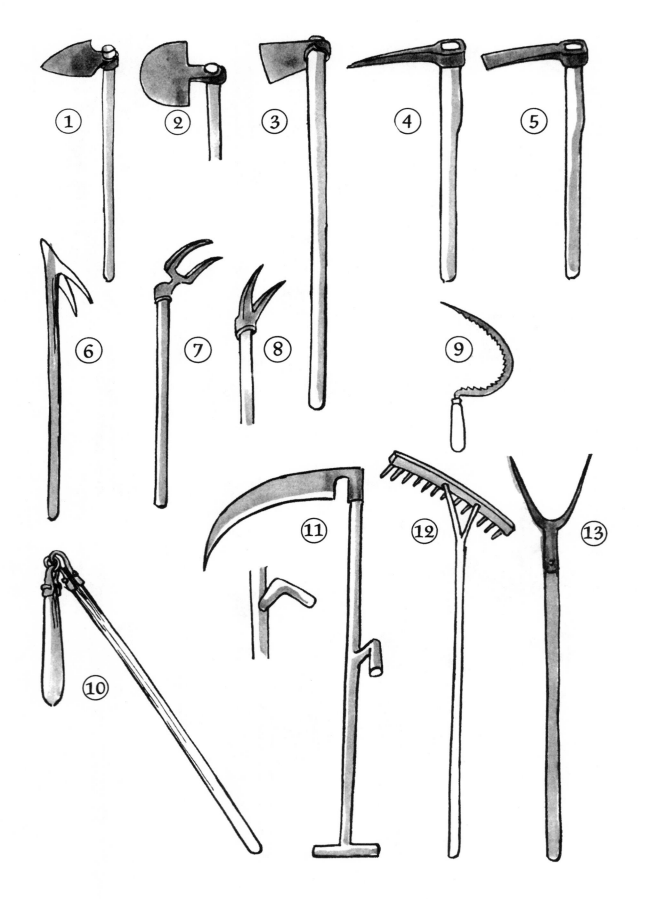

(1–2) Hoes from the Velislav Bible, dated about 1330. (3) A hoe in the painting "Autumn", by Francesca Cosso. (4–5) Pick-axes dating from about 1420, from "The Carrying of the Cross" and "The Finding of the Holy Cross" in the Raj-hrad altar-piece (Matějček, pl. 181 and 192). (6) Primitive wooden rake for raking (Niederle, *Slovanské starožitnosti*, p. 36, pl. 1). (7–8) Hoes from the second half of the 15th century from the Jena Codex, where they are depicted as imple-ments of torture. It is possible that these instruments, though there drawn out of proportion, were used for flaying the victim. (9) A sickle, from the Velislav Bible. (10–13) A flail, a scythe, a rake and a fork: from the same source.

PLATE 2 PART XI

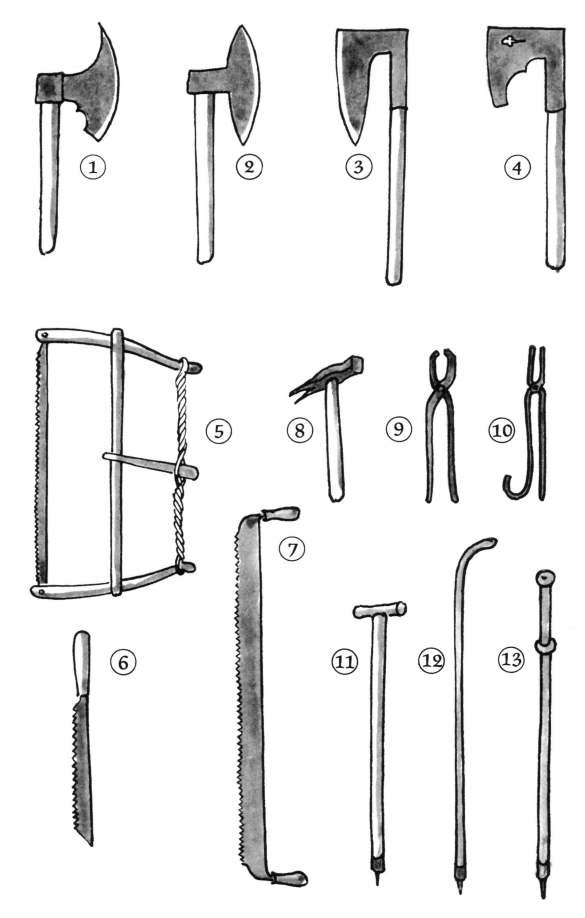

(1–4) Axes from illuminations in the King Wenceslas Bible. (5–6) 14th-century saws (*Die Geschichte der französischen Armee*, p. 87). (7) A saw from an illumination in the King Wenceslas Bible. (8) A 14th-century hammer as used by the blacksmith from the Krumlov MS, and the blacksmith from the *De moribus vivientium*. (9) Pincers from an illumination in the King Wenceslas Bible. (10) Pincers as depicted in the Krumlov MS. (11–13) Various types of cudgels from pictures in the Velislav Bible.

PLATE 3   PART XI

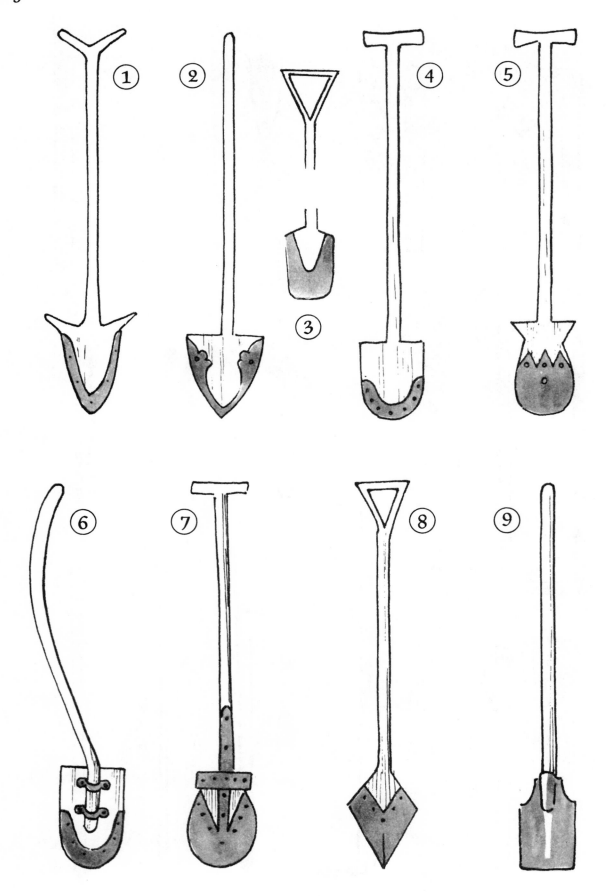

(1) A Polish spade (Niederle, *Slovanské starožitnosti*). (2) A spade of about 1330 (Velislav Bible). (3) A wooden spade, (4) A shovel from the illustration "The Siege of a 15th Century Town" (*Der Soldat*, p. 10, pl. 7). (5) A spade from the painting "Autumn", by Francesca Cosso. (6) A shovel from the end of the 15th century (Jena Codex). (7) A shovel, now the property of the Agricultural Museum in Prague. (8) An iron spade from a painting by Jacob Cornelisz of Amsterdam, early 16th century (*Alt-Niederländische Malerei*, pl. 140). (9) An iron shovel from an illumination in the King Wenceslas Bible; similar ones can be seen in the painting "The Carrying of the Cross" and "The Finding of the Holy Cross" in the Rajhrad altar-piece, dating from about 1420 (Matějček, pl. 181).

PLATE 4

PART XI

①

②

③

④

(1) Storage shelter of wattle, straw or bushwood, 16th century (*Der Soldat*, pl. 24). (2) A protective roofing of boards, from the late 15th century (*Mittelalterliches Hausbuch*, from the illustration "The Waggon Phalanx encamped"). (3) Wattle huts in a military camp, dating from the first half of the 16th century (Der Soldat, pl. 60). (4) A cauldron fixed over a camp fire, dated about 1540 (Jähns, p. 54, pl. 18).

PLATE 5   PART XI

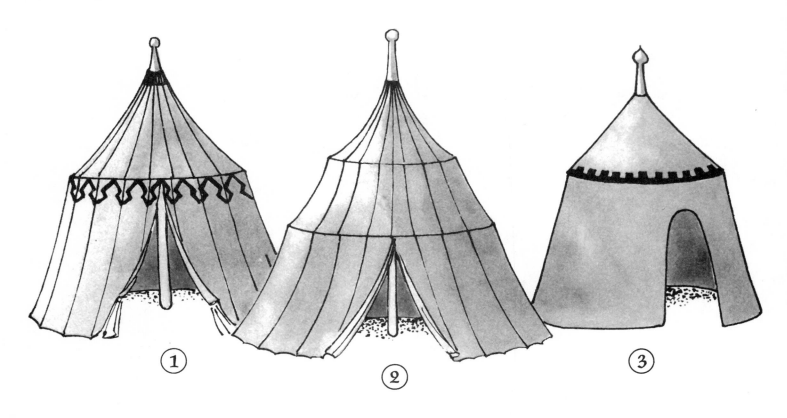

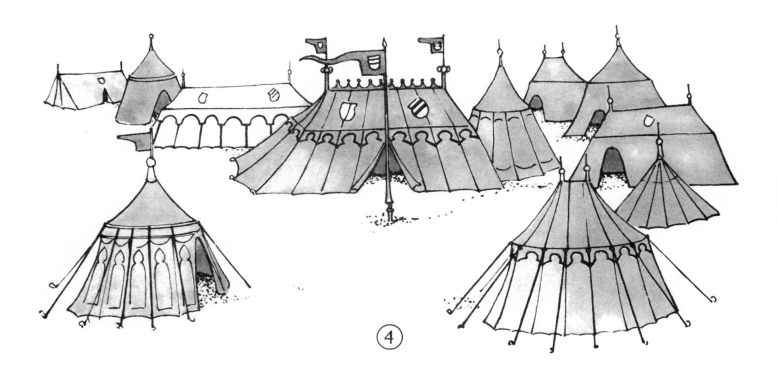

(1–3) 14th and 15th century tents, drawn from the illuminations in the King Wenceslas Bible. (4) The centre of a camp, including the commander's tent, adapted from an illustration in *Mittelalterliches Hausbuch*, "The Waggon Phalanx encamped".

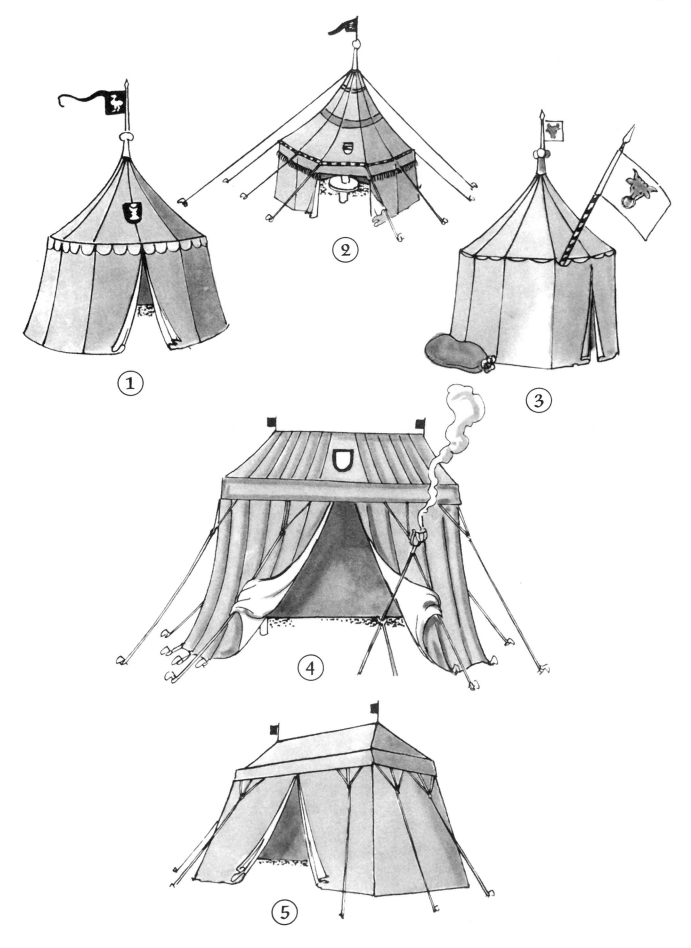

(1) A tent dating from between 1437–50 from an illustration in the Viennese MS "A Hussite Waggon Phalanx"
(2) A tent from the turn of the 15th and 16th centuries (*Deutsches Leben*, pl. 500). (3) A Swiss tent, of about 1450.
(Jähns, pl. 54, p. 18). (4) A 15th-century tent (*Deutsches Leben*, pl. 613). (5) A 15th-century tent (Viollet le Duc.)

PLATE 7

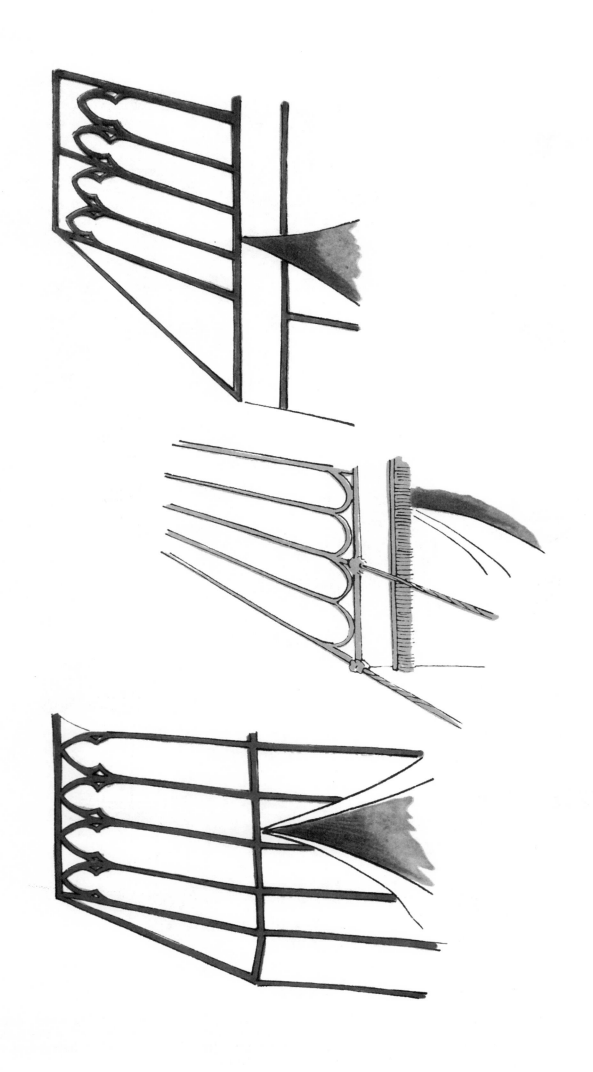

Tent decoration, dating from the second half of the 15th century, from the painting "The death of St. Ursula" by Hans Memling (1435–94).

PLATE 8 PART XI

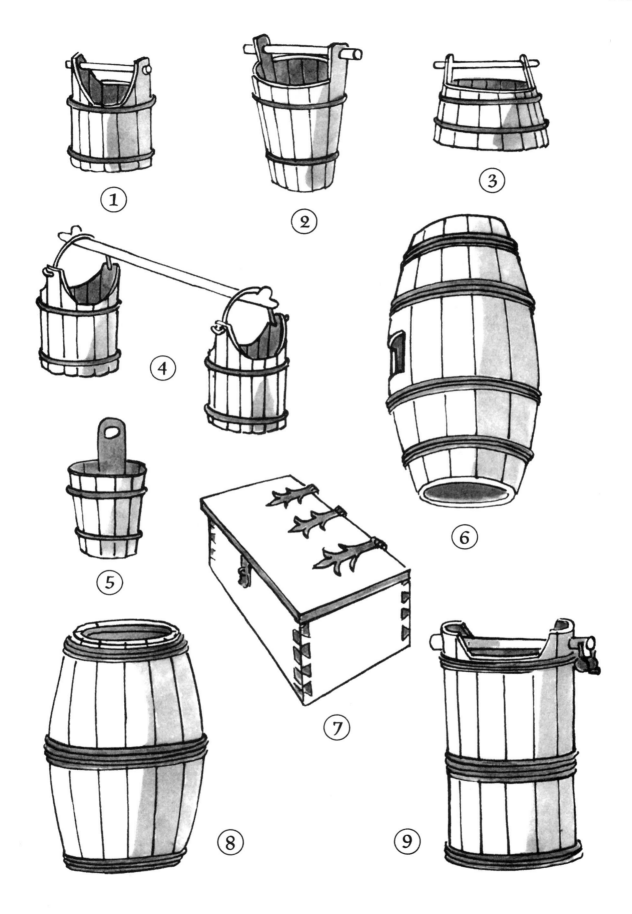

(1–3) Buckets from illuminations to the King Wenceslas Bible, circa 1400. (4) Buckets for carrying water, dating from 1330 (Velislav Bible). (5) A bucket, end of the 15th century, from the illustration "Monks bathing" in the Jena Codex. (6) A barrel, about 1405 (Bellifortis MS). (7) A chest, late 15th century (Jena Codex). (8–9) A barrel and vat, with a lock, also from the Jena Codex.

PLATE 9   PART XI

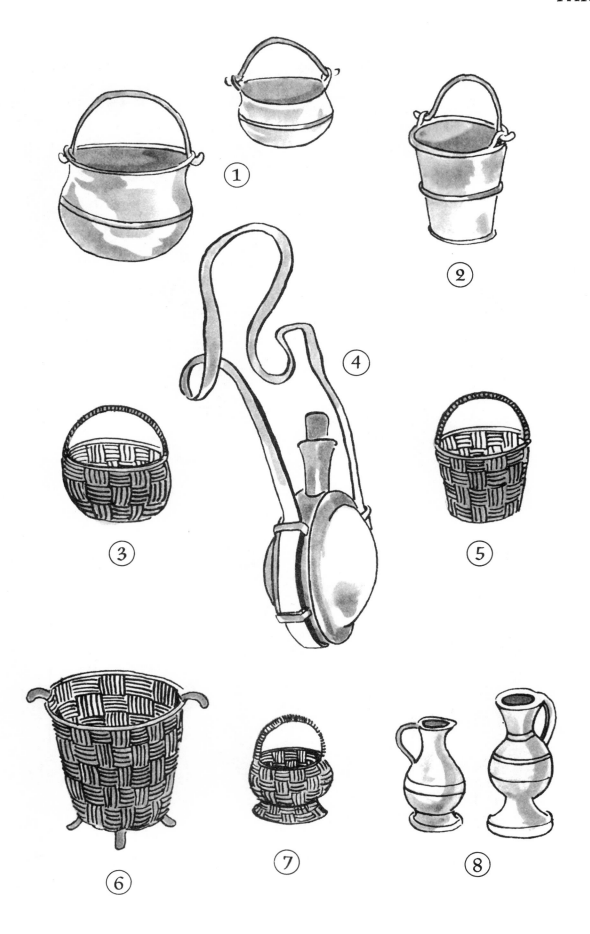

(1) Cauldrons from the Velislav Bible, 1330. (2) A metal bucket (*ibid.*). (3) A basket (*ibid.*). (4) A costrel of about 1405, from the illumination "Drunk Soldiers by the Vat" in the Bellifortis MS. (5) A basket, dating from 1405 (*ibid.*). (6) A hamper, of about 1330, from the Velislav Bible. (7) A basket, of about 1440, from the Aracoeli Madonna, St. Margaret and St. Dorothea (Matějček, pl. 121 and 122).

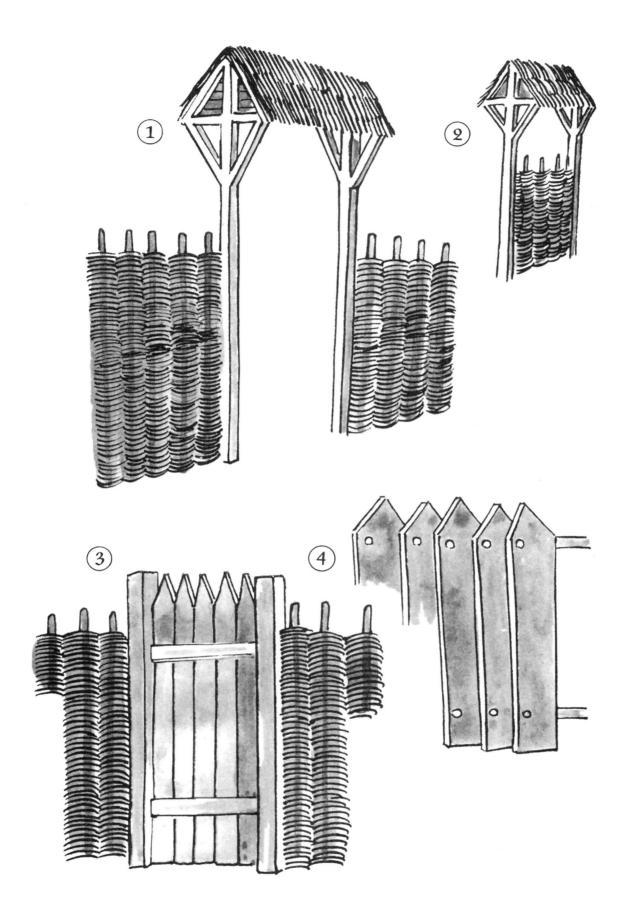

PLATE 10

PART XI

(1) A wattle fence and gateway, dating from the 14th–15th centuries, from an illumination in the King Wenceslas Bible.
(2) A closed wattle gate. (3) A wattle fence and wooden gate, about 1470 (*500 let maliarstwa polskiego*, p. 12). (4) A wooden paling, dating from about 1498 (Dehio).

412214